Inside

Warner Bros.

(1935–1951)

Inside
Warner

Selected, edited and annotated by

A FIRESIDE BOOK

Bros.
(1935–1951)

Rudy Behlmer

PUBLISHED BY SIMON & SCHUSTER, INC. • NEW YORK

Copyright © 1985 by Warner Bros. Inc.
All rights reserved
including the right of reproduction
in whole or in part in any form
First Fireside Edition, 1987
Published by Simon & Schuster, Inc.
Simon & Schuster Building
Rockefeller Center
1230 Avenue of the Americas
New York, New York 10020

Published by arrangement with Viking Penguin Inc.

FIRESIDE and colophon are registered trademarks of
Simon & Schuster, Inc.

The WB Shield Logo is a registered Trademark used by permission of
Warner Bros. Inc., 4000 Warner Boulevard, Burbank, California 91522

Manufactured in the United States of America

10 9 8 7 6 5 4 3 2 1

Library of Congress Cataloging in Publication Data

Inside Warner Bros. (1935–1951).

    Reprint. Originally published: New York, NY, U.S.A.:
Viking, 1985.
    "A Fireside book."
    Includes index.
    1. Warner Brothers Pictures, Inc.—History—
Sources. I. Behlmer, Rudy.
[PN1999.W3I5   1987]   384'.8'0979494   86-29676
ISBN 0-671-63135-7 Pbk.

Grateful acknowledgment is made to the following for permission to reprint copyrighted material:

The Hollywood Reporter: Edited version of an article by Darryl F. Zanuck from the "Holiday Number" of *The Hollywood Reporter,* December 24, 1932.
Selznick Properties Ltd.: Dictated letter from David O. Selznick to Jack L. Warner, March 8, 1938; letter from Ray Klune to David O. Selznick, May 19, 1941; telegram from David O. Selznick to Hal Willis, November 12, 1942.
Bob Thomas and the Associated Press: A selection from *Los Angeles Mirror* column by Bob Thomas, January 6, 1950.
Time Inc.: Edited version of "Warner Brothers," *Fortune,* December 1937. Copyright 1937 by Time Inc. All rights reserved.

For Curt and Anna
and for Betty

Contents

Photographs follow pages 112 and 238.

Introduction

This is the day-to-day story of a studio during its "Golden Age"—primarily the 1930s and 1940s. Warner Bros. was one of the big five of the time (along with MGM, 20th Century-Fox, Paramount, and RKO), a film factory turning out approximately fifty features a year for distribution in theatres they owned. These are the years of stars such as Bette Davis, Bogart, Cagney, Errol Flynn, and of films that have become perennial favorites, including *The Adventures of Robin Hood, Angels with Dirty Faces, Dark Victory, The Maltese Falcon, Now, Voyager, Yankee Doodle Dandy, Casablanca, Mildred Pierce, The Big Sleep, The Treasure of the Sierra Madre, Johnny Belinda, A Streetcar Named Desire*, and many others.

Warner Bros. called on their employees to commit their work to paper. Printed at the bottom of each sheet of interoffice correspondence was the reminder "Verbal messages cause misunderstanding and delays (please put them in writing)." And they did. This book is made up of some of those choice "writings."

The evolution of a script, the casting of the film, a director's approach and frustrations, the reaction to the screening of "dailies" or "rushes"—all of these became part of the record. Unhappy stars wrote to studio executives detailing their gripes. If there were problems on the set during filming, the unit manager attached to the film would explain them in his daily production report. Sometimes even telephone conversations and meetings were recorded and typed. Telegraph messages were sent between the Warners studio in Burbank and the corporate headquarters in New York. The correspondence takes us behind the scenes and allows us to eavesdrop on the inspirations, doubts, decisions, and turmoil that accompanied the making of a film, even as it reflects the varying conditions and evolution of the film industry as a whole. Taken all in all it provides us incomparable insight into a major studio at its peak and the professional life of some of the major figures in the history of motion pictures.

The richest years, from the standpoint of amount and kind of material in the studio files, are from 1935 to approximately 1951. Papers are relatively sparse before 1935, and the modus operandi of Warners evolved quite differently in the 1950s because of the radical changes that were taking place in the industry with the advent of television, post–World War II changes in recreational patterns, the divorcement and divestiture by government decree of motion picture production and distribution from exhibition, and the rise of independent production and foreign co-production.

Bosses Harry and Jack Warner issued commands aplenty. Harry was president, originally based in New York, and Jack, vice-president in charge of production and based at the studio in Burbank, had overall responsibility for running the studio and getting the films out. (A third brother, Albert [Abe], was treasurer in New York.) From 1927 to 1933, Darryl F. Zanuck was Jack's right-hand man and executive producer and as such was usually more involved in the actual producing of films on a day-to-day basis than his boss. Zanuck had a corps of "supervisors," as they were called during his reign, to handle details and follow-through. Hal B. Wallis replaced Zanuck as executive producer and later, after Wallis left, Steve Trilling became Jack Warner's executive assistant, but neither he nor anyone else was given the authority and control enjoyed by Zanuck and Wallis.

During Wallis's reign as executive producer (1933–1942), he flooded his staff of line producers (then called supervisors or associate producers), staff directors, writers, and others with memos. Since he was largely responsible for the "product" being made and had a good deal to say about it, he is heavily represented in these pages. Later Jerry Wald, although never an executive producer at Warners, would express himself in writing on anything and everything having to do with a film before, during, and after its production. Producers Mark Hellinger and Robert Lord were similarly inclined. Directors such as John Huston, Elia Kazan, Raoul Walsh, Ernst Lubitsch, and Michael Curtiz are represented in their own words, and there is a good deal of insightful correspondence about Howard Hawks, Sam Wood, and William Wyler, among others.

And the writers wrote, too. Fortunately, Casey Robinson, who enjoyed a close working relationship with Hal Wallis, expresses himself eloquently and at great length on some important projects. So do Norman Reilly Raine, Howard Koch, Lenore Coffee, Richard Brooks, Robert Buckner, John Monk Saunders, and others. And there are even a few choice items from the likes of William Faulkner, Tennessee Williams, B. Traven, James M. Cain, and Raymond Chandler.

The players did not send a steady stream of epistles to Jack L. Warner or Hal B. Wallis or anyone at the studio. Their agents usually acted as intermediaries and did the talking for them, but, as always, there were fascinating exceptions. Bette Davis, for example, often wrote directly to Jack L. or Hal B.—and she didn't mince words, as you will discover. She said what she thought and felt, as did Bogart, Flynn, Edward G. Robinson, Olivia de Havilland, George Raft, John Garfield, Claude Rains, Basil Rathbone, John Barrymore, and Paul Muni. Although Joan Crawford, Ronald Reagan, Jane Wyman, Lauren Bacall, Ida Lupino, and James Cagney didn't write directly, there is revealing correspondence about them in these pages, too.

The studio system of the twenties, thirties, and forties was essentially a factory-like method of turning out product to distributors and then to exhibitors for the public. Basically, it was not much different from the manufacturing of automobiles. But there was one difference: despite attempts at standardization, no picture could be *exactly* the same as another one on the assembly line. But similar formula elements—plots, incidents, characters—were used and then transposed from one genre to another: what worked in a Western could be used six months later in a gangster film.

Twists, blends, and cross-pollinations were the rule. When the script of *They Drive By Night* seems to run out of steam, the solution is to move directly into the third act of *Bordertown*, made five years earlier. When *Captain Blood* is a hit, do it again, more or less, as *The Adventures of Robin Hood* and then *The Sea Hawk*. When the gangster film is condemned by the Production Code Administration as well as by outside censorship organizations, revive it as the G-man film and then bring it back again in the guise of a sociological study of environmentally bred criminal behavior (*Angels with Dirty Faces*, inspired by the success of the play and film versions of *Dead End*.) If the husband–wife–best friend triangle in an action yarn proves effective in *Tiger Shark* (which derived from *They Knew What They Wanted*), repeat it, incorporating mild variations with a different dangerous profession as a background (*Manpower*, et al). When *Dodge City* works, follow it with *Virginia City, San Antonio*, and others. If Bette Davis dying from an incurable disease in *Dark Victory* is big box-office, repeat it in *'Til We Meet Again* (a remake of *One Way Passage*, except that Davis refused to do the picture and Merle Oberon had to be hastily substituted).

Remakes abounded at Warners, as they did at all the studios. *The Desert Song* was made four times, if you count one short subject version. *High Sierra* was filmed three times. *The Dawn Patrol* was produced twice with the same title, and all its spectacular air footage was lifted from the first version to fit neatly into the second. The prison drama *20,000 Years in Sing Sing*, filmed in 1933 with Spencer Tracy, became *Castle on the Hudson* in 1940 to accommodate a new star, John Garfield. If one biography, the 1936 *Story of Louis Pasteur*, was a hit, it was followed up with more—Zola, Florence Nightingale, Dr. Ehrlich, George M. Cohan, etc. Stories were revamped, inverted, musicalized, updated, bent, sequeled, made into series, converted to another time or place. But they kept coming off the assembly line.

Warners didn't invent the studio system, which had been around to a degree since the early days of motion pictures; by 1915, entrepreneur Thomas Ince and others had brought it to a surprising level of efficiency and sophistication. Warners had been using the system when it incorporated in 1923, and in the 1930s and 1940s it was a model of smooth, synchronized functioning. Nothing just happened; everything was planned, organized, and watched over carefully by a system of checks and balances.

The star system had been around for a long time, too—in movies since about 1910, but the legitimate theatre had set the pattern long before, as it had with various other aspects absorbed into the motion picture business. Film stars were "born" or manufactured and placed under seven-year contracts with options (the studio's, not the player's). If a contract player refused to do an assigned picture, he or she usually was suspended without pay, with the suspension time added to the seven years. If a leading player did one good film, he or she was then expected to do a couple of not-so-good or downright poor ones before being granted another quality item.

Players had a particularly rough time in the early 1930s and for several years after. When the Depression was at its worst and attendance at movie houses declined, actors were placed in a poor bargaining position; they occasionally suffered salary cutbacks. In the late 1940s and early 1950s, when movie attendance again declined, players were released from studio contracts to reduce overhead, and the established stars, due to changes in tax laws, found it more profitable to demand a percentage of a film's profit and even to become independent corporations.

The correspondence from the Warners files makes a remarkable record. What is even more remarkable is that it has been saved. Over the years, so much of the history of the various studios has been thrown out, lost, destroyed by periodic fires, or mishandled. So the existence of the

Warner files at the University of Southern California Archives of Performing Arts cannot be taken for granted.

Not every piece of paper in the Warner Bros. archives is a gem. The ephemeral, the routine, and the downright uninteresting abound. In selecting material for publication, I have concentrated on the more memorable films, players, directors, writers, producers, and other studio personnel. With so many films produced at Warners at the time, perhaps only two or three at best from any year are recalled by movie enthusiasts today. Naturally, many aspects of the business discussed in memos were similar for film after film, and for this book the redundant communications have been eliminated, except when they make a point. The emergence of "name" players is treated more extensively here than the rise of other stars who may have shined brightly—but only for a brief period.

Certain fondly remembered Warner personalities and films are conspicuous by their absence in this book—but this is not by design. Perhaps choice tidbits about them escaped from the files years ago; there was nothing of more than perfunctory interest (good or bad) about such luminaries, for example, as Doris Day and Al Jolson. Making only cameo appearances are Busby Berkeley, Dick Powell, Joan Blondell, and Ann Sheridan, to name a few other major personalities.

Alfred Hitchcock and Frank Capra, although strictly speaking not Warner Bros. producers and directors, made films at the studio, but based on the evidence, they must have taken most of their records with them when they left the lot. And files on one of the best remembered films of the late 1940s, *White Heat*, yielded nothing of interest, unfortunately. The coming of sound to motion pictures, in which Warners was so heavily involved, is not represented in these pages simply because there was nothing to be found that was appropriate for this book. The same applies to the use of the Technicolor process in 1929–1930 and the early musicals.

Because it falls outside the scope of this primarily production study, material on distribution and exhibition, housed mostly at Princeton University, has not been included. B movies, cartoons, and short subjects could be the topics of separate works, although there doesn't appear to be a great deal in the way of interesting correspondence regarding these areas in the files.

For those readers who would like more background on the early history of Warner Bros., the studio system of the time, executives, and talent, I suggest turning to the Interlude section (page 54), which is an edited reprint of an extremely interesting and informative 1937 *Fortune* magazine article about Warners.

Throughout this book bracketed material, italicized annotations, and occasional footnotes have been used to identify the person either sending or receiving correspondence and to provide background information. As a ready reference, the Index again indentifies key Warners people in the book by job description.

Several years ago I selected and edited for a book the papers of independent film producer David O. Selznick *(Gone With the Wind)*. *Memo from David O. Selznick* included only correspondence written or dictated by Selznick, whereas this book presents material from many people working at Warner Bros. But the introduction to that volume contained a paragraph that might well apply to the present collection, and I've reproduced it here, merely substituting "Warners" for "Selznick":

Anyone interested in the making of films can only be glad that Warners saved their carbons, for it is one thing to read or listen to reminiscences of someone noted in his field selectively recalling what happened many years before—with all the attendant inaccuracies and imbalances—but it is quite another when one is able to assess film history recorded at the time the events occurred, with the drama of the moment intact.

RUDY BEHLMER

Acknowledgments

As always in a project of this kind many individuals and organizations contributed to its realization.

While researching another book in 1976, I discovered that United Artists, owner of most Warner films produced up to 1950, had donated Warner Bros. scripts, still photographs, certain legal files, press books, 16mm prints, and other materials to the Wisconsin Center for Film and Theater Research at the State Historical Society in Madison. But there was little in the way of story correspondence and no production files, and these were what I needed for certain titles.

Then a friend, John Stephens, hearing of my plight, introduced me to Carl Stucke, a story editor at Warner Bros. who first arrived at the studio in 1933. When Carl took me to the storage area in the basement of the studio's carpenter shop and opened the file boxes for some of my requested titles, I asked what the clasped wad of correspondence sitting on top of the various drafts of the scripts was. "Oh, those are the story and production memos I have saved over the years," he replied. After riffling through the papers on *Casablanca*, I realized that here was more documented history on the creative aspects of those days than apparently still exists for other studios.

Then in 1977 those records and a great many others from Warner Bros. were inventoried and cataloged by Scriptorium and donated (by Warners) to the Archives of Performing Arts at the University of Southern California. I continued my research there, becoming more and more absorbed in pursuing papers on all the major films of the 1930s, 1940s, and early 1950s (and, as time went by, all the minor films as well), the separate files on personalities, the daily production reports, and various other records. By 1980 I was determined to do a book.

Dr. Robert Knutson, head of Special Collections at the University Library, U.S.C., was most supportive of my plan; he was instrumental in introducing me to Peter Knecht, general counsel at the time for the Warner Bros. studio in Burbank, to discuss the practical realities of doing such a volume of annotated correspondence. Mr. Knecht and James R. Miller, Studio Business Affairs, drew up a letter of agreement that made it possible for me to continue my research with a view to publication. Subsequently other Warner Bros. executives and personnel were extremely cooperative in aiding the project. In alphabetical order, they are: Stanley Belkin, Jess Garcia, Jack Kingsley, Dan Romanelli, Marshall M. Silverman, and Judith Singer.

Leith Adams, archivist for the Warner collection, went out of his way over a long period of time in acceding to my seemingly never-ending requests to scan more and more paper material and photographs—sometimes over and over again. His predecessor, Andrew Rosner, was also extremely cooperative.

Ned Comstock, in U.S.C.'s Department of Special Collections, constantly came up with important pieces of information, material from different collections, photographs, and a hundred aids to the project. Others in Special Collections who facilitated my work over the years in a thoroughly professional manner include (alphabetically) Joel Hailey, Ray Holland, Bill Jankos, Janet Lorenz, Lindy Narver, and Gaylyn Studlar.

During many fondly recalled visits to the Wisconsin Center for Film and Theater Research to screen and study Warner material, I was always warmly welcomed by the then director of the center, Professor Tino Balio, film archivist Maxine Fleckner, and her predecessor, Susan Dalton. They were most supportive and put in extra time to aid me. In screening 16mm prints of Warner films alone, I think I chalked up at least two hundred hours of viewing time over several years.

Mary Ann Jensen, the delightful curator of the Theatre Collection, Firestone Library, Princeton University, and her knowledgeable assistant, John Hein, allowed me to make the most of a week's memorable visit by having pertinent papers from Warners' New York office ready and waiting.

Clifford McCarty generously gave of his time to go through the manuscript, making many insightful suggestions. And so did Joanne Yeck, David Impastato, Ted Naron, Carl Stucke, and Tony Thomas.

In the area of photographic research, for materials other than those at the first-rate Warner Archive at U.S.C., I am indebted to the following individuals and organizations: the Wisconsin Center for Film and Theater Research, Malcolm Willits and Mark S. Willoughby (Collectors Book Store), George Pratt (George Eastman House), Mary Corliss (Museum of Modern Art), Marc Wanamaker (Bison Archives), Mary Julian, James C. Morehead, and James Silke.

Ann Pollack and Virginia Cook did the lion's share of the typing (from a labyrinthine manuscript), and Cheryl Hastings, Sally Hope, Donna Mulholland, and Sharon Straite also contributed on occasion.

Others who aided the cause in various ways include the Library of the Academy of Motion Picture Arts and Sciences, Brendan Carroll, Leonhard M. Fiedler, Ronald Haver, Charles Higham, Victoria Hochberg, George Korngold, Daniel Selznick, David Shepard, Bob Thomas, Time Inc., and Mel Tormé. And finally, a special salute to Walt Bode, my editor at Viking, who managed to offer constant encouragement and continued to persevere during the difficult periods.

Inside

Warner
Bros.
(1935–1951)

1 Prologue (1929–1935)

The years before 1935 are thinly represented in the Warner Bros. Archive—mostly some legal papers. Presumably many other files were destroyed years ago. The following correspondence represents a few highlights of what remains from the early years in the Warner collection at the University of Southern California and at Princeton University.

FROM P. A. CHASE [Warner executive, New York]

Mr. Ralph E. Lewis
Freston and Files [law firm]
650 South Spring St.
Los Angeles, Cal.

Re: Lee Duncan [Rin Tin Tin's owner and trainer]

December 6, 1929

Dear Mr. Lewis:

. . . We are about to start another Rin Tin Tin production, and after that picture is finished, we do not propose to make any more pictures with Rin Tin Tin appearing therein.

It has been decided that since the talking pictures have come into their own, particularly with this organization, that the making of any animal pictures, such as we have in the past with Rin Tin Tin, is not in keeping with the policy that has been adopted by us for talking pictures, very obviously, of course, because dogs don't talk. . . .

P. A. Chase

Rin Tin Tin had been Warners' most important commercial asset up until the introduction of sound.

FROM JOHN BARRYMORE

Mr. J. L. Warner [vice president in charge of production]

March 26, 1930

Dear Jack:

Received your letter, but regret you have made the question of my producing [a film version of] *Hamlet* a personal matter when it was only a business one. It is true, as Hotchener [his agent] said, that I have had an offer of more money; so it was natural that the matter be brought to your attention at this time. I simply requested Hotchener to go to you and say that as *Hamlet* would require an enormously greater amount of time, labor, and detailed attention on my part than an average play (which you yourself admitted to Hotchener), I thought I was entitled to get more money for it.

Shakespearean plays are my specialty; I have given long years to producing and acting them, with very great financial success both here and abroad. From this long experience I know that to put them on properly for talking pictures would require a tremendous amount of time and work—very much greater than for any other type of production, I do not think this could be reasonably expected of me under my present contract [with Warners], and when Hotchener told me of the other offer, entailing more money for this production, I naturally arranged that he should see you or Darryl [Zanuck] as your representative, as he is mine, to discuss the arrangements. I left the details to him to take up with you. I particularly want you to understand that I would very much prefer to do *Hamlet* with you, if you will meet my terms, which must be reasonable or such offers would not have come from other sources; and I think that you, Darryl, and myself could make something great out of it together.

There was never any question of my *breaking* my present contract with you, but only of *modifying* it, and it seems to me that considering the especial knowledge and experience I have with this play, and the attitude of the public towards my association with it all over the world (and particularly the success in England, which was so widely advertised in this country because it was the only time an American actor had ever accomplished it), and considering also the extra labor and concentration it would require from me, an additional $50,000 and 5% more of the gross are not unreasonable in view of the tremendous possibilities of this picture and the fact that we both realize that it is undoubtedly my "ace in the hole."

Am glad you like *Moby Dick* so far. I hope and believe it will be a great picture.

Usually, expressions of regard from actors to their producers have a slight favor of "bunk" and I am not in the habit of indulging in them, but I would like you to believe that I am perfectly sincere when I say that I would rather work with you personally than with anyone else in the business.

> All the best to you as always
> Jack Barrymore

Barrymore's film version of Hamlet *was not produced. Zanuck was associate executive in charge of production under Jack L. Warner, having worked his way up from a writer on Rin Tin Tin films. He joined Warner Bros. in 1924 and by the late 1920s was a major force at the studio.*

FROM JACOB WILK [Eastern story editor]

April 6, 1932

Dear Darryl [Zanuck, associate executive
in charge of production]:

The author of *I Am a Fugitive from a Georgia Chain Gang* is coming out to report April 13th. He has to be under cover and is traveling under a phoney name. That name is Richard M. Crane, though his name is Robert E. Burns. The reason he is traveling under a phoney name is because the State of Georgia is after him for having escaped. Will you please inform those people with whom he is to work that should Richard Crane call, he is Robert Burns, and they will know how to treat the matter from that point on.

In our contract with Burns, we are only paying his expenses out and back; no salary for his services. You may find Burns a little erratic, but you are used to all kinds of people so I am sure you will handle him and get the best out of him.

> With best wishes, I am
> Sincerely,
> Jacob Wilk

FROM RALPH LEWIS [Freston and Files, Warners' law firm, Los Angeles]

Mr. I. Howard Levinson [legal department]
Warner Bros. Pictures, Inc.
321 West 44th Street
New York, N.Y.

February 5, 1938

Dear Mr. Levinson:

Re: *Fugitive from a Chain Gang*

   . . . As part of the purchase but apparently by separate oral agreement, [Robert] Burns was employed to assist in the writing. [Jack] Warner believes he was given four weeks employment. Being a fugitive he worked and was known by a fictitious name. . . . Burns certainly came to the coast, and Warner thinks he contributed some ideas and information to the writers here and was of considerable use. Mr. [Hal] Wallis' recollection is that Burns merely sat in on a few story conferences. . . .

   Warner further states that the story was published at a time when they were promoting a cycle of similar pictures, but they were always on the lookout for this particular type and that the simultaneous transaction with [Paul] Muni was likewise a contributing factor, as the story and the actor would fit each other. The two deals may have been made a little apart in time, but nevertheless constituted part of the same transaction so far as Warner was concerned. . . .

Best regards,
Ralph Lewis

   A successful New York stage actor, Paul Muni's impact in the leading role of Howard Hughes' film Scarface *(1932) prompted Warner Bros. to sign him to a long-term contract and award him the rarely given script approval.*

FROM DARRYL F. ZANUCK

Mr. Edward G. Robinson [contract star]
Essex House
New York, N.Y.

October 26, 1932

Dear Eddie:

   . . . To start with the last paragraph of your letter first and then go backward, you accuse me of not submitting to you some of the pictures that we have made recently with other people which have turned out to be outstanding hits, and you state that you are certain that anyone of them would have been acceptable to you.

In the first place, you have no complaint as you have received absolutely nothing but the best in stories and, in the second place, you have repeatedly rejected stories that later turned out to be successful pictures. . . .

As I see it, Eddie, the whole fault lies in the fact that you want to be a writer. By this I mean that you want to put your views into whatever subject we purchase rather than to accept the views of the men I engage here who are specialists at a high salary in this specific work.

When I submit you a *Grand Slam* [1933], you say we have taken the wrong slant on the story—the idea is good but it should be something else. When I submit you a *Lawyer Man* [1933] or an *Employees' Entrance* [1933], you say the same thing.

By the way, *Lawyer Man* is the best picture [William] Powell has ever made and it would have been a perfect vehicle for you. It will be previewed in a week or so and I will send you the preview notices.

I have always wanted and asked for your suggestions and the suggestions of every star, as to story, etc., and those suggestions you made as to dialogue, etc., have, to my knowledge, for the most part been very effective and certainly appreciated by me.

The point I am trying to make is that when we submit a *Lawyer Man* or whatever it happens to be, you must have some faith in us. After all, our record of successes and box-office hits places us as the A-Company in the industry today, recognized thus everywhere. Our system, therefore, must be an ideal one. You can't make a lot of hits with a lot of different directors and a lot of different stars and some of them with no stars at all unless the "system" is a perfect one as, in our studio, it isn't just a case of one director or one star continually making a hit and the other ones flopping. This should be the greatest assurance in the world to you that our judgment is more or less correct, especially on the selection of stories and if I were in your shoes, I would be greatly guided by this "system."

After all, our sole interest is getting great pictures out of anything we select and we will accept anybody's ideas or suggestions, but the treatment of the subject in script form should be left largely to the judgment and intelligence of our "system," at least until the day comes—if it ever does—when our flops are more numerous than our hits. . . .

Sincerely,
Darryl Zanuck

Edward G. Robinson had been on the stage for years, but it was his first theatrical starring role as a gangster in The Racket *(1927) that led to several film roles (some as a gangster). Then* Little Caesar *(1930), produced by Warners, immediately made him a motion picture star and commenced his long career at Warner Bros.*

TO: [P. A.] Chase [Warner   DATE: November 11, 1932
    executive, New York]
FROM: [William] Dover [executive
    assistant to Zanuck]

Please draw a paper between Warner Bros. Pictures, Inc., and Darryl Zanuck wherein for the consideration of one dollar Darryl Francis Zanuck assigns all rights to his original story *Baby Face* to Warner Bros. Pictures, Inc. . . .

W. B. Dover

TO: Mr. Zanuck   DATE: November 11, 1932
SUBJECT: "Baby Face"   FROM: Howard Smith [screenwriter]

Following up the conference with [contract star Barbara] Stanwyck, I am sending you this note to remind you of the things she suggested, and which you suggested during this conference, for amplification and improvement of the story.

    1. The idea of Baby Face's father forcing the girl to dance at stag parties and to have affairs with the different men at the start of the story. The one definite situation where the girl's father beats her and forces her into a room where he knows a guy is waiting to spend the night with her—forces her into the room and turns the key in the lock after her. This is planted to definitely establish dialogue at the scene where the young banker asks Stanwyck to let him have the money he has given her in order to save him from prison. . . .

    2. The opening of the mills, the atmospheric idea of how this girl was forced by her no-good father to mingle with the lowdown—withal picturesque—characters of the mining town. How her father forces her to dance in the almost nude for the few shekels, which the men give her, and which shekels the father immediately brutally takes away from her.

    3. When the girl arrives in the city, the idea of her coming to the bank, the opening shot of this being the facade of the bank, panning shot from the basement to the top floor, showing the majesty, and imposing quality of the institution. . . .

Howard Smith

    Baby Face *was one example—of many—of the kind of sexually explicit material that was filmed by all of the studios in the early 1930s*

*—the worst years of the Depression. The Production Code, the indus-
try's attempt at self-regulation, was considerably strengthened in early
1934, thereby forcing studios to modify subject matter and treatment.
Warner Bros. and Columbia shared Stanwyck's contract in the early
1930s.*

Final Draft of an Article by Darryl F. Zanuck
for the "Holiday Number" of
The Hollywood Reporter,
December 1932

It is my sincere belief that the moving picture public will continue
to respond to the "headline" type of screen story that it has been the policy
of Warner Brothers-First National Pictures to produce during the past two
years.

A headline type of story must not be confused with the gangster or
underworld cycle of productions that have flooded the theatres in the past.
Somewhere in its makeup it must have the punch and smash that would
entitle it to be a headline on the front page of any successful metropolitan
daily.

Sometimes the story is a biography or an autobiography, like *I Am
a Fugitive from a Chain Gang.* Sometimes the story is that of a fictitious
character, based on headline incidents from the life of a real character,
such as *The Match King.* In the latter case, the story is deliberately veiled,
such as changing the character's name and altering some of the unimportant details, yet retaining enough of the original story matter so that
the average picture-goer easily grasps the identity of the notorious personality that is being exploited.*

Sometimes the story is of an exposé nature, like *Grand Slam,* which
endeavors to tear the lid off the contract bridge racket. In this case we use
a formula that calls for a mixture of drama and comedy, bordering slightly
on satire. . . .

The success of the innumerable pictures along these identical lines
that we have produced in the past encourages us to continue.

The first of these productions was *Doorway to Hell* [1930]. Then
came *Little Caesar, Public Enemy, Smart Money, Five Star Final,* etc.
We have touched on a great variety of subjects; . . . a maternity ward in
Life Begins, labor problems of the new South in *Cabin in the Cotton,*
etc., etc.

Of the productions we are handling at the present time, the most
pretentious are *Silver Dollar* and Warden Lewis E. Lawes' *Twenty Thou-*

---

*The film was fancifully based on the career of Ivar Kreuger.

sand Years in Sing Sing. One deals with the spectacular rise and fall of Colorado's most famous silver mining character,* and the other deals with Warden Lawes' greatly discussed "honor system."

We have just completed a musical exposé, *Forty-second Street*, which dramatically endeavors to lift the curtain and reveal the strenuous, heartbreaking efforts of a well known Broadway producer to stage a musical comedy in this year of depression. . . .†

Frisco Jenny, featuring Ruth Chatterton, is based on the life of a very notorious San Francisco Barbary Coast hostess. . . .**

It is my belief that the producer of pictures today, in searching for entertainment, finds himself in a position very similar to that of the editor of a metropolitan newspaper. By this I don't mean that romance and romantic stories are not "headline material". Love stories and sex stories make very good headlines, and sometimes very good pictures. *Baby Face* with Barbara Stanwyck, and *Ex-Lady*, with Bette Davis, are two of these particular types we are now producing. . . .

You can't go on telling the same story forever. The triangle is rusty. That is why we originally adopted the headline type of story, and that is why we intend to continue with it.

All the pictures mentioned above were made between 1930 and 1933. The policy continued.

FROM JACK L. WARNER
    HOLLYWOOD, CALIFORNIA
TO EDWARD G ROBINSON, PERSONAL
    ESSEX HOUSE, NEW YORK

                       MARCH 9, 1933
FOR THE PAST THREE DAYS AND NIGHTS MOTION PICTURE PRODUCERS HAVE BEEN MEETING FOR THE PURPOSE OF TRYING TO DEVISE PLANS TO TRY AND KEEP STUDIOS OPEN, AND LAST NIGHT THEY MET WITH BOARD OF DIRECTORS OF THE ACADEMY OF MOTION PICTURES ARTS AND SCIENCES WHO ADOPTED A RESOLUTION FOR THE ENTIRE INDUSTRY ENDORSING A PLAN WHICH MUST BE SUCCESSFUL AND IF NOT WILL RESULT IN THE IMMEDIATE DISCONTINUANCE OF ALL MOTION PICTURE PRODUCTION. AS YOU KNOW, THIS CONDITION IS CAUSED BY NATIONAL EMERGENCY, AND BUSINESS AT THE THEATRES [upon] WHICH WE DEPEND FOR COMPLETE SOURCE OF INCOME HAS BEEN DEMOR-

---

*Loosely based on the legendary H. A. W. Tabor.
†"Suggested by" Florenz Ziegfeld.
**"Suggested by" Tessie Wall, but more accurately by the fictional *Madame X*.

ALIZED MAKING IT IMPOSSIBLE TO TRANSFER MONIES TO LOS ANGELES. THE ACADEMY'S RESOLUTION WHOLEHEARTEDLY AND UNANIMOUSLY URGE THE ENTIRE INDUSTRY TO AID IN KEEPING THE STUDIO OPEN, AND EVOLVED THE FOLLOWING PLAN: THAT EVERYONE CONNECTED WITH PRODUCTION OF PICTURES, WHETHER UNDER CONTRACT OR NOT, ACCEPT A FIFTY PERCENT REDUCTION IN SALARY FOR EIGHT CON-SECUTIVE WEEKS COMMENCING MARCH SIXTH. IF PEOPLE ARE ON VACATION THEY ARE TO AGREE TO DEDUCT FIFTY PERCENT [of] THEIR SALARIES FOR FIRST EIGHT WEEKS AFTER THEY RETURN FROM THEIR VACATIONS. IT IS UNDERSTOOD UPON EXPIRATION OF SAID EIGHT WEEKS PERIOD YOUR CONTRACT WILL BE IN EXACTLY THE SAME STANDING AS BEFORE THIS TEMPORARY MODIFICATION. MASS MEETINGS HELD AT ALL STUDIOS TODAY, INCLUDING OUR OWN, WHEN ALL STARS, EXECUTIVES, DIRECTORS, WRITERS, AND FREE LANCE PLAYERS AND ALL BRANCHES OF MECHANICS ATTENDED AND APPROVED ACADEMY'S PLAN TO MEET THIS EMERGENCY WITH WHOLEHEARTED APPROVAL AND HAVE SIGNED ACCORDINGLY. UNLESS YOU ARE IN ACCORD WITH THIS ONE HUNDRED PERCENT AND RESPOND BY IMMEDIATE TELEGRAM SUBSCRIBING AND ACCEPTING THIS NOT LATER THAN FRIDAY NOON MARCH TENTH LOS ANGELES TIME, WE WILL BE FORCED TO SUSPEND ALL CONTRACTS UNDER SUSPENSION AND EMERGENCY PROVISION DUE TO NATIONAL EMERGENCY, AND WHICH WILL DEFINITELY AND IM-MEDIATELY RESULT IN THE CLOSING OF OUR ENTIRE STUDIO. REAL-IZING YOUR BEING AWAY FROM HERE MAKES THIS DIFFICULT, BUT SITUATION SO SERIOUS THAT UNLESS DRASTIC ACTION ON OUR PART IS CARRIED TO ITS FULFILLMENT WE CANNOT CARRY ON. YOUR CON-TRACT, AS YOU KNOW, IS ON FORTY WEEK BASIS, WHICH YOU ARE TO MAKE THREE PICTURES IN THE FORTY WEEKS. THEREFORE, IN ORDER TO DETERMINE WHAT REDUCTION YOU WILL TAKE WE HAVE COMPUTED YOUR YEARLY SALARY AND DIVIDED IT INTO FORTY WEEKS. AND WE WISH YOU TO WAIVE FIFTY PERCENT OF EIGHT OF THESE FORTY WEEKS TO BE DEDUCTED WHEN YOU RETURN FOR WORK.

WARNER BROTHERS PICTURES, INC.
BY J L WARNER, VICE PRESIDENT

This plan was put into effect at all of the studios. When the above telegram was sent, America was at the nadir of the Depression. On March 4 every bank in the nation, by order of President Roosevelt, was forced to close its doors. Four days later Roosevelt enacted his emergency banking bill to strengthen America's financial system. It was the beginning of the New Deal.

FROM HARRY M. WARNER [president of Warner Bros.]

Mr. Will H. Hays [president]
Motion Picture Producers &
Distributors of America, Inc.,
28 West 44th Street,
New York City.

June 9, 1933

Dear Mr. Hays:

You will remember the discussion at lunch the other day with yourself and others in regard to the activities of the Twentieth Century Pictures Company.

Darryl Zanuck had been employed by our company for a number of years and his contract had three years to run. At the time he resigned from our company [April 14, 1933] we were paying him salary at the rate of $4,000 per week and his contract called for a higher salary in the future. Mr. Zanuck stated to us that he had been offered twice as much from others than we were paying him and furthermore had indicated his desire to raise the salaries of actors and personnel in the motion pictures we were producing. You will recall Mr. Zanuck clashed with us at the time we were at the West Coast discussing the termination of the bank holiday salary reduction which resulted in Mr. Zanuck's resignation from our company.*

A few days after accepting his resignation we find that a new production company had been organized, called the Twentieth Century Picture Company with Mr. Joe Schenck as President and Mr. Darryl Zanuck as Chief producing executive.

Twentieth Century Pictures have approached contract and non-contract employees of our company at the Coast, not only actors, directors and writers, but even stenographers. One of the most aggravating single incidents of taking an important employee from another company, is the signing by Twentieth Century Pictures of a contract with George Arliss, an actor who had been associated and identified with us since 1928 and in whom we believed we were in the process of developing an important motion picture asset. . . .

Nevertheless, without any final word from him, or any notice by the Twentieth Century Pictures Company, we were suddenly informed that he had signed a contract with them. Similarly Twentieth Century Pictures have signed a contract with Loretta Young while she was still employed by us under an extension of her contract and we had made her a bona fide offer for a new contract.

*Warners refused to accept the date set by the Academy of Motion Pictures Emergency Committee for the full restoration of salaries. Zanuck resented the repudiation of an agreement, openly stated so, and then resigned.

I have been told and it is common rumor in the industry that Twentieth Century Pictures has been chiefly financed by a loan by Nicholas Schenck, President of Loew's Inc. and by Louis B. Mayer, head of production of Metro-Goldwyn-Mayer, to the President of Twentieth Century Pictures who is the brother of Mr. Schenck and to William Goetz of Twentieth Century Pictures, who is the son-in-law of Mr. Mayer. . . .

Without adding anything further to the above statement it is obvious that things have happened which should not happen in a well organized industry, the heads of which sit down together in your presence in the office of the Motion Picture Producers & Distributors of America, Inc. and attempt to lay out and abide by a course of fair dealing and business ethics. The doing of such things is only an incentive, in fact a compelling incentive, to companies who are the unfortunate victims of such circumstances, to retaliate or to appeal to another tribunal for protection. . . .

Very truly yours,
Harry M. Warner

Three days later Joseph Schenck wrote to Will Hays, having read a copy of Harry Warner's letter, and said that he had never spoken to Zanuck while he was in the employ of Warner Bros. regarding the formation of Twentieth Century or any other company, nor did he in any way induce or encourage Zanuck to leave Warner. "In fact, as I understand it and was told to me by Harry Warner himself, Darryl Zanuck did not voluntarily leave Warners. Warner was anxious to accept his resignation."

Schenck related that Zanuck came to his apartment to ask Schenck advice about various offers. Since Schenck was at that time out of the business of producing films, Zanuck felt he would receive good and unbiased counsel. "Only after two and one-half hours of conversation did I start to think about going back into the producing game with Zanuck and made that suggestion to him. He readily accepted and we signed the contract."

Schenck stated that both George Arliss and Loretta Young were signed after their contracts had expired at Warners.

Schenck resented Warner's statement that he (Schenck) borrowed money from his brother to form the company. "It is absolutely none of his business." Schenck claimed that when he signed Zanuck neither his brother nor Louis B. Mayer knew anything about it. And he engaged William Goetz because he considered him "a clever young man" who would eventually turn out to be a good producer.

Twentieth Century was a successful company, and in 1935 it merged with Fox Film Corporation.

Hal Wallis replaced Zanuck at Warners. He had joined the company in 1923 as assistant to the head of publicity, worked his way up, moved

*into production, and eventually became the senior supervisor (producer)
under Zanuck.*

TO: William Wellman [director]   DATE: July 5, 1933
FROM: Hal Wallis [associate   SUBJECT: "Wild Boys of The Road"
    executive]

Dear Billy:

I am just looking at the stuff where the train passes over and cuts
the kid's [Edwin Phillips] leg off. There is no doubt about it, it is effective
but if we ever left this in, there would be more premature births in the
theatre and more people dying than were killed in the World War. I know
that you are protected all around so that we can cut this any way, but we
still have to tone it down a little. . . .

I hope . . . you will get it over more by suggestion. . . . The picture
looks so great to date that I know we don't have to resort to going too
heavy on this particular type of scene, as you have such marvelous shots
in your train stuff. As a matter of fact, if you handle them without
pounding them over so hard, I feel that it will be a lot better for the
picture.

The pan-shot of the freight train where the brakeman starts throwing
coal at the three kids, and they hop off the train, is marvelous. This
particular type of shot, these long shots that you are getting in the picture
are making it a big thing. It gives the picture a background and a sweep
bigger than I ever thought it was going to have. . . .

Hal Wallis

TO: [Michael] Curtiz [director]   DATE: October 21, 1933
FROM: Hal Wallis   SUBJECT: "Mandalay"

I am just looking at your dailies. . . .

Generally your stuff is beautiful and I don't want to start limiting
you and restricting you. . . .

However, when you show [contract star] Kay Francis in the bathtub
with [contract star Ricardo] Cortez in the shot and a close-up of Kay
Francis in the tub and show her stepping out of the tub and going into
Cortez's arms, then you get me to the point where I am going to have to
tell you to stick to the script and not to do anything else. For god's sake,
Mike, you have been making pictures long enough to know that it is
impossible to show a man and a woman who are not married in a scene
of this kind. The situation itself, is censorable enough with Cortez and
Francis living [together]. . . .

Hal Wallis

Curtiz had been a European director before being signed by Warner

Bros. in 1926. He went on to become the studio's most important director over a long period.

TO: [Robert] Presnell [screenwriter] DATE: October 21, 1933.
FROM: Wallis SUBJECT: "Mandalay"

. . . Naturally, in the scene in the Orient Cafe, it should be shot carefully, that is, making it more of a night club and gambling house than to indicate that it is a hook shop.* I don't feel we are sacrificing anything by doing this because people will put their own interpretation on it and know what kind of an establishment it is and what Francis is doing there. . . .

Hal Wallis

TO: [Hal B.] Wallis [associate DATE: March 8, 1934
    executive]
FROM: Mr. Warner

I am now looking at *It Happened One Night* [a Columbia Picture] with Clark Gable and Claudette Colbert. . . .

Wish you could see it Thursday. It has eleven reels [105 minutes]. In other words, maybe we are cutting our pictures too fast and making them too snappy—you can't tell though, maybe we are right. . . .

In seeing Clark Gable tonight in this picture I think we should definitely have [contract player] Lyle Talbot grow a mustache just like his. It gives him a sort of a flash and good looks. . . .

J. L. Warner

TO: Mr. Wallis DATE: October 5, 1933
FROM: Mr. Warner SUBJECT: "Convention City"

We must put brassieres on [contract star] Joan Blondell and make her cover up her breasts because, otherwise, we are going to have these pictures stopped in a lot of places. I believe in showing their forms but, for Lord's sake, don't let those bulbs stick out. I'm referring to her gown in *Convention City*.

J. L. Warner

TO: Archie Mayo [director] DATE: September 13, 1934
FROM: Hal Wallis SUBJECT: "Bordertown"

I don't like the way you played Bette Davis at all in the scene in the construction set. It's about time she's starting to crack, and if she's getting the willies from walking around the house she certainly don't show it in this scene. She plays it like Alice in Wonderland.

*House of prostitution.

I want you to take this scene over and make it in a more emotional-hysterical way. . . . I agreed with you when you softened her up in earlier scenes when she was on the make for him, but now that the murder has been committed it is time for her to start cracking. You can't do it all at once in the court-room. You don't have to re-shoot all the angles just take over the angle shooting over her shoulder. . . . She should begin to look a little careless about her appearance. I know you are going to tell me that she is hysterical when she drives up to the house and tells him to stop the car, but I still tell you she should have been a little more wild-eyed and hysterical in the office scene.

Hal Wallis

Bette Davis had signed a long-term contract with Warner Bros. in 1932, after being with Universal for a short period and before that a stage actress.

TO: Mr. Wallis   DATE: September 13, 1934
FROM: [Robert] Lord [supervisor*   SUBJECT: "Bordertown"
    and screenwriter]

Dear Hal:

I emphatically disagree with your criticism of the way Miss Davis is played in script scene 159. I think Archie has directed the scene perfectly. At least, he has directed the scene as I, who wrote it, intended it to be directed.

Before Miss Davis arrives at the construction shed, we see her at home . . . where we underline her growing insanity in such a manner that no audience can possibly miss it. These scenes have not yet been shot.

After the scene in the construction shed, we have two more scenes between Mr. Muni and Miss Davis . . . in which we underline her growing insanity before the courtroom scene. We also have script scene 161 for the same purpose.

My point is very clear and logical: if we start Miss Davis cracking up and screaming too early, we will have absolutely nothing left for her in the later, clinching scenes. We will arrive at a climax in her characterization a full reel before we intend to. We will also face the danger of making her character tiresome and monotonous.

Hal, believe me, I know something of psychopathic women. I did not create this character without careful documentation and study. I will

---

*"Supervisor" was the title for a staff producer working under the executive producer at some of the studios during this period. The term "associate producer" also was used in some organizations.

be the first one to protest if Archie is playing her badly. In my opinion, he is playing her with great discretion and effectiveness—and the lady is giving an outstanding performance.

I am sorry if I seem so obdurate about a relatively slight retake but, in this particular case, I am positive that we are right and you are wrong.

Lord

From the available evidence, which is the released film, the retake if made, was not used. Robert Lord joined Warner Bros. in 1927 as a writer and later became an important producer ("supervisor") at the studio.

TO: [Ray] Enright [staff director]   DATE: July 19, 1934
FROM: Mr. Wallis   SUBJECT: "Perfect Week-End"
    [*The St. Louis Kid*]

Dear Brick:

Your first two days' dailies, generally, look very good. The action is good and your set-ups are OK but there is one major criticism and that is in Cagney's characterization. I have an idea that this is inspired largely by himself because I know that, when he first read the script, he objected to playing another tough character and I can see that he is doing his best to soften him up and make him as much of a gentleman as possible and still keep him a truck driver. . . .

He doesn't have to go around talking out of the side of his mouth or slugging people but let him show a little guts and let him get hard once in awhile as the picture loses a punch by having him playing it so gentlemanly. . . .

It is true that we don't want to play him as tough as he usually plays these things as there is naturally an objection to slugging dames and all of that stuff today but, at the same time, we don't want to lose Cagney's real characterization which is a semi-tough character and which we definitely are doing in these first two days stuff. It is going to hurt the picture considerably unless you change immediately. . . .

Hal Wallis

James Cagney was brought to Warners from the New York stage in 1930. The Public Enemy (1931) made him a major star.

TO: [Sam] Bischoff [supervisor]   DATE: June 14, 1934
FROM: J. L. Warner   SUBJECT: "The Case of the
    Howling Dog"

Be sure that Bette Davis has her bulbs wrapped up. If she doesn't do it, we are either going to retake, or put her out of, the picture—and if you talk with her, you can tell her I said so. . . .

In pictures, never let anyone cover their eyes with hats.

J. L. Warner

Davis refused to work in The Case of the Howling Dog *and was suspended after she "failed to report for wardrobe fittings." Contract player Helen Trenholme was cast in the role of Della Street.*

TO: Harry Joe Brown [supervisor] DATE: July 6, 1934
FROM: Mr. Wallis SUBJECT: "The Thin Man"

I saw *The Thin Man* [MGM] tonight and it would certainly be great if you could [get] the treatment into *The Case of the Curious Bride* that they got into that picture. The treatment of the subject absolutely made the picture and if you can get that lightness into the character of Perry Mason and let him solve *The Case of the Curious Bride* in that manner, it will make twice as good a picture as if it is handled in the usual straight, detective story fashion.

Hal Wallis

TO: [Leo] Forbstein [music director] DATE: November 20, 1934
FROM: Mr. Wallis SUBJECT: "Gold Diggers of 1935"

This morning I got a call from [director Busby] Berkeley and [supervisor Robert] Lord on the song that [contract star] Dick Powell did in the motor boat, and I find that the record for this, which was played back with Powell singing to it, was made only the night before. The complaint was that the orchestra recorded the number with a straight tempo and did not permit for any business on Dick's part or for the proper rendition of the song, and also that the orchestration was not good, that someone other than [Ray] Heindorf had made it.

My purpose in writing the letter is for a couple of reasons. In the first place, the *Gold Diggers* is perhaps the most important property that we make all year, and, regardless of the fact that Heindorf broke an ankle, this number should have been arranged by him, not in the past week, when his ankle was broken but four or five weeks ago. . . .

Incidentally, this is just one more argument against making a record on the recording stage and then playing it back for someone to sing to, as, if we had had a standard recording orchestra on the stage this morning to do the number, we might have played around with it and got the tempo a little different and rehearsed the thing as it should have been rehearsed and done it properly instead of by engineering methods and experimentations by our sound department. I saw the rehearsal of the number and Dick Powell seems to be rushed all the way through it because he was singing to a mechanical orchestra being played back to him instead of singing to an orchestra to follow him and do the number properly, and probably some day I can convince our sound department that that is the way important numbers in important pictures should be done. . . .

The one important thing that I think should be given consideration is the fact that our first big important number that Dick Powell sings in the picture, in a very romantic scene, is recorded the night before he is to shoot it, and the arrangement is made by somebody over night—two nights before he is to sing it, without ever having talked over the situation where the song comes in in the script or anything else, and it is just an automatic process and the orchestration should have been made weeks ago.

Hal Wallis

At this time, at all of the studios, most musical numbers were pre-recorded and then filmed to playback of the recording.

TO: Wallis   DATE: January 11, 1935
FROM: Jack L. Warner

I overheard a typical Mike Curtiz–Harry Joe Brown squawk about not wanting to use Errol Flynn in *The Case of the Curious Bride*. I hope that they did not change you because I want him used in this picture, first because I think it is a shame to let people like Curtiz and Harry Brown to even think of opposing an order coming from you or myself and, secondly, when we bring a man all the way from England he is at least entitled to a chance and somehow or other we haven't given him one. I want to make sure he is in the picture. Let me hear from you on this the next time we see each other.

J. L. Warner

Since arriving from England in 1934, Flynn had small parts in The Case of the Curious Bride *(1935) and* Don't Bet on Blondes *(1935), two modest Warner program pictures.*

2

Jack L. and Hal B. in Stride (1935–1938)

CAPTAIN BLOOD

FEBRUARY 20, 1935

FROM JACK L. WARNER [vice president in charge of production]
MR. W. R. HEARST [publisher]
SAN SIMEON, CALIF.

DEAR MR. HEARST
    WE GOING [to] PRODUCE RAFAEL SABATINI [novel] "CAPTAIN BLOOD" WITH ROBERT DONAT. WOULD MISS MARION DAVIES BE INTERESTED IN PLAYING IN THIS IMPORTANT PICTURE? THERE IS AN EXCELLENT FEMININE PART FOR HER. HOWEVER, WE CAN GO OVER ALL THIS IMMEDIATELY UPON MY RETURN.

Hearst's Cosmopolitan Productions and Marion Davies recently had moved from MGM to Warner Bros. Olivia de Havilland eventually was assigned the role of Arabella Bishop, the feminine lead in Captain Blood. *She had been under contract since late 1934 when Warners signed her to reprise her stage role of Hermia in Max Reinhardt's film version of* A Midsummer Night's Dream *(1935).* Captain Blood *was her fourth picture.*

TO: Hal Wallis [executive
    producer]
FROM: Harry Joe Brown
    [supervisor]

DATE: June 11, 1935
SUBJECT: "Captain Blood"

Dear Hal:

In going quickly over the names since you spoke to me of it this noon at lunch, I still feel that Leslie Howard is the number one man [for the role of Captain Blood]. I can't help but feel that he is getting an excellent follow-up after *Scarlet Pimpernel* in *Captain Blood*. I am sure we would make a much greater picture than *Scarlet Pimpernel*, and Mr. Howard could play any scene in this picture as well as any star, and better than most of them.

A good proportion of these scenes such as the courtroom, the love scenes, scenes with his men, are all sensitive scenes and should be played as such. Howard also has the intelligence that a man such as this leader must have. I cannot think of any scene that he could not play.

With [Fredric] March out of the picture, my next choice would be Clark Gable, and next, Ronald Colman. I fully understand the terrific effort in even starting to negotiate for these men [under contract to other studios], but I still feel that no man in the business is too big to go after for *Captain Blood*. I am confident that it is one of the best stories of its kind ever written.

After that ilk of players, there is also an English player who should by all means be given a test, and that is Brian Aherne. He is in the [Robert] Donat-Howard class of actors, and has just missed going over the top, due, I would say, to a lack of vehicles and studio consideration of him.

Robert Donat originally had been signed to play Captain Blood, but based on inconclusive and varying reports regarding his health, personal life, and/or his contract, he bowed out prior to shooting. Leslie Howard was not available or not interested; Brian Aherne was tested.

TO: Mervyn LeRoy [director]
FROM: Wallis

DATE: June 11, 1935
SUBJECT: "Captain Blood"

I would like to have a couple of very good tests made on Thursday of George Brent and Errol Flynn for the part of Captain Blood in the picture of that name.

As you know, Curtiz is shooting the picture and I will appreciate it if you will arrange to shoot these.

Hal Wallis

George Brent and Errol Flynn were both under contract to Warner Bros. Brent had played leads for a few years, but Flynn had done only two small parts in the United States.

TO: Harry Joe Brown,   DATE: June 20, 1935
    Michael Curtiz   SUBJECT: "Captain Blood"
FROM: Wallis

We are going to make another series of tests with Errol Flynn for the part of "Captain Blood." . . .

Have a wig fixed properly for Flynn, even if we have to make one; get some good clothes for him without all those spangles and gold braid on them. In other words, dress him pretty much as he will be dressed in the picture.

Also, between now and the end of the week, Harry Joe should get Flynn in and lay out the scenes which Flynn will be required to do. There should be two or three scenes of different types so that we can test Flynn exhaustively, and definitely decide if he can do the part.

(1) There should be one scene between "Blood" and "Levasseur" with somebody to play "Levasseur's" part also.
(2) There should be a scene between "Blood" and his men.
(3) A scene between "Blood" and the girl.

In other words, pick out material that will give Flynn the opportunity to get over every emotion. We want [contract player] Jean Muir to work with him again in the test.

When making the tests, Mike Curtiz should move the people around, instead of just parking Flynn in front of the camera and shooting a close-up. He should actually play the scene.

Please let's not have any slip-ups on this series of tests, as the result of them will determine whether or not Flynn is to do the part, and let's have everything right; have Flynn up in his scenes and really do this thing correctly so that we won't have a lot of excuses next week as to why we did not do this or why we did not do that. . . .

Hal Wallis

After testing Flynn again and contract player Ian Hunter, Flynn was cast as "Blood."

TO: Curtiz   DATE: August 18, 1935
FROM: Wallis   SUBJECT: "Captain Blood"

Dear Mike:

. . . I think Flynn is doing very well, except that in the court-room I thought you played him down a little too much, particularly those speeches where he talks about having been in prison for three months, and a little later on, where he says, "Very well, then," and where he tells the Judge that he is a doctor and tells the Judge about his own condition. It seems to me you could have gotten a little more fire in him . . . let his eyes light up a little, get a little more fire in his eyes in scenes of this kind. He plays a little too much in a monotone. These repressed scenes are good, but they should be varied.

I know that he can do this, it is just a matter of direction. There is a test here that was made of Flynn in England, where he played a great scene, with lots of guts and a lot of fire, and I wish you would look at it to prove to yourself that he can do those things. . . .

Hal Wallis

TO: Curtiz   DATE: August 28, 1935
FROM: Wallis   SUBJECT: "Captain Blood"

I am looking at your dailies, and, while the stuff is very nice, you got a very short day's work. I suppose this was due to bad weather.

However, I don't understand what you can be thinking about at times. That scene in the bed-room, between Captain Blood and the governor, had one punch line in it; the line from Blood: "I'll have you well by tonight, if I have to bleed you to death," or something along these lines, anyhow. This is the one punch line to get over that Blood had to get out of there by midnight, even if he had to kill the governor, and instead of playing that in a close-up—a big head close-up—and getting over the reaction of Errol Flynn, and what he is trying to convey, and the crafty look in his eye, you play it in a long shot, so that you can get the composition of a candle-stick and a wine bottle on a table in the foreground, which I don't give a damn about.

Please don't forget that the most important thing you have to do is to get the story on the screen, and I don't care if you play it in front of BLACK VELVET! Just so you tell the story; because, if you don't have a story, all of the composition shots and all the candles in the world aren't going to make you a good picture. . . .

Hal Wallis

TO: Curtiz   DATE: September 9, 1935
FROM: Wallis   SUBJECT: "Captain Blood"

The dailies in the garden, between Blood and the girl [Olivia de Havilland]—generally—were good. . . .

He plays the scene at the carriage very well . . . and if you will work with the boy a little, and give him a little confidence, I know he can be twice as good as he is now, but the fellow looks like he is scared to death every time he goes into a scene. I don't know what the hell is the matter. When he has confidence and gets into a scene, he plays it charmingly.

Hal Wallis

TO: Curtiz   DATE: September 30, 1935
FROM: Wallis   SUBJECT: "Captain Blood"

I have talked to you about four thousand times, until I am blue in the face, about the wardrobe in this picture. I also sat up here with you one night, and with everybody else connected with the company, and we discussed each costume in detail, and also discussed the fact that when the men get to be pirates that we would not have "Blood" dressed up.

Yet tonight, in the dailies, in the division of the spoil sequence, here is Captain Blood with a nice velvet coat, with lace cuffs out of the bottom, with a nice lace stock collar, and just dressed exactly opposite to what I asked you to do.

I distinctly remember telling you, I don't know how many times, that I did not want you to use lace collars or cuffs on Errol Flynn. What in the hell is the matter with you, and why do you insist on crossing me on everything that I ask you not to do? What do I have to do to get you to do things my way? I want the man to look like a pirate, not a molly-coddle. You have him standing up here dealing with a lot of hard-boiled characters, and you've got him dressed up like a God damned faggot. . . .

I suppose that when he goes into the battle with the pirates (the French) at the finish, you'll probably be having him wear a high silk hat and spats.

When the man divided the spoils you should have had him in a shirt with the collar open at the throat, and no coat on at all. Let him look a little swashbuckling, for Christ sakes! Don't always have him dressed up like a pansy! I don't know how many times we've talked this over. . . .

I hope that by the time we get into the last week of shooting this picture, that everybody will be organized and get things right. It certainly is about time.

Hal Wallis

TO: Wallis   DATE: December 10, 1935
FROM: [Robert] Lord [writer
      and supervisor]

Dear Hal:

Why do you have so much flogging, torturing and physical cruelty in *Captain Blood?* Do you like it? Does Mike like it or do you think audiences like it? Women and children will be warned to stay away from the picture—and justly so.

                                                                    Lord

TO: Writers, Supervisors, Directors,   DATE: August 10, 1935
    and Department Heads   SUBJECT: Previews
FROM: J. L. Warner

I will appreciate it for the good of the work we are all accomplishing, if you will make it your business to be present . . . at all our previews, because, in my opinion, we can certainly all learn.

A preview is the place where you can gain more real knowledge in one hour than from any other form of making pictures, as it is here where the audience reacts one way or the other.

                                                            J. L. Warner

TO: [William] Keighley [director]   DATE: March 7, 1935
FROM: Wallis   SUBJECT: "G" Men

. . . you are still playing Cagney too much of a gentleman. I can't seem to get you to let the fellow be a mug from the East side. After all, he is supposed to be an East side mug who was put through law school by a lot of crooks and he is playing it like a white collared gentleman in a drawing room. It seems to me that in this opening sequence where Cagney is talking to the jury, we can have him a little more of the old Cagney character, with a little tougher accent and not being so perfect in his English. . . . It can be taken for granted that after he gets into the Department of Justice he tries to conduct himself and act more like a gentleman, which will be all right.

                                                            Hal Wallis

Keighley, a stage director, signed with Warner in 1932 as a dialogue director, but was soon directing some of the studio's more important films (as well as routine works).

TO: [J. L.] Warner   DATE: September 27, 1935
FROM: Wallis   SUBJECT: "Enemy of Man"

With further reference to the title of Pasteur picture, I feel definitely that we should call it *The Story of Louis Pasteur.*

Of course, every time we go into a subject of this kind, the Sales Department brings up the arguement: "Nobody knows Pasteur" or 'it doesn't mean anything," et cetera, et cetera; but the same thing could have happened to:

> *Disraeli*
> *House of Rothschild*
> *Les Miserables*
> *David Copperfield*
> *Anna Karenina*
> *The Barretts of Wimpole Street*

I feel that if Metro or the other companies had asked exhibitors or others what they thought about the above titles, the chances are none of them would ever have reached the screen, and they would all have been called *I Loved A Woman* [1933].

After all, we are making a story with a big theme and a story concerning a world famous figure, so let's give it a title of importance and possibly we can get a good grossing picture out of it. . . .

Hal Wallis

The picture, starring Paul Muni, was released as The Story of Louis Pasteur *(1936) and started a biographical cycle at Warner Bros. and other studios.*

TO: Wallis   DATE: December 23, 1935
FROM: [Roy] Obringer   SUBJECT: Leslie Howard
      [general counsel]

Just to remind you of our existing contract with Leslie Howard relative to the previews on *The Petrified Forest.*

The picture, as you know, is to be previewed with both the happy and unhappy endings to determine which ending is more acceptable to the public. Howard should be notified as to the time and place of these previews, in order that Howard will not complain of not having the opportunity to be present and note the reaction of the audience.

If, after both previews, we are unable to come to an agreement with Howard as to which ending shall be adopted for the release, then, within

one week after such second preview, we will leave the issue to a board of
3 arbitrators whose decision will be binding upon both ourselves and
Howard.

R. J. Obringer

*Wallis, writing on the above memo, replied that they had already
decided to use the unhappy ending, in which the character portrayed by
Howard is murdered by the character played by Humphrey Bogart. Howard
had starred in the play on Broadway and specifically requested the above
provision in his contract for this film only. He also insisted that Bogart
reprise the role he created on Broadway. Warner then signed Bogart to a
long-term contract.*

FROM BETTE DAVIS

June 21, 1936

Dear Mr. [Jack] Warner:

In reference to our talk today—it seemed to me our main
problem is getting together on the money. You as Head of your firm,
naturally know what your concern can afford and what they can't.

I have no desire to be "off your list" and I feel sure—you do not
wish it either. I agree lots of harm can be done thru publicity. Believe
me when I tell you I have thought and prepared for every angle of this
for a long time now. I also know you have the right to keep me from
working—a great unhappiness to me because I enjoy working—
especially after my long vacation. I am so rested it hurts! However,
there comes a time in everyone's career when certain things make
working worth-while. I am now referring to the very few rights I have
asked for—when I saw you in your office the other day you assured me
you would do all the things I wanted anyway with the exception of the
loan-out [to other studios], so it is hard for me to understand why you
object to putting it in writing. Five years is a long time—anything can
happen—so you must see my side of it—protection. You can't blame
anyone for protecting themselves. If I am worth anything to you at
all—you can't mind letting me know it in writing—if I'm not this
letter is in vain.

As to the "loan-out clause," I am the kind of a person who
thrives under change. I have never wanted this clause because I wanted
to feel I was my own boss—have authority of my own—quite the
contrary. I like a boss—someone to look up to whose opinion I respect
as I do yours. Mentally—a change does me good—makes me do better
work, I like working with new directors, new casts, etc. I also am
ambitious to become known as a great actress—I might, who can tell.
Every once in a while a part comes along peculiarly suited to me. I

want to feel, should a role come my way, I am at liberty to take advantage of it. If no such part ever appears in five years, then I will not take advantage of my right. In that case I am very anxious to travel, thus the request for three consecutive months vacation. Travel is also change—good publicity for you and me both and particularly important to me during the next five years as I have never been out of this country—it is broadening to one's intellect and will help me I'm sure in my work and thus help you. I am an essentially high-strung person—for that reason—change means rest and I must have rest.

To get back to our call and the purpose of this letter, I would be willing to take less money, if in consideration of this, you would give me my "rights." You have asked me to be level headed in this matter. I feel I am extremely and I hope you can agree that I am. I am more than anxious to work for you again, but not as things stand. I really would be unable to do justice to my work at all—as I would feel I was coming back—not entitled to the things I sincerely believe I deserve.

As a happy person, I can work like Hell—as an unhappy one, I make myself and everyone around me unhappy. Also I know and you do too—in a business where you have a fickle public to depend on, the money should be made when you mean something, not when the public has had time to tell you to "go to hell." . . .

Bette

Following this letter, Bette Davis refused to report to work for God's Country and the Woman *(1936) and was suspended by the studio. She then went to England to make a film. In September, Warner Bros. sued her for breach of contract. She lost the court case and returned to work in* Marked Woman *(1937) in November—without loan-out privileges. The Little Foxes (1941), her one film away from Warners from 1934 until the end of her contract in 1949, was a special deal arranged by the studio with Samuel Goldwyn in exchange for Gary Cooper to star in* Sergeant York *(1941).*

THE CHARGE OF THE LIGHT BRIGADE

TO: [Sam] Bischoff [supervisor]   DATE: January 8, 1936
FROM: Wallis   SUBJECT: "The Charge of the Light
                                            Brigade"

I am going to run *Lives of a Bengal Lancer* [Paramount, 1935] at my house tonight. Would you like to see it again, in view of our getting ready for *Light Brigade*?

Hal Wallis

Paramount's Lives of a Bengal Lancer *was a major success and started a cycle of adventure films that glorified British imperialism in India and Africa.*

TO: Bischoff   DATE: February 13, 1936
FROM: Wallis   SUBJECT: "The Charge of the Light Brigade"

. . . I am still somewhat concerned over the historical inaccuracies, as covered by our London office letter of November 27th—particularly the total disregard for historical facts on the battle of Balaclava and "The Charge of the Light Brigade," the motivation therefore. . . .

I realize that we have a highly fictionized story and that it bears no relation to historical facts but, at the same time, if we are to save ourselves from a lot of grief and criticism in England, we must make our picture as historically accurate as possible, or at least surround our Battle of Balaclava and The Charge of the Light Brigade with historically correct incidents and details, which will take the curse off of our one major invention—that of having "Geoffrey" [Errol Flynn] secure the signature of Lord Raglan at the War Council.. . . .

Hal Wallis

TO: Hal Wallis   DATE: March 10, 1936
FROM: Jack L. Warner

I had a general conversation with Mike Curtiz in the usual Curtiz manner in the dining room at noon, and all he talked about were the sets and that he wants to build a fort somewhere else, and all a lot of hooey. I didn't hear him say anything about the story. In other words, he's still the same old Curtiz—as he will always be! Bischoff was there at the time, and I told him that we don't want to go any place for the fort or any other locations, other than the ones you have already picked out, so for Lord's sake, get ahold of this Mike and set him on his pratt and let him make the story and not worry about the sets. Let the Art Director worry about this; he's getting paid for it. You know what I mean.

I am now looking at the new tests of Errol Flynn with his mustache darkened and he looks very good. As far as I am concerned, I think it would be a good idea to leave the mustache on. It gives him a little more punch in this particular role. What do you think? Let me know.

I am now looking at the helmet with the sash on, and Flynn looks excellent. The mustache certainly looks good; I am sure that the mustache is the thing for this picture.

J. L. Warner

The mustache remained, and with rare exceptions was a permanent fixture throughout Flynn's career.

TO: Hal Wallis   DATE: March 28, 1936
FROM: Rowland Leigh   SUBJECT: "The Charge of the Light Brigade"
      [screenwriter]

Dear Hal Wallis:

I hope you will not think I am interfering gratuitously, but might I make a few comments with regard to the casting for *The Charge of the Light Brigade?* The parts I refer to may already be definitely set, in which case, naturally there is nothing to be done.

1. The part of "Elsa." It is difficult to explain why, but I can promise you that an English audience will never accept Anita Louise as Colonel Campbell's British daughter brought up in England. Whereas they would accept Olivia de Havilland. It is not so much a question of accent as of intonation. Miss Louise is an awfully good actress but to English eyes and ears she is one hundred per cent American. Whereas Miss de Havilland both in looks and voice could, with careful handling, easily be accepted as a young English woman of the Victorian era.

2. The part of "Randall." This part was written by Mr. Jacoby and myself with David Niven in mind so we were naturally delighted when we heard that he had been engaged to play it. We understand now that he is to play "Barclay," who is more or less nondescript walk-on. . . .

3. This is a delicate point but would it be possible for me to see the tests along with either Curtiz or you because time and again people who are quite good actors play parts for which their definite cockney accents render them unsuitable. Curtiz naturally doesn't know the shadings of English accents, and in a film like this where the person playing an "officer and a gentleman" must be a gentleman as well as military, it is frightfully important that the actors should speak the Queen's English.

The rest of the casting has been so brilliant and I naturally am so intensely interested in the success of the film that I hope you will forgive me for these few criticism and suggestions.

Very sincerely,
Rowland Leigh

Niven, borrowed from Samuel Goldwyn, did play the role of "Randall."

FROM JACK L. WARNER

MARCH 27, 1936
WARNER TO WALLIS—WE DEFINITELY WANT YOU TO USE OLIVIA DE HAVILLAND IN "CHARGE OF THE LIGHT BRIGADE" WITH ERROL FLYNN

AS WE MUST HAVE COMBINATION, BECAUSE "BRIGADE" FOLLOW-UP PICTURE TO "CAPTAIN BLOOD" AND INTEND TO HANDLE THE CAMPAIGN THAT WAY. THIS IS IN NO WAY ANY REFLECTION ON [contract player] ANITA LOUISE, WHOM WE ALL ADMIRE AND TO WHOM WE LOOK FOR BIG THINGS, BUT BECAUSE OF THE FOREGOING WE MUST INSIST ON USING DE HAVILLAND.

Olivia de Havilland was cast opposite Flynn. Anita Louise remained under contract until 1938, after which she free-lanced.

TO: Curtiz   DATE: April 17, 1936
FROM: Wallis   SUBJECT: "The Charge of the Light Brigade"

. . . Are you trying to cut in the camera and pick out just those portions of the scene that you want to play in closeup? Apparently this is it, otherwise you would let the scenes run full.

I remember about four months ago when you came to my office and pleaded to be allowed to make this picture and promised me that if you got it you would absolutely behave and do everything that you were told to do, and I would not have any trouble with you on the picture, but I have had just one headache after another. I certainly am not going away with any feeling of security over this picture, because every day that you have shot so far there has been something wrong. . . .

Let me tell you now that for the balance of the picture I want you to let all camera angles run full. I don't necessarily mean long shots to run all through a scene, but when you move into close-ups I want you to shoot the entire scene in close-ups so that we can cut it the way we want. Let us have a break on playing with the film.

Hal Wallis

FROM JOSEPH I. BREEN [director of the Production Code Administration]

Mr. J. L. Warner
Warner Bros.
Burbank, Calif.

August 24, 1936

Dear Mr. Warner:

Mr. [Harold] McCord [editorial supervisor] has phoned in, requesting a Certificate to permit the re-issue of your picture *The Public Enemy* [1931].

As you will recall, this picture definitely falls into the category of gangster pictures, which the [Motion Picture Producers and

Distributors] Association agreed to discontinue some time ago. In view of this fact, we naturally could not issue a Certificate at this time authorizing its re-issue. . . .

Cordially yours,
Joseph I. Breen

The Production Code Administration was created in 1930 by the Motion Picture Producers and Distributors of America. The Public Enemy was not reissued until 1953.

TO: [Lloyd] Bacon [director]   DATE: January 10, 1937
FROM: Wallis   SUBJECT: "Marked Woman"

I saw the fog test and generally it looks okay, except that the cameraman should wet down the stairs and the building so that we get the feeling of moisture. As it is, it is too dry. It doesn't quite get the effect over. Also, they ought to put glycerine or something on the electric lights so we get that murky halation—that effect of halation. Also, he did not have the big electric light fixture on the street lighted. I suppose you will do that when you are ready to shoot and let him get that so we can get drippy feeling too. I would have him wet down the sidewalk, the stairs and the building, the pillars and around the doorway—all of that—and then I think it will be all right and have him be careful and not pump too much fog into the foreground in gusts as it did in this test. . . .

Hal Wallis

TO: Wallis   DATE: January 29, 1937
FROM: [Robert] Lord   SUBJECT: "Tovarich"

Dear Hal:

I have been studying the play *Tovarich* very closely and I am more convinced than ever that it can be made into an outstanding picture.

I saw announced in the newspapers that the following people have been engaged for it: Claudette Colbert as Tatiana, [Charles] Boyer as Prince Mikail, and [Basil] Rathbone as the Commissar. This is probably just another false newspaper rumor; but if it is true, two of the people are quite wrong for the parts.

The ideal actor, in fact the inevitable actor, to play the Commissar is Edward G. Robinson. He must be gross, earthy, coarse, brutal, from the gutter—but a brilliantly educated man. Everything about Rathbone suggests the aristocrat. Rathbone playing the Commissar will throw your piece completely off balance.

Now about Boyer: He is a sad, meek, little man, about five feet, seven or eight—unless I am completely misinformed. Prince Mikail is a Russian cavalry officer, big, dashing, aristocratic and handsome—everything that Boyer is not. Freddy March, Brian Aherne, Rathbone, or even Ian Hunter is much closer to the character than Boyer. I know that Boyer has a good name and is adored by women; nevertheless this is one of the best stories we have had in years and it would be a shame to weaken it by casting the wrong man for Prince Mikail.

I am sorry to start my association with the picture by making trouble, but I sincerely feel that these matters deserve serious consideration.

Bob Lord

Claudette Colbert, Charles Boyer, and Basil Rathbone were cast. None was under contract to Warner Bros.

TO: Lord
FROM: [Walter] MacEwen
[executive assistant
to Hal Wallis]

DATE: March 5, 1937
SUBJECT: "That Certain Woman"

Dear Bob:

Before he left for New York, Mr. Wallis asked me to talk to you when you got back about an alternate ending for *That Certain Woman*.

Owing to the fact that in the picture *Marked Woman* Bette Davis walks off into the fog for a sort of indefinite finish, and again in *Kid Galahad*, Eddie Robinson is killed and Davis walks down an alley to an uncertain future, Mr. Wallis feels that to give her an uncertain finish for the third time in a row in *That Certain Woman* might not be good audience psychology.

What he had in mind was a happy ending more along the lines of the old *Trespasser* [1929—upon which *That Certain Woman* was based] script—a quick, short scene in which she gets her man and baby back again. I am sure you will understand from this note what Hal is driving at, but if it isn't clear to you, maybe I can embroider it verbally for you.

Walter MacEwen

The character portrayed by Bette Davis does "get her man [Henry Fonda] and baby back again" at the conclusion of the film.

TO: Wallis   DATE: March 19, 1937
FROM: MacEwen   SUBJECT: "One Hour of Romance"

[Supervisor Henry] Blanke suggests the title *Confession* for use instead of the title *One Hour of Romance*. He thinks it is much more suitable for the *Mazurka* story than the title *One Hour of Romance*.

 Confession is a title Geza Herczeg coined for *The Great Lie*. Blanke would rather see us use it on the [Kay] Francis picture, and use the title *One Hour of Romance* on *The Great Lie* which he thinks it suits best.

Walter MacEwen

How's that again? The picture, an adaptation of the German film Mazurka *(1935), was released as* Confession *(1937). The* Great Lie *became the title for a 1941 Warner film.* One Hour of Romance *was never used.*

TO: Mr. Wallis   DATE: March 25, 1937
FROM: T. C. Wright   SUBJECT: "One Hour of Romance"
 [studio production manager]   [*Confession*]
            Joe May

As Mr. Blanke is home sick, I am writing to you about the amount of work which [director] Joe May did yesterday. . . .

 He made 6 [camera] set-ups all day long. Another thing he did which I think is the most damn foolish thing I have ever heard of in pictures, and I have heard of a lot of them—he took Basil Rathbone, at five grand a week, when we had a perfectly good double on the set, and insisted on Rathbone doing the fall down the stairs. Both the Unit Manager and [assistant director] Sherry Shourds wanted him to use the double that we had provided. Rathbone, however, said he was willing, and Joe May wanted to shoot the picture *his* way, so he had Rathbone roll down the stairs not once for the long shot, but *10* times. #6, #7, and #10 were HOLD takes, and two hours was spent for these 10 shots of the roll down the stairs.

 I am giving this to you for your own information, but I am instructing both [unit manager Al] Alleborn and Shourds that if this guy has anything else like this, to let me know, and I am going to get you to go down on the set. . . .

T. C. Wright

 This was the first and last picture Austrian director Joe May made for Warner Bros.

THE LIFE OF EMILE ZOLA

FROM MORRIS EBENSTEIN [Legal Department, New York]

Mr. Henry Blanke
Warner Bros. Pictures, Inc.,
Burbank, Calif.

February 18, 1937

Dear. Mr. Blanke:

I have now completed reading the final version of the *Zola* script. . . .

We are unfortunately confronted here with a very serious problem. I have just learned . . . that Lucie Dreyfus, wife of the late Captain Alfred Dreyfus, is still alive. Now, she plays quite a prominent role in our script. As I wrote you in one of my recent letters, there is quite an unfortunate twist in the American law on the subject of using in a film an impersonation of a person who is actually alive. Under our law you cannot use the actual name of a living person in a photoplay or impersonate an actual living person in a photoplay, without his written consent and it makes no difference whether you say good or bad things about the person in such a case. Even though nothing derogatory is said about the person, he will have the absolute right to enjoin the showing of the picture if his name is used to any extensive degree, or if he is impersonated in the picture by another actor, unless his written consent is obtained in advance. You simply must not use the name of a living person to any extensive degree in a photoplay and further, you must not impersonate a living person in a photoplay.

In view of this state of the law, it appears that Madame Dreyfus will have the absolute right, if she is so minded, to enjoin the showing of our film. She may have the same rights in England. Incidentally, this is not the case in France and other European countries, but is a peculiar twist of the American law.

The question then is what to do about it. . . .

Sincerely,
Morris Ebenstein

Henry Blanke accompanied director Ernst Lubitsch to America in 1922 and then to Warner Bros. in 1923 as Lubitsch's assistant. He remained with Warner in a variety of capacities, eventually being named a supervisor in 1933. Blanke was associated with many important pictures at the studio.

Whenever a legal complication seemed to warrant it, background material regarding the evolution of a project was researched, organized, and presented to the general counsel at the studio in memo form.

FROM FINLAY McDERMID [story editor]

August 8, 1938

Report regarding *The Life of Emile Zola*

On November 22, 1936, Pierre Dreyfus, son of the celebrated central figure of the Dreyfus Case, wrote a letter to the well-known lawyer, Samuel Untermeyer of New York. . . .

As a result . . . Warner Brothers subsequently turned over to Mr. Dreyfus, a copy of the final script. Certain changes were suggested by him and were duly made.

Pierre Dreyfus accepts on March 9, 1937, the final script of *Zola* in behalf of himself, his mother and his sister, as a true dramatic presentation of the affair. Himself an author, he realizes the dramatic necessity of taking a notable historic liberty in making Madame Dreyfus the person who appeals to Zola to arouse his interest in her husband's cause. He also accepts certain other dramatically important changes, but agrees with us that we have succeeded in maintaining the true spirit of the story and of the characters involved therein. . . .

Now, while it is true that our picture is exceptionally true to the *spirit*, the *background*, the *meaning* of Zola's character, life and times, it is also true that—but, only *after learning the facts*—we took great liberties in other respects.

For every biographer there are certain historic gaps to fill, certain interpretations of motives which must be made. And for a biographer who employs any form of dramatic presentation, problems of selection, chronology, emphasis are particularly acute.

Briefly, the picture *Zola* has little in common with accurate chronology or factual history, however faithfully it may interpret the spirit of that history or the heroic meaning of Emile Zola's life. There are many additions, many omissions in the picture. No mention, for example, is made of Zola's "other" love affairs or his period of domestic unhappiness nor to any elements in his life not germane to the vigorous and simple theme of the picture.

Chronologically the picture takes enormous liberties for dramatic purposes. *Nana* appears as the novel which skyrocketed the author to fame and fortune before the Franco-Prussia war; in reality *Nana* was written long after Zola had won a place for himself, and the war had become history.

Even the date of his death is advanced. . . . Zola is shown literally at work in his study. (Actually he and his wife had retired for the night.)

Zola was buried in the Montmartre Cemetery. Not until 1908 were the remains transferred to the Pantheon. At the funeral Anatole France delivered an oration, a small part of which is used in our picture. But once again scenes and events have been merged; the Pantheon is used by us as the scene of the oration and a portion of our speech stems not from Anatole France but from Zola's "Letter to Youth."

Historically, Zola did not meet Madame Dreyfus until after he had been arraigned for trial; her moving appeal to Zola for help—as shown in the film—is entirely fictitious. . . .

Throughout the picture the forces arrayed for and against Zola are frequently shown as one character instead of two, three, or a dozen. . . . Cezanne, in a measure, stands not only for himself but for other friends of Zola's youth.

The character of Nana—except as Zola's fictional heroine—and the part she played in Zola's career, are pure invention; the meeting between the two during a police raid never took place. Zola did witness such a raid and in all biographies mention is made of Zola's securing material for his book by paying note-taking visits to prostitutes. But the inspiration of building from the Nana scene the episode shown in our picture was an entirely original dramatic liberty, as was the entire idea of using *Nana's* success as a turning point in Zola's life. It meant a drastic revision of *all* chronology as regards Zola's literary output.

As characters are blended, so too, are places. . . .

Throughout our picture we have attempted, not to depict a "hero". Our protagonist is a man, with a man's weaknesses. We have "debunked" him—in the manner of the modern *printed* biography. He puffs and he groans, he laments and he wails before he abandons the happily slothful way of life into which he has fallen. . . .

TO: Perc Westmore   DATE: March 2, 1937
   [make-up artist]   SUBJECT: "Zola"
FROM: Wallis

I saw the test of the double with the [Paul] Muni make-up, and while I do not doubt that it is a very splendid piece of work so far as you are concerned, I really do not believe it is necessary to go into this sort of make-up for Muni.

My feeling is that I would rather take Muni as he is and make him up for the character so far as the hair and the beard is concerned and still retain the impression for the audience that Paul Muni is playing the part than I would to try to reproduce Zola exactly and so disguise Muni and make over his facial characteristics as to lose the Muni personality. Of course, this is not altogether so because Muni's personality and voice and all of that would still come through, but I would not go to such effort to disguise Muni and try to reproduce exactly the character of Zola.

Also, even though the additional flesh composition that you put on to the man was very good, there is still an element of fakiness which would be still more apparant when you get into closeup action such as we will have all through the picture. In other words, this phoney flesh does not look the same, and you will lose the control of the facial muscles, et cetera.

In other words, let us keep away from using that stuff and just make Muni up so far as the beard and the hair are concerned.

Hal Wallis

Wallis's wishes were followed.

TO: J. L. Warner   DATE: April 13, 1937
FROM: Miss E. Williams
      [representing Cosmopolitan
      Productions at Warner Bros.]

Dear J.L.:
Mr. Hearst has asked me to tell you how he feels about material that Marion [Davies] has had to date at Warners. He said one thing that Metro did was to get stories for Marion, realizing that she was a star and the stories were about and for her, and he would much prefer not to do any more pictures until some such story is obtained for her. If it would make it easier, he would like a release from you so she could feel free to negotiate on the outside.

He said he has been very unhappy on this last picture [*Ever Since Eve*] fighting for everything he has gotten and trying to convince the powers that be that all he was asking for was something for Marion to do in the picture and not everyone else, and having Marion look like a stick. That was his reason for having the ending rewritten, in order that Marion would have something to do. He said, "Maybe this is what they want here. Maybe they would prefer getting out of our contract."

I tried to reach you today to tell you this, but as this was impossible, thought I would send this note to you. May I see you tomorrow?

Sincerely,
E. *Williams*

Shortly afterward, following four starring roles at the studio, Marion Davies left Warner Bros. She did not appear in any further films.

FROM S. CHARLES EINFELD [director of publicity and advertising,
New York]

April 12, 1937

Dear Jack [L. Warner]:

When I wrote you the other day that we had a smash on our
hands with *Marked Woman* I was pretty certain of what I was saying
but didn't want to go on record and predict any such business as we are
doing at the New York Strand. . . .

Of course in this case we must give a great deal of the credit to
Bette Davis. If you could hear the comments of women at the Strand,
you would be convinced of what I am going to say in the balance of
this note. They don't talk about how beautiful she is, but how realistic
she is.

You hear women say, "There's a gal who doesn't need a lot of
junk all over her face and who doesn't have to put on the glamour to
hold us in our seats. . . . She isn't afraid to let people see her as the
tawdry character she is supposed to represent."

In other words, where the average glamour girl fears to tread,
Bette Davis steps in and "takes over." We should let her stay that way
and under no conditions, try to make a "Garbo" or "Kay Francis" out
of her. Bette Davis is a female Cagney and if we give her the right
parts, we are going to have a star that will pay off the interest on the
bonds every year.

I hope when we get to *Jezebel*, we'll let her bust wide open.

With kindest regards,

Sincerely,
S. Charles Einfeld

FROM BETTE DAVIS
Hollywood, California,

July 26, 1937

Dear J.L.:

I have worked very hard to become known as a dramatic actress. I
wanted to do the comedy with Leslie [Howard—*It's Love I'm After*,
1937] and hoped I could prove my versatility. I hope I have. But for
you to want me to become a slap-stick musical comedy actress—an
entirely different type of comedy from Leslie's—I cannot understand.

If the two girls in *Hollywood Hotel* [1937] were written well I
could see some point to your request, but one girl (Beatrice) is
ridiculous, in that there is no living actress such a fool, and the
waitress almost entirely spoils the plot—a dull person. There isn't even
a real love story between the boy and girl. If the waitress were a sweet,
charming person, she would be a great contrast to the actress, but she

isn't; and, also, you know that Mr. [Busby] Berkeley will want me to do some kind of a musical number in the Hollywood Bowl sequence, and I could not even attempt it. This fact will annoy him, and rightfully so. *You need* a girl trained for this kind of work.

Please reconsider for both our sakes. It would be a great mistake if I start slap-stick comedies—my real value to you will soon be lost.

Sincerely,
Bette

Rosemary and Lola Lane were cast in the look-alike roles intended to be played by Bette Davis.

JEZEBEL

TO: Wallis   DATE: February 15, 1935
FROM: [Walter] MacEwen   SUBJECT: "Jezebel"

Have now read the full play script of *Jezebel* and it is not very good. Nevertheless, there is no denying that it could be improved a great deal in transference to the screen and that it would provide a good role for Bette Davis, who could play the spots off the part of a little bitch of an aristocratic Southern girl. She should also look swell in the gowns of the period (1853).

The trouble is that there is really no one in the play to pull for, to offset the bitchiness of the leading part, and although the resulting picture might look very good to us in the projection room, I'm very much afraid audiences in general would not appreciate it to the point of making it a box office success. Maybe I'm a Pollyanna, but I suspect that box office history in the past would prove that audiences prefer to sympathize with their leading characters, and find a little warmth and honest sentiment in them. In other words, while Bette Davis receives acclaim for nasty supporting roles, I doubt if a picture built solely around her in an unsympathetic part would be so well liked.

There is, however, a possibility that in adaptation the part of Julie in *Jezebel* could be given a slant which would make it more acceptable to audiences. She could start off as a spoiled little vixen, for which there is some justification because of factors in the girl's upbringing and background. Enough of the "Jezebel" in the characterization could be retained to make it interesting (she is crossed in love just about the time she is ready to come to heel, which at least partially justifies some of her nastiness) and then, by certain modifications, one could fairly logically get a good deal of sympathy for her, and leave one feeling that a touch of the good old regeneration through suffering is going to make her a wiser and more palatable person after the final fade out. . . .

Walter MacEwen

The final screenplay was constructed to allow Davis's character a "regeneration through suffering," thereby making her sympathetic.

TO: [Henry] Blanke   DATE: October 28, 1937
FROM: Wallis   SUBJECT: "Jezebel"

[Director William] Wyler came up to talk to me and explain that he wanted John Huston to sort of represent him in preparing the last half of the script in collaboration with the writers and yourself. In other words, he apparently knows Huston personally, spends a great deal of time with him, and will see him at night, and he maintains that Huston knows exactly his feelings and thoughts about the script, and his views on the last half of it. He explains that he himself cannot devote the time to consult with the writers, and Huston apparently will be a sort of a go-between operating between the writers, and you, and himself. In view of this, and in order to keep Wyler happy on the picture, and to get a script out as quickly as possible, I have agreed to put Huston on the picture, and told Wyler we would try it out. . . .

Hal Wallis

Huston recently had sold a treatment of his original story, Three Men and a Girl, *later retitled* Three Strangers *to Warner. He went to work at the studio writing the screenplay of that property when Wyler requested his services on* Jezebel. *Huston eventually received a collaborative writer's credit on* Jezebel *and signed a contract with the studio as a writer. Wyler had been borrowed from Samuel Goldwyn to direct* Jezebel.

TO: Blanke   DATE: November 4, 1937
FROM: Wallis   SUBJECT: "Jezebel"

Do you think Wyler is mad at [free-lance star] Henry Fonda or something because of their past? It seems that he is not content to okay anything with Fonda until it has been done ten or eleven takes. After all, they have been divorced from the same girl [actress Margaret Sullavan], and by-gones should be by-gones. I wonder if he wouldn't be satisfied to okay a fourth take or a fifth take occasionally. I am sure Fonda is a good actor, and I think if we will try printing up an occasional third or fourth take, after Wyler has okayed a tenth or an eleventh take, you will find that the third or fourth is just as good.

Possibly Wyler likes to see these big numbers on the slate, and maybe we could arrange to have them start with number "6" on each take, then it wouldn't take so long to get up to nine or ten. Will you please talk to Wyler and see if you can influence him a little on this score.

Hal Wallis

TO: Blanke   DATE: January 8, 1938
FROM: Wallis   SUBJECT: "Jezebel"

In spite of hell and high water and everything else, Wyler is still up to his old tricks. In last night's dailies, he had two takes printed of the scene where Donald Crisp leaves the house and Davis comes down the stairs and finds out that Pres [Henry Fonda] is coming. The first one was excellent, yet he took it sixteen times.

Doesn't this man know that we have closeups to break up a scene of this kind, and with all of the care he used in making the closeups, certainly he must expect that we would use the greater portion of the scene in closeup. Yet, he takes the time to make sixteen takes of a long shot. What the hell is the matter with him anyhow—is he absolutely daffy? Is he on the level when he says he is going to speed up and try to get through? If he is, this is a poor indication of it. Will you please tell him I said so.

Hal Wallis

As reflected in the Daily Production Reports, there seemed to be an attempt to accelerate. However, the film finished January 17, 28 days over the allotted 42 day schedule.

FROM WILLIAM SCHAEFER [Jack L. Warner's executive secretary]
March 8, 1938

TO: Mr. Warner

Mr. David Selznick [producer of *Gone With the Wind*—1939] telephoned and dictated the following letter to you, because he was afraid a wire might miss you. The letter as dictated is as follows:

Dear Jack:

Reiterating what I told you last night, I think it would be a very great pity indeed from your own standpoint, for so distinguished and costly a picture as *Jezebel* should be damned as an imitation by the millions of readers, and lovers, of *Gone With the Wind*. And I am fearful that this is what may happen due to a few completely unnecessary bits. The picture throughout is permeated with characterizations, attitudes and scenes which unfortunately resemble *Gone With the Wind* regardless of whether or not they were in the original material. But I am referring to a few specific scenes such as the very well remembered piece of business in which Scarlett pinches her cheeks to give them color.

More importantly, there is the scene of the men around the dinner table which actually is a slow spot in your picture, if you will forgive my saying so. I refer to the dialogue scene dealing with the difference between the North and the South, the discussion of an imminent war, and the prediction by the Southerner that the North will win because of its superior machinery, etc. The scene is lifted practically bodily out of *Gone With the Wind* in which it's an important story point leading to Rhett Butler's behaviour, in its entirety, during the war, whereas it has nothing to do with either the original play *Jezebel*, or with your adaptation, and is a completely irrelevant point that can have no reason for being in the picture except for its attempt to give it further flavor of *Gone With the Wind*. The war is never even mentioned again in the rest of your picture, the time of its conclusion of which is long before the beginning of the Civil War.

If you like, I would be very happy, indeed, to study your picture further, and to give you page references from *Gone With the Wind* on these, and other points, because I sincerely think it would be important from your own standpoint, as well as ours, that success which your picture deserves should not be marred by any appearance of an attempt to capitalize on a work for which the American public has demonstrated such a great love.

I am assuming that these suggestions which are advanced in good faith will be given no publicity by your people.

Once again many congratulations to your organization on a fine job.

Cordially yours,
David O. Selznick

FROM JACK L. WARNER

Mr. David O. Selznick
Selznick International
Culver City, California

March 8, 1938

Dear David:

Concerning our talk last night following the preview, this morning I immediately investigated the dialogue pertaining to the "Industrialist of the North" etc., etc., during the dinner table sequence in *Jezebel* and I find this whole sequence was taken bodily from the Owen Davis play of *Jezebel* in Act II, Scene I, and I am herewith enclosing the mimeographed copy of this scene from the Davis play, which we literally transposed into our picture.

I just received your memorandum, over the phone, and I believe my letter answers it.

Thanking you again for your splendid interest.

Sincerely,
Jack L. Warner

THE ADVENTURES OF ROBIN HOOD

TO: J. L. Warner   DATE: July 19, 1935
FROM: Dwight Franklin
[special visual consultant
on *Captain Blood*]

Don't you think that Cagney would make a swell Robin Hood? Maybe as a follow up to the [*Misdummer Night's*] *Dream*. With the gang as his Merry Men. [Frank] McHugh, [Allen] Jenkins, [Ross] Alexander, [Hugh] Herbert, etc.*

Entirely different from the [1922 Douglas] Fairbanks picture.

I have a lot of ideas on this if you are interested.

Dwight Franklin

Shortly afterward Cagney was announced as the star of the upcoming Robin Hood, *but in November, in a contractual dispute with Warner, Cagney walked out and did not return to the studio for two years.*

FROM HAL B. WALLIS

JACK L WARNER
RITZ TOWERS HOTEL NYC

JANUARY 8, 1936
. . . HAD ALREADY SPOKEN TO WRITERS ON "ROBIN HOOD" REFERENCE DOING THIS FOR FLYNN AND FEEL SURE WE WILL HAVE THIS TO FOLLOW "LIGHT BRIGADE." ALSO THINK IT GOOD TO PUBLICIZE THIS NOW AND LET CAGNEY KNOW HE IS LOSING THESE PROPERTIES BY HIS ATTI-TUDE. . . .

HAL

---

*All were Warner contract players.

TO: Blanke   DATE: March 16, 1937
FROM: Wallis   SUBJECT: "The Adventures of Robin Hood"

I read the [Rowland Leigh] script of *Robin Hood* and I am frankly not too enthusiastic about it.

The development of the romance between Marian and Robin is too quick. She sees him when he is first brought in and given a beating and then has him freed and the next time she meets him there is a passionate love scene in Sherwood. It seems to me there should have been an earlier meeting between these two. . . .

The episodes leading up to Robin Hood becoming an outlaw do not seem important enough. . . . It seems to me that in this story they will expect to see Robin in action—robbing the rich, giving to the poor, and doing the things for which the character was famous. We see nothing whatever of this and there is a lot of dull stuff in the script which could come out to make room for some more adventurous episodes and action. I have not read the original manuscript for years but it seems to me that it contained a lot of material that should be in a script of this type.

The most important matter is that of the dialogue. This is too poetical and too much like *Midsummer Night's Dream*. I would not want to make the picture unless we went through the entire script and did considerable modernizing of the dialogue.

You cannot have the maid or anyone else reading lines such as, "Oh, M'Lord, tarry not too long for, I fear, in her remorse, she may fling herself from the window—some harm will befall her, I know!", with Sir Guy answering, "Then will I go to her at once. Wait on me, De Lacey!", etc., etc. This may be all right if we were doing the picture as an operetta, but as a straight movie it won't do.

Hal Wallis

Norman Reilly Raine and later Seton I. Miller were assigned to write the script, and they avoided the problems referred to in the above memo in subsequent drafts.

TO: Mr. Wallis   DATE: September 7, 1937
FROM: T. C. Wright [studio   SUBJECT: "Robin Hood"
    production manager]

I wonder if we are wrong in allowing *Robin Hood* to be shot at Chico [approximately 350 miles north of Los Angeles]. As you know, Curtiz did not do much Saturday [filming *Gold Is Where You Find It* on location] on account of rain, and from all indications now *Robin Hood* will not start until the later part of this month, September, and the rains generally set in around the first of October.

If it rains one day, it will take another day to dry out, particularly in the woods, under the trees.

Do you think that the locations there are so vastly superior to the ones we can secure down here in [Lake] Sherwood [local location area].

I mean by this,—is it worth gambling on the weather?

Also, we must consider the additional cost of transportation, etc., that we will be burdened with.

I think that you should give this very careful consideration before you make up your mind, as truthfully I am a little worried about weather conditions during the month of October up and around Chico. . . . .

T. C. Wright

Chico was used for many of the Sherwood Forest sequences.

TO: Wright   DATE: September 16, 1937
FROM: Wallis   SUBJECT: "Robin Hood"

Olivia de Havilland will definitely play the part of "Maid Marian" in *Robin Hood*.

I don't want you to send any notification on this out, however, until Mr. Blanke has called Anita Louise in and explained to her that she will not do the picture and the reasons therefor.

Hal Wallis

The teaming of Flynn and de Havilland in Captain Blood *and* The Charge of the Light Brigade *had been extremely successful, and the projected high budget on* The Adventures of Robin Hood *suggested that the studio protect its investment with a proven co-starring team.*

TO: Mr. Wallis   DATE: September 23, 1937
FROM: T. C. Wright   SUBJECT: "Robin Hood"

Before you came in last night at the meeting, there was quite a discussion between the writer on this picture [Norman Reilly Raine] and Mr. Blanke and Mr. Keighley [the director]. We were talking about where we could save money to reduce the Budget to what you want it.

The writer just couldn't see why the Jousting Tournament was necessary in the picture. Of course, Mr. Keighley argued that it was the big production splash in the picture but the writer said you had a good story without it. Whether he is correct or not I do not know, that is your business, not mine, but I am forwarding this information to you.

My suggestion is this: Let the Jousting Tournament stay in to pacify Mr. Keighley. Let him go north and do all of the exteriors, as the Jousting sequence is a separate sequence. Then, when he comes back and makes preparations to go to Busch Gardens [location in Pasadena] to shoot the Jousting sequence and the Archery Tournament, then possibly, if you agree and so desire, you can tell him to let the Jousting Tournament go until the very end of the picture and you would by that time determine whether or not you had sufficient footage and material for making a picture. . . .

T. C. Wright

TO: Hal Wallis   DATE: September 23, 1937
FROM: Norman Reilly Raine   SUBJECT: "Robin Hood"
       [screenwriter]

Since I feel very strongly on the subject of Mr. Keighley's sincere but misguided attempts, further to bugger up *Robin Hood,* and having spent a considerable portion of last night analyzing his desires and how they would affect the facts, I would like to direct your attention to the following:

THE TOURNAMENT (JOUSTING)

According to what Mr. Keighley replied to my question at the budget meeting last night, the reason he wants this in is threefold: (a) People remembering the [1922 Douglas] Fairbanks picture will expect something spectacular. (b) It puts over the life and pageantry of the period as well as telling story. (c) It is necessary, because the balance of the script is so weak that we have to give the audience something at the beginning that will carry over.

My reply to these is: (a) People do not remember the details of the Fairbanks picture; therefore, the pageantry and color and chivalry inherent in the background itself if we follow the revised final will satisfy them, especially as it is to be in color. (b) Story can be told much more effectively *and entertainingly* at the supper in the great hall as in the revised final. (c) Before Mr. Keighley got the jousting tournament bee in his bonnet he thought the old beginning (since improved tremendously in the revised final) was, to quote his own words: "*Great!* I could go out and shoot it tomorrow just as it stands!" Mr. Blanke will bear witness to this.

The jousting tournament never can be anything but a prologue which, if done with the magnificence Mr. Keighley sees, will have the disastrous effect of putting the climax of the picture at the beginning— and I'll be goddamned if that is good construction dramatically in fiction, stage or screen, because the only way you could ever top it would be to have a slam-bang hell of a battle or something equally spectacular—and expensive—at the end. Maybe I'm crazy—but what we set out to tell was the story of Robin Hood . . . the swashbuckling, reckless, rakehell type of character who, *by his personal adventures* has endeared himself to generations. It is not by thoughts of knights and castles and tournaments that this character has lived; he has lived because he was a vital, human character who soaked the rich to help the poor; who was a daredevil that stuck his head in a noose for the sheer hell of it; who gathered to himself faithful comrades—Friar Tuck, Little John et al. *These* are the things people have remembered and loved. *THEY ARE ROBIN HOOD*—yet these are the things Mr. Keighley mistakenly wants to sacrifice in order to get in his "spectacle." But I maintain that it is the *human* element that makes great drama and great entertainment . . . the conflict, and growing of love between boy and girl; the *characterization of Robin in his scenes with his men* so we understand why this great *human* story came down through the ages . . . and if these things are entertainingly told as I firmly believe they are in the revised final, we'll get all the spectacle naturally we want in the *archery* tournament *as now written.* But the archery tournament will certainly suffer pictorially if we stick a jousting tournament in the beginning. Christ's second coming in a cloud of glory would seem tame if we showed the creation of the world first. . . .

The Fairbanks picture, *in order to live up to its tournament fade in* had to ring in the whole goddamned Crusades; and a slight taste of the real Robin Hood story was dragged in as a tag at the end to justify the use of the name. . . .

Norman Reilly Raine

Raine, before coming to Warner Bros. in 1936, wrote numerous short stories for The Saturday Evening Post *(the "Tugboat Annie" series, among others).*

FROM HAL B. WALLIS

TO: BILL KEIGHLEY
WARNER BROTHERS LOCATION
CHICO, CALIFORNIA

OCTOBER 6, 1937

DEAR BILL: I DON'T WANT TO START WORRYING YOU OR RIDE OR CROWD YOU BUT WHILE THE FIRST THREE DAYS' DAILIES ARE GORGEOUS AND JUST THE LAST WORD, AT THE SAME TIME IT HAS TAKEN THREE DAYS TO SHOOT THE MEETING BETWEEN ROBIN AND LITTLE JOHN, AND IT WAS NOT YET COMPLETE AT END OF THREE DAYS' WORK. I DON'T HAVE TO TELL YOU THAT AT THIS RATE WE WILL BE ON LOCATION UNTIL IT SNOWS, AND NATURALLY CHANGE IN BACKGROUNDS WILL BE SO GREAT AS TO MAKE THE DIFFERENCE MARKED. DON'T KNOW WHAT YOU CAN DO ABOUT IT EXCEPT TO CUT DOWN ANGLES AND NOT SPEND SO MUCH TIME ON THIS SORT OF STUFF, BUT BELIEVE YOU WILL AGREE

THAT AT THE RATE OF THREE DAYS TO SHOOT ONE LITTLE SEQUENCE
WE HAVE CAUSE FOR WORRY. . . . REGARDS

HAL WALLIS

There were some weather problems on location at Chico.

TO: Blanke   DATE: October 7, 1937
FROM: Wallis   SUBJECT: "Robin Hood"

. . . Take out the jousting tournament and go back to the original version
where the scenes now played in the box at the jousting tournament are
played in the banquet hall instead. . . .

Hal Wallis

FROM ERROL FLYNN
Richardson Springs
Chico, Cal

October 24, 1937

Dear Hal [Wallis]
    First let me thank you again for fixing things re the radio
deals. . . .
    Now one other minor, but to me very important, squawk. My
wig . . . I loathe the bloody thing. With the hat on it's fine, and the
alteration I want to suggest does not affect any of the stuff we've shot so
far—the part that's wrong is hidden by the hat. The centre part in the
wig is my chief complaint. I would like an almost unnoticeable part on
either side so that one side or the other could sweep back off the
forehead. The fringes would then, when the hat is removed, not look
like fringes but just a few locks of loose hair carelessly falling over the
brow. My drawing of course is hopeless but I've explained to the make
up here who say they will write to the studio and explain it.
    The point is, I haven't had my hat off yet and when I do, the
new wig would match. Would you ask them to make me one like that
described and send it up so we can get it right before we come down?
I'm quite certain you will think it an improvement, Hal. If you don't—
nothing has been lost. I hate this present one so much I shudder every
time I see the Goddam thing—and I've had nothing but comments
from people, when they see it with the hat off, about the stupid looking
fringe and centre part. So there must be something to it.
    I feel like one of the oldest inhabitants of Chico now—we all do.
And we're all very sick of it but consoling ourselves with the report or
rather rumour that you like the stuff down there. Is it so?
    All the best Hal and kindest personal regards.

Errol

*The new wig, per Flynn's request, was used for all scenes played
without cap.*

TO: Mr. Blanke   DATE: November 10, 1937
FROM: Mr. Wallis   SUBJECT: "Adventures of Robin Hood"

I imagine that we are about two weeks behind schedule on *Robin Hood*
so far. After yesterday's talk, you know what this will amount to in dollars
and cents.

I wish you would go through the script again and have a talk with
Keighley and see if there aren't some additional scenes or sequences that
we can cut out of the picture at this time. Perhaps by now, Keighley has
a different perspective on the stuff, and what is not needed, and he may
have some ideas for cuts.

Hal Wallis

TO: T. C. Wright   DATE: November 30, 1937
FROM: Al Alleborn [unit manager] SUBJECT: "Adventures of Robin
                                             Hood"

Report for 11-29-37 [the unit had returned from Chico]:
    Keighley company called 9:00 AM, first shot 9:30, finished shooting
6:20 PM. Worked INT. LADY MARIAN's APT. on STAGE 4 and INT.
CORRIDOR OUTSIDE APT. . . .
    I was with Mike Curtiz and [assistant director] Jack Sullivan regarding
his [Curtiz] taking over the picture and going over necessary details in
order to start with him on Wednesday morning. We are starting on
Wednesday morning in the INT. CASTLE—BANQUET SCENE—the
deer sequence, and will open up in there with the entire cast . . . at 9:00
AM, and Flynn at 10:00 o'clock. . . .

Al Alleborn

TO: T. C. Wright   DATE: December 1, 1937
FROM: Al Alleborn   SUBJECT: #186 "Adventures of Robin Hood"

Report for 11-30-37:
    Keighley company called 9:00 AM. . . .
    Worked in the INT. MARIAN's APT.—sequence where Rathbone
comes in and catches her with written note regarding Robin Hood. . . .
    Curtiz looked over the Castle set and lined up every shot which we
are doing today. Looked at rehearsal of the men who are dueling; also

looked at the cast for their fight which takes place in the END sequence. Cameraman, [Sol] Polito, lined up the Castle set and this morning, Wednesday, had an early call so we would be ready to shoot at the earliest time possible.

At this writing, Polito is taking over the picture [from cameraman Tony Gaudio] and first shot, a long boom, taking in the entire Castle set, was OK'd at 11:00 AM. . . .

We are planning on working several nights during the week, if only for a couple of hours, without Flynn or De Havilland, to try and speed up and shorten the schedule . . .

Al Alleborn

Curtiz replaced Keighley on the film.

TO: Mr. Blanke   DATE: December 3, 1937
FROM: Mr. Wallis   SUBJECT: "Adventures of Robin Hood"

There is one thing that we will have to watch with Mike. In his enthusiasm to make great shots and composition and utilize the great production values in this picture, he is, of course, more likely to go overboard than any one else, because he just naturally loves to work with mobs and props of this kind. . . .

I don't have to tell you again that the cost on this picture is mounting at a tremendous rate, and it is up to us to see that we economize where economy is possible. I did not try to stop Mike yesterday when he was on the crane and making beautiful production shots, because they were establishing shots and because they moved up to our principals and we immediately got into the story, but I do object to wasting time and money on unimportant characters and unimportant action. . . .

Also, when he gets into the fight stuff, please be sure that Mike doesn't over-shoot and get a thousand daffy shots of impossible gags, which as you know are liable to boomerang and make our scenes ridiculous. We must be very careful not to make the thing too wild with Robin escaping from a hundred men, so the quicker he gets out of the room [in the castle] and up on the balcony the better, and don't let him have Robin holding off a hundred men with a bow and arrow, or the audience will scream, and from that point on you won't ever get them back into the story again. This must be handled very carefully and worked out very carefully.

Hal Wallis

TO: Mr. T. C. Wright   DATE: December 4, 1937
FROM: Al Alleborn   SUBJECT: #186 "Adventures of Robin Hood"

Report for 12-3-37:
    . . . I think this company with a new crew is moving along 100%
better than the other crew, and everyone is endeavoring to make a comparative showing.
    The balance of the work that is left to do in the Castle has been
walked through and explained to the cameraman and everyone concerned,
including Mr. Wallis and Blanke who have approved of the way Mike is
to play it and the number of set-ups necessary for the action. . . .

Al Alleborn

TO: Mr. Warner   DATE: January 21, 1938
FROM: Mr. Wallis   SUBJECT: "The Adventures of Robin Hood"

My suggestion for billing *The Adventures of Robin Hood*, with Errol Flynn,
Olivia de Havilland, and so forth, selling the bigness of the subject, seems
to be borne out by the big hits today—*Hurricane*—*Wells Fargo*—and
now *In Old Chicago*, all of which are selling the title and the subject
matter, with the cast following.
    I still think it is a good idea.

Hal Wallis

    *Wallis's suggestion was followed. The Adventures of Robin Hood
was the studio's most expensive ($2,033,000) picture up to that time.
Fortunately, it was an extraordinary success.*

FROM ERICH WOLFGANG KORNGOLD [composer]

February 11, 1938

Dear Mr. Wallis:
    I am sincerely sorry to have to bother you once more. I do
appreciate deeply your kindness and courtesy toward me, and I am
aware of the fact that you have made all concessions possible to
facilitate my work.
    But please believe a desperate man who has to be true to himself
and to you, a man who knows what he can do and what he cannot do.
Robin Hood is no picture for me. I have no relation to it and therefore
cannot produce any music for it. I am a musician of the heart, of
passions and psychology; I am not a musical illustrator for a 90%
action picture. Being a conscientious person, I cannot take the
responsibility for a job which, as I already know, would leave me
artistically completely dissatisfied and which, therefore, I would have to
drop even after several weeks of work on it and after several weeks of
salary.

Therefore, let me say "no" definitely, and let me say it today when no time has been lost for you as yet, since the work print will not be ready until tomorrow. And please do not try to make me change my mind; my resolve is unshakable.

I implore you not to be angry with me and not to deprive me of your friendship. For it is I who suffers mentally and financially. I ask you to weigh the pictures for which I composed the music, such as *Midsummer Night's Dream, Captain Blood, Anthony Adverse, Prince and [the] Pauper,* against the one I could not make, *Robin Hood.* And if during the next few weeks you should have a job for me to do, you need not cable all the way to Vienna.

> With my very best regards, I am,
> Gratefully and sincerely yours,
> Erich Wolfgang Korngold

Korngold was an esteemed composer of operatic and concert works. His contract with Warner Bros. was for no more than two pictures per year.

TO: All Concerned   DATE: February 14, 1938
FROM: Henry Blanke   SUBJECT: "The Adventures of Robin Hood"

Korngold is now definitely set to do the music on *Robin Hood.*

> *Henry Blanke*

Korngold, who won an Academy Award for his Robin Hood score, was convinced by an impassioned plea from the head of Warners' Music Department, Leo Forbstein, who had been sent to Korngold's home by Wallis and Blanke. But the principal deciding factors were the political events taking place in Austria. Shortly afterward, Korngold's property in Vienna was confiscated by the invading Nazis.

Interlude

WARNER BROS.
From *Fortune* magazine, December 1937

Harry M. Warner, its President and boss, explains the ten-year zoom of Warner Bros. Pictures, Inc., from a rank outsider to the biggest thing in show business by telling you that he and Abe and Jack have always been great dreamers. As you reach for your hat, he detains you with a leer and some such succinct enlargement as this: "Listen, a picture, all it is is an expensive dream. Well, it's just as easy to dream for $700,000 as for $1,500,000."

Which explains a lot, though not everything. Warner Bros. has larger gross assets ($177,500,000) than any other movie company. It has been among the giants for nine years now, so that a quick reference to *The Jazz Singer*, whose unexpected success found Warner Bros. with a long headstart on the talking-picture field, no longer suffices to dismiss its curious primacy. To Hollywood and Broadway, Warner's primacy is an odd and faintly distasteful fact. People in show business, by and large, are inclined to resent the Warners. Many of Hollywood's first citizens, especially over at the Metro-Goldwyn-Mayer studio (*Fortune*, December, 1932), think that Harry's cut-rate dreaming is the worst possible formula for making pictures. And yet by all movie standards—Hollywood's, the box office's, and the critics'—Warner Bros. is conceded to make very good pictures indeed.

This is all the more aggravating to Hollywood because the Warner studio, besides lacking a proper disregard for production costs, is conspicuously without that other prime necessity, a producing "genius." (The special case of Mervyn LeRoy, who answers the description, will be considered later.) Warner used to have one of these in Darryl Zanuck, but he left in 1933 to join 20th Century Pictures and later to merge with Fox, where, the local wits have it, he is currently sitting on the Blarney stone of Hollywood. Zanuck has never been officially replaced at Warner and the studio continues in the hands of a jocose penny watcher, Jack Warner, his methodical assistant, Hal Wallis, and half a dozen almost anonymous supervisors, none of whom is nearly nervous or worried enough to be a genius as Hollywood understands the term. And yet the Warner product, as its pictures are collectively known, has been getting better, not worse, ever since Zanuck left. The inexpensive topical stories that Zanuck so successfully snitched from the day's headlines (*Doorway to Hell*, *Public Enemy*) are still pouring from Burbank in a uniformly profitable stream (*G-Men*, *Black Legion*, *Marked Woman*, *China Clipper*). In the field of ambitious superspecials Warner can preen itself for A *Midsummer Night's Dream*, *Green Pastures*, *Anthony Adverse*, and currently *Adventures of Robin Hood*.

But furthermore, in pictures like *Black Fury* (mine labor trouble), *They Won't Forget* (sectional prejudice in the Deep South), and *Zola* (the Dreyfus case), Warner has touched movie critics and fans on a nerve that had almost been atrophied by the average producer's chronic cynicism— the nerve that quickens to serious social issues. Most Warner executives are quick to disown the role of crusader for social justice; they protest that their only purpose in treating these "controversial" themes is a harmless passion for gold. The amount of salt with which this denial should be taken will appear when we examine Harry's subtle and race-conscious mind. But except for MGM with its one brave picture *Fury*, Warner is the only major studio that seems to know or care what is going on in America besides pearl-handled gunplay, sexual dalliance, and the giving of topcoats to comedy butlers.

The Ford of the Movies is how Major Abe Warner likes to think of Warner Bros., which turns out sixty pictures a year for him to distribute. Warner pictures are not so much alike as so many Fords but they are almost as easy to recognize; they lead the low-price field and the profit to Warner is in the volume rather than in an occasional smash hit. "We've made a staple of entertainment," says Harry Warner. The average Warner picture costs about $400,000, even though occasionally a *Zola* or a *Submarine D-1* may reach $1,000,000. By never buying unnecessary stories, rarely making retakes, and always knocking temperament on the head where they can, the Warners probably get more production money onto the screen than any other studio.

Warner Bros. is the only big company without a newsreel, but it is more expert than most newsreels in capitalizing on the news. Many a Warner script is invented whole by the boys at the studio around some current scandal or timely and dramatic locale. Warner pictures are hence as close to real life as Hollywood ever gets. In *Marked Woman* you are looking at what is really a portrayal of five prostitutes, as everyone who had heard of Lucky Luciano knew, although for Hays office purposes they were called night-club entertainers. *Black Legion* was in production before last year's scandal in Detroit was off the front page. Even Warners' *The Prince and the Pauper*, the lavender romance by Mark Twain, came out with a big coronation sequence just in time to collar the crowds who couldn't go to London [for the coronation of George VI].

In Wall Street, meanwhile, the Warner paradox has a different twist. In the big three-way movie consolidations of the twenties, when almost every studio of importance was swallowing (or being swallowed by) a countrywide distributing system and chain of theatres, the Warner acquisitions were conspicuously late, hasty, and gluttonous. . . . The almost comical way in which the brothers hunched forward together in their oversized golden saddle seemed to betoken an early fall. Having earned what was then the record movie net of $17,000,000 in 1929, Warner Bros. piled up losses of $31,000,000 in the four years 1931 through 1934. Litigious stockholders tried to put the brothers in the street and a federal antitrust suit threatened to put Harry in jail. "Management has shown less than average acumen," said *Barron's Weekly* as late as 1935. And yet Warner Bros. has been the only big theatre-owning company— again excepting MGM's parent, Loew's, Inc.—to have ridden the depression without resorting to bankruptcy, receivership, or reorganization of any kind. It has not even changed hands, and Harry, backed by Brother Abe and Brother Jack, is still in both managerial and financial control. The ride has left Harry with a nervous stomach, which keeps him at times on a light diet of steak and potatoes. . . .

The huge 135-acre studio at Burbank operates somewhat like a moated feudal city, from which raids have occasionally been conducted against their more easygoing competitors, but which has not often been raided from without. Their production methods, in many respects unique, are mostly self-developed. Their personnel turnover is small, their interior discipline almost grim. The Warner brothers trust few people outside their own camp, but in each other they have the most implicit confidence. "Warner brothers personally," as Harry once put it, "have always construed themselves as one."

There were originally six Warner brothers, but only four to keep in mind. Beginning with the oldest, they are Harry, who is something of a martinet; Albert (Abe), massive, genial, and bumbling; Sam, who is dead; and Jack, who lives in Hollywood and wears dishrag sport shirts in the Hollywood manner. Their father was a Polish farmer who emigrated in 1883 in search of religious freedom and became a butcher in Ohio. Harry was at first a shoemaker; later he went to work for Armour. But Abe and

Sam, the mechanically-minded Warner, got a projection machine and began to make a few dollars exhibiting *The Great Train Robbery* and other early films, in 1905 acquiring a nickelodeon in Newcastle, Pennsylvania, where Jack sang in the pit, and Sister Rose played the piano. Harry soon joined them as the business manager, and by 1917 the four boys had their own distributing company in New York, selling the products of small independents and a few pictures of their own. That year James W. Gerard published *My Four Years in Germany*. By ringing Gerard's doorbell and offering him a share in the profits, Harry secured the rights; and by taking the old-time movie speculator Mark Dintenfass to a stand-up lunch in a saloon he secured the studio and laboratory in which he made the picture. It was a sensation, grossing nearly $800,000, of which the brothers cleared $130,000. Soon they had John Barrymore, Rin Tin Tin, Lenore Ulric, Ernst Lubitsch. In 1925, the second year after their incorporation, they made $1,000,000. There their real story begins.

When Waddill Catchings met the Warner boys in December, 1924, they were selling their pictures through franchise holders—powerful independent distributors who also advanced them some of the money to make their pictures, but not enough. "Most of our time," complained Harry to Catchings, "was spent in obtaining money from loan sharks"; it cost them as much as 40 percent. Even in those days the Warners were conspicuous for the reverence in which they held their budgets: *School Days* cost $50,000, *Why Girls Leave Home* $33,000, and both grossed around half a million. Impressed by this and by the frugal private lives that Harry forced the brothers to lead, Catchings took them in hand and raised some real money for them. With $800,000 of it they bought the Vitagraph Co., which had a nationwide system of exchanges and enabled them to free themselves from the franchise holders. By 1928 they were a $16,000,000 corporation. Within two years they were to be a $230,000,000 corporation. There has never been anything quite like that, even in the movie industry. . . .

Even in 1928, had the corporation been forced to liquidate, the common stockholders would have got nothing and the preferred stockholders would have had to take part of their equity in good will. It is said that Al Jolson, while making *The Jazz Singer* in Hollywood, was being paid by checks on a New York bank; but when he was in New York on payday the check was on a Hollywood bank. The opening of *The Jazz Singer* on October 6, 1927, was of course the official debut of modern movie history, because Jolson talked for the first time in a feature picture. He said "Come on, Ma, listen to this" just before launching into "Blue Skies," and the Warner audience was quietly electrified. It should have been a thrill for the brothers too, but it wasn't, because Sam had died the day before.

The whole thing had been Sam's idea. He had persuaded Harry to listen to a device that the Bell Laboratories had invented and that the more respectable studios had already listened to and nixed. Sam had conducted the work that made the device practicable—quieting the Kliegs and the camera, adapting the synchronizing technique to studio conditions. In this work Sam got help from the telephone company engineers. . . .

When *The Jazz Singer* sent his persecutors yapping on a new scent, Harry knew he could not hold his lead for long. As soon as the big-timers could make enough talkies to supply their chains, Warner Bros. would be just another independent producer once more. To forestall this, in one furious burst of family pride and financial sorcery, Harry became overnight one of the bigtimers himself.

Harry's buying spree, which lasted from 1928 through 1930 and ran Warner's gross assets up to $230,000,000, was conducted with less cash than confidence. Without the stock market, he would have had less of both. Back in 1926, when Barrymore's *Don Juan* was shown with a musical score, Warner Bros. common had begun to behave very fancily on the curb, and the brothers (somewhat reluctantly) had learned a play from Catchings that was to stand the company in good stead more than once. That was to sell their personal holdings and lend the proceeds to the company. It was these loans, amounting to $5,000,000 in 1928, that enabled Vitaphone to survive its early persecutions. In 1928 Bryan Foy, directing shorts in Hollywood, happened to spin a two-reel talking melodrama called *The Lights of New York* into five reels, and thus made the first "all-talking" feature. The total cost was $21,000. It did a $75,000 business in a single week at the Strand in New York and ultimately grossed about $1,000,000. That spring the Big Five gave in and wired their studios and chains for sound. On the strength of these phenomena and various merger rumors that summer, Warner Bros. stock went from 39 to 139 a share. And on the strength of *that* phenomenon Catchings actually swung the merger that put Warner Bros. once and for all on its financial feet.

That was the acquisition of the Stanley Co. of America, which controlled some 250 theatres and also owned a third of First National Pictures, a first-class studio whose leading star was Richard Barthelmess and whose producing reputation made Warner Bros. look like celluloid butchers. With cash from the banks and from sales of his stock Harry bought out the scattered holders of another batch of First National for $4,000,000; later he acquired the final third from William Fox for $10,000,000. With some debentures and a lot of common stock, he also bought enough new theatres to run his chain up to more than 500 houses. During the first half of 1930 he was averaging better than one new theatre a day. He bought Witmark, Remick, Harms, and other music publishers. For its patents, its record factory, and its stillborn sixteen-millimeter home talkie projector, he bought the radio, record, and phonograph divisions of the Brunswick-Balke-Collender Co. and lost $8,000,000 on the deal. He bought radio companies, foreign sound patents, and a lithograph company; he produced *Fifty Million Frenchmen* and other Broadway shows. He raided Paramount and bought Kay Francis, William Powell, and Ruth Chatterton with contracts whose generosity was limited only by their agents' imaginations. He shot, in short, the works. *Variety* dedicated an entire issue to the Warner brothers. They had arrived.

Harry Warner is a small, strong, swarthy man of fifty-six with a deceptive cupid-bow mouth and a vague resemblance to George Arliss. Willful and a worrier, constantly preoccupied with his own thoughts, he often fits that Hollywood definition of a producer: a man who asks you a question, gives you the answer, and tells you you're wrong. He has two major interests, business and morals; in lighter moments these take the form of speculation on the price of the billiard table Paul Muni gave him or of heavy epigrams on how to handle women. Having worked himself since he was eight years old, he is in despair at the indolence and lack of initiative he beholds around him since the new labor movement. "Hard work never hurt me," he says; "on the contrary, it developed me very fine." By dint of primogeniture, an iron will, and a non-money-making father, he has been the head of the house of Warner since its earliest days. That responsibility has relaxed a little; he is now merely the court of appeals, or trouble department. "They never bring anything to me," he explains, "until it's already wrong." But Harry Warner is still the undisputed boss of Warner Bros. and is in many quarters conceded to be the No. 2 man—second only to Nicholas Schenck of Loew's—in America's most influential industry. . . .

The movie business [in 1931] got rapidly worse. As theatre receipts dropped nearly half their length, Harry's $106,000,000 of funded debt looked more and more mountainous. Other chains were going into receivership, and . . . it seemed a tempting way out for Warner Bros. But Harry, remember, is proud. He would never have been happy with a safe fortune. . . . Besides, he and his brothers had all that common stock. Accordingly, he gave his brothers a lecture on the family honor and they all went to work.

If show business had forgotten that the Warners could be tightwads, it learned it again now with a vengeance. . . . Executives and errand boys took cuts; even the high-priced contract stars took a 50 percent cut for eight weeks, although the stars had Zanuck on their side in resisting it and he made it his ostensible reason for quitting. . . .

Warner Bros.' gross consolidated income for the year ending last August [1937] was about $100,000,000. Probably $54,000,000 of this, and about half the company's $6,000,000 profit, came from its chain of 480 theatres. . . .

Distribution . . . is one department in which Harry seldom has to shoot trouble. It is headed by Albert, the second Warner, who, Harry once wrote Catchings, was known as "honest Abe" and was "the most popular man in the movie industry." ("As for myself," Harry added, "I may be disliked by some of the big men.") Honest Abe, who is also treasurer of Warner Bros., is not so active in the sales end as he used to be, and he is now generally called Major Albert; but he is still the best liked of the Warner brothers anyway. The Major's title is genuine, having been given him by the army in return for the Warner's propaganda pictures. Harry, who was out of town on that occasion, ordinarily represents the family when such honors are bestowed.

Jack Warner, supreme head of Warner Bros. production, is the youngest of the brothers and the most engaging. He is in fact a comedian of almost professional pretensions, with that sunny gift for slangy self-exposure that only show people ever really master. He once advised a novice writer, just arrived at Universal, to look back in the files if he ever got stymied for ideas. "That's how we do it," he explained cheerfully. "Whenever I go by the projection room and hear them running off *Moby Dick* I know the boys are working on *Captain Blood*." Jack has other moods however. He is usually the hero of the Happy Gateman story. He has a habit of patrolling the lot and seeing that no unnecessary lights are on and that everybody is at work. On one such trip he heard the new gateman singing Verdi arias in a beautiful voice. Engaging him in talk he learned that the man was indeed a serious student of voice and practiced daily. "Which would you rather be," asked Jack, "a singer or our gateman?" The man, all warm inside, said "Oh, a singer." "You're fired," said Jack simply.

Jack, in fact, would not be Harry's brother if he did not look upon the making of movies as like any other kind of factory production, requiring discipline and order rather than temperament and talent. His job is not to make artistic triumphs ("We're not running any museum," as the Major puts it) but to make sixty pictures a year on a budget of $25,000,000. Warner's budget is not the smallest in the industry, but it is the smallest per picture in relation to what the average Warner picture grosses. Of the 214 Warner pictures released from January 1933, to the end of last year only one has not yet returned its negative cost and 85 percent have returned more than negative and distribution cost, thus contributing to the corporate profit. This does not mean that they were good pictures. It means that they didn't cost very much to begin with and that every one of them hit its budget on the nose. That is a famous Jack Warner specialty.

To begin with, Jack's 135-acre lot at Burbank is in many respects the best equipped studio in Hollywood. . . .

The very size and scope of the Warner lot, in fact, are merely means to a million small economies. Everything in creation is stored there so that practically nothing ever has to be bought. Bert Teitlebaum's art directors are sent on a tour of the crammed scenery docks every week, so that when they start sketches on a new script they will be thinking of what's on hand rather than what would be nice. . . .

But Jack's important savings come from the way he handles talents and ideas, which are the really expensive ingredients of a movie. . . . Paramount, for example, operates more or less as a loose federation of powerful producers, each of whom runs amuck as his own temperament dictates. But at Burbank it is a point of dogma that the company is bigger than any individual. Jack permits no temperaments around him exept his own.

Jack does not even call his men producers nor does he like to give them screen credit; until recently they were officially "supervisors," which in Hollywood is almost a term of abuse. For creative men in so close an atmosphere, these supervisors are a surprisingly contented lot. Take Henry Blanke. He gets some of the most artistically ambitious assignments, being a former Lubitsch assistant and the possessor of a German accent and a cultivated face. Yet he does not rebel when assigned to do a piece of straight commercial bushwa like *The Green Light* [1937], nor yet when his plans for *Adventures of Robin Hood* are pared after the budget meeting. He eliminated $50,000 worth of campfires from that script with as good a grace as if he had never heard of Lubitsch. He even states as a general rule that economies make for improvements. For example, he wanted 400 people milling in the street outside the courtroom during the trial scene in *Zola*, and was told he could have only 200. So he changed the lighting to make it a rainy day and got from the prop department 400 umbrellas, only 200 of which had people under them.

Perhaps the most typical of Jack's producers is Sam Bischoff, who was a C.P.A. until he found himself owning an independent studio fifteen years ago. He is certainly the hardest-working, averaging twelve to fourteen productions a year, all of them A's and some of them fairly ambitious. When he first came there in 1932 and brought in *Murder in the Clouds* at $80,000, Harry Warner carried the cost sheet around in his pocket for days. Bischoff says his job is no different from running a silk mill, and that he's good at it not because he's a genius but because he's Jewish and shares the racial sense of drama.

Sam made *The Charge of the Light Brigade* with no original story cost at all, making the whole thing up (with the help of some writers) to fit a ready-made climax that he remembers as "Theirs was not to ask, theirs but to do and die." But it is Lou (Red, White, and Blue) Edelman, another supervisor, who really specializes in free plots. He makes two types of movie, both usually low cost. One is the "service" picture, glorifying some branch of the uniformed forces of the nation: *Devil Dogs of the Air, Here Comes the Navy, Submarine D-1.* Given Pat O'Brien or Dick Powell, the setting, and the technical cooperation of the government, Lou can let the story take care of itself, and brings in some of his assignments at as little as $300,000 apiece. The sales department, which ascribes their monotonous success to a growing nationalist sentiment, keeps asking for more. Lou's other specialty is the headlines, which also give him ready-made plots. "Anything worth newspaper space is worth a picture," he says, and keeps a scrapbook full of current clippings from six daily papers. He made *G-Men* in eight weeks, starting with nothing but the title and the death of John Dillinger. For *Marked Woman* Lou drew on the [Special Prosecutor Thomas] Dewey vice investigation in New York and he is currently worming a script out of what Dewey has told the world about the poultry racket. The Warner story department seldom has to buy anything for Edelman.

A still more spectacular corner cutter is Bryan Foy, whom we met above as the director of *The Lights of New York*. Foy learned to respect the dollar by being brought up in vaudeville (his father was Eddie Foy), and later became a shoestring independent producer of the most opportunistic stripe, with titles like *Sterilization, What Price Innocence?*, and *Elysia* (made in a nudist camp) to his credit. He picked these subjects because he "needed something to take the place of Clark Gable." He boasts that he heard of technocracy on a Thursday, shot a short about it on Friday, and booked it on Monday. Such was Foy's training for his job at Warner, which is to produce no less than twenty-six features a year at a total cost of about $5,000,000. Foy, in short, heads up all Jack's B pictures, as he hates to hear them called, and thus guards the real backlog of the whole Warner progam. "You can run a movie business without any A's at all sooner than you can run it without any B's," points out Harry. Some of Foy's pictures get A promotion and play A dates, such as *Alcatraz Island*; but you will notice that they are all strong on "inserts" (e.g., newspaper clips, to save the cost of acting out episodes) and close-ups (to keep your eyes off the sets). His story costs are virtually nil. About half his pictures are merely new treatments of pictures that Warner has already made before, such as *West of Shanghai*, a timely quickie of last October, which was a remake of the elderly drama, *The Bad Man*, with China substituted for Mexico. Foy's adroitness at such switches keeps him serenely ahead of his seemingly crushing assignment.

Such, in brief, are a few of the men who make Jack's pictures for him. Over them all, under Jack, sits Hal Wallis, who used to be the studio publicity man and is now called Associate Executive in Charge of Production. Wallis initiates many scripts and passes on all of them, dickers with stars, assigns budgets, and in fact takes bows for the whole Warner picture program, excepting Foy's B's. Things are so smoothly organized at Burbank that when Jack is in Europe (where he goes annually to see the shows and returns with so many antiques that his Beverly Hills home is nicknamed San Simeonette), Wallis can run the studio without him, and vice versa. There are also, of course, the twenty-odd directors, among them a few topnotchers like Dieterle, Curtiz, and Lloyd Bacon; but none of them is permitted to do anything more than follow the script. Nor is anyone permitted to make retakes at Warner Bros. unless the preview is extraordinarily sour. At MGM they scarcely start work on a picture until after the preview; but at Burbank, where Jack or Wallis sees all rushes daily and retakes are made the next day, a picture whose shooting schedule is over is definitely "in the can."

The dispatch with which Warner pictures go through the mill is in one way counted a blessing by the actors. They are not much coached or argued with because their time is expensive, and they consequently have more freedom to act. In Dick Powell, [Pat] O'Brien, [Joan] Blondell, Glenda Farrell, George Brent, Kay Francis, and others Jack has assembled a sort of permanent stock company who fall efficiently into each new role with an easy feeling that they have seen it before and will get home for dinner. But when he gets hold of a star with the authentic afflatus Jack is likely to have more than his share of trouble. He had most with Cagney, who got sick of being typed as a girl-hitting mick and of making five pictures a year instead of four. He expressed his dissatisfaction in such ways as growing a mustache, talking to Jack in obscene Yiddish, and finally suing his way out of his contract on a technical breach of the billing clause. Jack is still after him in the courts. The Bette Davis case was somewhat more pathetic. In the hope of adding a few cubits to her reputation by making a picture for Korda, she took to the law in England, paid most of her fortune to get beaten, and is now back at the old grind under Jack, who has exchanged with her profuse expressions of forgiveness. Kay Francis is trying to sue her way out, and Paul Muni keeps happy largely because his contract gives him a veto on his roles, which he has exercised more than once.

Now Jack's bargain-counter dictatorship has produced some excellent pictures, as we have noted. If he does not allow much liberty of temperament on his lot, he is very far from discouraging liberty of imagination. But there is one man there who enjoys both. Mervyn LeRoy, a small and jumpy man of thirty-seven who looks younger and smokes gigantic cigars, is Harry Warner's son-in-law. Before he married Doris Warner, in the presence of a Vitaphone camera and a microphone at the Waldorf-Astoria in 1934, he had won a reputation as Hollywood's boy genius by directing Gold Diggers of 1933, I Am a Fugitive from a Chain Gang, and others. LeRoy is on excellent terms with Harry, but his producing reputation owes nothing to the kinship, and he is recurrently rumored to be on the point of leaving Warner for another studio. He has one of the two private bungalows on the Warner lot. (The other is Marion Davies's and was moved in pieces from MGM at a cost of $12,000 when Hearst's Cosmopolitan Productions transferred its mixed blessings to Burbank in 1935). LeRoy produces what he wants to, makes his own budgets. . . .

Harry [Warner] has a profound urge to stamp his feelings on the world as well as on his family. He says now that it was the educational possibilities that first attracted him to talking pictures; he is working on an ambitious program of schoolroom films; and . . . he believes that all Warner pictures contain some moral lesson. "The motion picture," he says simply, "presents right and wrong, as the Bible does. By showing both right and wrong we teach the right."

Although he can relapse with startling suddenness from this plane to the details of a real-estate deal, there is no reason to doubt the genuineness of Harry's messianism. It has two bases. One is his own lack of schooling; the other is his violent hatred of all forms of human prejudice and persecution. But Harry is not headlong about his screen preaching and it is never obvious. . . . Harry is so violently anti-Nazi that his incalculable influence could be all too quickly enlisted in America if the democratic nations should go to war. But in time of peace, if you see Harry's proselyting hand in a movie, it will be raised against the injustice that he has had to feel and hopes you will not have to. And when, as is usually the case, his pictures pretend to nothing more than entertainment, you may be sure you are getting a lot for his money.

High Visibility
(1938–1940)

TO: Mr. Blanke   DATE: May 25, 1938
FROM: J. L. Warner   SUBJECT: "Four Daughters"

. . . The park sequence [in *Four Daughters*] is very good but it could have been shot on our lot here. We have a better looking park and it is all in close shots so why go on location. In the future I wish you fellows wouldn't talk Tenny Wright out of these things when we spend a fortune building a park in the studio and then everybody wants to go on location. The other fellow's grass seems the greenest. . . .

J. L. Warner

TO: Lord-Keighley   DATE: June 28, 1938
FROM: Wallis   SUBJECT: "Brother Rat"

    I am looking at the tests of Jane Wyman, and her wardrobe for *Brother Rat*.

    Don't you think all of her outfits are too smart and too cute for the character she is playing, at least up to the point of where she takes her glasses off and becomes attractive to the boys? After all, she is supposed to be the plain, unattractive girl, and she looks gorgeous in these different costumes. She looks very smart in the sport clothes; there is Change #6 on here with a big picture hat, and certainly rather than being the wall-flower type whom the boys all shy away from and hide away from on blind dates, this girl is terrifically attractive. Every one of her costumes is smart, and she looks lovely in them, and it seems to me that we are defeating the whole purpose of our story situation and characterization with this girl's clothes. Even if she wears glasses, it isn't going to hide the fact that she is very attractive. . . . Her hair is fixed beautifully, and all in all, I am very much afraid that it is going to throw our whole story out of key. . . .

Some modifications were made. Jane Wyman had been under contract to Warner Bros. since 1936. During this period and for a few years in the early 1940s she played supporting roles in A pictures and leads in Bs and modest program pictures.

ANGELS WITH DIRTY FACES

FROM JOSEPH I. BREEN [director of the Production Code Administration

Mr. J. L. Warner,
Warner Brothers,
Burbank, Calif.,

January 19, 1938

Dear Mr. Warner:

This goes to you in confirmation of my telephone conversation today with Mr. MacEwen with regard to the [first] script *Angels with Dirty Faces*, which you submitted for our consideration. As I told Mr. MacEwen, while it might be possible to make a picture from the basic story which would meet the requirements of the Production Code, the script, in its present form, is not acceptable on a number of counts. I list these briefly below:

It is important to avoid any flavor of making a hero and sympathetic character of a man who is at the same time shown to be a criminal, a murderer and a kidnaper. In order to achieve this, great care will be needed both in the writing and actual shooting of the picture. . . .

The present script also violates the Association's ruling re "Crime in Motion Pictures" on a number of points, as follows:

The successful kidnaping for ransom.

The gun battle with the police, in the course of which a policeman is shown dying at the hands of the criminal.

The unpunished gangster murder of the man in the telephone booth.

It is our understanding that you intend to rewrite this script very considerably. However, just for the record, we set down the following minor items, in addition to the above mentioned major difficulties:

. . . Page 49: Political censor boards will probably delete all suggestion of a strip poker game. We suggest that you change it. . . .

Page 74: There should be no machine gun in the hands of the gangsters, and this killing should not be shown in such detail, but merely suggested.

Page 79: This scene of Rocky [James Cagney] manufacturing a bullet-proof vest should be omitted.

Page 87: There should be no scenes of policemen dying at the hands of Rocky.

Page 94: Political censor boards everywhere will delete these details of the preparation for the electrocution.

Page 101: This flippant reference by Rocky to God should be changed.

We will be happy to read any revised treatment of this story you may prepare.

Cordially yours,
Joseph I. Breen

TO: Mr. Wallis   DATE: April 4, 1938
FROM: [Walter] MacEwen   SUBJECT: "Angels with Dirty Faces"

At Sam Bischoff's request, I sent Joe Breen a copy of the [revised] treatment on *Angels with Dirty Faces*.

Breen has called up very concerned about this treatment, which he regards as the gravest problem that has confronted them in the last couple of years. He furthermore thinks that Howard Hughes would have a case for plagiarism against us because of certain incidents in the treatment which are dangerously similar to some things in *Scarface*. I haven't read the treatment, but Breen also claims that warnings which were sounded in his original letter of January 19th on the story which we bought [from another studio, Grand National], have been completely ignored.

I asked Joe not to send out any tough letter on this treatment, but instead to have a conference with Bischoff and the writers, as I was sure none of the difficulties were insuperable. Breen will get together with Sam on Wednesday.

This is for your information.

Walter MacEwen

*Compromises were made on both sides, and the film was produced.
The reference to certain incidents being similar to parts of* Scarface *(1932)
seems to be not warranted. Actually,* Angels with Dirty Faces *was con-
sciously or unconsciously influenced by MGM's* Manhattan Melodrama
(1934), both the play and Samuel Goldwyn's film version of Dead End
*(1937), and a dash of the then timely Father Flanagan, founder of Boys
Town, Nebraska, and the crusading radio priest, Father Coughlin.*

TO: Mr. Bischoff   DATE: April 28, 1938
FROM: Mr. Wallis   SUBJECT: "Angels with Dirty Faces"

In the development of *Angels with Dirty Faces*, be sure to instruct
the writers that the boys in the story, when Cagney returns to his neighborhood, are to be made as prominent as possible in the script. Give them
as much as possible to do, and keep in mind the fact that we want to use
four, five, or six of [the] "Dead End" boys, so instead of writing it for just
two or three boys, let's use the whole group, which will be a terrific selling
point in connection with Cagney and [contract star Pat] O'Brien. In other
words, Cagney and O'Brien and the Dead End kids in *Angels with Dirty
Faces* is sure box-office.

Incidentally, we are previewing *Crime School* [with The "Dead End"
Kids] Monday night at Warner's Hollywood, and I would like you and
the writers of *Angels* to be there. Tell them definitely I want them there,
and I don't want any alibis on Tuesday that they had dinner appointments,
or something.

Hal Wallis

TO: Mr. Roy Obringer [general   DATE: June 2, 1938
       counsel]   SUBJECT: "Angels with Dirty Faces"
FROM: Mr. MacEwen

Dear Roy:

Rowland Brown conceived and wrote the story *Angels with Dirty
Faces* some time around the beginning of August 1937. His conception
of this story idea was inspired by Mervyn LeRoy's need for a story for the
"Dead End" kids whom he had just signed.* Subsequently, Brown refused
to submit the story to LeRoy because the latter indicated that he would
not pay any substantial prices for it.

The story was also submitted to Emanuel Cohen, then with Paramount, also Grand National who later dealt for the story. . . .

Walter MacEwen

*LeRoy left Warner Bros. in early 1938.

The story was purchased by Grand National as a vehicle for James Cagney, who during one of his disputes with Warner Bros. was making films at the small studio for a salary and percentage of the profits. When Cagney returned to Warners the property went with him.

TO: Mr. Bischoff   DATE: June 28, 1938
FROM: Mr. Wallis   SUBJECT: "Angels with Dirty Faces"

I talked to Cagney today, and he has two or three good ideas which were in the original [Rowland Brown] story of *Angels with Dirty Faces* and which have not been incorporated into our final script.

One of these was the idea of using a loud speaker on the street when the officers talk to Cagney up in the warehouse, and when O'Brien comes along, he talks to Cagney over this loud speaker, which is a good piece of business.

Another, was the idea of changing the finish [of this sequence] so that Cagney comes out on the street holding O'Brien off at the point of a gun, and then tries to escape, etc. I will talk to you about this in person, but within the next couple of days, I want to get together with you, Cagney, Mike [Curtiz] and the writer, and let's incorporate some of these good, gutty ideas which will undoubtedly help the picture.

Hal Wallis

The ideas were incorporated.

TO: Mr. Curtiz   DATE: July 13, 1938
FROM: Jack L. Warner   SUBJECT: "Sister Act" [*Four Daughters*]

Dear Mike:

After I had the nice talk with you in the lobby last night, I want you to show me you can make the picture you are now shooting [*Angels with Dirty Faces*] in 30 days. You are two days behind now, and I know you can make it up if you will just shoot the story that has been so well written.

If you will stop all that superfluous roaming camera, Mike, you will make a great picture, as you always have. For your information, in the case of *Sister Act* [*Four Daughters*] 2000 feet had to be cut out of everything you worked so hard and wasted your time on, which we could not leave in the picture. As an example, the reflection shot of Jeffrey Lynn at the piano was 64 feet long, took several hours to get ready and we had to take it out.

I could pick 10 or 15 more shots that we cut out, which you worked hard to do and wasted time on. Do you call this good business and intelligence properly displayed? You know it isn't, so let's buckle down and really shoot the story.

J. L. Warner

TO: T. C. Wright   DATE: July 29, 1938
FROM: Frank Mattison [unit   SUBJECT: "Angels with Dirty Faces"
    manager]

Report for 7-28-38:

. . . Company is now 4 days behind schedule.

You can tell from yesterday's report that Mike spent the day adding shots that were not in the script and building up the sequence, all of which takes a great deal of time. . . .

Mr. Curtiz is yelling for iron doors and bars along the prison set for the doors thru which Cagney passes on his way to the [electric] chair. [Art director] Bob Haas is doing the best he can but I am sure you do not want to go outside and build any new iron gates. . . .

From present indications we will finish this picture on Saturday, August 6. This is 5 weeks and 5 days, so you see my estimate of 36 days to shoot the picture is very nearly correct. We are going to run over the Budget but not a very great deal unless Mike goes screwy when we get outside on the New York Street [back lot] to continue the gun battle.

I think Mike should be ashamed of himself for telling you yesterday he received no cooperation, for if we gave him only what is in the script we should have finished with the Warehouse day before yesterday.

While the shots he has added are no doubt building up the sequence, there is no mind-reader on the lot that can keep ahead of Mike when you turn him loose with machine guns, revolvers, bullets and gas bombs. I think he would rather play cops and robbers than eat.

Frank Mattison

FROM M. B. BENJAMIN [Loeb and Loeb, law firm]

Warner Bros. Pictures, Inc.,
Burbank, California

August 26, 1938

Gentlemen:

Samuel Goldwyn Inc., Ltd. has called to our attention the fact that in the advertising and publicizing of your motion picture *Crime School* you are using the words "The 'Dead End' Kids" and featuring the same in large type; also that it understands that you intend to use similar advertising in connection with other motion pictures being produced or to be produced by you.

Our client recently produced the motion picture entitled *Dead End* which was based upon the very successful play *Dead End*, and has the exclusive right to the use of this title in motion pictures. The advertising of any of your pictures, including *Crime School*, in the manner above referred to, is unauthorized, misleading and is in unfair competition with our client's motion picture *Dead End*.

We request that you immediately desist from such form of advertising and that you eliminate and discontinue the use of the words "The 'Dead End' Kids."

Very truly yours,
M. B. Benjamin
of Loeb and Loeb

FROM ROY OBRINGER

Mr. Ralph Lewis
c/o Freston & Files [Warners law firm]
1010 Bank of America Bldg.
Los Angeles, California

August 27, 1938

Dear Ralph:

Herewith is a letter from Loeb and Loeb, representing Samuel Goldwyn, which is self-explanatory. . . .

In the first instance, while Goldwyn may have purchased a copyrighted property from the author of the stage play *Dead End* and may have the exclusive right to the title *Dead End*, two things should be borne in mind. First, we have under contract and have used in the picture, *Crime School*, and also *Angels with Dirty Faces* six of the original Dead End Kids who appeared in the legitimate stage play in New York entitled *Dead End*. Secondly, we are not adapting the words, "Dead End" as the title of either of our photoplays, but they are entitled *Crime School* and *Angels with Dirty Faces*, and reference is made in connection with said titles to the fact that appearing therein are the Dead End Kids. Is it not a fact that we can truly represent to the public that the Dead End Kids are in our picture and that they are the Dead End Kids who appeared in the legitimate stage play, *Dead End*. . . .

R. J. Obringer

P.S. As a matter of fact, I think we should charge Goldwyn, since he apparently doesn't like our free advertising of his picture. In other words, I think that our *Crime School*, with its reference to the "Dead End" Kids, is keeping his picture alive.

Warner Bros. continued to refer to and bill the actors as The "Dead End" Kids.

FROM WILLIAM DIETERLE [director]

July 21, 1938

Dear Hal [Wallis]:

It seems to me that it would be of great advantage to our friendship if I write you this letter.

And let me emphasize right here—that whatever you decide—it will not harm my feelings for you, for they are based on human values—not on business relations.

The basis for my present contract was my profound admiration for you as man and creative producer. My apprehension in case you should leave the lot was calmed down when you told me that you had just signed a new long-term contract. Thereupon I gave up all other negotiations, to try it again with Warners, provided they would meet my little list of "wants."

They were such things as:

1. [A William] "Dieterle Production" (Credit on the screen and in advertising and publicity)
2. To work only under H. Blanke
3. Story agreement
4. Never a gangster—or Reno picture, and different other things. . . .

Finally when all was settled except the most important points— you called me in again and convinced me that no director on the lot has and will have a "Production" credit—and about the other points you told me that I would work only with Blanke and never have to direct a picture I didn't like—so believing you I signed the new contract. You went away on a vacation, and my first assignment was *The Great O'Malley* [1937]. In spite of the fact that I did not like it and Blanke was not supervisor, I made the picture, hoping you would come back and all would be alright. *Another Dawn* [1937] was my next assignment and I don't have to tell you again how much I disliked the story, but I made the picture for your sake.

In the meantime, newcomers like Mr. Litvak and later Mr. Wyler, received "Production" credit, which was denied to me. And pictures like *Tovarich* and *Robin Hood* were given to others, in spite of having been promised to me on the occasion when Mr. Warner, for family's sake, had to take *Anthony Adverse* [1936] away from me.*

The same happened when I was hurriedly called back from my

*Mervyn LeRoy directed *Anthony Adverse*.

vacation—after the *Zola* picture. After many months of waiting I was offered *White Banners* [1938], whereas Mr. Wyler, loaned from an outside lot, directed *Jezebel*.

This short history of my new contract may tell you why I finally had to go out to another lot and do *Blockade* [Wanger, 1938].

Now as for the rest of this contract—I beg you to consider the understanding between you and me, upon which I decided to stay on the Warner lot: please do find means and ways that the unpleasant things of the past do not happen again—or else let us part as good friends.

Always yours,
William Dieterle

Dieterle left Warners in 1940 to free-lance. He had been with the studio since 1930.

TO: J. L. Warner   DATE: April 30, 1938
FROM: Hal Wallis   SUBJECT: "The Dawn Patrol"

I wish you would think seriously about the re-making of *The Dawn Patrol* [1930], so that we can make a decision on this. . . .

Certainly, if they are considering reissuing it [the original 1930 version] in England, they must consider the subject matter very timely. By using our exterior shots from the [original] *Dawn Patrol*, and just re-making the interiors, which consist almost entirely of the little head-quarters shack, we should be able to re-make the picture for a "quarter."

I wish you would look at the print that we have here this coming week, as I would like to get a good writer to do a little polishing on the script and begin planning it for production as with Errol Flynn, Patric Knowles, Bruce Lester, James Stephenson, and in fact practically our entire stock company, we could knock out a very great picture in a very short time, and one that I think would bring us a fortune now when the whole world is talking and thinking war and re-armament.

Hal Wallis

TO: Hal Wallis   DATE: September 21, 1938
FROM: Seton I. Miller [screen-   SUBJECT: "Dawn Patrol" credits
    writer]

Dear Hal:

Bob Lord just spoke to me about *The Dawn Patrol* credits and asked me to write you a note concerning them.

If I had completely rewritten the script, I would ask for sole credit, but seeing that I used so much of the original [1930] script with very little change from the way [Dan] Totheroh and I wrote it, I feel that he should have second credit. The situation seems to parallel the revival of a stage play in which the cast would be changed, but the co-authors would both receive credit even though only one of them had made the revision necessary for the new production.

I sincerely appreciate your wishing to give me single credit but feel that Totheroh's name should be on there too.

Seton Miller

Dan Totheroh's name was on the credits. See page 337 regarding the genesis of the original 1930 Dawn Patrol.

TO: Mr. [Lloyd] Bacon [director]   DATE: October 20, 1938
FROM: Hal Wallis   SUBJECT: "The Oklahoma Kid"

The new dailies look very much better. . . .

There is just one thing that bothers me, and I think possibly this will be corrected after our talk last night. That is, the manner in which Cagney is playing the part, and of course, this is tremendously important. I just cannot get any kick out of him playing the scenes with that grin on his face in the serious moments when he should be grim and I know definitely that if he plays them with a grimness and with a definite purpose, they will be twice as powerful. I refer, of course, of where he is talking to [Donald] Crisp. I am so sure about this, because we just had an identical situation in *Angels with Dirty Faces*, as I told you, where he was playing the picture much the same manner, and we went back and did two or three days work over and played it more grimly, and everybody will tell you that the picture was helped tremendously by so doing, and the scenes were a hundred percent better, more effective, and more believable.

Somehow or other, Cagney grinning all through these scenes doesn't particularly characterize him as the happy-go-lucky, dashing bandit of the early days—it just doesn't come off, so let's play it straight for drama.

Hal Wallis

DARK VICTORY

TO: Hal Wallis   DATE: January 14, 1938
FROM: [Walter] MacEwen   SUBJECT: "Dark Victory"

Thinking of [contract star] Kay Francis stories, may I again call to mind *Dark Victory*. I have followed up on this a couple of times with Mr. Warner since it was last discussed, but with the New York boys coming out, etc., he stalled me on it and I have not had an opportunity to mention it for several days.

If Casey [Robinson] were to be available to do the script, and we could buy it for around $20,000, I think you would have a good Kay Francis picture in a reasonably short time, and one that would not cost a fortune to make. Moreover, Kay herself is, I understand, very much in favor of it.

Walter MacEwen

TO: Mr. Obringer　　　　　DATE: May 16, 1938
FROM: Walter MacEwen　　　SUBJECT: "Dark Victory"

Dear Roy:

We have made a deal to acquire from David Selznick a piece of story property entitled *Dark Victory* for a total consideration of $27,500. This story was a produced play and Selznick also has some treatments and scripts on it which we will get. . . .

Walter MacEwen

Selznick intended to star Merle Oberon, but there were complications.

TO: Hal Wallis　　　　　　　DATE: August 19, 1938
FROM: Casey Robinson [screen-　SUBJECT: "Dark Victory"
　　　writer]

Dear Hal:

I note that at M.G.M. they have postponed *Northwest Passage*, leaving Spencer Tracy without an assignment. They are trying to put him into the Joan Crawford picture, but he is refusing the part [*The Shining Hour*]. That seems to leave him open for borrowing, and I plead with you to make every possible effort to land him.

Please forgive my pushing my nose into casting which, strictly speaking, is not my concern, but you know that you and I have nurtured *Dark Victory* along for three years and I am concerned about it as I have never been concerned about any other picture. It is, above all things, a tender love story between a Long Island glamor girl and a simple, idealistic, more-or-less inarticulate New England doctor. If we don't capture this feeling in the proper casting of Doctor Steele, I know we will wind up with a tragic flop instead of a truly great picture.

I don't know if you've found time yet to read the entire script, but if you have I'm sure you will agree with me that Tracy was born to play this part—and of course I don't need to tell you what the combination of the names of Bette Davis and Spencer Tracy on the marquee would do to the box office.

Sincerely,
Casey

Tracy was loaned to Twentieth Century-Fox for Stanley and Livingstone *(1939) and was not available for* Dark Victory. *Northwest Passage (1940) was reactivated a year later. Casey Robinson had been one of the top writers at Warners since* Captain Blood.

TO: [David] Lewis [associate producer]*
FROM: Hal Wallis

DATE: August 22, 1938
SUBJECT: "Dark Victory"

Will you please get together with [director] Eddie Goulding and arrange for [free-lance actor] Basil Rathbone to make a test for *Dark Victory* within the next day or two. Goulding can do this tomorrow or Wednesday evening.

Make a couple of scenes with him, and particularly get one of the tender scenes with the girl toward the latter part of the story.

Bette Davis is probably leaving town today or tomorrow for about ten days so we will have to have another girl work with Rathbone. Have [contract player] Gale Page play it, or possibly [Olivia] de Havilland.

Hal Wallis

British director-writer (and sometime composer) Edmund Goulding signed with Warner Bros. in 1937 after years at MGM (Grand Hotel— 1932) and other studios. He left in 1943.

FROM BASIL RATHBONE

Mr. Jack L. Warner
Warner Bros. Studio
Burbank, Calif.

August 31, 1938

Dear Jack:

Thank you for your letter of August 29th. I just hope you are going to be as happy about *Dawn Patrol* as we have all been in making it. . . .

And now, Jack, I would like to ask you a favor. Would you either let me have, or destroy yourself, the test I made last Saturday night for *Dark Victory*. The whole thing has made me very unhappy. In the final analysis, I have no one to blame but myself, as I should never have made the test. In the first place, the scene that Mr. [David] Lewis insisted that I make was not a good one for me, but Mr. Lewis seemed

*The title "associate producer" rather than "supervisor" had been in use for about a year.

to have such very definite and complicated ideas as to the playing of
the part that I felt there must be some good reason for his choosing
that particular scene. There was, indeed, a good reason, and it was a
very simple one, too. Mr. Lewis does not and never has wanted me to
play Dr. Steele in *Dark Victory*, for he told me quite frankly before I
made the test that he could not see me in the part, but since it was
decided by him and others whose authority was necessary, that such a
test should be made, I do feel that to an actor in my position in our
business, more consideration should have been shown. The test, as you
probably know by now, was unbelievably bad. Photographically, I
cannot remember when I ever looked worse. The angle from which I
was shot was the worst angle of my face that could have been chosen.
You might reasonably ask me how it comes that I was not aware of this
when testing. Jack, when I am playing a scene, I am interested in the
job I have to do. I am not a camera hound and I trust implicitly, those
whose job it is to make the best of me, photographically. I can't be
looking for the camera and be sincerely concentrated on giving a good
acting performance. I asked Mr. Lewis, knowing that he was against
my playing the part, not to attend the making of the test; nevertheless,
he turned up and sat there through its entire making. . . . The script
which Miss Gale Page and I had learned was materially altered and
had to be relearned by us on the set. Whether this was for the good of
the scene I can't say as I was much too tired, after a long day at
Calabasas [the Warner Ranch], on location for *Dawn Patrol* with the
temperature of 105° in the shade. I also had the regretful feeling of
trying to make good in a part which Mr. Lewis had previously told me
Mr. Spencer Tracy would be ideal in. If Mr. Spencer Tracy was ideal
for the part, what was I doing, making a test for it at all, and wasting
your money? My work is well known to all those in authority at your
studio and unless there was a very reasonable chance of my meeting
with the approval of those in authority, I should never have been put
through that dreadful evening. Again, I say I blame no one but myself
and it has been a severe lesson to me for I now realize that a test is not
a test of one's ability, and not necessarily a fair example of one,
photogenically. I don't know who was to blame for making me look so
horrible, but one would only have to look through the camera to
realize that in a long scene taken, one presumes for the object of
watching my reaction, my eyes were hardly ever seen. It was an
abominable piece of mis-management since not only could no one tell
what I felt or thought, but nothing could be seen of Miss Gale Page
but the back of her head. This might have been permissible if you
could have seen me, but you couldn't.

I was told that it was necessary for me to make the test at the latest on Saturday night so that Mr. Wallis could see it on Monday. Mr. Wallis is in Mexico City! There was trouble on the set all evening as it appeared that the test was costing too much money, and there were rows going on about time, and overtime, etc. [Cameraman] Tony Gaudio told me he was amazed that no close ups were made. It was Mr. Lewis who said they were not needed and that the "two shot" would be quite sufficient. I suppose it was sufficient for him for he probably appreciated the bad angle of my face and didn't want it mitigated by a good close up. I am told on the best authority that other tests are to be made for Dr. Steele and that the scene chosen for the tests is one in the earlier part of the script giving Dr. Steele a far better opportunity to show himself. I would have chosen a scene from the earlier part of the script but Mr. Lewis insisted on the one I did *which is the woman's scene,* in which I could only react to her and these reactions are valueless unless you could see my eyes, which you could not. If it appears to you that I am making a mountain out of a molehill, I can only ask your appreciation that one's pride has been very deeply hurt. It is a sorry lesson to have to learn, but I have learned from it. If I have not by now proven my ability, no purpose can be served by making any further efforts and I would never make a test again for anyone, under any circumstances. I am very unhappy that all this should have occurred just when your studio and I were getting together on a matter which I had hoped and believed would be beneficial to both our interests.

This letter is in no way personal, Jack. . . . I am putting it out of my mind from tonight, but I could not let it go completely without writing to you. I tried to see you today but you were so very busy with conferences, and I apologize for having burdened you with yet another letter from me.

My sincere good wishes to you,
As ever,
Basil

FROM HAL B. WALLIS

Mr. Basil Rathbone
5254 Los Feliz Boulevard
Laughlin Park
Hollywood, California

September 12, 1938

Dear Basil:

I have a copy of your letter to Jack concerning your *Dark Victory* test, and I am sorry that you feel so upset about it.

Please don't let it concern you as you have made a lot of pictures here in the past, and will, I hope, make a lot more in the future. If a test for a particular part is not just right, certainly we know your capabilities and a test is not going to influence us aversely.

> Hope to have a talk with you about this soon.
> With kindest regards,
> Sincerely,
> Hal

George Brent, under contract to Warners since 1932, was cast as Dr. Steele. Brent appeared in eleven pictures with Bette Davis from 1932 to 1942.

TO: Hal Wallis   DATE: September 26, 1938
FROM: Roy Obringer   SUBJECT: Bette Davis

Inasmuch as Kay Francis is leaving the lot for good upon finishing her present picture, Bette Davis's attorney, Oscar Cummins, asked me if we would not grant Bette the favor of giving her Francis's dressing room.

I do not know the status of Davis's present dressing room, nor are dressing rooms in general within my province and I will leave it up to you, but if Francis's dressing room is available, then I am of the opinion that Bette Davis, being our top rank female artist, would undoubtedly be entitled to it.

Will you let me know on this.

> R. J. Obringer

Apparently Davis was given Francis's dressing room.

TO: Hal Wallis   DATE: October 17, 1938
FROM: Orry-Kelly [dress designer]   SUBJECT: "Dark Victory"

I agree with you about the changes, particularly the velvet dress for Miss Davis. The only reason this one was made was because she asked for a very naked dress, and practically designed it herself. However, I will change the whole top in the morning.

> Orry-Kelly

DODGE CITY

FROM NOLL GURNEY [agent]

Mr. Jack L. Warner,
Warner Bros. Pictures, Inc.,
Burbank, California

September 1, 1938

Dear Jack:

Re: *Errol Flynn—Dodge City*

Errol asked me to have a talk with you about the above whenever convenient to you. He seems a little dubious about his ability to play a part that is so essentially American—or accentuated as he puts it—but Bob Lord is so enthusiastic about Errol for this part, and I know you are too, that I feel if we have a talk together it will give Errol some confidence. Bob thought perhaps we had better wait a day or two, maybe until next Tuesday, as the work in *Dawn Patrol* is pretty heavy going at the moment and it might be best if Errol concentrate on the job at hand for a little while longer. However, when and if I am needed I will come over.

I do hope you are feeling better.

Very best,
Noll Gurney

Flynn was cast in Dodge City *and went on to make seven other Westerns over the years that were, for the most part, extremely popular.*

FROM S. CHARLES EINFELD [director of publicity and advertising]

Mr. J. L. Warner [on vacation]
4537 Collins Avenue
Miami Beach, Florida

March 20, 1939

Dear Jack:

We're going ahead full steam with plans for [the premiere and promotional festivities of *Dodge City* in] Dodge City and I think I can safely say this is going to be one of the biggest things that has ever been put on in the history of show business.

The train schedules have been definitely set. The contingent from Chicago will be in Syracuse, Kansas at 5:30 A.M. Saturday morning. The two Eastern cars will then be hooked on the Hollywood train and the complete train will arrive in Dodge City at 10:00 A.M. on Saturday, April 1st. [Representatives will be coming] from Texas to join the representatives from New York, Chicago, Hollywood and the midwest. . . .

You may already know about the N.B.C. [radio] coast to coast hookup for Saturday night, April 1st. . . .

We are going to have a parade and already there are 400 horses entered and approximately 45 bands. Add to this, stage coaches, buckboards, Indians, etc., and you'll get some idea of what a spectacle it will be. Secretary Dunkley of the Chamber of Commerce estimates that it will be about 4 miles long and take two to three hours to pass.

The hotels in Dodge City have been sold out for 10 days and every resident has already booked several out-of-town guests for the weekend. I figure there will be 100,000 people to witness the event.

Sheriff Dowdy okayed deputizing everyone in our delegations and we have ordered appropriate badges. . . .

We've rented the largest room at the hotel which will be converted into a barroom with Santa Fe porters as bartenders. Besides the newspaper people in our parties, there will be correspondents of every description and rank from all over Kansas and Colorado clamoring for interviews. . . .

Our entrance into Dodge City is going to be sensational. Fifty miles from the town a convoy of 50 decorated planes will sweep down from the clouds and accompany the train to the depot. Five miles from town 50 masked horsemen will sweep out from the prairie shooting guns and pacing the train.

The Governors of two, or possibly three states, together with the Mayor, Chief of Police, etc., will be in the greeting committee.

We're going to have a beauty contest which should be good for nation-wide art breaks.

Another terrific attraction will be a rodeo. That is expected to bring out a minimum of 10,000 customers for the stadium which seats 7000 tops.

The town is adding several hundred additional policemen and deputies to keep the crowds under control. . . .

All the citizens of Dodge City are growing beards. . . .

[Record breaking runner] Glenn Cunningham will definitely race the train into Dodge City. All the guests will stay over night in the train cars.

All of the party and the citizens of Dodge will wear frontier costumes.

We definitely expect the Secretary of War, Woodring, and the Secretary of Agriculture, Wallace, and the President of the U.S. Chamber of Commerce, Charles E. Baker, to attend. We are taking 7 special policemen with us to take care of the crowds for fear of moral turpitude. We are also carrying a doctor and nurse—just in case. . . .

Hope you're having a nice vacation.

S. Charles Einfeld

P.S. I could have gone on for 15 or 20 pages but I think you get the idea.

FROM CLAUDE RAINS [contract player]

AUGUST 31, 1938

JACK WARNER,
VICE PRESIDENT, WARNER BROTHERS FIRST NATIONAL PICTURES
DEAR JACK. HAVING THOROUGHLY ENJOYED MY ASSOCIATION WITH
THE STUDIO AND TOED THE LINE TO COOPERATE TO THE BEST OF MY
ABILITY, I FEEL THAT YOU SHOULD KNOW OF MY INABILITY TO UN-
DERSTAND BEING CAST FOR THE PART OF PHELAN IN "THEY MADE ME
A CRIMINAL." FRANKLY, I FEEL THAT I AM SO POORLY CAST THAT IT
WOULD BE HARMFUL TO YOUR PICTURE. YOU HAVE DONE SUCH A GOOD
JOB IN BUILDING ME UP THAT IT SEEMS A PITY TO TEAR THAT DOWN
WITH SUCH A PART AS THIS, AND I AM CONFIDENT THAT YOUR GOOD
JUDGMENT WILL RECOGNIZE THIS. DOGS DELIGHT TO BARK AND BITE
AND I THINK I HAVE BEEN A GOOD DOG FOR THREE YEARS, SO PERHAPS
YOU WILL GIVE ME FIVE MINUTES TO TALK IT OVER.

CLAUDE

Rains was kept in the picture. Many thought he was miscast.

FROM EDWARD G. ROBINSON

October 20, 1938

Dear Hal:

. . . I'll do *Brother Orchid* [1940—in which he would play
another gangster], and I do not object to doing that genre, but I feel
that I should not be forever circumscribed within these limits. I want
the gamut broadened, not from conceit or actor's temperament, but in
order to do justice to my capacities, as a whole.

While on the subject of stories, I want again to express a strong
desire to appear in the International Spy Ring story you are going to do
[*Confessions of a Nazi Spy,* 1939]. *I want to do that for my people.*
You mentioned that the story may not be too good, but I see no reason
why effort should not be expended to make it a knock-out of a
story. . . .

With kindest regards,
Cordially
Eddie

Robinson was cast in Confessions of a Nazi Spy.

TO: Hal Wallis   DATE: January 4, 1939

FROM: Norman Reilly Raine   SUBJECT: "Each Dawn I Die"

Dear Hal:

I have moderated the three scenes we discussed this morning—in court, on the train, and facing the Warden; and if [rising contract star John] Garfield or someone milder plays that part it'll probably be all right; but if Cagney plays Ross I think it a definite mistake to dilute his character. What audiences love about the guy [Cagney] is that they get instant blistering, crackling action from him the moment his toes are stepped on. In this story he's not a gutless piss-ant who wonders, starry-eyed, how he came to be in this spot. He's a hard-boiled police reporter who's been framed into it by political forces he's been fighting tooth and nail for a long time—and he just wouldn't take it lying down, or being silent, or gentlemanly. He'd shout at them in court; he'd jump down and carry the fight to them. He'd hate them, and hate every part of his punishment that they were responsible for and he'd throw that hate and defiance in their teeth. He'd start popping and keep popping. He'd be cocky; sure of himself; sure no power could keep him down. He's a realist, a tough newspaperman. In the train he'd knock Stacey's [George Raft] teeth out if he talked out of turn, just as he'd do the same thing in a barroom, or anywhere else reporters gather. That's what audiences like and demand of him. Confronting the Warden his viewpoint would be; I did nothing, I don't belong here, I have a right to a soft job. What he expects he asks for—even demands. That's Cagney.

Mr. Keighley quotes his performance in "G" Men as a sample of how he *gradually* got tough, thereby lending lights and shadows to the character. But my recollecion of that picture is that in the first few hundred feet he beat the bejusus out of a hooligan who asked him to defend him in a wife-or-mother-beating case. It was swift, decisive, tough action and the audience ate it up. So far as the characters of Ross and Stacey being similar, thereby necessitating a different shading for Ross, that shading already exists. Cagney (Ross) is quick to resent indignities and injustice. He's belligerent and tough. Stacey also is tough—but in a quiet way. He doesn't rant and kick up a noise. He's subdued—and deadly. But both are tough, which is swell.

Let's not get arty about this picture. It isn't a gloved hand in any part. It's a bunched fist; brutal, violent and direct. And I have an immovable conviction that Cagney as Ross should [be] tough, realistic and dangerous to cross right from the opening bell. And we show the change in character, not of a passive guy, a nice guy, whom a system makes savage, but of a tough, cocky guy who thinks he's strong enough or clever enough to beat the system—and instead it beats him. And if that isn't better drama I'm wasting time trying to write.

Norman Reilly Raine

Cagney continually tried to modify the "tough guy" image as presented in his films.

TO: Warner-Wallis   DATE: April 10, 1939
FROM: [Steve] Trilling [casting   SUBJECT: Ann Sheridan
      director]

David O. Selznick Productions would like to borrow [contract player] Ann Sheridan for the part of "Belle Watling" in *Gone With the Wind*. I was advised that the part actually works only about ten days but was spread over three to four weeks. . . .

Are we at all interested—before I go to the trouble of getting a script to find out how important the part really is. So far as billing is concerned, only the stars, Gable, Leigh, Howard and de Havilland [loaned from Warner], have been guaranteed billing so we could probably demand fifth billing.

Steve Trilling

There is nothing in the files to indicate what happened with the apparent firm offer. The role was played by Ona Munson.

[circa March 1939]
Cutting Notes from Mr. [Paul] Muni [after viewing a rough cut of *Juarez* in which he played the title role].

COACHMAN SCENE. (Tears) CLOSE SHOT takes away from effectiveness of dialogue. . . . Also the following scene with Uradi [Joseph Calleia], I'm certain can be greatly improved by checking over other takes carefully. . . .

ESCOBEDO's [John Miljan] TENT. This scene was a little hammy on my part and out of tone with my other scene. Perhaps the LONGER SHOT would be less phoney. I also believe seeing the group and the surroundings will add value. (Bella [Muni's wife] recommends using longer shot). . . .

JUAREZ-DIAZ [John Garfield] SCENE was very disappointing, I'm sure there are better takes and a much better scene can be had. I felt much warmer than it appeared on the screen. A look into his eyes may help certain scenes.

SPECULATOR'S SCENE. Recommend looking at other takes. . . . *Eyes* should [be] expressive there. . . .

My first speech to the crowd in Matamores shocked me—it was so bad. I don't know whether it was printed, but I tied in this same speech in a few takes with Uradi in another angle. I'm sure there was a better quality there. I'd advise checking up on it. . . .

GENERAL COMMENTS. Mexico and its people are missing in the picture. Juarez would become a greater figure if the audience would have a few visual glimpses and know that Juarez is not simply building up a cause, but that there *is* a cause; a cause which should make every right thinking person feel that he would like to do what Juarez is doing. At present Mexico is hazy and the people foreigners, and as such, it will be very difficult to win sympathy. Actors can only do *so* much with dialogue. What a vivid flash can do, no actor can do.

The awesomeness and grandeur of the country; its gigantic trees that are thousands of years old; the mysterious Aztecs—something of that must be seen—we can't only take Maximilian's [Brian Aherne] and Carlota's [Bette Davis] word for it.

It is not certain from the existing records if any editorial modifications were made to Juarez *as a result of Paul Muni's (and his wife's) recommendations. Muni's wife had a strong influence on his work. The above cutting notes represent the only recorded instance from the files where an actor comments on his performance during or following a screening to my knowledge.*

THE OLD MAID

TO: Steve Trilling [casting director]   DATE: February 17, 1939
FROM: Wallis   SUBJECT: "The Old Maid"

I want you to make an intensive search for someone to play the part of CLEM in *The Old Maid*. We will probably have to line up some free-lance artist to do the part, but it will have to be someone very good of the type of George Brent or David Niven [under contract to Samuel Goldwyn]. Get a list together, and I will wait for you to get in touch with me on it. Don't wait for me to follow you up on it. . . .

Hal Wallis

TO: Steve Trilling   DATE: February 22, 1938
FROM: Wallis   SUBJECT: "The Old Maid"

We will use [contract player] Humphrey Bogart for the part of Clem Spender in *The Old Maid*. . . .

Hal Wallis

TO: T. C. Wright   DATE: March 20, 1939
FROM: Al Alleborn   SUBJECT: "The Old Maid"

REPORT for 3-18-39 fourth shooting day:

. . . This morning, MONDAY, company opened in the train shed, first sequence, CLEM returning. . . . We will . . . rush the first dialogue scenes with BOGART to the Lab so that Mr. WALLIS and BLANKE can see them tomorrow, TUESDAY, and they will make a decision as to whether he remains in the picture or there is a recast. . . .

I do feel Tenny, however, that they will recast the part tomorrow that BOGART is in, and have advised Trilling to check on a man named [Alan] MARSHAL who was tested for this part and whom [Bette] DAVIS and [director Edmund] GOULDING feel is the perfect "CLEM." . . .

Al Alleborn

TO: T. C. Wright   DATE: March 22, 1939
FROM: Al Alleborn   SUBJECT: "The Old Maid"

REPORT for 3-21-39:

. . . Messrs. WALLIS, BLANKE and GOULDING looked at the scene with BOGART in the R. R. STATION and decided to take him out of the picture. Our schedule will be away from this character until it has been recast. . . .

Al Alleborn

TO: Wallis   DATE: March 22, 1939
FROM: [Edmund] Goulding   SUBJECT: "The Old Maid"

Dear Hal:

As I told you, I talked to George Brent. . . .

In the present stress and with the general line-up, I do feel that the picture needs George—because, as we all agreed, the picture is based on the two girls falling in love with a man. That man must be important both in name, performance and appearance. He must be someone to remember throughout the play. That was why my first impulse was to suggest David Niven to you. Unless the man has the requisite strength and personality to be remembered—and is a man whom the women in the audience will believe could have been this important to our two girls— the picture will lose something of what it requires. . . .

I know that I could go to work on the part with George, take time with his photography and arrange his scenes so attractively with Bette and [contract star Miriam] Hopkins that the audience will wish him back in the picture—just as the girls in our story do. . . .

Eddie

George Brent was cast for the role of "Clem," who dies early in the film. Niven had gained stardom in Warners' The Dawn Patrol (1938), directed by Goulding, and Brent had been very effective in Dark Victory, also directed by Goulding. Bogart at this stage of his career was playing mostly supporting roles or leads in B pictures.

TO: T. C. Wright   DATE: March 28, 1939
FROM: Al Alleborn   SUBJECT: "The Old Maid"

REPORT for 3-27-39:
    This morning, TUESDAY, the company opened in the train shed again. . . .
    Working with these two ladies [Davis and Hopkins] and BRENT is a slow drag because every scene has to be rehearsed well and certain things ironed out to get the best out of it for all concerned. . . . Goulding has a tough job on this picture with these two girls. Not that they want to cause him any trouble or worry, but each one is fighting for a scene when they go into it. . . .

Al Alleborn

TO: T. C. Wright   DATE: April 29, 1939
FROM: Al Alleborn   SUBJECT: "The Old Maid"

REPORT for 4-28-39:
    39th shooting day. . . .
    We had to quit at 5:40 PM because Miss HOPKINS' makeup went bad.
    Immediately on finishing, the cameraman [Tony Gaudio], Miss HOPKINS, GOULDING and myself discussed the makeup of HOPKINS—that she was changing her makeup from an old maid to a younger character. In other words, not leaving it as it had been tested and approved by Mr. WALLIS and the Supervisor on the beginning of the picture.
    I had [make-up artist Perc] Westmore come over to the stage and he and Goulding talked with Mr. WALLIS and Westmore was instructed this morning, SATURDAY, when Miss Hopkins came in to make sure that her makeup was as tested and OK'd by Mr. WALLIS. . . .

Al Alleborn

TO: Walter MacEwen   DATE: May 4, 1939
FROM: Casey Robinson   SUBJECT: Writing credits—"The Old Maid"

Dear Walter:
    . . . When the purchase of the rights to THE OLD MAID were up

for consideration first by the studio, I was sent a copy of a Paramount screenplay.* . . .

I do know that it was this script which both Miss Bette Davis and Miss Miriam Hopkins refused to play and which the Studio regarded as needing a complete re-treatment—which I performed. . . .

As you, or anyone else who has read the various material on THE OLD MAID can instantly see, the *story* told in both scripts is the same story told in Zoe Akins' stage play and, in fact, the same story which Edith Wharton told in her novel. There is, however, a great difference in the basic conception of the Paramount screenplay and the Warner Bros. screenplay. The Paramount screenplay concentrated on the character of Charlotte [Davis] and the various things that life did to her in turning her into an old maid and making her lose her child. The Warner Bros. screenplay is the story of the hatred which develops between two women through jealousy.

When we were considering buying the property and it was sent to me for my opinion, I was at first against the purchase of this property which seemed a rather old-fashioned sob story—until I fell upon this general conception of the story which seemed to make it worth while. You will, of course, find the roots of this jealousy-hatred motive in the stage play, though in it this theme was not given sufficient development—and you will also find some remnants of it left in the Paramount screenplay, though the writers of that script saw fit to lay even less emphasis on it than Miss Akins did in her stage play.

It was my opinion that this hatred-jealousy theme should be seized upon, enlarged and built into the basic treatment of the story. . . .

Whatever merit this conception of mine may or may not possess, the fact remains that it was this conception that persuaded Miss Davis and Miss Hopkins to play in the picture and the Warner Bros. Studio to make it—thus taking THE OLD MAID off the Paramount shelf where it had lain for a good many years. . . .

Sincerely,
Casey Robinson

Casey Robinson received sole screenplay credit on The Old Maid.

TO: Sam Bischoff
FROM: Bob Fellows [unit manager]

DATE: May 31, 1939
SUBJECT: "20,000 Years in Sing Sing"

Dear Sam:

In accordance with Mr. Wallis's wishes and your request, I just

*Not produced.

finished looking at the above picture [made in 1933] with John Hughes, the art director, and Jack Killifer, the cutter.

After a long discussion, we are going to follow this routine [for the remake, *Castle on the Hudson*]:

Killifer is getting the print of the [original] picture and is going through sequence by sequence, checking the print against the present script. He is having all the scenes printed up that can possibly be used again. When he has this film together, he will contact you and I would suggest that you and the director make your final selections. Hughes has the stills from the original picture and is going to duplicate these sets that have to be built, leaving out such set-ups that involve shots covered by the present picture. Naturally, some of the sets will be affected by the final selection you and the director make, so I would also suggest that you have Hughes present when Killifer shows you the selected shots.

Naturally, Killifer is selecting every possible shot indicated in the script, by the selection of medium and long shots in the prison—even with the old principals in them, a considerable saving can be effected. In most shots a similar hat and the same type of dark clothes will make it possible to get by with these scenes, and naturally be quite a saving in set construction. . . .

In addition to this saving, the director can save a week's shooting time by matching these selected cuts. This will require the use of a Moviola [small screen viewing machine] on the set and it will necessitate the casting office matching approximately the general size and build of some of the bit players, but it can save in the neighborhood of $80,000 on the cost of the picture.

Bob

This was the same procedure used in the remake of The Dawn Patrol *and* The Crowd Roars *(1932)—the latter called* Indianapolis Speedway *(1939).*

TO: Mr. Blanke   DATE: June 3, 1939
FROM: J. L. Warner   SUBJECT: "We Are Not Alone"

I thought *We Are Not Alone* [with Paul Muni] ended at page 143, but much to my amazement, I find that there is another part to come. It appears to me we will have so many pages on this script that we are going to have a repetition of *Juarez* and waste a fortune on the cutting room floor.

I am not childish and going to keep Muni and anyone else happy, but this script must be down to where the picture is 9000 to 9200 feet when finished. In fact, that is going to be too long for this type of suffering picture.

I will not permit a repetition of *Juarez* as long as I am in the picture business—just to satisfy Muni, it was criminal and we wasted a fortune. . . .

J. L. Warner

Muni had asked that his role in Juarez *(1939) be expanded. The script was overly long and a vast amount of material was cut after shooting. Considering the cost, headaches, and the less than strong commercial acceptance,* Juarez *was not a successful enterprise.* We Are Not Alone *did poorly.*

THE ROARING TWENTIES

The following is an introduction to an outline for a film eventually to be called The Roaring Twenties. *Hellinger was a popular syndicated Broadway columnist who recently had been signed by Warner as an associate producer.*

The World Moves On
Original Story for the Screen
by Mark Hellinger

This is a big picture. It is either big—or it is nothing at all. For, while it deals with a specific set of humans, the background is far more important than the characters. And the background is the history of an era.

The World Moves On [*The Roaring Twenties*] deals with Prohibition. Oh, yes—it deals with men and women who live and love, who gloat and emote, who suffer and succeed. The ingredients of the successful picture are ever present. But over everything hangs the shadow of an era that the world of tomorrow will find it difficult to believe. The era of Prohibition.

So, before proceeding with this outline, you must answer one very important question: Is it yet time for such a picture? There will be those who say no; that the period in question is still too close to be treated as history. This opinion may be correct. Until such a picture is made, no one will be able to state definitely. But I hold the opposite view.

I hold the opposite view for specific and detailed reasons. They are:

1. During the Prohibition era, itself, some of the most successful films of the day were those that dealt with that very subject, or with characters developed under that regime. Surely no one will argue that point with me.

2. The man who says that any certain subject cannot be box-office, is setting himself up for a helluva kick in the rump. They said you couldn't make money with a horse race yarn—and along came *Broadway Bill* [1934]. They said you couldn't do a thing with a prize fight tale—and along came *Kid Galahad* [1937]. They're always saying those things until one that "can't possibly succeed" does succeed. Then you have an epidemic of similar yarns.

3. *The World Moves On* covers a period of twenty years. From 1919, directly after the World War—until 1939, when the picture is released. You are watching history being enacted, even though you may recognize many of the characters who walked in life beside you. Does that make the subject less fascinating? I think otherwise. I think it was [journalist] Frank Munsey who, years ago, realized that people would always buy papers to read about that which they themselves had already seen. Surely this is a truism that holds good for the screen as well. Our vanity will always drag us to spots in which we can say "I once knew that guy myself"—or "by golly, that's right. I saw it happen, myself."

4. If you will grant that my last point is correct, you will have to agree with me on this statement: The youth in your audience of 1939— ages fifteen to twenty-one—never knew what Prohibition was! Strange to say; yet consider: Prohibition went out around 1934. Your boy of twenty-one today, was sixteen at the time. While he was growing up—thirteen to sixteen—Prohibition was dying. In other words, it is fairly safe to say that the youth of today has no conception of what the speakeasy era actually was. He might *think* he knows, but he doesn't. It's difficult to believe, but there it is.

5. I was too young to fight in the [First] World War. I was very close to the big fight; yet I couldn't make it. Did that spoil my enjoyment of *The Big Parade* [1925], *What Price Glory?* [1926], *Journey's End* [1930], *All Quiet on the Western Front* [1930]? Hell, no. . . . Was the earthquake too close for me to enjoy *San Francisco* [1936]? Did the fact that Ziegfeld died only a short time before destroy the notion that *The Great Ziegfeld* [1936] was a glorious musical?

6. If youth is interested in a film because youth is curious—and if the rest of us are interested in order to see what was so close to us—and if the foreign market always enjoys Uncle Sam in one of his silliest moves— what type of audience do we fail to attract? You tell me.

7. The moral of *The World Moves On* is that, no matter how thin you slice it, crime does not pay. It raps booze, which should cause the drys to endorse it heartily. It favors the Administration, because it was the Administration that put an end to Prohibition. It will please the wets because it demonstrates that, under the modern set-up, the gangster element has vanished from the liquor trade.

8. I have always wanted to write this picture. There may be others who have studied the subject more closely in a bookish way. But I can promise you that nobody has *lived* it more closely than I. . . .

(Incidentally—and here I go again—do you see the *Alexander's Ragtime Band* [1938] motif as it runs through here? Popular war songs when we open—1920 songs . . . Songs of 1924 . . . Songs of 1927. . . . Hell, stick 'em in as you see fit—and with more logic than in *Alexander's Ragtime Band*. For this is the story of an era.) . . .

TO: Bob Lord DATE: July 25, 1938
FROM: Niven Busch [screenwriter] SUBJECT: "The World Moves On"
[*The Roaring Twenties*]

Dear Bob:

If you will walk up to a mirror and take one of those long, horrifying looks into your soul that a writer has to take occasionally, you will realize that you don't like the treatment you wrote on *The World Moves On*. Much as I love you, I don't like it either.

I don't have to tell you what's the matter with it. You have tried valiantly to put screen construction on a sketchy but suggestive sales brochure [referring to Hellinger's original story]. To do that in four days was a task that would challenge the talents of Henrik Ibsen. In fact Ibsen would be so far behind, it wouldn't even be a photo finish. (Question from Hellinger: Where is this Ibsen running and who's got the leg up?)

I am not saying that we can't take three guys and through their lives get the story of the prohibition era. It's a challenging, exciting subject, but I feel strongly that in boiling down the wildest decade that this country ever lived through, we can't do it justice if we focus the whole story on a gangster's love affair. Most of the things that can be done to such a subject have been done in one way or another countless times upon the screen. In your eagerness to make the story definitive you have boiled it down to cut rate Cagney—a Roosevelt era Little Caesar modified to the censorship requirements of 1938. What's more I have a feeling that no matter what we did in the screenplay, working on these lines, it would give us the same thing—that unhappy paradox, a quiet gangster picture.

Maybe if we took an average guy and his two friends—one of them a gangster, and followed them through ten years, cueing in new events for time dissolves as Hellinger suggested, we might get the feeling of an epic into a story. We would have to make a hero's life an interesting and exciting thing, and yet construct it so that it could only have happened at that particular time in the nation's history. This story has yet to be written. To create it might pay dividends. It would also involve a period of floundering, a period of humble and patient work and effort to arrive at something new. If the studio wants to gamble on an enterprise of this kind, I will be glad to do my damndest. But I don't think we're on the right track now.

Niven Busch

Jerry Wald, Richard Macaulay, and Robert Rossen wrote the final screenplay of The Roaring Twenties, *which was a modification and embellishment of Hellinger's outline.*

TO: [Raoul] Walsh [director]   DATE: July 20, 1939
FROM: Hal Wallis   SUBJECT: "Roaring 20's"

The scenes with Cagney, the woman [Gladys George], and [Frank] McHugh outside the jail, and the balance of the stuff that day were good. The stuff has kick to it.

However, I don't like your [camera] setups; those straight-on two-shots, and individual closeups are going to get monotonous and make for choppy cutting. For example, in the courtroom instead of just shooting a big, choker head of the judge, why didn't you shoot over-the-shoulders of Cagney and Jeffrey Lynn up at the judge. Get a little composition in the thing and a little grouping so that we don't have to cut from one big closeup to another and just have a series of portraits on the screen with the people speaking the lines. . . .

Hal Wallis

This was director Raoul Walsh's first film for Warners, although he had been directing motion pictures since 1914. Walsh was subsequently put under long-term contract.

TO: Walsh   DATE: August 29, 1939
FROM: Wallis   SUBJECT: "Roaring 20's"

We want to retake the finish of the picture on the church steps along the lines discussed in the projection room today.

The scene, as it is, is undershot. It all happens too quickly, and with Gladys [George] and the cop running into that one angle where Cagney is stretched out on the stairs, it is all over so quickly and not built up at all, and the finish becomes flat.

I think it will help considerably if we will do the following:

When Cagney comes into the church steps, instead of that close shot on the stairs where he runs into it and then runs up a few steps and then falls down, pick Cagney up down the street and pan with him as he staggers into the shot of the church steps, let him stagger up against a pillar on the left of the church, where we will distinctly see that it is a church, then let Cagney go up two or three steps and stagger half way across the stairs and fall and roll down. Then cut to Gladys George, picking her up down the street where you picked Cagney up, and pan her into the shot on the church steps and let her go in and kneel down beside Cagney as she did in the other stuff.

Also, I would like to get another cut of Gladys George running down the other street where Cagney stumbled against a mail box and let her run around that corner and exit in the direction that he did.

Then we will need a cut of the cop coming in from another direction to the church steps, and then go into your scene. In playing the scene, don't have Gladys George looking up at the cop answering his questions emoting, but rather have her pick Cagney up as she does, she looks down at him and probably runs her hand through his hair, and then as the cop starts to ask her questions "Who is this fellow?" she looks straight ahead of her straight past the camera with tears in her eyes but with her voice almost in a monotone as if she is answering mechanically and thinking of the past. When the cop asks who it is, have her say "His name was Eddie Bartlett," and when the cop says "What did you have to do with him?" have her say "That's something I never could figure out."

At the end of the scene from her closeup, after she reads the line "He used to be a big shot," pull back and up into a long shot, so that we leave the three small figures on the church steps, the girl holding Cagney in her lap, the cop standing alongside, and we can use that for our fadeout shot. . . .

Be sure and shoot this both ways, however, (1) without any people in . . . and (2) the whole scene with people in the background.

I want to be sure to get this right, because so much depends on having an effective finish, and I want to be sure to get it shot now while Cagney is here, as upon completion of the picture he is going away for a couple of weeks and I don't want to have to make any retakes again when he comes back.

Hal Wallis

The retake without any people in the background was used in the released film.

THE PRIVATE LIVES OF ELIZABETH AND ESSEX

FROM JACK L. WARNER

March 7, 1939

Dear Hal:

. . . What do you think of making *The Knight and the Lady* in color? Or have you any suggestions to offer for the next color picture? You want to be very careful to pick a subject that will not cost a great amount at any time as I feel in *Dodge City*, for a picture of its magnitude we have a great deal for what it costs, while *Valley of the Giants* [1938], *Gold Is Where You Find It* [1938], and *Heart of the North* [1938] will not be commercially successful. All of them will lose money.

In fact, outside of *God's Country and the Woman* [1937] and *Robin Hood* [and the as yet unreleased *Dodge City* (1939)], none of the [Warner] color pictures have been any where near successful or where we got our money back and unless we have the right type of picture we are going to avoid making any picture in color, irrespective of our contract. Technicolor will just have to extend it. . . .

Jack

The Knight and the Lady *(later retitled) was made in Technicolor.*

TO: T. C. Wright DATE: April 5, 1939
FROM: Wallis SUBJECT: "The Knight and the Lady"

In planning your sets for *The Knight and the Lady*, please plan these on stages where they can be saved after this production as we will be able to use practically every set over again for *The Sea Hawk* and this will save a fortune.

Hal Wallis

FROM BETTE DAVIS

JACK L WARNER, PERSONAL
WARNER BROS STUDIO

APRIL 28, 1939

I HAVE BEEN TRYING . . . FOR SOME WEEKS TO GET AN ANSWER FROM YOU CONCERNING THE TITLE OF MY NEXT PICTURE. I FELT CONFIDENT THAT YOU WOULD OF YOUR OWN VOLITION CHANGE IT, CONSIDERING THE FACT THE PLAY FROM WHICH IT IS TAKEN WAS BOUGHT FOR ME AND WAS CALLED "ELIZABETH THE QUEEN." I HAVE FOUND OUT TODAY YOU ARE NOT CHANGING IT. YOU OF COURSE MUST HAVE REALIZED MY INTEREST IN THE TITLE CHANGE CONCERNED THE BILLING. . . . THE SCRIPT "THE KNIGHT AND THE LADY," LIKE THE PLAY, IS STILL A WOMAN'S STORY. I THEREFORE FEEL JUSTIFIED IN REQUESTING FIRST BILLING, WHICH WOULD AUTOMATICALLY CHANGE THE TITLE, AS THE PRESENT TITLE IS OBVIOUSLY ONE TO GIVE THE MAN FIRST BILLING. I FEEL SO JUSTIFIED IN THIS FROM EVERY STANDPOINT THAT YOU FORCE ME TO REFUSE TO MAKE THE PICTURE UNLESS THE BILLING IS MINE. IF YOU WOULD LIKE TO DISCUSS THIS MATTER WITH ME I WOULD BE MORE THAN WILLING.

BETTE DAVIS

FROM GRADWELL SEARS [general sales manager, New York]

May 8, 1939

Dear Jack:

The subject of titles is really becoming a serious problem. Almost every good title you get seems to have some kind of an impediment. . . .

I also read in [Louella] Parsons's column that you are trying to get the title *Elizabeth and Essex* in place of *The Knight and the Lady*. I implore you not to make this change. *The Knight and the Lady* with [Errol] Flynn and Davis indicates a romantic swashbuckling sort of thing, while *Elizabeth and Essex*, except to the classes, indicates something entirely different. *The Knight and the Lady* undoubtedly would have mass appeal while *Elizabeth and Essex* is limited entirely to class appeal. . . .

Sincerely,

G. L. Sears

FROM ROY OBRINGER

May 9, 1939

MEMORANDUM

At 12:45 P.M. Saturday, May 6, 1939, Mr. J. L. Warner phoned from his home to Bette Davis, who was having luncheon at the studio restaurant, and the substance of his conversation was as follows:

(a) That Bette Davis would receive first billing in her next picture.

(b) That the title, *The Knight and the Lady* would definitely not be used (Mr. Warner states that he did make some comment, however, as to the possible necessity of using the title *The Lady and the Knight*).

(c) That we were considering and making an effort to see if we could not use the title *Elizabeth and Essex*, but there was no definite commitment on this, due to the possible legal obstacles and excessive costs to acquire the right to use this title, should any other person have a prior legal right to its use.

R. J. Obringer

FROM JACK L. WARNER

Mr. Gradwell Sears
321 West 44th Street
New York City, N.Y.

May 19, 1939

Dear Grad:

. . . In the first place, they want $10,000 for the title, *Elizabeth and Essex*, as it is a title of a well-known book [by Lytton Strachey]. Secondly, we are billing the picture as follows:

Bette Davis and Errol Flynn
in
The Lady and the Knight

TO: T. C. Wright   DATE: June 12, 1939
FROM: Frank Mattison   SUBJECT: "The Knight and the Lady"

Report for 6-10-39:

. . . I had [a] . . . display of temperament late SATURDAY afternoon from Miss DeHAVILLAND; to wit—at 5:15 PM when we started to rehearse a scene between her and Miss FABARES [Nanette Fabray], she informed Mr. Curtiz that she positively was going to stop at 6:00 PM, but Mr. Curtiz told her that unless she stayed and finished the sequence he positively would cut it out of the picture. Miss DeHAVILLAND expressed herself before the company and Mr. Curtiz came right back, with the result that . . . it became necessary for me to dismiss the company at 6:15 without shooting this sequence.

Inasmuch as this sequence of 2 pages was inserted at Miss DeHAVILLAND'S request, I believe that we definitely should not shoot it and uphold Mr. Curtiz in the matter. I think this will put Miss DeHAVILLAND in a proper frame of mind so that she will take direction and instruction hereafter.

Relative to Miss DAVIS' refusal to cooperate with us in our schedule, I have laid the shooting schedule out in direct continuity as she would like to have us do it. . . . I believe we will get better results by spending the money and cooperating with Miss DAVIS for, as you know, she only has to delay us ½ a day between now and the finish of the picture to cost us many times the amount mentioned. . . .

Frank Mattison

FROM BETTE DAVIS

[To] J L WARNER

JUNE 30, 1939

I HAVE WAITED NOW SINCE DAY PICTURE STARTED FOR TITLE TO BE SETTLED. I WAS PROMISED IT WOULD NOT BE "THE KNIGHT AND THE LADY." THE PRESENT TITLE "THE LADY AND THE KNIGHT," AS ANNOUNCED IN PAPER AND CALLED SUCH IN FAN MAGAZINES, I CONSIDER THE SAME THING. . . . YOU HAVE THE CHOICE OF "ELIZABETH AND ESSEX," "ELIZABETH THE QUEEN," OR "THE LOVE OF ELIZABETH AND ESSEX." IF MR. MUNI IS ALLOWED THE TITLE "JUAREZ," ANOTHER HISTORICAL PICTURE . . . YOU NEED HAVE NO WORRY ABOUT THE BOX OFFICE WITH THE TITLE "ELIZABETH AND ESSEX" WITH FAR MORE WELL KNOWN PEOPLE THAN "JUAREZ."

BETTE DAVIS

*The "well known people" presumably refer to the characters of Eliz-
abeth and Essex and Juarez rather than the people playing these roles.*

TO: Gradwell Sears   July 14, 1939
FROM: Jack L. Warner

. . . Note, we have secured the right to use *Elizabeth and Essex,* and I
have added the words, *Private Lives of* to it. We ran into a big snag in
using *The Lady and the Knight,* which I could not overcome. Furthermore, in case we both do not know, you cannot call a Queen a lady. . . .

Best wishes.
Sincerely,
Jack

FROM OLIVIA DE HAVILLAND

July 18, 1939

Dear Mr. Warner—
It is a shame that you are so busy this week that it is impossible to
arrange a luncheon engagement. I should have enjoyed the experience
so much.
There is something I would like to straighten out with you,
something that is, I feel very important to both of us. I have not been
at all happy about the situation that existed during *The Lady & the
Knight.* I feel that a misunderstanding was created between us that had
no business to be there. As you know, when you called me on the
phone, full of indignation, I wanted to talk to you in person, rather
than discuss so vital a matter through such an unsatisfactory medium,
but you were busy or preferred not to do so. . . .
The first time you called, the conversation concerned my starting
date on *The Lady & the Knight.* As I explained to you, I had, four
weeks before, forseen the problems that would arise between the
schedules of *G.W.T.W.* [*Gone With the Wind*] and *The Lady & the
Knight* and had discussed the matter with Mr. Wallis, Mr. Lord & Mr.
Curtiz and come to a conclusion satisfactory to all of us. My principle
in being concerned was simply this: I wanted to do a good job in
G.W.T.W. for it was a solemn responsibility, & I wanted to do my best
in *The Lady & the Knight,* for it is one of your big pictures for the
year, & a bad performance on my part could weaken the film
perceptibly. As you know it is impossible to perform two decided and
different characters at the same time, so our problem was to work out
the schedules so that they would not conflict. . . .

When I started my first important day's work on *The Lady & the Knight*, not having had a vacation since September, I was quite nervous, and as one always is on the first day of a picture, somewhat apprehensive of my first consequential scene. And that scene was a charming, well-written one, & I wanted to do it well.

I arrived at the studio at 6:45 A.M. shot a number of reaction shots beginning at 9. The morning passed, the afternoon passed, & finally at 5:30 P.M. with my nose shiny, my makeup worn off, my vitality gone, & my tummy doing nip-ups, we prepared to line up the charming scene. I mentioned that it was nearing six, that everyone was tired, and I hoped that we could shoot the scene another day since it required virtually no set. However, when the lights were arranged, at 6:15, with everything against me technically, I limped on the set prepared to go through with this thing. Unfortunately, to make matters much worse, I found that a certain man who means well wanted to get this charming scene over in a hurry—and then, *bang!* he said something very tactless, and to my horror I found myself shaking from head to foot with nerves, & unable to open my mouth for fear of crying—which would never do in front of so many people. The man, who meant well, realized he had gone too far, apologized, & dismissed the company assuring me that he could quite well shoot the scene another day for it required no set & could be done in a short time. He had said the same kind of thing a few days before to a famous blond actress who had gone home with the tears streaming down her face.*

And someone went to you about all this! I know that if you had been present on that set, and had realized my problem, you would have dismissed the company rather than shoot that scene so late in the day. I know, too, that you understand that an actress, no matter how talented she is, is dependent very seriously upon her appearance & her vitality for the quality of her performance. When those two things leave her, whether it is after five years work or at the end of a day, she has nothing to rely on. And when I make suggestions to anyone at the studio, it is for the good of the whole. . . .

You have a tremendous business to conduct, one that you have built to astounding success & complexity, & your time is not to be wasted with trivialities.

> My very best wishes to you,
> Olivia de Havilland

---

*The "certain man" presumably was director Michael Curtiz; the "famous blond actress" presumably was Bette Davis.

FROM GRADWELL SEARS

August 14, 1939

Dear Jack:

I hate to keep harping on this subject, but I feel I owe it to you and the company to do so.

The reaction to the title *The Private Lives of Elizabeth and Essex* is extremely bad. I am getting letters of protest from every part of the country and my own people tell me that wherever they go exhibitors are objecting to this title. They say that it smacks of Alexander Korda* and that in the south, mid-west and small towns particularly, it will be confused with an English picture, which as you know do very little business especially in small towns.

I recognize the value of the title *The Private Lives of Elizabeth and Essex* for the foreign market, but I implore you Jack, not to use this title for American consumption, because it will cost us hundreds of thousands of dollars. *The Lady and the Knight, The Knight and the Lady* or any other title which suggests romance and adventure will serve far better than the present title which positively identifies the material as an English historical drama. . . .

Sincerely,
Grad

FROM JACK L. WARNER

August 16, 1939

Dear Grad:

. . . I assure you that a picture entitled *The Old Maid* [1939] would not have gotten a quarter if it did not have a cast consisting of Bette Davis, Miriam Hopkins and George Brent, and I am sure that *The Private Lives of Elizabeth and Essex*, starring Bette Davis and Errol Flynn, will do just as much business as it would under any other title, because after all these people are the attraction and not the title, which I think you will agree with. . . .

The picture was released as The Private Lives of Elizabeth and Essex, *and considering the stars, lavish production, Technicolor, and heavy promotion, the film did not do outstanding business.*

---

*The producer who made, among many other motion pictures, a series of historical films: *The Private Life of Henry VIII* (1933), *The Private Life of Don Juan* (1934), *Catherine the Great* (1934), etc.

TO: [Mark] Hellinger   DATE: July 18, 1939
    [associate producer]   SUBJECT: "Nevada" [*Virginia City*]
FROM: [Robert] Lord

Dear Mark:

Your basic story line [of *Virginia City*] is about as good (perhaps a little better) than the basic story line of *Dodge City* and *Union Pacific* [1939]. That is to say: "It stinks and they stank."

To be quite realistic, the basic story line of most westerns, including the successful ones, is prone to be somewhat feeble-minded. Why not—since they cater to the lowest common denominator of our mass audience?

My guess is that with extraordinary work, effort, sweat and pain—a very acceptable western could be made from your story-line. It would be a back-breaking job both in the writing of the script and in the actual production of the picture.

I personally would not shoulder the responsibility of going ahead with the story in view of Mr. Wallis's opposition to it. . . .

> In all sincerity,
> *Bob*

TO: Mr. Wallis   DATE: October 23, 1939
FROM: [Robert] Buckner   SUBJECT: "Virginia City"
    [screenwriter]

Dear Hal:

Everyone's had a crack at you on these many changes for *Virginia City* except me. I know that we are very close to starting production now and that you may not care to re-open the present revised beginning as written by [Norman Reilly] Raine under Curtiz's instructions. But I feel very strongly that a great mistake is being made, and since I shall be solely responsible for the screenplay I must state my reasons. . . .

The picture should start with the stagecoach sequence, as did the original story. Libby Prison, Jefferson Davis's office, Richmond park, the tunnel and escape, Hooker's tent—all these scenes are completely unnecessary. Beyond that, I believe that the revised scenes are dramatically unsound, both from the point of characterization, dialogue and their effect on the story as a whole. We use up 50 valuable pages to establish three minor story points; (1) The South must get gold, (2) Vance [Randolph Scott] is to try to get it, [Errol] Flynn to stop him, and (3) Julia [Miriam Hopkins] falls in love with Flynn.

I say they are minor points because all three can be made on the stagecoach and in Virginia City in 24 pages where they belong. This is not a War picture, but a Western. The long nostalgic love scene between Julia and Vance is pure piffle straight from *Gone With the Wind*. Julia is played up as a fine lady of ye olde aristocratic South. She's not. She's a Western girl with a Southern tradition about which she is not drippingly sentimental. She's tough, not common but hard and realistic.

Libby Prison serves absolutely no story purpose and never did. It was written for *Dodge City* for an entirely different reason [but not used]. It is now badly overwritten and gives undue emphasis to what is merely a prologue. The dynamiting of the powder-magazine is phoney and merely helps Mike [Curtiz] out of a jam.

But the main reason why this new beginning is all wrong is this: It kills my opportunity to develop properly the 2nd and 3rd parts of our story. Now I must condense the Virginia City sequences out of all proportion to their importance, and also the chase of the Gold Train, which last I have just completed and which I believe you will agree is the most exciting and colorful part of the picture.

Robert Buckner

The prologue with Libby Prison, etc., remained. At this time, the influence of Gone With the Wind *(1939) was considerable. Robert Buckner signed with Warner Bros. in 1937. Previously he had been a contributor of fiction to American and British magazines.*

FROM BRYAN FOY [head of B pictures]

March 10, 1939

Dear Jack:

. . . I think there is a picture in the life of Father Duffy, the Chaplain of the 69th Regiment [of World War I]. We could call the picture *The Fighting 69th*. . . . I hope that you won't think I'm shooting too high when I ask for [contract star] Pat O'Brien, because you must understand that I have to invent my own Muni's. Think of that sensational exploitation it would mean to me: Pat O'Brien, Jane Wyman, and an ALL STAR CAST. (By all star cast, I mean all our stock players). . . .

Warners' program of approximately twenty-five B films a year began in 1935 under Foy's supervision. In the 1940s Warner B pictures virtually disappeared, due to changes in the amount and kind of films being made during World War II, among other reasons. However, modestly priced pictures continued to be made at the studio.

FROM JACK L. WARNER

Mr. Darryl Zanuck, [vice president in charge of production,
Twentieth Century-Fox]
20th Century-Fox
Beverly Hills, Calif.

July 12, 1939

Dear Darryl:

It is very unfortunate that someone did not call your attention to
the announcements we had about our story, *The Fighting 69th*, in all
the New York papers and *Variety* of March 22, 1939. . . .

We are preparing to make a very important picture with James
Cagney, Pat O'Brien and George Brent. . . .

While copyrighted material takes precedent over registrations at
the Hays Office in New York, this may or may not play a part in our
particular situation, but the point that I am dwelling on, Darryl, is that
ten weeks or so before you made any announcement of your story, we
had already announced ours. . . .

With all these facts, I am sure you haven't any moral right to go
ahead and make your picture because it would be a sad state of affairs
in the picture industry if every company would jump out, knowingly or
unknowingly, dealing with the same idea before their competitors were
able to complete their picture, and which competitors had made prior
announcements with respect to such proposed picture. . . .

Sincerely,

*Fox did abandon their project and Warners produced the very suc-
cessful* Fighting 69th *(1940).*

DR. EHRLICH'S MAGIC BULLET

FROM WILL H. HAYS [president,
Motion Picture Producers and
Distributors of America, Inc.]

Mr. Joseph I. Breen
5504 Hollywood Boulevard,
Hollywood, California

August 22, 1939

Dear Joe:

. . . In my opinion there is a distinction between a picture in
which a venereal disease is the subject and a picture in which the
discovery of a cure for a venereal disease is an incident. There is a

difference too, between an incident, as in *Dead End*, where the girl [played by Claire Trevor] had syphilis, and the inability of her lover [Humphrey Bogart] to kiss her was a dramatic piece of business, and a picture about the life of a great bacteriologist [Paul Ehrlich], whose many great discoveries and contributions to society happen to include the discovery of a cure for a venereal disease; also a difference between the latter and the kind of a reference that was involved in pictures as far back as *The Green Hat* [A *Woman of Affairs*, 1929].

To make a dramatic picture of the life of Dr. Ehrlich and not include this discovery among his great achievements would be unfair to the record; to omit the reference to syphilis in the fictional picture, *Dead End*, with its great basic theme, was no such dis-service.

Obviously is warranted our careful study of this whole matter, to the end that if possible an accurate picture may be made of the life of this renowned scientist, showing his great service, true to the historical record and yet being strictly within the Code. . . .

We remember, too, that all the arguments and the facts relative to the value of the great humanitarian service that might be the result of a public campaign against syphilis do not prove that a motion picture producer making an entertainment picture on the subject of syphilis, is not influenced by the profit motive.

It must be that regardless of our sympathy with the objectives of the campaign against syphilis, we cannot avoid the responsibility of starting that which results in the opportunity for 16,000 exhibitors to exploit the disease in their neighborhood theatres, where the shock and profit purpose obtain.

> With kindest personal regards, I am
> Sincerely yours,
> Will H. Hays

FROM HAL B. WALLIS

Mr. Will Hays
Motion Picture Producers' Ass'n.
23 West 44th Street
New York City, N.Y.

August 24, 1939

Dear Mr. Hays:

Reference the copy of your letter to Joe Breen, which he sent to me, dated August 22nd, regarding *The Story of Dr. Ehrlich*, this letter is to confirm our understanding that we will not send out any advertising, exploitation or publicity matter on this subject that deals with syphilis, sex hygiene, venereal diseases, or anything pertaining thereto. We also agree that all such advertising matter will be submitted to the Advertising Code Administration either here or in New York for approval before it is sent out.

We will work over the script immediately and will reduce all reference to venereal diseases to a minimum.

We will re-write the script and change, or eliminate, any clinical scenes dealing with syphilis patients or treatment of syphilis so that they will not be objectionable.

We will also endeavor to confine the references to syphilis to the actual development of the cure by Dr. Ehrlich and to scenes necessary to show his fight to develop a cure. . . .

> Best Wishes,
> Sincerely,
> Hal Wallis

FROM FINLAY McDERMID [story editor]

October 27, 1941

REPORT [regarding *Dr. Ehrlich's Magic Bullet* (1940). Another instance of legal complications.]

. . . Already forwarded . . . I understand, is the letter from [writer] Norman Burnside which originally interested the Coast branch of the studio in the area of an Ehrlich biography. It was Burnside's idea to develop an anti-Nazi theme out of the Ehrlich material and quite obviously, for Burnside's purpose, the reasons for picking Ehrlich as a protagonist had very little to do with syphilis and its cure. Ehrlich happened to be a great humanitarian and a German Jew. Had his life's work been a cure for tuberculosis or cancer or even something entirely remote from the field of medicine, the basic Burnside theory would not have been affected one whit.

The studio, although dubious, was still sufficiently interested to hire Burnside to develop his idea. And, as it did develop, producer opinion began to crystallize; it would be a mistake to make a political propaganda picture out of a biography which could stand on its own feet. Heinz Herald, co-author of *Zola* and John Huston, a co-author of *Juarez*, were assigned to the Ehrlich story to bring to it the dignity and human warmth which characterized these two earlier Warner biographies. . . .

The Ehrlich picture, as far as the studio was concerned, was one in a series of successful biographies presented with a maximum of sincerity and "social consciousness." *Pasteur, Zola, Florence Nightingale* [*The White Angel*], *Juarez* had preceded it. A medico-chemist, a nurse, a writer, a statesman.

It is generally true of the 1938 period that all biographical material submitted to the Story Department was carefully examined, and a great many biographical stories were either purchased, developed or given experimental treatments during this time. Roughly 40 such biographies (including Christ, Beethoven, Alexander Hamilton) were contemplated to the point of purchase or partial research development. . . .

Medical biographies were very much under consideration at this time. *Yellow Jack*, the popular play about the research history of yellow fever, had been considered by all studios and purchased by M.G.M. (released in May 1938). Paul de Kruif, one of the play's co-authors, had written many books on medical research containing "popular" biographies of the various research heroes. In the wake of *Pasteur*, de Kruif's and all similar books were examined or re-examined by various studios. . . .

It is, I believe, true that *Ehrlich* was the first motion picture to deal sincerely and openly with syphilis. . . .

On July 6, 1919, Warner Brothers released a picture on syphilis entitled *Open Your Eyes.* . . . *Damaged Goods* [1913] by Eugene Brieux is the only one with any pretensions of more than a sensationalist value. . . .

Since that day, the independent producers have had the field pretty much to themselves, selling "states rights" "For Men Only" pictures. . . .

Even adaptations of such a play as Sidney Kingsley's *Dead End* or Michael Arlen's novel *Green Hat*—in both of which syphilis played an important plot part—avoided giving the disease a name. . . .

In the July 1936 issue of *Reader's Digest* appeared an article by [Surgeon General Thomas A.] Parran, entitled, "The Next Great Plague to Go." On December 29, 1936, he convened a National Conference of Venereal Disease Control. From then on, all nationally circulated magazines joined in the fight. . . .

By the years 1937–9, syphilis has become a truly popular subject. . . .

Ehrlich was a blending of three distinct trends—the biographical (already established by *Pasteur*, *Zola*, etc.) the *medical* biography (popularized by many books such as *An American Doctor's Odyssey*) . . . the books of Dr. A. J. Cronin and their successful picture adaptation—*The Citadel*—as well as a swarm of medical-background pictures such as the *Kildare* series. Warners' *Green Light*—fictionalization of the Rocky Mountain fever research story—*Yellow Jack* and Warners' *Pasteur* plus the specific "publicize syphilis" trend of the press and periodicals. . . .

Against the pre-Parran background of 1936, had I—as a motion picture story editor—received the suggestion of a story on venereal disease, I know that I would have written a courteous rejection and forgotten the matter within ten minutes. By August of 1938, I should certainly have been affected by the fact that even in the *Ladies' Home Journal* and from the pulpits of the churches, syphilis had become the subject of an open crusade and those I imagine were precisely the respective reactions of the two studio representatives who *were* faced by these respective stimuli.

Finlay McDermid

FROM BETTE DAVIS

September 1, 1939
Franconia, N.H.

Dear J.L.,

Have just finished talking to Hal [Wallis]. I must explain one thing—for the first time in my life I don't care whether I ever make another picture or not. I am that overworked. I have given you a lot of honest effort in the past eight years. The time has come when I feel I have earned some privileges in writing. These I must have.

My contract is ridiculous. I have no protection whatsoever. I must have limited pictures—I must have time off between. I think two [per year] is all I should make with a possible third if all conditions are favorable. The Wood Bros. [managers] know all the conditions—and were given to understand some weeks ago that you were willing to write a contract for me that would not be very far from what I wanted.

It is up to you. I am very serious about all this because I must be for my own good. If necessary I am even willing to stand the gaff of unemployment. Health is one thing that can't be manufactured. I am very serious about mine—and willing to go to any length to protect it. And staying in Hollywood working almost forty weeks of the year does not make sense—from your standpoint—box office can be ruined by too many pictures—as you well know.

Would appreciate your not communicating with me—it upsets me very much. I must be allowed to completely forget business . . . Also arguing with me is no use—nor do I want to come back until it is settled.

Sincerely,
(signed) Bette Davis

Davis was exhausted after completing five pictures in twelve months, and she did not want to do 'Til We Meet Again (1940). Davis took a prolonged vacation in New England, finally consenting to see Jack Warner in late October at an inn in New Hampshire. She agreed to return to work in January.

THE SEA HAWK

FROM HENRY BLANKE

Mr. Morris Ebenstein
Warner Bros. Pictures, Inc.
321 West 44th Street
New York, N.Y.

September 25, 1939

Dear Mr. Ebenstein:

. . . Enclosed please find our *Sea Hawk* script which, by the way, has no resemblance in any shape or form to the old *Sea Hawk* [1924] picture or script made by First National before. . . .

In regard to your questions, let me state that nothing in our script is 100% historical. One could say, as you know, that the relationship between Spain and England which forms the broad pattern of our story is more or less historical. Our leading character called "Thorpe" [Errol Flynn] is taken after the character of Sir Francis Drake, and the Panama sequence resembles slightly the Drake adventure in Panama; also Thorpe's attitude toward Spain resembles that of Drake; also his attempts to take action against Philip of Spain by using his influence on the Queen are patterned after those of Drake. Everything else is purely fictitious. I would say that Thorpe is a mixture of invention and the real Drake, and that the same applies to Queen Elizabeth [free-lance actress Flora Robson]. I would say that Wolfingham [free-lance actor Henry Daniell] and the other characters are fictitious. . . .

As ever yours,
Henry Blanke

TO: T. C. Wright
FROM: Frank Mattison [unit manager]

DATE: February 19, 1940
SUBJECT: #296—"The Sea Hawk"

Report for 2-17-40

Saturday . . . the company . . . made 16 set-ups . . . of the duel. . . . This duel has turned into a matter of a walk. Mr. Daniell is absolutely helpless and his closeup in the duel will be mostly from the elbows up.

Mr. Curtiz was greatly discouraged with his results on Saturday, as well as Friday, but there is nothing we can do as it will be impossible to go back and change to someone else in this part. . . .

The Casting Office and everyone connected with the picture were duly warned of Mr. Daniell's inability to fence long before the picture started, and we knew of him being taken out of a part in *Romeo & Juliet* [1936] because he could not handle a sword. Nevertheless, he is playing the part and it is going to take two more full days to finish the duel at the rate we worked on it Saturday and last Thursday. . . .

Frank Mattison

TO: Mr. Wallis   DATE: March 14, 1940
FROM: Blanke

Dear Hal:

As per our conversation this morning I explained to you which shots I can use from *Captain Blood* [for insertion in *The Sea Hawk*]. They were as follows:

1. Shots of fellows swinging over during the battle.
2. Inserts of guns firing.
3. Shots showing the effect of these cannon balls on the boat: wreckage, masts falling, etc.

Besides the above, I have some MEDIUM and LONG SHOTS which were originally taken from [*The*] *Divine Lady* [1929] but which you also used in *Captain Blood*. The action of these shots is general battle action, and certain sailors falling into the water, etc. All these shots are very good to help build our battle into an effective one, but as I explained to you, the action of the two boats coming together where the principals swing over, and all the action that the script still describes for the principals during the first battle, and which Mike [Curtiz] to date has not shot, has yet to be taken. . . .

Blanke

TO: Mr. Wright   DATE: March 14, 1940
FROM: Hal Wallis   SUBJECT: "The Sea Hawk"

For the past few days, I have been getting a lot of reports via the grapevine about Errol Flynn. Also, Mike has told me he loses hours every day on account of Flynn and is days behind because of him, that he doesn't know his lines, etc.

I also understand that Flynn is late on the set practically every day, that he was called to work the other afternoon at 4:30, and at 9:00 o'clock said he was cold and that he was going home and proceeded to leave before the set was finished. . . .

Do you know about these things? Do your assistants or Unit Managers tell you what is going on, and if you do, why don't you do something about it? If you can't do anything about it, why don't you at least let me in on it so that I can? Why do you as Studio Manager tolerate a condition of this kind?

Hal Wallis

FROM SETON I. MILLER

Mr. Walter MacEwen
Warner Brothers Studio

March 18, 1940

Dear Walter:

I can't understand upon what basis Mr. [Howard] Koch claims
sole [screenplay] credit on *Sea Hawk*. Taking it for granted that Mr.
Koch is a gentleman of honesty and integrity, it occurs to me that
either he has not been in Hollywood long enough to understand the
basis and ethics of credit—that he considers dialogue the only
important element in a screenplay, or that he is under the impression
that the story and screenplay which he cut down, reconstructed to
some extent, and re-dialogued to a large extent was Mr. [Rafael]
Sabatini's instead of being entirely original with me. There is not one
word of Sabatini's novel in the script. If Mr. Koch had gone back to
the Sabatini novel or had thrown my story and script out and written a
new one about, for instance, some episode in the English navy under
Edward VIII, he would be entitled to sole credit. But he didn't.

The characters and characterizations are the same from the
heroes to heavies . . . except for the shading on Elizabeth, who is not
played with my bellicoseness, and Alvarez [Claude Rains] and
Wolfingham being more mild and diplomatic. And Maria's [contract
player Brenda Marshall] Spanish servant has become an English
companion [free-lance actress Una O'Connor].

The inter-relationship between the characters is the same.

Koch has introduced new business, such as the [navigation] charts
and [Thorpe's pet] monkey, but has retained the major portion of
mine.

The story and plot are exactly the same except that Koch uses the
threat of the Armada against England instead of Alva's land army.

The main item is, however, that Koch used my screenplay
construction and progression of sequence practically step by step, and
in many sections even sequence of scenes. In the process of shortening
and tightening he dropped some sequences, replaced a few and added
the chartmaker routines. His most important sequence reconstruction
was sinking the first Spanish boat, having Thorpe take Maria aboard his
own and was thereby able to get the romance much further advanced
in the early part of the script and to have a few more scenes between
Thorpe and Maria. A swell asset. Koch effectively built up a lot of the
scenes in his re-dialoguing, but many of the lines carry the same

connotation and many were retained from my script with little or no re-wording.

To me the fair credit would be Original Story by Miller—Screenplay by Koch and Miller (story suggested by the Sabatini title or novel). I regret losing the Original credit but can understand the sales value the studio places on the Sabatini name. . . .

If, however, Mr. Koch still wishes to make an issue of sole credit, I'm perfectly willing to abide by the decision of the Screen Writers Guild Conciliation Commission or any completely neutral jury you care to name.

Best regards,
Seton I. Miller

P.S. Although I based Thorpe's character on [Sir Francis] Drake, [Sir John] Hawkins and [Martin] Frobisher, I believe it is a mistake to openly identify Thorpe with Drake in a sub-title. The raid on Panama is from Drake, but otherwise Thorpe's adventures vary so widely from Drake's history that the British may resent taking large dramatic liberties with their naval hero, where they wouldn't with a presumably fictitious character.

The released film did not contain a title identifying "Thorpe" with an historical character.

TO: Walter MacEwen   DATE: March 20, 1940
FROM: Howard Koch   SUBJECT: "The Sea Hawk"

Dear Walter:
. . . Miller is right in many of his facts. He is mistaken, I believe, in most of his conclusions. . . .

What I feel Miller fails to realize is that a situation may look similar because of its place, order and participating characters, but at the same time be so vastly different in its motivations and dramatic content as to constitute a change in plot.

Actually, Miller's conflict is with Sabatini and not with me, since Sabatini is getting credit which has no basis in fact—credit for original material that I believe Miller should have.

Judging from his letter it seems that he misunderstood my attitude. I have not wanted him to lose credit for the material he furnished. If he can't get this credit on the actual basis of original material, I have already offered to share in the credit for the screenplay. At the same time, I feel it would be entirely unreasonable to ask me to give up *first* screen credit in order to compensate him for his concession to Sabatini. . . .

Sincerely,

FROM SETON I. MILLER

Mr. Walter MacEwen
Warner Brothers Studios

March 26, 1940

Dear Walter:

Have just read Mr. Koch's rebuttal to my letter. . . .

Under the circumstances, I don't wish to prolong the incident by requesting an arbitration hearing. My main desire for an arbitration was in case Mr. Koch persisted in his claim for sole credit. I have never felt that first or second place in a two name credit on Screenplay meant a great deal of difference, so if Mr. Koch is unwilling to flip a coin, and feels that first position is so vital, by all means let his name be first . . .

Best regards,
Hap

The final credit read "Screen play by Howard Koch and Seton I. Miller." There was no original story credit or Sabatini credit. Koch, in 1939, had been put under contract to Warner Bros. This was shortly after the sensational response to the Orson Welles 1938 radio broadcast of War of the Worlds, *which Koch had adapted. Miller was employed at Warners nonexclusively since 1930 and the original* Dawn Patrol. *From 1935 until 1940 a great deal of his work was done for Warner Bros.*

TO: Mike Curtiz   DATE: March 27, 1940
FROM: Hal Wallis   SUBJECT: "The Sea Hawk"

Dear Mike:

I am quite concerned over the great amount of whipping you are doing in the scenes in the galley. In almost every scene you have these men going up and down in long shots, medium shots and closeups, with the whips coming in and hitting the men as they are rowing. As you know, we have been cautioned by the Hays office against too much brutality, and the way you have been shooting the stuff, we won't be able to cut it out. You have far too much of it, and it's going to become offensive and repulsive. . . .

Left to right: Production Head Jack L. Warner, Producer-Director Ernst Lubitsch, President of the Motion Picture Producers and Distributors of America Will H. Hays, President of Warner Bros. Harry M. Warner, Chief Executive Sam Warner (1925). (Bison Archives)

The front of Warner Bros. Studios on Barham Boulevard in Burbank in the early 1940s. Today, Warners shares the same lot with Columbia Pictures, and it has been renamed The Burbank Studios. (Bison Archives)

Albert Warner, the fourth brother and treasurer of the company. (Warner Bros. Archives)

WARNER BROS. PICTURES, INC.
BURBANK, CALIFORNIA

INTER-OFFICE COMMUNICATION

To Mr. _____ TRILLING _____   Date _____ February 14, 1942

From Mr. _____ WALLIS _____   Subject _____ "CASABLANCA"

Will you please figure on HUMPHREY BOGART
and ANN SHERIDAN for "CASABLANCA", which
is scheduled to start the latter part of
April.

HAL WALLIS

HW:og

VERBAL MESSAGES CAUSE MISUNDERSTANDING AND DELAYS
(PLEASE PUT THEM IN WRITING)

Note the directive at the bottom of the page, which appeared on all Warner Bros. interoffice correspondence.

Cinematographer Sol Polito (left) planning a camera angle with Director Michael Curtiz on location in Chatsworth in the San Fernando Valley for *The Charge of the Light Brigade* (1936). (USC Archives of Performing Arts)

Darryl F. Zanuck (left, ca. 1931) was in charge of production at Warner Bros., under Jack L. Warner (right) from 1927–1933. (Bison Archives)

Filming *Jezebel* (1938): far left, cinematographer Ernest Haller; sitting on stool, Director William Wyler (on loan from Samuel Goldwyn Productions); in front of camera, free-lance star Henry Fonda and Bette Davis. (The Museum of Modern Art/Film Stills Archive, courtesy Warner Bros.)

Contract players Anita Louise (left) and Olivia de Havilland in the mid–1930s when both often were considered for the same role. (Wisconsin Center for Film and Theater Research)

Above: Filming *The Adventures of Robin Hood* on location in Chico, California, in late September 1937. Alan Hale (left) as Little John confronts Errol Flynn as Robin. Director William Keighley on stool.

Left: If-Looks-Could-Kill Department: Miriam Hopkins (left) and Bette Davis on the set of *The Old Maid* (1939). Director Edmund Goulding serves as conciliator. (Warner Bros. Archives)

Right: Composer/conductor Max Steiner working on his score for *Life with Father* (1947).

Below: Composer/conductor Erich Wolfgang Korngold (right) on a re-recording stage at Warners where the dialogue, music, and sound effects tracks for *Juarez* (1939) with Paul Muni (on screen) are being mixed. (Tony Thomas)

Left: Ann Sheridan (against leaning board to protect her gown between scenes) chats with costar Humphrey Bogart during the filming of *It All Came True* (1940). (Warner Bros. Archives)

Right: Harry and Jack Warner at a broadcast at Warners' Sunset Boulevard lot in Hollywood (now KTLA and KMPC) in late September 1940, for the benefit of the Canadian Red Cross. (The Museum of Modern Art/Film Stills Archive)

Photographing a scene for *The Sea Hawk* (1940) on the recently built Stage 21. Called the "Maritime" sound stage, it could be filled with water, while tracks and hydraulic jacks could rock a ship (or two ships) from side to side. Painted sea and sky cyclorama in background. Stage 21 was destroyed by fire in May 1952. (USC Archives of Performing Arts)

Free-lance Director Howard Hawks and Gary Cooper (borrowed from Samuel Goldwyn Productions) on the firing range at the Warner Ranch in Calabasas during the filming of *Sergeant York* (1941). (USC Archives of Performing Arts)

Publicity pose of George Raft, non-Warner star Marlene Dietrich, and Edward G. Robinson in *Manpower* (1941). The behind-the-scenes fireworks were considerably more interesting than the film (see page 143). (Warner Bros. Archives)

Jane Wyman joins husband Ronald Reagan for a party on the set at the completion of filming *Kings Row* in October 1941. Both were under contract and had been married about a year and a half at the time.

KNUTE ROCKNE—ALL AMERICAN

FROM ROBERT BUCKNER [screenwriter]

Rev. Hugh O'Donnell, C.S.C.,
Vice-President, University of Notre Dame,
Notre Dame, Indiana

July 26, 1939

Dear Father O'Donnell:
[Business Manager of Notre Dame] Art Haley's letter has just reached me, with the news of your suggestion that Pat O'Brien would be the university's first choice for the Rockne role, together with the reasons which underlay the choice.

I would like to present the "interior" situation here at the studio which motivated our preference of James Cagney to Pat O'Brien, in hopes that you, as a part-time business man, may understand the vitally important economic reasons for our position.

Frankly, and this is of course confidential, Pat O'Brien possesses only a fractional degree of Cagney's popularity, both in this country and abroad. Cagney is now among the first three or four male stars in the industry. Pat is not among the first fifty. The picture's cost has been estimated at $750,000, with the strong possibility that it may run higher. The studio could not afford the extremely dangerous gamble with Pat. In fact, it is a certainty that neither our sales organization nor the thousands of exhibitors would react favorably to the idea. In effect, it is a simple matter of arithmetic. Cagney would insure the picture's success. O'Brien would not.

So much then, for the purely economic angle. Now, as to the faithfulness and effectiveness of the characterization of Rockne. . . .

It is a common and easy mistake to identify an actor with the type of roles which he has made famous. It is also a great tribute to his acting ability. The studio sees *The Life of Knute Rockne* as the first big step in a new career for Cagney. The next picture for him is *John Paul Jones*. We agree entirely with you that one of the basic ideas in the picture is to show Rockne as he was in life, a great hero to the youth of the nation. But knowing both actors intimately, through years of experience with both men, we believe that Cagney can give it all the heart and warmth and sincerity that any friend of Rockne's could wish. Cagney realizes his responsibility and believes strongly in his ability to give the best performance of his life.

No decision has been made, since we all wish to defer to your opinion in the matter. . . .

Sincerely,
Robert Buckner

FROM J. ARTHUR HALEY [business manager]

Mr. Bryan Foy [head of B picture unit]
Warner Brothers Pictures Inc.
Burbank, California

August 2, 1939

Dear Brynie:

As you perhaps know, there have been several letters written by Bob Buckner in behalf of Cagney's playing the role of Rockne. The university definitely cannot see this selection. I do not mean to say that Cagney is not a great actor, for we know that he does rank among the tops.

There are two very strong points which they have; first, the fact that Cagney received a lot of publicity during the war in Spain because of his support of the Loyalist Cause. Secondly, the fact that Cagney has been cast in roles that have been of the gangster type, and in this particular picture, which is to appeal to the youth of the nation, this would not be of benefit to the picture.

Concerning the publicity given to Cagney and his support of the Loyalist Cause, I did mention this fact today when writing to Bob about the matter of publicity. I did not mention the fact that there are hundreds of Catholic newspapers printed throughout the land, which gave publicity to this connection of Cagney's. The university, knowing this fact, do not feel that they can jeopardize their reputation because of the publicity thus received. In fact, they feel that the studio would take more of a gamble in casting Cagney in this particular role following such publicity. . . .

Yours very sincerely,
J. Arthur Haley
Business Manager

FROM HAL B. WALLIS

Mr. J. Arthur Haley
University of Notre Dame
Notre Dame, Indiana

August 11, 1939

I have your letter addressed to Brynie Foy and concerning the casting of the role of Rockne. . . .

You are familiar, of course, with the efforts we have made to get Spencer Tracy [under contract to MGM] and we should like nothing better than to have him play Rockne. However, so far our efforts have availed us nothing and we have had no encouragement or word of any kind from Metro as to the possibilities of getting Tracy.

Naturally, in making the picture we want to work closely with the University and we don't want to do anything that will be displeasing to you.

Consequently, we will keep trying to get someone for the part who will be not only an important name for the good of the picture, but one who will also be acceptable to you.

With kindest regards,
Sincerely,

TO: Hal Wallis   DATE: January 23, 1940
FROM: Bob Fellows [associate   SUBJECT: "Knute Rockne"
     producer]

Dear Hal:

[Casting director Steve] Trilling believes that he can find a double for O'Brien, but it is going to be very difficult. I don't believe that you can tell the story of Rockne without telling of his formative years at Notre Dame, his courtship, etc., etc., which necessitates the character to look around twenty-three years old.

I understand that O'Brien has made the statement that he would rather play "Rockne" than any other role. His activities on his own behalf have shown that he is quite anxious to do the picture. Therefore, wouldn't it be feasible to get O'Brien in a trainer's hands. . . . If he would be willing to cooperate, and I am sure he would, I know we could get those double chins off and knock ten or fifteen years off his looks. In any event, I think this suggestion is worth a try.

Bob

O'Brien played the role, and the relatively inexpensive production did extremely well.

In 1956, when Warners sold their pre-1950 films, certain scenes involving George Gipp (Ronald Reagan), including "win just one for the Gipper" references and some additional material, were cut from the picture because of legal complications.

At the time of the original production, the studio purchased some material from a December 1938 Cavalcade of America radio script about Rockne. The screenwriter, mistakenly assuming all of the radio script had been bought, closely based other bits and pieces of his screenplay on the radio script, and when the film was released in 1940, the writer of the dramatization threatened to sue.

A subsequent settlement granting Warners motion picture rights to the entire radio script did not include a provision for television, which was not commercially developed at the time. Hence, in 1956, when the Warner pre-1950 library was sold—to be used primarily for television—some scenes and portions of scenes were deleted by the studio before transferring the film elements to the purchaser, Associated Artists Productions, who later sold the entire package to United Artists.

FROM GEORGE RAFT

Mr. Jack Warner
Waldorf-Astoria Hotel,
New York City

October 17, 1939

Dear Jack:

. . . [Agent Noll] Gurney had told me that there was no need to have written into my contract the fact that I would not have to play heavies. For three weeks I had refused to sign the contract because of the studio refusing to put in a paragraph to that effect. When I saw you at your house you told me, in the presence of Noll Gurney, that I would not have to play any dirty heavies and if anyone at your studio ever submitted a script to me in which I was to play a dirty heavy I was to bring the script to you and you would take me out of it. I remarked at that time to you that I was afraid the studio would put me into parts that Humphrey Bogart should play and you told me that I would never have to play a Humphrey Bogart part.

A situation has arisen where the studio has given me a script *The Roaring Nineties* [not produced] in which the part that I am asked to play is really as dirty a heavy as I have ever known and I am sure that if you had read the script you would not have allowed the studio to submit it to me. . . .

Please straighten out this matter for me. I need your help because you are the only one who knows of our understanding at your house.

Warm regards,
George Raft

Raft had been under contract to Paramount from 1932 to 1939.

TO: Hal Wallis   DATE: October 23, 1939
FROM: Robert Lord   SUBJECT: "No Time for Comedy"

Dear Hal:

One of the delights of this business is the fact that a person is continually faced with new kinds of trouble.

No Time for Comedy seems to offer a kind of trouble new for me, at least.

It is a brilliant play which can be closely followed to make a screenplay with very little effort. A great deal of the excellent dialogue can be retained. Instead of using two sets, we can move our characters around through nine or ten.

You cast the picture with extremely good actors and have a director guide their talking through nine or ten sets. Then, what have you?

In my opinion, you have a photographed stage play which will prove a bitter disappointment commercially. How dare I make such a statement?

Simply because, in the past, the Lubitsch type of sophisticated light comedy has almost always failed to impress mass audiences. Critics like it, studio executives like it, our wives like it—but the cash customers don't like it!

As much as I dread the job, I believe that the [S. N.] Behrman play should be pretty radically altered—vulgarized—to make it understandable for a mass audience. In the vulgarizing process, much of the smart dialogue will be lost, because characters and situations will be changed.

New York critics and Cafe Society will accuse us of being button-hole makers. Mr. Behrman will be pretty damn sore at us. It is a difficult and completely unsympathetic task—one which I should like to avoid. But one which I feel to be necessary unless we deliberately set out to make a picture for the critics and our wives.

I think you and Casey [Robinson] and I had better have a brief discussion of this problem.

Bob Lord

No Time for Comedy *(1940) was altered in part to fit James Stewart's personality, and, in comparison with the original, "vulgarized."*

TO: Hal Wallis   DATE: December 13, 1939
FROM: [William] Cagney [brother   SUBJECT: "Torrid Zone"
       of James Cagney and
       associate producer]

Dear Hal:

The following is submitted most respectfully:

Mr. McEwen sent me 103 pages of *Torrid Zone* which I have read, and must report that this is just the type of story that made Cagney want to leave the studio upon the expiration of his last contract [in 1939]. There is no real substance or importance in the entire 103 pages, and I know that Jim will only be enthused by plot and development that is worthy of his talent.

I can't go to too great a length to explain the importance of our realizing the necessity of submitting material that is dramatically sound and worthwhile to Cagney. In addition to all the other previous reasons which you know about, he is constantly besieged with offers to do the most important vehicles at other studios and therefore would naturally feel that if we don't supply him, others will.

Torrid Zone is what has been known for so long as a typical Cagney vehicle and that is just the reason he would refuse to do it—the only difference being that it is set in a banana country. I personally feel that it is about as good a vehicle for George Raft as I have read in a long time, and feel too that with nothing of importance to start with, the folks who have worked on it have done a very good job.

Bill Cagney

Torrid Zone *(1940) was produced with James Cagney and did well at the box office. The basic idea, some of the characters and the locale were reminiscent of MGM's* Red Dust *(1932). Another influential plot device appeared to be from the play,* The Front Page *(1927).*

THE LETTER

FROM JOSEPH I. BREEN
[director of the Production Code Administration]

Mr. Jack L. Warner
Warner Brothers Pictures, Inc.
Burbank, California

April 18, 1938

Dear Mr. Warner:

We have read with great care the playscript of *The Letter*, by W. Somerset Maugham. . . .

As we read it, this is the story of a wife, who murders her lover, but who, by lying, deceit, perjury, and the purchase of an incriminating letter, defeats justice, and gets off "scot free."

In the development of this story we have the murder of the lover; all the sordid details of the illicit sex relationship between the married woman and her lover; and very pointed and very numerous references to the second mistress of the murdered man, who is characterized as a China woman. . . .

Because of all this, we could not, of course, approve a motion picture, based upon this story.

In this connection, you may be interested in knowing that when this picture was produced by Paramount [starring Jeanne Eagels], at its Long Island Studios in 1929, it caused very considerable nation-wide protest. In addition, it was rejected, in toto, in England, in Canada, and in Australia, and the company had much difficulty in securing permission to exhibit it in a number of other foreign countries. The British objection seems to hinge upon the characterization of the several British people, engaged in an illicit sex relationship, and, more importantly, in the suggestion that Hammond, the murdered man, maintained a China woman as his mistress.

We have no reason to believe that the official attitude throughout the British Empire will be any different now, than it was in 1929 and 1930.

Very truly yours,
Joseph I. Breen

TO: Hal Wallis   DATE: December 20, 1939
FROM: Robert Lord   SUBJECT: "The Letter"

Dear Hal:

I had quite a chat with [director] Eddie Goulding about *The Letter*. His ideas on the play are a trifle radical.

Since I am so enthusiastic about the play, I persuaded him to let me try a treatment which follows the play very closely indeed. In this treatment, I will try a scheme which I believe will enable us to get by the censors. I do not guarantee that we will get by, but it is certainly worth trying; because, in my opinion, if we can follow the play very closely and manage to get by the censors, we will have one of the most powerful and different motion pictures ever made.

[Howard] Koch is tied up for a day or so, writing some scenes for *Virginia City*, but he has read the play and is very enthusiastic about it. As soon as he finishes with *Virginia City*, I will get him started on such a treatment which should take two or three weeks to write.

I hope this meets with your approval.

Bob Lord

Lord and Koch changed the murdered man's Chinese mistress in Maugham's story to his Eurasian wife (Gale Sondergaard). At the conclusion, the murderess (Bette Davis) is killed by the Eurasian wife, who in turn is taken away by the police. William Wyler was borrowed once again from Samuel Goldwyn to direct.

TO: Hal Wallis   DATE: April 29, 1940
FROM: Lord   SUBJECT: "The Letter"

Dear Hal:

Mr. [William] Wyler and I have been discussing the actual procedure of work in shooting *The Letter*—and have decided that the following plan will enable us to make the best picture for the least expense in time, money, nervous strain, etc.

A. Before starting to concern himself with any actual physical production details—except *casting*—Mr. Wyler would like to work with Howard Koch for about ten days on the script.

This work is to be done at Mr. Wyler's house or somewhere away from the studio where they will not be disturbed.

Mr. Wyler will keep in constant touch with me so that I will always know what changes are being made in the script.

B. Before actually starting photographing the picture, we would like to have one full week's rehearsal with all the principals in the cast.

C. We should like to have a schedule of eight weeks, independent of the one week rehearsal period.

Naturally, if it is physically possible to bring the picture in under eight weeks, we will make every effort to do so.

D. If possible, we should like to borrow Gregg Toland from Goldwyn for the cameraman on this picture. Mr. Wyler has made many pictures with Toland; finds him to be extremely fast as well as good.*

I realize that most of these points do not coincide with our method of making pictures at this studio. This is why I am putting them on paper to show to Mr. Warner and yourself.

If there is any disagreement, dissatisfaction, etc., with our requests, the sensible time to discuss them and attempt to reach an understanding is right now—not several weeks hence.

Bob Lord

TO: Mr. Wyler
FROM: Hal Wallis
DATE: May 1, 1940
SUBJECT: "The Letter"

Dear Willy:

I am so sorry that we cannot work out the one week's rehearsal plan. I am more than anxious to have your engagement here a happy one, but there are certain limits to what we can do.

I hope you will realize our position and that you will settle down to the preparation of the picture, so that we can go ahead as scheduled.

Hal Wallis

TO: Mr. Wright
FROM: Mr. Wallis
DATE: May 23, 1940
SUBJECT: "The Letter"

I note that you have laid out *The Letter* schedule in eight weeks.

With this script being in 124 pages I want it scheduled in seven

*Staff cameraman Tony Gaudio was assigned to the film.

weeks, and not only do I want it scheduled but I want it shot in seven weeks.

Hal Wallis

The film was photographed in seven weeks and three days.

TO: Mr. Wallis
FROM: Robert Lord

DATE: May 28, 1940
SUBJECT: "The Letter"

Dear Hal:

Take 14 of the dolly shot [at the opening of the film] I thought was a little better and faster than Take 3. Also, the parrot reacted more strikingly to the sound of the shots.

I honestly think that Wyler is doing pretty well to date—for Wyler. He is by nature a very deliberate man. I think he is doing the best he knows how. If that is not good enough, we will simply have to change directors. The quality of his work, as always, I think is excellent.

Bob Lord

TO: [S. Charles] Einfeld [director
    of advertising and publicity]
FROM: Hal Wallis

DATE: November 14, 1940
SUBJECT: William Wyler,
    "The Letter"

Dear Charlie:

When I made the deal with Wyler to direct *The Letter,* a consideration that was more important to him than almost anything else was that he be given the proper billing and publicity. He is one of those chaps to whom this means more than salary or anything else and I told him that he would be properly taken care of.

I think you will agree that this has not been the case so far as the names of everyone except Davis have been very much subordinated. I know that this is because of the type of ads you have been running but we may want Wyler again sometime, especially if *The Letter* does business, and unless we keep the promises we make these people it makes it difficult to do business with them later on. The next time it will be a matter of putting in the contract the size of type to be used, etc., etc., and so I would prefer to do it the easier way.

Will you please extend yourself a little so far as Wyler is concerned and give him a little more of a build-up in this stuff.

Hal Wallis

TO: Walsh   DATE: May 6, 1940
FROM: Hal Wallis   SUBJECT: "They Drive By Night"

Dear Raoul:

The dailies have been coming through very nicely—the action is good, the tempo is good, and the setups are nice.

One thing I have been missing, however, and that is establishing long shots or showing some of the action in long shots. This is particularly lacking in the market sequence. I remember okaying a budget of $10,000 or $15,000 to fix up the street down there and get a little bit of atmosphere into it, but so far, I have seen nothing but close shots of the cab, the boys getting out of it and panning them into close action with other people as in the scene where they sold the lemons to George Tobias. Also, the shot where Raft drives in to park the truck and has the fight. Everything is done in short pan shots without any of the atmosphere of the street being shown, and for the amount of background that has been shown in this stuff so far, we could have used the New York street [on the back lot] without spending any money on it. It isn't so much that I'm trying to get our money's worth out of the set, as it is that I'm trying to get the atmosphere into the picture, and I wish that when you go back there you would watch this and get some interesting setups, some long shots of the street, and then when the truck comes into it you can pan with it, but at least let's get back a ways and see what the boys are coming into and establish the fact that it is a market.

Hal Wallis

FROM JAMES M. CAIN

2966 Belden Drive
Hollywood, California

May 23, 1940

Briney: [Bryan Foy, in charge of
       B pictures at Warners]

Have just read [Robert] Presnell's script on [Cain's 1938 magazine story] *Money and the Woman,* and just wanted to let you know that I think he made a fine job of it.

He did one thing that interested me very much. When I planned this story, before any of it went on paper, I mean, I relied on the plotting of the lovers, to put the money back, for love scenes of a whispery, conspiratorial quality. But I never was quite able to pull them off . . . and they died on me. So I cut them out, and never pulled them up into close focus. But Presnell . . . has caught the very thing I was after, and done it beautifully.

He solved other sticks very neatly too. . . .

Well, congratulations, and I think you are going to get a good picture. . . .

> Yours,
> Jim Cain

This was before Cain's Double Indemnity, Mildred Pierce, *and* The Postman Always Rings Twice *were filmed in the mid-1940s.*

FROM BRYAN FOY

May 24, 1940

James Cain
2966 Belden Drive
Hollywood, California

Dear Jim:

Thanks for your letter, and if you'll remember, I screamed my head off that I wanted to do the original story, which I think we have captured.

You probably are well aware that we used 80% of your dialogue of your original.

Thanks for reading the script.

> Regards,
> Bryan Foy

FROM JACK L. WARNER

To: Foy

July 26, 1940

Last night I came back to the Studio and ran *Money and the Woman*. It's a damned good picture.

Four or five little things could have been cut out of the picture, which would have moved it along a little faster, and above all, you did not need the last newspaper insert, because the story told itself without the newspaper insert. In the future, P L E A S E don't use newspaper inserts unless they are absolutely essential.

> J. L. WARNER
> (formerly with the newspaper
> Guild against newspaper
> inserts by Foy)

Foy was famous for using newspaper insert shots in his B pictures. Money and the Woman was—and still is—a considerably better than average B.

TO: Hal Wallis   DATE: July 20, 1940
FROM: [Wolfgang] Reinhardt   SUBJECT: "Hornblower" director
      [associate producer]

Dear Hal,

As [*Captain Horatio*] *Hornblower* seems to be without a director after [William] Dieterle's leaving the studio, I should like to let you know that I have just learned that Wyler is available for another picture. I understand that he has changed radically from his former practices, that he has finished *The Letter* on schedule and came out below the budget.

In view of these circumstances I thought that you might want to venture putting him on another picture. He would certainly be able to do a wonderful job with *Hornblower*, especially if we should get [Laurence] Olivier and [Vivien] Leigh. A lot of the naval stuff might be handled by a second unit, so that his work could be concentrated on the principal parts without risking his getting lost in "an epic of the seas." Anyway his leaning towards expensiveness is of a different nature than Mike's [Curtiz]: Wyler would not be tempted to do terrific mass-stuff and the like. His drawback is rather his slowness with the actors—but he seems to have conquered this weakness.

If you think there is anything in the suggestion I might give him the script to read and find out in which way he feels it could be done. If the thing that appeals to him should be the magnitude of the action, we had better forget about him. If, on the other hand, he saw a way of doing this story by relying mainly on the human aspects of it, then we might come out cheaper than with Curtiz doing it.

By the way, as regards dropping the wife out of the story, I have become convinced that that would be a mistake. It seems that we would lose too many sentimental values and some surefire scenes. So unless I hear from you to the contrary, [John] Huston will retain her in the new version.

Wishing you an enjoyable vacation and with best regards.

Sincerely,
Wolfgang Reinhardt

Production on Captain Horatio Hornblower *was postponed until after World War II. It was produced by Warners in England with Gregory Peck in the lead and Raoul Walsh directing; Hornblower's wife was dropped.*

TO: Mr. Blanke   DATE: November 18, 1940
FROM: [Edmund] Goulding   SUBJECT: "Far Horizon"
                                 [*The Great Lie*]

I think it is a strong, fine scene—beautifully written and very playable.

I am wondering whether Lenore [Coffee]—having once written it and put everything she has into it—couldn't go back over it, remembering our thought to make the reactions of these women strictly modern—1941. It is only in the vernacular and phrasing that it might be sharpened. In reading the scene, one is conscious of the spontaneous logic of the two women—the capability of expression. As I don't want to touch the writing of the scene, I wonder if Lenore could disturb some of the rather flowing and steadily thoughtful speeches—in other words, jack them up. Such lines as "That you might die," are terrific punch lines.

Play two instruments against each other. Make Sandra [Mary Astor] completely staccato—and Maggie [Bette Davis] completely legato. Phrase it for hysteria—and pause—and the searching for a word. It would be awfully hard, in directing these scenes carefully as written and arranged, to get the uncertainty of the next line. There should be one place in which the characteristic feminine tangent is provided—something that is completely irrelevant—and the other one says, "I don't understand,"—and the first one says, "I didn't mean that."

It merely means to take the scene—touch nothing of its essence—but, in its orchestration, to sharpen—slow—speed—speed up—stop—pause. A certain amount of this can be done in the direction and performance, but the best one to do it is the person who wrote the scene. . . .

Eddie

4

Bogart (and Others) Rise to the Occasion (1940–1942)

HIGH SIERRA

TO: Mr. Wallis
FROM: [John] Huston

DATE: March 21, 1940
SUBJECT: "High Sierra"

Dear Hal:

I just finished *High Sierra* and I think it is a very fine book indeed. I must admit to being a pushover for W. R. Burnett's stuff, however.

It would be very easy for this to be made into the conventional gangster picture, which is exactly what it should not be. With the exception of *Little Caesar*, all of Burnett has suffered sadly in screen translation. . . .

Take the spirit out of Burnett, the strange sense of inevitability that comes with our deepening understanding of his characters and the forces that motivate them, and only the conventional husk of a story remains. . . .

This might easily be the lot of *High Sierra*. On the other hand, if it's gone at with real seriousness—the seriousness Burnett deserves—I think it could be made into a fine and outstanding picture.

John Huston

TO: Hal Wallis   DATE: March 29, 1940
FROM: Huston   SUBJECT: "High Sierra"

Dear Hal:

[Associate producer] Mark Hellinger told me that you called him and wanted to know whether or not I was doing a treatment* of *High Sierra*. That idea never crossed my mind. It seems to me that the book itself is a very complete treatment.

I am already well along in the screenplay. What I have done is very rough. I wouldn't want anyone to see it but I am delighted with the way it is going and to change form at this time might stop the flow. If it continues to move at this rate, you can expect to have a screenplay in a few weeks—and that without *too* great haste on my part.

If it is that you would like to have something to show Muni, I suggest that you let me write him direct, telling him about my approach to the material and assuring him, if he needs such assurance, that it will not be along the lines of a conventional gangster story. . . .

John Huston

FROM HUMPHREY BOGART

NORTH HOLLYWOOD CALIF. MAY 4, 1940
HAL WALLIS—WARNER BROS. STUDIO
DEAR HAL. YOU TOLD ME ONCE TO LET YOU KNOW WHEN I FOUND A PART I WANTED. A FEW WEEKS AGO I LEFT A NOTE FOR YOU CONCERNING "HIGH SIERRA." I NEVER RECEIVED AN ANSWER SO I'M BRINGING IT UP AGAIN AS I UNDERSTAND THERE IS SOME DOUBT ABOUT MUNI DOING IT. REGARDS.

HUMPHREY BOGART

Paul Muni did not want to portray another gangster—regardless of the treatment. Bogart was given the role. Author W. R. Burnett claimed in 1982 that Bogart talked George Raft out of taking the part because it didn't suit him. Muni left Warners shortly afterward when his contract was canceled "by mutual agreement."

FROM MARK HELLINGER

Undated, circa May 1940
Hal:

On Saturday morning, you returned a script of *High Sierra* to the

---

*The intermediate stage between a synopsis (or outline) and a screenplay.

studio. You ordered it mimeographed as a final. You ignored me completely in the matter.

I do not question your right to do these things. I do not question your authority in any way. . . .

What I question is the motive for such an insult to a man who has tried his damnedest to understand you, and to help you. . . .

Is it possible that—as you have done with most of your producers—you wish also to make a messenger boy of me? . . . Because, as I told you in my note, I'm not taking that from you or anybody else. . . .

I am not going into a resume of the items that led up to this dispute. Your resentment of every mention of me in conversation or in print is too patently obvious. When I advertise, you send me a note to advertise properly, which means that I must use your name. . . . When we click with *They Drive By Night*, your only reaction is to quote stingingly from a review that credited me wrongly with picking a technical staff. . . .

In *Brother Orchid*, you burned mightily because I fought bitterly for Ann Sothern over your choice of Lee Patrick. And when I finally tackled Jack Warner on the idea, you cautioned me never to go over your head again. . . . And—oh, what the hell. I could go on with items such as these for page after page—and nobody knows it better than you. . . .

I have written you this letter because, under the option just picked up, I have another year to go with the company—and I cannot go on working under you if you expect to continue your present policies in regard to me. . . .

I do not expect to say yes to you when my opinion is no. . . .

I want to continue to make money for Warner Brothers—and I want your help and guidance. Keep on using your other producers as messenger boys and involuntary ass-kissers . . . —but credit me with just a little more manhood and honesty.

With this assurance from you, we will begin all over and forget everything. I hope for that assurance, because everyone will be happier in the long run. . . .

Mark Hellinger

Hellinger and Wallis temporarily patched up their differences, at least on the surface.

TO: Mr. Warner   DATE: September 18, 1940
FROM: Hal Wallis   SUBJECT: "High Sierra"

Don't you think we ought to reverse the billing on *High Sierra*, and instead of billing Bogart first, bill [Ida] Lupino first?

Lupino has had a great deal of publicity on the strength of *They Drive By Night*, whereas Bogart has been playing the leads in a lot of "B" pictures, and this fact might mitigate against the success of *High Sierra*.

The billing has just gone through with Bogart's name first, and I think we should reverse it.

Hal Wallis

The billing was reversed with Lupino's name in first position. On the strength of her performance in They Drive By Night, *she had been signed by Warner to a long-term contract. Previously Lupino was under contract to Paramount (1933–1937).*

FROM WALTER MacEWEN

Mrs. H. B. Nash,
Milwaukee County
Better Films Council,
Milwaukee, Wisconsin

March 7, 1941

Dear Mrs. Nash:

I have your recent letter commenting upon our picture *High Sierra*, and I do appreciate your thoughtful attitude towards this production.

You may be sure that the picture could not have been released had it been in violation of our Production Code, but I think upon analysing it you will agree that the proper moral values are sustained in that the criminal activities of the leading character inevitably leads towards his violent death.

We do check and double-check all of our stories and pictures most carefully, and it is our feeling from a sound psychological point of view, that this type of picture does not tend to make crime attractive. Rather, it is our belief that a crime picture of this type has a cathartic effect upon young minds with an incipient criminal tendency, since the vicarious enjoyment of the crime thrills on the screen is, according to one important school of thought, a form of release which reduces the necessity upon the part of the criminally inclined observer to commit criminal acts himself.

As to the fact that the leading character in *High Sierra* has a most normal and kindly side to his nature, do you not feel that it is better to present a fully rounded picture of this type of individual? After all, were he to be portrayed only as a vicious and completely unsocial person, the tendency upon the part of audiences would be to make it impossible for them to identify themselves with such a character. On the other hand, if he is shown in some of his moods to be a more ordinary type of human being, I believe the audience will tend to feel, if only subconsciously, that everyone must be on their guard against letting the wrong side of their nature, or their bad instincts, prevail, since once they permit this to happen, the end can only be tragic.

We do appreciate the cooperative attitude of your organization as evidenced by your letter, and I trust that my analysis of this particular picture may be helpful to you in your future activities.

Sincerely,

Walter MacEwen

TO: Raoul Walsh   DATE: November 8, 1940
FROM: Hal Wallis   SUBJECT: "The Strawberry Blonde"

Dear Raoul:

In last night's dailies, it seemed to me that you missed the most important shot in front of the barber shop. What you should have had was a pan shot picking up Virginia [Rita Hayworth, on loan from Columbia] and panning with her as she came by the barber shop, and then as she came in front of the shop with the men in the background, you could have moved the camera up on the group as their heads turned and followed her down the street. Instead, we have to cut from them to her walking down the street, and then we cut back to a shot shooting straight at the men, and then a blur goes by that is supposed to be Virginia. . . .

I don't understand how you miss these things. Put the camera on a dolly and move it a little bit—move up on people instead of those short cuts from one to another all of the time.

I don't know of any other way to shoot a scene of this kind. It is such an obvious thing to do. We really should go back and do this thing over, but I suppose it means calling back a lot of expensive bit people and again taking a half day to pick up something that we should have had in the first place, and I don't want to have to keep going back and doing everything twice. I'd like to get it the first time. . . .

I wish you would think out ahead of time every sequence you go into from now on, and figure the best way in which to shoot it to get the most out of it in the way of business, camera angles, and everything else. Let's try to get some composition, and some moving shots, and some interesting stuff in the picture.

Hal Wallis

Ann Sheridan, during a salary dispute, had turned down the role played by Rita Hayworth.

THE SEA WOLF

FROM PAUL MUNI

The Ambassador
Park Avenue
51st to 52nd Streets
New York, N.Y.

M. C. Levee [agent]
1300 N. Crescent Heights Blvd.
Hollywood, Calif.

November 1, 1937

My dear Mike:
       From the first paragraph of your letter to me anent Rafael
Sabatini or Sidney Howard or Eugene O'Neill regarding Sea Wolf, I
was tempted to say "okey dokey" but then my experience and my
realistic tendency reminded me that neither Sabatini nor Howard, and
certainly not O'Neill, would be interested in writing a screenplay from
that story. Of course I don't want to seem to you like a wet blanket,
but I can't afford to share your optimism and rely on mere hearsay.
       You know my feeling about The Sea Wolf, since that story has
already come up before, and you would readily understand that when I
refused to consider Selznick's offer [to do the picture for him when he
owned the property] there would be no reason to assume that its
chances are any better under the present set-up. For me to okay a story
based on a book whose screenplay will be so remote from the original
that it may not even be recognizable, is rather a precarious proposition.
Certainly it has an enticing element, but how can I, at this time,
definitely decide to okay it?
       Perhaps were I to be guaranteed that one of these three men will
positively be assigned to the story I would feel confident in gambling
on its chances and okay the story without reading it. On the other
hand, it seems to me that it would be unwise to okay any story because
I would have no opportunity to even confer with the writers, producers
and director, because of my being en route.
       I share with you the belief that the background and the character
hold great potentialities, but I do not share the belief that I can assist or
suggest by the way of collaboration, once the screenplay is written
unless I am together with the writers before they start writing. I see no
way of undoing something that may be basically opposed to my
opinion.
       Under the circumstances, however, I will reiterate what I have
said before, that if I can be assured beyond doubt that one of these

three writers will be assigned to the screenplay, I am willing to okay it as my next picture, and should it be accomplished I will take my chances on straightening out anything that may come up when I am back in Hollywood.

As for the direction, while you know how I feel, I would accept Mervyn LeRoy's direction, because I feel that he is a competent director, and, properly guided on story problems, he is capable of turning out a fine film.

But let us not permit the time element to interfere with the possibilities of assuring ourselves of a film for which we should all have great optimism. We have experienced disappointments before, mainly due to the fact that we were afraid of losing time. I am sure you understand just what I mean. . . .

Yours
(Signed) Muni

The Sea Wolf *was postponed.*

FROM GEORGE RAFT

HAL WALLIS
WARNER BROS STUDIO

OCTOBER 23, 1940

MY DEAR MR. WALLIS, JUST READ "SEA WOLF." YOU TOLD ME IN YOUR OFFICE THAT IT WOULD BE A FIFTY FIFTY PART [the role of "Leach"]. I AM SORRY TO SAY IT IS JUST THE OPPOSITE. AS I EXPLAINED BEFORE, I WANT TO WORK BUT THIS IS JUST A LITTLE BETTER THAN A BIT. I'M SORRY TO SAY I DON'T BLAME THIS ON YOU BECAUSE YOU'RE A NICE GUY, AND I KNOW YOU TRIED YOUR BEST FOR ME. HOPE YOU ARE IN THE BEST OF HEALTH. AT SHERRY NETHERLAND HOTEL NY.

GEORGE RAFT

FROM HAL B. WALLIS

TO: GEORGE RAFT
SHERRY NETHERLANDS HOTEL
NEW YORK CITY

OCTOBER 23, 1940

DEAR GEORGE:
AM SORRY YOU FEEL THE WAY YOU DO ABOUT PART IN "THE SEA WOLF." I CANNOT AGREE WITH YOU THAT PART IS ONLY A BIT. EVERY- ONE CONCURS IN MY OPINION THAT IT IS A GREAT PART IN A GREAT SCRIPT AND SHOULD BE ONE OF MOST IMPORTANT PICTURES OF YEAR AND YOU SHOULD BE IN IT. IT IS THE KIND OF PART YOU HAVE BEEN

WANTING TO PLAY, NAMELY THE ROMANTIC LEAD IN A GOOD GUTTY
PICTURE. YOU ARE NOT A HEAVY AND YOU GET THE GIRL. POSSIBLY
IN ACTUAL NUMBER OF LINES IT ISN'T THE BIGGEST PART BUT I ASSURE
YOU IT WILL COME THROUGH EQUALLY AS IMPORTANT AS [EDWARD
G.] ROBINSON. REGARDS.

HAL WALLIS

*John Garfield was cast in the reasonably good role. He was now a
rising star at Warners after his appearance in* Four Daughters *(1938).*

TO: Mr. Wallis   DATE: November 14, 1940
FROM: J. L. Warner

I have a good, hot hunch that we should change the title of *The Sea
Wolf* to

THE LAW OF THE SEA

My reason is this; we have released *The Sea Beast* twice, we have
just released *The Sea Hawk*, and the title *The Law of the Sea* is a big,
resounding mouthful to me. Also, it doesn't point up an individual performance as *The Sea Wolf* does, but gives us a chance to cash in on a
big, sweeping epic title. I was never so sold on a title in my life as this
one. The only thing that worries me is that someone else must have
thought of it before and have written two or three novels under this title.
Robinson stated this in last night's dailies, and that is where I got it from.

J. L. Warner

TO: Mr. Wallis   DATE: November 15, 1940
FROM: Blanke   SUBJECT: Re: "The Sea Wolf"

Dear Hal:

Mr. Warner was kind enough to show me a note that he had written
you about changing the title of *The Sea Wolf*.

I tried to get my point clear to him, but I don't know how far I got.
I don't have to tell you how popular that book is and that the publication
figures must be way ahead of *Gone With the Wind*, and changing the
title of *The Sea Wolf* I would consider a blasphemy. Not only would we
be criticized for this, but I should think it would be a detriment to the
box office. It would be the same had Mr. Selznick changed *Gone With
the Wind* to *Molly from the South.*

I think that everyone of us is familiar with the *classic* aspects of *The
Sea Wolf*—a book which has been translated into every language of the
world, and has in its time been a sensational success—keeping this success
through the years since its publication.

Mr. Warner's point in changing the title was to avoid the similarity to the title of *Sea Hawk*, but as I suggested before, this picture should be publicized and exploited as Jack London's *Sea Wolf*, and if this would be done I believe all similarity would be destroyed.

Blanke

The Sea Wolf *was retained as the title.*

TO: Mr. Blanke   DATE: November 20, 1940
FROM: Mr. Wallis   SUBJECT: "The Sea Wolf"

Mike's [Curtiz] dailies are coming along nicely. The scene with Van Weyden [free-lance actor Alexander Knox] and Robinson was very good.

However, there is one thing we will have to watch, and that is tempo.

Whenever Robinson gets into these philosophical discussions, particularly with Van Weyden, the tempo seems to lag, and Robinson seems to change his character. In the other scenes on deck, he was swell, he was tough and hard, and as soon as he gets into these philosophical discussions, he changes character, and you can close your eyes and think that the scene is being played in a drawing room. Eddie starts dropping his "R's," he becomes very "New Yorky," and I wish Mike would watch this very closely.

Let's at all times keep Eddie in character. Keep him hard, tough, and don't let him become too much of an intellectual when he gets into these scenes with Van Weyden. Leave that part of it to Van Weyden. . . .

Hal Wallis

TO: Hal Wallis   DATE: February 17, 1941
FROM: Mark Hellinger

Dear Hal:

In reference to the blue pages [script revisions] on *Affectionately Yours*, both [director] Lloyd Bacon and I agreed that the scene was necessary. In your absence, I put it through.

I hold no brief for the scene. You are the executive producer and, if you don't want it, that's up to you.

I do object most strenuously, however, to your method of announcing to both the director and production manager that I am little more than a . . . messenger boy around here. As the associate producer on the picture, I do my best to turn out a good film. And when you do not agree on some point, *I* am the one to be talked to—and not the director and production manager. Small wonder that there isn't a director on the lot who gives a good God damn for anything your associate producers say.

Why should a director care—when you arbitrarily reverse your associate producers without so much as giving them a chance to discuss a situation?

Would you mind very much if I finished the Dietrich-Raft picture [*Manpower*] and then got out of here? I honestly feel it would be much better for all concerned.

Mark Hellinger

Copy to: J. L. Warner

On March 8, the studio announced that Hellinger had resigned. Hellinger returned to Warners in 1942 after Wallis was no longer executive producer.

KINGS ROW

TO: Hal Wallis　　　　　　　　DATE: July 3, 1940
FROM: Wolfgang Reinhardt　　　SUBJECT: "Kings Row"
　　　　[associate producer]

Dear Hal,

It is only with reluctance that I bring myself to report unfavorably on a prospective assignment as important as *Kings Row*. Yet I prefer not to kid myself or you regarding the enormous difficulties that a screening of this best seller will undoubtedly offer. As far as plot is concerned, the material in *Kings Row* is for the most part either censurable or too gruesome and depressing to be used. The hero finding out that his girl has been carrying on incestuous relations with her father, a sadistic doctor who amputates legs and disfigures people willfully, a host of moronic or otherwise mentally diseased characters, the background of a lunatic asylum, people dying from cancer, suicides—these are the principal elements of the story. The balance of the plot-elements, the ones that are not objectionable, unfortunately are very much on the hackneyed side: A banker who steals trust funds, real estate speculations and some other typical occurrences of a small town. In my opinion the making of a screenplay would amount to starting from scratch, practically writing an original story about the life of a small town, using the same characters but inventing more or less new circumstances for the action. . . .

The quintessence of the author's [Henry Bellamann] ideas is an accusation against the hypocrisy, the narrow-mindedness and the cruelty of the typical midwestern rural town or if you will, of American society as a whole. In the novel this is done in a rather mellow way, without too much bitterness, in the style of a philosopher who knows too much about the evilness of men to get too excited about it.

In the picture we would have to hit much harder, we must let facts speak for themselves, as we cannot rely on a Greek chorus to explain the meanings of the plot. We would have to build up dramatically the contrasts that are rather mildly touched upon in the novel. . . .

W. Reinhardt

TO: Mr. MacEwen　　　　　　　DATE: January 16, 1941
FROM: Mr. Wallis　　　　　　　SUBJECT: "Kings Row"

Will you get a copy of the script on *Kings Row* and send it to [free-lance star] Ginger Rogers. . . .

Hal Wallis

FROM JOSEPH I. BREEN

Mr. Jack L. Warner
Warner Brothers Studios
Burbank, California

April 22, 1941

Dear Mr. Warner:

We have read with great care the final script, dated as of April 13th, for your proposed production titled *Kings Row*, and I regret to be compelled to advise you that the material, in our judgment, is quite definitely unacceptable under the provisions of the Production Code and cannot be approved. A picture, following along the lines of this script, would, necessarily, have to be rejected. . . .

Before this picture can be approved under the provision of the Production Code, *all the illicit sex will have to be entirely removed*; the *characterization of Cassandra* will have to be *definitely changed*; the mercy *killing* will have to be *deleted*; and the several suggestions of loose sex, chiefly in the attitude of Drake with reference to the Ross girls, will have to be *entirely eliminated*. In addition, the suggestion that Dr. Gordon's nefarious practices are prompted by a kind of sadism will have to be *completely removed from the story*.

You will have in mind, also, I am sure, that a picture of this kind could not be released in Britain, where *any* suggestion of insanity is always *entirely eliminated* from films.

In this same connection, I throw out for consideration the very important question of industry policy, which is involved in an undertaking of this kind. Here is a story based upon a so-called best-selling novel, which is identified in the public mind as a definitely repellent story, the telling of which is certain to give pause to seriously thinking persons everywhere. . . . To attempt to translate such a story to the screen, *even though it be re-written to conform to the provisions*

of the Production Code is, in our judgment, a very questionable
undertaking from the standpoint of the good and welfare of this
industry. Such a production may well be a definite *disservice* to the
motion picture industry for, no matter how well the screenplay is done,
the fact that it stems from so thoroughly questionable a novel is likely
to bring down upon the industry, as a whole, the condemnation of
decent people everywhere.

Because this story suggests an important question of industry
policy, we are referring that phase of the undertaking to Mr. [Will]
Hays for a decision as to the acceptability of *any* production based
upon the novel, *Kings Row*. This means that even though your present
script is re-written to bring it within the provisions of the Production
Code, it will still be necessary, before approval can be given to the
script, that a decision as to its acceptability, *from the standpoint of
industry policy*, be rendered by the Board of Directors of this
Association in New York.

I am sending a copy of this letter to Mr. Hays for such comment,
or observation, as he may care to make in the circumstances.

Very truly yours,
Joseph I. Breen

Will Hays's reply is not in any of the files.

FROM JOSEPH I. BREEN
Mr. J. L. Warner
Warner Brothers
Burbank, Calif.

April 24, 1941

Dear Mr. Warner:

This goes to you in confirmation of our conference yesterday with
Mr. Wallis, Mr. [Casey] Robinson, and Mr. [David] Lewis [associate
producer], with regard to your proposed picture *Kings Row*, and our
letter of April 22nd, covering the same.

With a view to bringing the proposed picture within the
requirements of the Production Code, and also of avoiding any possible
danger of a seriously adverse audience reaction to the finished picture,
the following changes in the script were agreed upon.

Mr. Wallis assured us that there would be absolutely no
suggestion or inference whatever of nymphomania on the part of
Cassandra. To this end, her illness will be definitely identified as
something else, possibly dementia-praecox, and certain lines in the
picture which might possibly be interpreted as referring to

nymphomania, will be changed, so as to remove any possibility of this flavor persisting in the finished picture.

It was agreed that, while it is necessary for the proper telling of your story, that there be an indication of one sex affair between Cassie and Parris [Robert Cummings, borrowed from Universal], Mr. Robinson will inject a new scene into the picture, probably between Parris and Drake [rising contract star Ronald Reagan] in which Parris will definitely condemn himself for this affair, condemning the affair as wrong, and will indicate his feelings of impending tragedy. This will tie in directly with the later scene in which they learn that Cassie has been killed by her father, Dr. Tower [Claude Rains].

The suggestion of a sex affair between Randy [Ann Sheridan] and Drake will be eliminated entirely.

The suggestion of a mercy killing of the grandmother [free-lance actress Maria Ouspenskaya] by Parris will be eliminated entirely.

We list below the various lines and scenes which seem to us to give the unacceptable flavor referred to in our first letter. These are for the guidance of Mr. Robinson in his revisions:

Page 3: There must be no suggestion of nude bathing on the part of these children. . . .

Pages 48 and 49: We suggest a careful rewriting of this scene, to delete any lines which might give an objectionable flavor to Cassie's characterization. Specifically, we mention the following:

"Then other times she's so different she scares me. She's so wild—as if all she wanted— When she's like that, she's—just a kind of excitement that I dread and wish for at the same time"; "Sure, bo— like me and Poppy Ross. Times I could eat her alive, and times I could throw her out on her ear" "Funny she keeps after you. Generally, nice girls—you know what I mean. I think Cassie's nice all right, but generally—well, the ones I've known, like Louise [contract player Nancy Coleman]—gosh, you just look at them and they act as if you're yanking their clothes off. Maybe old Cass is cooped up so much that when she does get loose she's all the way loose."

In addition to being very questionable from the standpoint of characterization, the above dialogue is absolutely impossible from the standpoint of censorship, and will be eliminated everywhere. . . .

Page 83: It was agreed, in this scene, that it would be definitely indicated that Dr. Tower knew about the affair between Cassie and Parris, and that this had something to do with his killing of the girl. . . .

Page 120: This action of Dr. Gordon [free-lance actor Charles Coburn] striking Louise should be masked, as if done in a full shot it will be deleted by censor boards.

Page 166: In order to clear up the relationship between Randy and Drake, please omit the line "I had given him everything with gladness." . . .

We will be happy to read any revised script you may prepare on this picture, and to report further, whenever you have it ready.

Cordially yours,

Joseph I. Breen

The above points were followed in the final screenplay.

TO: Hal Wallis   DATE: June 26, 1941

FROM: Sam Wood [director]   SUBJECT: "Cassie"—"Kings Row"

Dear Hal:

I think it most important to get Miss Lupino for "Cassie" if possible. When I was talking to Miss de Havilland today, I kept thinking how much older and more matured she was than Cassie should be and in addition Lupino has a natural something that Cassie should have.

Am shooting tests today, but if you want to discuss this, give me a ring on Stage 2.

Sam Wood

Wood was a free-lance director brought in to do Kings Row. *His recent credits included* A Night at the Opera *(1935),* Goodbye, Mr. Chips *(1939),* Kitty Foyle *(1940), and an uncredited thirty-two minutes of* Gone With the Wind *(1939).*

TO: Mr. David Lewis [associate   DATE: August 20, 1941

    producer]   SUBJECT: "Kings Row"

FROM: Mr. J. L. Warner

The dailies last night of Nancy Coleman and Coburn were excellent. This is a great scene.

We must get one thing settled in the next few days and stop all this nonsense as we have never done business this way and I am not going to permit it to start.

By this I mean the setting of the part of Cassie. We definitely will not have Bette Davis do it and de Havilland will not do it, therefore I see one of the following people as the best we can get to play the part:

Joan Leslie

Susan Peters

Priscilla Lane

We still have to make a test of [contract star] Priscilla Lane, but one of these will have to do the part.

Furthermore, Wood is 11-½ days behind on a 48 day schedule. This is really something I cannot understand irrespective of the delays that have occurred.

J. L. Warner

TO: Mr. Lewis
FROM: Wallis

DATE: August 28, 1941
SUBJECT: "Kings Row"

I had a session yesterday with Ida Lupino and [her agent] Arthur Lyons, and I believe I used every possible argument to convince her that she should do the picture, but all to no end.

Her agent notified us this morning that she will not play it and we must therefore cast the part of "Cassie" from whoever else is available.

The list seems to boil down to Joan Leslie and Susan Peters and we will have to set one of these girls unless Wood has someone better to suggest. If he has no other suggestions, then I am going to set one of these two girls this week so that we can get started on wardrobe.

Hal Wallis

According to some references at the time, in memos from casting director Steve Trilling, Lupino didn't "want to do the small and secondary part of Cassie . . . also, she didn't want second billing to Sheridan." In another memo, her agent reported that "she could not feel the part or see herself doing it."

Betty Field, who was just finishing work on Blues in the Night *for Warners, was again borrowed from Paramount for the role.*

TO: Mr. Obringer
FROM: Hal Wallis

DATE: October 2, 1941
SUBJECT: Ida Lupino

Dear Roy:

Regardless of what we do legally on the Ida Lupino situation, I want you to answer Lyons's wire and I want you to reject categorically and individually the arguments put forth in his telegram. . . .

He continually refers to the submission of *Juke Girl* [1942] on top of "Cassandra" [in *Kings Row*] as though both of these properties should never have been submitted to her and were beneath her as an artist. As for "Cassandra," Bette Davis pleaded to be allowed to play this part and I believe she enjoys a somewhat better position—at least at this time— than does Miss Lupino. As to *Juke Girl*, Ann Sheridan is going to play the part and I believe she likewise is in a fairly good position insofar as her career is concerned. . . .

TO: T. C. Wright   DATE: October 7, 1941
FROM: Frank Mattison [unit   SUBJECT: #364—"Kings Row"
    manager]

Report for 10-6-41:
    . . . Today, Tuesday, the company is shooting on Stage 14, the
EXT. [Dr.] TOWER HOME, the INT. TOWER HOME. . . .
    This will finish this picture.
    This will be 23 days over the schedule and very considerably over
the Budget.
    Considering the broken manner in which this show has been shot
as regarding sets, cast, etc., I only hope it fits together right. I have never
seen a picture shot in such a hurried manner as this picture has been
made. Most of these circumstances were beyond our control and the
insistence of Mr. Wood that we have Robert Cummings play the lead in
this picture.

Frank Mattison

    Cummings was concurrently filming It Started With Eve *at Universal
and was shuttling back and forth between the two studios. Also, Ann
Sheridan was working on* The Man Who Came To Dinner *at the same
time.*

Article in Los Angeles DAILY NEWS,
by Harry Mines

October 22, 1941
    . . . Here's something unusual: Henry Bellamann, author of *Kings
Row*, heads west to help Erich Wolfgang Korngold on the scoring of the
movie adaptation of the novel at Warners. Bellamann, before he sat down
to his typewriter, was on the faculty of the Curtis Institute of Music in
Philadelphia and at the Juilliard Music foundation.

FROM ERICH WOLFGANG KORNGOLD [composer]
October 25, 1941

Dear Mr. [Robert] Taplinger [director of studio publicity]:
    . . . I am enclosing an amusing newspaper clipping.
    Isn't it too bad that Shakespeare couldn't do the same as Mr.
Bellamann and "head west" just to help me score A *Midsummer
Night's Dream?*
    But, seriously: should I really stop working and wait for the arrival
of Mr. Bellamann? Amazing isn't it, that he didn't seem to care about
the script, the cast, shooting or directing—he's just crazy about music.

Besides, he was on the faculty of the Curtis Academy of Music and I, myself, was professor on the music academy in Vienna—so, maybe, we'll win the Academy Award for 1941—together.

However, if he shouldn't arrive in time to help *me*, I shall certainly be ready to "head east"—perhaps *I* could help *him* in writing his new book!!

Please forgive this outburst of sarcasm and once more thanks and best regards!

> Sincerely yours,
> Erich Wolfgang Korngold

FORM LETTER

Prepared August 23, 1942

Dear ————:

Many people have written to our Music Department, telling us how much they enjoyed the music in *Kings Row*. We appreciate your interest in the picture, and do want you to know something more about the music.

The incidental music that continued on through the picture was written by our own Erich Wolfgang Korngold. This music was not published and, consequently, can not be purchased; nor was the music recorded for commercial distribution, we are very sorry to say. . . .

The Music Department feels that the work being done by its musical directors is, indeed, a contribution to creative musical endeavor; and we do appreciate your consideration.

> Sincerely,
> The Music Department

At the time, with rare exception, dramatic film scores were not published or recorded for commercial distribution. This score elicited unusual interest.

TO: J. L. Warner
FROM: Blanke

DATE: January 31, 1941
SUBJECT: "Gentle People"
[*Out Of The Fog*]

Dear Mr. Warner:

 . . . Casting Garfield for the part of "Goff" [in *Out Of The Fog*] would, as you know, relieve us of the problem of convincing Lupino to play with Bogart. Too, one of the original suggestions by Wallis for the part of "Goff" was John Garfield. . . .

> *Blanke*

Garfield was cast for the role; Bogart was slated for Manpower.

MANPOWER

FROM HUMPHREY BOGART

LOS ANGELES CALIF.

MARCH 6, 1941

HAL WALLIS, WARNER BROTHERS STUDIO
DEAR HAL, I AM SENDING YOU THIS WIRE BECAUSE I AM EXTREMELY
UPSET AND WANTED YOU TO KNOW THE TRUE FACTS, AND YOU CAN
TAKE MY WORD FOR IT THAT ANY STATEMENTS TO THE CONTRARY
ARE UNTRUE. ANY REMARKS AND ACCUSATIONS BY MACK GRAY, GEORGE
RAFT'S STAND-IN, WHICH WERE ATTRIBUTED TO ME, ARE COMPLETELY
AND ENTIRELY UNTRUE. I HAVE NEVER HAD ANYTHING BUT THE VERY
FINEST FEELING OF FRIENDSHIP FOR GEORGE. I UNDERSTAND HE HAS
REFUSED TO MAKE THE PICTURE [*Manpower*] IF I AM IN IT. I HAVE
BEEN TOLD THAT FOR SEVERAL WEEKS HE'S BEEN TRYING TO GET ME
OUT OF THE PICTURE. . . . GEORGE ALSO TOLD MY AGENT SEVERAL
WEEKS AGO THAT HE DIDN'T THINK I SHOULD DO THIS PART AS IT WAS
COMPLETELY WRONG FOR ME AND WOULD HURT ME. I TRIED TO GET
GEORGE TO TELL ME THIS MORNING WHAT HE WAS ANGRY ABOUT AND
WHAT I WAS SUPPOSED TO HAVE SAID BUT HE WOULDN'T TELL ME. I
FEEL VERY MUCH HURT BY THIS BECAUSE IT'S THE SECOND TIME I
HAVE BEEN KEPT OUT OF A GOOD PICTURE AND A GOOD PART BY AN
ACTOR'S REFUSING TO WORK WITH ME.* I WAS ON THE SET PREPARED
TO MAKE THE TEST WHEN MACK GRAY CAUSED THE SCENE AND NOBODY
MADE ANY EFFORT TO STOP IT. IT SEEMS TO ME IT'S A FINE STATE
OF AFFAIRS WHEN AN ACTOR WHO IS PREPARING TO GO TO WORK HAS
TO PUT UP WITH SUCH A SITUATION AS OCCURRED THIS MORNING ON
THE SET. I COULD SEE NO WAY TO PROTECT MYSELF AGAINST THESE
INSINUATIONS AND ACCUSATIONS AND I THINK IT'S UP TO THE COMPANY
TO PROTECT ME INASMUCH AS WE ARE ALL CONCERNED IN THE BUSI-
NESS OF MAKING GOOD MOTION PICTURES. REGARDS

HUMPHREY BOGART

*Bogart was replaced by Edward G. Robinson. Ida Lupino did not
want to work with Bogart again after his alleged abusive verbal treatment
of her during the filming of* High Sierra, *and preferred John Garfield for
the role of Goff.*

TO: Mr. Obringer   DATE: March 17, 1941
FROM: [Steve] Trilling [casting director]   SUBJECT: Humphrey Bogart

We delivered a script of *Bad Men of Missouri* to Humphrey Bogart on
Thursday, March 13, and notified him through his agent that he was

*The first was *Out of the Fog* (1941).

assigned to the part of "Cole Younger" in said production. We requested that he come in to see Mr. Enright the director this morning, the 17th, to discuss with him the part, advance preparation, etc.

About 1:00 P.M. today, a messenger returned the script and the attached memo to my office in which Bogart advises:

> "Are you kidding—This is certainly rubbing it in—Since Lupino and Raft are casting pictures maybe I can. . . .
>
> > Regards,
> > Bogie"

His house advised when I telephoned that Bogart is on his boat at Balboa. I tried to reach him there by phone at 1:20 P.M. and was notified that the boat was cruising and that they would leave a message for Bogart to call me back immediately the boat docked—time indefinite.

Mr. Warner requests that you immediately wire Bogart, legally notifying him to report tomorrow morning at 10:00 A.M. for wardrobe, advance preparation, etc., at my office, and if he should fail to do so, take the necessary steps to place him on suspension.

Steve Trilling

TO: Mr. Warner DATE: April 18, 1941
FROM: Mr. Obringer SUBJECT: Humphrey Bogart

As you know, Humphrey Bogart was suspended March 18, 1941, because he would not appear in *Bad Men of Missouri*. Bogart attempted to come back Apr. 2nd, but we continued his suspension until the time it will take [contract player] Dennis Morgan to finish the picture. . . .

R. J. Obringer

TO: T. C. Wright DATE: April 1, 1941
FROM: Frank Mattison [unit SUBJECT: #358 . . . "Manpower"
manager]

Report for 3-31-41:

. . . Yesterday we had considerable upset with Miss [Marlene] Dietrich in the trying on of her wardrobe. I find that after Mr. Wallis OK'd a change for her, when the time comes to shoot the scene she refuses to wear the wardrobe. Furthermore, when sketches are OK'd by Mr. Wallis, [costume designer] Milo Anderson consults with her and she changes the gowns so they are not made up to look like the sketches. We have case in point now in the making of her wedding gown which I am sure Mr. Wallis is going to reject when he sees it on the screen. Miss Dietrich has an idea that she is to be dressed like a clothes horse stepping out of a page of *Vogue*, rather than the wife of a lineman who makes $200 a month and who, no doubt, could never afford to buy her the clothes she wants to wear in this picture.

I talked with her yesterday endeavoring to have her wear the gowns Mr. Wallis had OK'd, but she told me "there is no sense in my wearing dirty and drab clothes when Geo. Raft is dressed up and looks like he just stepped out of *Esquire*." I find that Mr. Raft also wears pointed collars, even after he was told not to do so by Mr. Warner. The wardrobe man has one hell of a time; the suits belong to Mr. Raft, and even tho he has short pointed collars on some of his shirts, he evidently refuses to wear them. Yesterday we finally got Miss Dietrich into her change which she liked very much, and which she wanted to show to Mr. Wallis. We got her up to Mr. Wallis's office and he OK'd it so that we could go ahead with the scene.

Miss Dietrich told me yesterday, also, that she always has several fittings on her gowns and was not used to having them fitted just once and then put on her and tested. She feels she should have some days in between to straighten out the other two changes for her wardrobe. She also told me she had never worked in a Studio yet where things are rushed thru as they are here. I told her that was the Studio's system.

Frank Mattison

Marlene Dietrich, under contract to Universal at the time, was fulfilling a one-picture commitment with Warners.

FROM ROY OBRINGER

Screen Actors Guild
care, Kenneth Thomson, Executive Secretary,
1823 Courtney Avenue
Los Angeles, California

April 30, 1941

Gentlemen:

On or about March 24, 1941, the undersigned corporation commenced photography on its motion picture entitled *Manpower*, with Edward G. Robinson, Marlene Dietrich, and George Raft, as principal players. . . . As production on this motion picture progressed it became apparent to a number of persons engaged in and about the production that a feeling of hostility was being evidenced by Mr. Raft against Mr. Edward G. Robinson. . . . The situation culminated in an unusually heated and disagreeable verbal attack by Mr. George Raft upon Mr. Edward G. Robinson on April 18, 1941, on the premises of the undersigned Company at Burbank, California, and immediately outside Stage No. 11, on which the production was then being photographed. . . . The controversy at that time appeared to arise over the inclusion or deletion of a certain line of dialogue in the final script covering said photoplay. Apparently, Mr. Raft was of the opinion that the line should not be spoken, although assigned to Mr. Robinson, whereas Mr. Robinson took the view that the line was in the script and was satisfactory to him, and that inasmuch as he considered the line an important one, he preferred to speak the line. Mr. Robinson then said, in substance, to Mr. Raft, "Look, George, you may think the line does not make any sense, but I have to speak it and it is all right with me." Thereupon, in the presence of the persons above named, and perhaps in the presence of other persons engaged on said production, Mr. George Raft directed toward Mr. Robinson a volley of profanity and obscene language with the express purpose and intent of embarrassing and humiliating Mr. Robinson and lowering his professional dignity and standing in the eyes of all those persons with whom he was obliged to work and come in contact in connection with the production of said photoplay.

In the opinion of those persons to whom representatives of the undersigned corporation have talked, the attack on Mr. Raft's part was wholly uncalled for and actually brought about a very serious disturbance in the production of said photoplay. The interruption and disturbance of production of the picture became so serious because of the situation that Mr. Hal B. Wallis, Executive Producer of the undersigned corporation, was called into the controversy, Mr. Edward G. Robinson left the set and went to his dressing room, and the entire production was stopped for several hours, resulting in a great and substantial loss to the undersigned. Several hours after the controversy had been temporarily quieted, production was proceeded with and approximately a week passed and, except as called for by the script and by the Director, Messrs. Robinson and Raft did not speak to one another, although the script proceeded upon the theory that the characters portrayed by Messrs. Robinson and Raft were close friends.

Just prior to twelve o'clock noon on Saturday, April 26th, while the cast in said production was engaged on said Stage 11, Mr. Robinson was rehearsing a scene wherein the script called for him to be provoked by one of the other characters. The script called for Mr. Robinson to attack this character and during the attack the script required that Mr. Raft, playing the part of "Johnnie" in the production, make his entrance and seek to quiet the disturbance. Instead of conducting himself as called for by the script, Mr. Raft immediately undertook to and did violently rough-house and push the said Edward G. Robinson around the set in an unusually vigorous and forceful manner, with the showing of a great deal of personal feeling and temper on Mr. Raft's part, causing Mr. Robinson to wheel around and say to Mr. Raft, "What the hell is all this?" In reply to Mr. Robinson's question to Mr. Raft, Mr. Raft thereupon told Mr. Robinson to "shut up," and in the immediate presence of the persons hereinafter mentioned, directed toward him a volley of personal abuse and profanity, and threatened the said Edward G. Robinson with bodily harm, and in the course of his remarks directed and applied to Mr. Robinson in a loud and boisterous tone of voice, numerous filthy, obscene and profane expressions. Thereupon, Mr. Robinson walked into his dressing room on the set. A minute or so later Mr. Robinson returned to the set and addressed himself to Mr. Raft, substantially as follows: "George, what a fool you are for carrying on in such an unprofessional manner. What's the use of going on? I have come here to do my work and not to indulge in anything of this nature. It seems impossible for me to continue." Following such remarks Mr. Raft directed another volley of profanity and obscene language toward Mr. Robinson, whereupon Director Raoul Walsh, Assistant Director Russell Saunders, and others, fearing further personal violence on the set between the two men, jumped in and separated them, and Mr. Edward G. Robinson left for his dressing room off the set and the entire production was stopped. . . .

As a result of the controversy between the two Principals on Stage 11, all further work involving the two principals was suspended from just prior to noon on Saturday, April 26, 1941, until Monday morning, April 28, 1941, and the general confusion, etc., on the set was such that the undersigned corporation lost an entire day in production, resulting in a large financial loss to the undersigned corporation. The effect of the disturbance was such that Mr. Robinson became highly nervous and such nervous condition affected his voice and made the same husky so that he was unable to properly and clearly speak his lines and otherwise give the artistic and creative performance of which he is capable. The said Edward G. Robinson, by reason of the above-mentioned occurrences, has demanded of the undersigned corporation that it give him full protection on the set from bodily harm and insulting demeanor from Mr. George Raft, making the position of the Company an extremely difficult one in its effort to produce a photoplay of artistic merit under the circumstances shown. . . .

The undersigned feels that the above occurrences are of such serious import that they should be officially called to the attention of the Screen Actors Guild. . . .

> Yours very truly,
> WARNER BROS. PICTURES, INC.
> By: Roy Obringer

TO: Mr. Hal Wallis   DATE: April 28, 1941
FROM: Raoul Walsh   SUBJECT: "Manpower"

Dear Hal:

Robinson and Raft shook hands this morning and we are off to a good start. I will try to make up the time we lost.

Raoul

TO: Mr. Wallis   DATE: June 12, 1941
FROM: Mr. Obringer

In connection with the recent [Screen Actors] Guild letter covering the Robinson-Raft episode during the production of *Manpower*, Ken Thomson [of the Guild] called me and stated that he was under the impression that Robinson had told you or that you intended to talk to Robinson about authorizing the Guild to disregard the investigation or hearing as you felt it might result in very bad publicity. . . .

R. J. Obringer

In Lewis Yablonsky's book George Raft *(1974), the author states that "Mirroring their screen roles [in* Manpower*], wariness developed between Raft and Robinson. Raft was enamored of Dietrich; and he believed, perhaps with reason, that Robinson also was interested in their leading lady. It was this unstated rivalry for Dietrich that might have provided the spark to their animosity." Raft told Yablonsky in the early 1970s, "I never thought Robinson was right for the role, which was written to be played by a big guy. I'm not sure why I got mad at Robinson. I resented his trying to put me down with advice, you know, how to handle lines and business. He made me madder and madder."*

Yablonsky quoted Robinson: "He [Raft] believed so completely that he was George Raft in the role, not George Raft playing a role, that there were times when he could get carried away from his inner forces. . . . Also, we had that misunderstanding that I can't figure out. . . . I think George just resented my being in the picture. He once told me later on that he felt my role called for a bigger guy, someone like Victor McLaglen, whom he wanted. I guess tension built up and we clashed."

TO: Mr. Obringer   DATE: June 14, 1941
FROM: Frank Mattison   SUBJECT: "Manpower"—George Raft

Yesterday, about 12:30 noon, Mr. Walsh had lined up a closeup of Mr. George Raft in this picture where he was holding Mr. Robinson by the belt before the scene where Mr. Robinson's body is dropped from the top of the tower. When Mr. Raft was put in place and told the business of letting the belt slip through his hand, Mr. Raft said, "Wait a minute. This has been changed from the way we had it before." There was some further discussion; it was Mr. Raft's understanding in the picture that while he was holding Mr. Robinson in the air by the belt that it was the belt that broke so that the body fell to the ground by accident and not by means of the belt slipping out of the hand of Raft. "This will make me a heavy," said Mr. Raft. Mr. Raft refused to do the shot saying that it was his understanding that the belt was to break and the break being the cause of the death of Mr. Robinson rather than the fact of the belt slipping out of Mr. Raft's hand. He refused to do the shot, and after considerable argument and talk, pro and con, he said "The hell with it!" and away he went.

Everything else in spite of him was shot.

It appears that Mr. Raft's principal objection to the shot was the fact that he would have let Robinson's life drop through his hands rather than the death being an accident. Mr. Raft refuses to be a heavy.

In the released version of the film, the death is definitely depicted as being the result of an accident.

THE MALTESE FALCON

TO: Mr. Wallis
FROM: Mr. Blanke

DATE: May 19, 1941
SUBJECT: Re: Mary Astor

Dear Hal:

As you know, I had [free-lance actress] Mary Astor in on Friday and gave her the script on *Maltese Falcon* as well as on *The Gay Sisters*. I told her that on *The Gay Sisters* some additional work will be done which will strengthen her part.

She called me this morning saying that she thinks *Maltese Falcon* a "humdinger" and would love to do it. She also likes the script *The Gay Sisters* very much.

This is for your information.

Blanke

P.S. We are waiting to hear from [contract player Geraldine] Fitzgerald today in regard to *Maltese Falcon* so that we can then make up our minds.

TO: Mr. Trilling DATE: May 19, 1941
FROM: Mr. Wallis SUBJECT: Mary Astor

If we do not get an okay from Geraldine Fitzgerald on *The Maltese Falcon*, we will use Mary Astor. . . .

We also want a hold on Astor for *The Gay Sisters* and this starting date also is to be flexible. We do not know just when we will start it because of [Bette] Davis's illness, etc., but our plans are to put it into production July 7th. . . .

Hal Wallis

TO: Mr. Wallis DATE: June 7, 1941
FROM: Mr. Blanke SUBJECT: "The Gay Sisters"—
Bette Davis

Dear Hal:

When you got me on the dictaphone yesterday to inquire about the Bette Davis situation in regards to the *Gay Sisters* script, I forgot to tell you a rather important point which she made in her telephone conversation with me.

She stated that she likes Mary Astor very much and—as I could prove—helped her in every way on *The Great Lie* to make a success. So—this as a preface in order not to misunderstand her motivations on the following point:

She is now in *Little Foxes* [For Samuel Goldwyn], playing an elderly woman and one of her main objections on the *The Gay Sisters* was that she was afraid in "Fiona" she would again have to portray an aged woman.

I set her at ease on this point by telling her that in the story she is six or eight years old at the time of 1918, which makes her for the most part of the story around thirty to thirty-two years old.

This set her at ease in regards to this point, but brought her to the criticism of casting Mary Astor as Evelyn, her next younger sister. Her point is that Mary Astor, no matter what we do, will always photograph older than Bette, and that Bette automatically would have to age herself considerably in order to make it believable that she is older than Mary Astor, and by doing this we would get to the result that she is afraid of— namely, that she will arrive at an age similar to the one she is putting on in *Little Foxes*. . . .

The roles slated for Bette Davis and Mary Astor were played by Barbara Stanwyck and Geraldine Fitzgerald. Astor was signed for The Maltese Falcon.

FROM GEORGE RAFT

Mr. Jack Warner
Warner Bros. Pictures, Inc.
Burbank, California

June 6, 1941

Dear Jack:

I am writing to you personally because I feel any difference of opinion that may have arisen between us can be settled in a most friendly manner. As you know, I strongly feel that *The Maltese Falcon*, which you want me to do, is not an important picture and, in this connection, I must remind you again, before I signed the new contract with you, you promised me that you would not require me to perform in anything but important pictures—in fact, you told me, in the presence of Noll Gurney, you would be glad to give me a letter to this effect. A long time has passed since you made this promise to me and I think you should let me have this letter now.

I understand that you are quite agreeable to use someone else in *The Maltese Falcon*, provided you get an extension of my time. This I think is only fair. . . .

Very sincerely,
George Raft

Humphrey Bogart was taken off suspension and cast in the role of Sam Spade, which had been slated for George Raft.

TO: Mr. Blanke   DATE: June 12, 1941
FROM: Hal Wallis   SUBJECT: "The Maltese Falcon"

[Director John] Huston's second day's dailies are better than the first, but I still feel that they are too leisurely in tempo. I think my criticism is principally with Bogart, who has adopted a leisurely suave form of delivery. I don't think we can stand this all through a picture, as it is going to have a tendency to drag down the scene and slow them up too much. Bogart must have his usual brisk, staccato manner and delivery, and if he doesn't have it, I'm afraid we are going to be in trouble. All of the action seems a little too slow and deliberate, a little labored and we must quicken the tempo and the manner of speaking the lines. Even the little scene where Bogart answers the telephone at two in the morning, his partner has been shot. The delivery of the lines was a little too slow where he speaks off stage and says, "where" etc., etc., and then before he finally picks up the phone and dials it again to tell somebody else about it, his secretary, there is a long pause and this does not make for the punchy, driving kind of tempo that this picture requires. We must get away from this method of delivering the dialogue, particularly on the part of Bogart and whenever we have pieces of business, it must be fast, there must be action in the picture. . . .

The actual scene, the setups, etc., are fine. It is primarily a matter of tempo and delivery.

cc: Mr. Huston   *Hal Wallis*

This was Huston's first opportunity to direct a feature film.

TO: Mr. Wallis   DATE: June 13, 1941
FROM: Huston   SUBJECT: "The Maltese Falcon"

Dear Hal:

Regarding your note yesterday—I am shrinking all the pauses and speeding all the action. You understand, of course, that so far I have done only the slow scenes of the picture. Unless that's kept in mind, a false impression of monotony might easily arise. For instance: Between the telephone business in Spade's apartment and the scenes of Spade and Iva [free-lance actress Gladys George], and Spade and Effie Perine [free-lance actress Lee Patrick] in his office, there are two scenes—those between Spade and the coppers—which will go so fast they will make sparks.

After the sequence I am doing at present—Brigid's apartment—the story really begins to move. By the time we reach the Cairo-Brigid-copper sequence in Spade's apartment, it will be turning like a pinwheel.

I mention these things only to reassure you that as I am making each scene, I am keeping the whole picture in mind. This picture should gain in velocity as it goes along. Otherwise the very speed with which I intend playing the coming sequences would become monotonous.

Nevertheless, I am doing as you said in your note—making Bogart quick and staccato and taking the deliberateness out of his action.

I think if we had been shooting in sequence and you had seen the Spade-copper scene in his apartment by this time, all your anxiety regarding tempo would have been dispelled. You may be sure that after I saw the first day's rushes, I was well aware of the perils of slow timing.

John

TO: Mr. Blanke   DATE: June 24, 1941
FROM: Mr. Wallis   SUBJECT: "The Maltese Falcon"

The scene in the apartment with Bogart, Astor and [contract player] Peter Lorre, is very good. I don't think it is too slow. It could stand just a little speeding up, the speaking of the lines seems a little languid, and he could pick up a little on this.

One thing that bothers me, however, is the way in which Mary Astor is speaking her lines. She seems to be playing it just a little too coy and ladylike. I think she is going overboard a little on this, in the soft quality of her voice, and obviously playing a part for all of the characters with whom she comes in contact with in the picture, and I think she overdoes it to the point of where the people she is playing with, would know that she was putting on an act. If this is not entirely clear to you I will discuss it with you in person.

Hal Wallis

TO: Mr. Wallis   DATE: June 30, 1941
FROM: Mr. Blankc   SUBJECT: "The Maltese Falcon"

Dear Hal:

By tonight the Huston troupe will be a little better than two days ahead of schedule and we figure now that by the time he finishes the picture, we will be four or five days ahead; but, in order to do this, I am coming to you with a request for an unorthodox procedure, and therefore need your okay for same.

The way we are going at present we will finish in Gutman's apartmcnt at 1 o'clock tomorrow, and we are then going back into Spade's apartment which involves one solid sequence of thirty-five pages of script and every member of the cast is in it.

Since this is Huston's first picture and it is the toughest part to shoot in order to keep it interesting for the entire thirty-five pages, we would all like to do the following: Huston will move into Spade's apartment at noon, and with all members of the cast present, he will rehearse the entire thirty-five pages until Wednesday at 1 o'clock (or for a full day) and then start shooting same. Thc director knowing what he shall do, the actors all knowing their little moves and being up on their dialogue, will enable us to pick up more valuable time than the day lost in rehearsal.

Repeating again that this is Huston's first picture, and knowing that we will profit in the end in regard to quality of performance, as well as in time, I know that you will grant me this request. Kindly advise.

Blanke

From all evidence, this suggested procedure was followed.

TO: T. C. Wright   DATE: July 19, 1941
FROM: Al Alleborn [unit manager]   SUBJECT: #369—"The Maltese
                                          Falcon"

Report for 7-18-41:

34th shooting day. . . .

The picture is finished, but at Blanke's and Huston's rcquest we eliminated the ending, as written in the script, which takes place on Stage

3 in Spade's office [as in the novel]. These gentlemen feel they can cut the picture without this ending, and if necessary they can always get Bogart. Their feeling, however, is that the picture will not need the ending written for Spade's office. . . .

Costs as of Thursday's work, July 17, stand at $327,182, or $54,000 under the Budget, which should see us through. No department has gone over its gross budget to any appreciable extent. This, in my opinion, is very gratifying. Production finished 2 days ahead of schedule.

Al Alleborn

TO: Al Alleborn   DATE: July 30, 1941
FROM: H. Blanke   SUBJECT: "The Maltese Falcon"

Dear Al:

John Huston and I have had our meeting with Mr. Warner in regard to retakes on *The Maltese Falcon* and the things definitely decided to do are as follows:

1. . . . Archer [free-lance actor Jerome Cowan] will be standing at the railing and we will shoot it so that we will presume that the camera is Mary Astor. He will come towards the camera as if he is about to embrace her when a pistol will appear in front of the lens, shoot several times, Archer will stumble back against the railing, the railing will give way and he will tumble down the hillside. . . .

2. A shot of Miles Archer lying dead on the ground as seen by Spade with the ambulance driver's and the policeman's feet milling about. . . .

3. A closeup of Gutman [contract player Sydney Greenstreet*] sitting in the chair while Bogart is phoning Effie to bring the Falcon over to the apartment. Besides this, I will need a wild track† of Gutman indicating that this is the false Falcon made entirely out of lead. (John Huston will know the right line.)

4. The tag: Instead of playing the tag of the picture as originally planned in Spade's office, we will also play this in Spade's living room and the scene more or less will pick up as in Script Sc. 123. The scene had already been shot, but on account of this being the finish it will have to be restaged.

For the scene we will require Mary Astor, Humphrey Bogart, Barton MacLane, Ward Bond. . . .

The scene will play as indicated in Sc. 123, but as I said before it will have to be staged differently, as with their exit out of the room we

---

*This was Greenstreet's first film role.
†A voice recording without photography or synchronization.

will continue in the corridor to the elevator. Mary Astor and Dundy [Barton MacLane] will get into the elevator as Bogart and the other detectives come out into the corridor and see Dundy and Astor descend in the elevator with last looks between Bogart and Astor played between them.

Blanke

FROM HENRY BLANKE

August 14, 1941

My dear Hal:

Weeks have passed and I haven't heard from you, and I presume that you have had a good time [on vacation] and that you are recharging your nerve batteries in order to be set for the things to come.

Luckily, I didn't have to write to you about anything "professional" so far as everything has run comparatively smoothly and I have not been in contact with Mr. Warner more than two or three times. . . .

The Maltese Falcon has finished long ago, and I also believe it turned out to be a very good picture. Mr. Warner made me shoot a few little things for some spots that he believed were told too much by suggestion—whether he is right or not, I won't argue. . . . Not knowing when you will return, I don't know whether you will be here for the preview or not. . . .

Always,
Henry Blanke

TO: Mr. Wallis

September 6, 1941

FROM: J. L. Warner

Dear Hal:

Last night after the preview [of *The Maltese Falcon*] I thought for about an hour, and believe we should positively make over the opening close-ups of Mary Astor and tell the audience what the hell it is all about instead of picking up with a lot of broken sentences with confusing words. . . .

Many of the cards stated they were very confused in the beginning, and I am sure we throw them off. Therefore, why be so clever, as we have a hell of a good picture. . . .

We should do these retakes the first thing Monday.

Jack

FROM SAM JAFFE   [agent (not the actor)]

Mr. Steve Trilling
Warner Brothers Pictures, Inc.
Burbank, California

August 4, 1941

Dear Steve:

I talked to Bogart last night and everything is pleasant and he's starting the picture [*All Through the Night*] this morning, however, he is unhappy about the idea of doing a role only because George Raft refused to do it.

I had a long discussion about *All Through the Night* with him, and I felt this would make a pretty fair picture though he didn't actually think so. My point in writing you about it is only that I think you should bring this matter to the attention of Jack Warner and point out to him that a story should be prepared for which they have Bogart in mind and no other actor because it seems that for the past year he's practically pinch-hitted for Raft and been kicked around from pillar to post, and I am thinking mainly of the *Manpower* situation.

Warmest regards,
Sam Jaffe

TO: T. C. Wright
FROM: Al Alleborn

DATE: September 11, 1941
SUBJECT: #369—"The Maltese Falcon"

Report for Wed., 9-10-41:

RETAKES

Company was called for 9:00 A.M. on Stage 6, INT. SPADE'S OFFICE, lined up and started shooting at 11:56 A.M. This delay was due to the cameraman having to see the film [originally shot] for matching purposes. . . .

We finished shooting at 4:00 P.M. and Bogart was turned over to the other company [*All Through the Night*] and there was no delay to the [director Vincent] Sherman company due to his working with the Huston company.

Company made 7 set-ups on Scene 3, working with Mary Astor, Bogart and Jerome Cowan, all of which were finished.

Al Alleborn

FROM HAL B.WALLIS

Mr. Jack L. Warner [on vacation]
Arlington Hotel
Hot Springs, Arkansas

October 8, 1941

Dear Jack:

According to some of the reviews and other press notices from
New York on *The Maltese Falcon*, the picture came in "under wraps,"
"on rubber heels," "was a delightful surprise because it came in
unheralded," etc., etc.

You probably have seen the reviews, which are wonderful, and
have seen the figures, which are also wonderful, and it is too bad that
they were apparently not sufficiently sold on the picture in New York
to get behind it importantly.

Now that it has opened and has proven to be a hit, I thought
perhaps you might want to give them a slight goose and let them get
behind this picture in other situations and give it the importance which
it deserves.

With kindest regards, and take it easy.
Sincerely,
Hal

FROM JACK L.WARNER

FEBRUARY 14,1942

TO [Jacob] WILK [story editor, New York]: IS THERE ANY CHANCE GET
DASHIELL HAMMETT TO WRITE A SEQUEL TO "MALTESE FALCON."
WHAT I MEAN BY THIS IS HE CAN TAKE ALL THE CHARACTERS, WITH
THE EXCEPTION NATURALLY OF MARY ASTOR AS SHE IS SUPPOSED TO
RECEIVE A DEATH SENTENCE, AND GO RIGHT ON FROM END OF OUR
PICTURE. IF HAMMETT WOULD BE INTERESTED IN THIS TYPE OF PROP-
OSITION LET ME KNOW QUICK. WE WOULD USE BOGART, GREENSTREET
AND REST OF CAST. HOWEVER, WE DON'T WANT THIS TO INTERFERE
WITH HAMMETT'S ADAPTATION OF "WATCH ON RHINE." THIS CAN ALL
HAPPEN AFTERWARDS. . . .

FROM JACK L. WARNER

MAY 19, 1942

TO: TO WILK: WON'T GIVE HAMMETT OVER FIVE THOUSAND DOLLAR
GUARANTEE FOR "FALCON" SEQUEL. IF HE HASN'T CONFIDENCE IN HIS
ABILITY TO WRITE AN ACCEPTABLE STORY, LET'S FORGET IT. ADVISE.

FROM JACK L. WARNER

JUNE 17, 1942

TO: TO WILK: WE WILL DROP THE DASHIELL HAMMETT "MALTESE FALCON" SEQUEL IDEA FOR TIME BEING. . . .

TO: Roy Obringer   DATE: January 14, 1943
FROM: H. Blanke   SUBJECT: "Three Strangers"

Dear Roy:

As you know, several years ago [1937] we purchased an original, called *Three Strangers*, from John Huston.

You may also know that Mr. [Frank] Gruber, a writer on the lot, is now working on this story for me. To the characters John Huston had, we have added a private detective on the order of the one portrayed by Humphrey Bogart in *The Maltese Falcon*. It would enrich my story manifold if we could make him identically the same character as in *The Maltese Falcon* and even give him the same name.

The Maltese Falcon, as you know, was written by Dashiell Hammett, and the character of the private detective was Spade. The question I want to ask you is whether or not I have the legal right to use this character's name again in the new story of *Three Strangers*.

Kindly advise as this is very important to me for the further development of the story.

Henry Blanke

TO: Mr. Henry Blanke   DATE: January 18, 1943
FROM: R. J. Obringer

Dear Henry:

With reference to your memo of January 14, 1943 making inquiry as to whether or not we can use the character of the detective "Detective Spade" from the literary property of *The Maltese Falcon* in the script *Three Strangers*.

Originally when I asked on this I was advised that the character "Detective Spade" only appeared in *The Maltese Falcon* by Dashiell Hammett, and if this would have been true there would have been no reason why we could not have used this character as we bought all picture rights on *The Maltese Falcon*.

However, upon further investigation I find that "Detective Spade" is a character which has been used on more than one occasion by Dashiell Hammett. As a matter of fact, Hammett wrote a story entitled "A Man Called Spade" in 1936, six years after our [original] contract on *The Maltese Falcon*. This story appeared in a collection of short stories by

Frank L. Mott. Consequently, with respect to this character, you run into the same problem you would on the Penrod and Sam stories, the Charlie Chan stories, the Torchy Blane stories, etc. In other words, the author did not divest himself of the privilege of using the character "Spade" when he sold us *The Maltese Falcon,* as this character is one which appears to have established a secondary meaning in the public mind, and which character cannot be used by the buyer of a book containing such character for the purpose of sequels. We have no sequel rights on *The Maltese Falcon.* I appreciate that you merely propose to use only the character "Spade" of *The Maltese Falcon,* and that as far as you are concerned your proposed use does not constitute a sequel. However, from Hammett's point of view this would constitute a sequelization of his character and you could not make such use without some consent on the part of Hammett.

Perhaps you can devise some rough and boisterous character who would be a detective, but certainly not with the name of "Spade" and not with the characteristics that Hammett has given to "Spade."

R. J. Obringer

The Sam Spade character was not used in Three Strangers.

FROM FINLAY McDERMID [story editor]

Comparison
Wings of the Navy
(Final Script)
with
Beyond the Blue Sky [*Dive Bomber*]
(Original Story by Frank Wead)

December 5, 1940

Beyond the Blue Sky [*Dive Bomber,* 1941] resembles *Wings of the Navy* [1938] in precisely the same manner that almost every service picture resembles its cousins. The primary concern of a service picture is to put over a background which is novel and thrilling to the layman, and almost inevitably it falls back on one of the simplest and surest story formulas to highlight that background.

I doubt that we could claim exclusive rights to the formula—although we've used it in at least twenty pictures; since it is equally popular on other lots and in fiction. It is used in almost any action picture which depicts an out-of-the-ordinary and dangerous occupation—shark-hunting, flying, submarining, etc.

Briefly, the original formula goes like this: Two friends—or brothers—are taken up with their jobs. The one who is *most* taken up with his job also gets the girl first—sometimes marrying her. At this point the girl and the best friend discover their mutual love and fight nobly not to let the husband—or fiance—know. If they do decide to tell, the husband (or fiance) is always involved in some sort of occupational accident which makes the lovers think they can't let him lose everything. The fiance, however, does discover how things stand, and—possibly after conquering a jealous impulse—sacrifices his life in some spectacular occupational job that needs doing.

Naturally, there are variations in each story. Sometimes it is the friend who obligingly removes himself in spectacular style. In *Wings* [*of the Navy*], the friend doesn't quite succeed, and the fiance gives up the girl. In *Sky*, the friend has had an equal chance with the girl from the beginning; the girl, throughout, is in love with the man who is to die, and the motive for this man's suicide is connected entirely with the occupational facet of the story; only incidentally, not by intent, does his death clear the way for a marriage between the girl and the friend. The occupational accident (in this instance an occupational disease) which precedes the final suicide does not have the usual effect of binding the girl more closely to the invalid in spite of her real desires.

In general, I should say that the formula has been used too often to give us any monopoly on it, and that there are sufficient variations of detail between the two story skeletons to nullify any claim we might make on the score of identity of plot.

On the other hand, when the similarities of background and incident are added to the plot similarities, the two properties show a much more striking likeness. In other words, if *Sky* happened to be set against a background of smuggling or lion-taming or oilwell drilling, it would bear no more than the usual generic likeness which crops up in most hazardous-occupation yarns.

But both *Sky* and *Wings* have Pensacola as a setting. Both stories rely for background color on the training of cadets. Both have scenes in which the cadets undergo physical examinations and both show the rejection of cadets for minor disabilities which would pass unnoticed in civilian life. Finally, both have as their biggest action moments scenes showing an airplane being tested in a power dive. . . .

Both films were produced by Warners. The final script for Dive Bomber *was considerably modified.*

TO: Mr. Wallis
FROM: Mr. Lord

DATE: March 4, 1941
SUBJECT: "Flight Patrol" [*International Squadron*]

Dear Hal:

I don't think we have to worry too much about Mr. Foy's production, *Flight Patrol*. The final situation is stolen from *Dawn Patrol* rather than *Ceiling Zero* [1936]. In other words, the script consists of: first half, *Ceiling Zero*; second half, *Dawn Patrol*.

Bob Lord

FROM JACK L. WARNER

TO BRYAN FOY

NEW YORK MARCH 5, 1941
RELAY FOLLOWING WIRE TO ZANUCK—DEAR DARRYL: REPLY YOUR WIRE REFERENCE OUR PICTURE "FLIGHT PATROL." IN FIRST PLACE, FOY MAKING A PICTURE ADAPTED FROM TWO OR THREE OF OUR OLD SCRIPTS. HE HAS MADE HUNDREDS OF PICTURES FOR US AND NATURALLY HAVE TO TAKE HIS WORD FOR OUR STORY. I HOPE YOUR STORY [*Yank in the RAF*, 1941] DOESN'T CONTAIN THE INGREDIENTS OF OUR SCRIPTS. SECONDLY, BELIEVE YOU UNDULY ALARMED BECAUSE YOUR PICTURE WILL BE OF SUFFICIENT IMPORTANCE WITH TYRONE POWER TO OFF-SET ANY LOW BUDGETED PICTURE MADE BY US OR ANYONE ELSE WITH A WAR-AIR BACKGROUND, AS THERE ARE IN THE MAKING OR WILL BE MADE DOZENS OF THIS TYPE PICTURE. YOU MUST REMEMBER, DARRYL, THE SECOND WORLD WAR WAS NOT PUT ON SCHEDULE SO THAT YOU OR I OR ANYONE ELSE COULD HAVE AN EXCLUSIVE ON THE RAF OR ANY OTHER BRANCH OF THE ARMY, NAVY, MARINE OR AIR CORPS. . . . MY SUGGESTION IS YOU GO RIGHT AHEAD AND MAKE YOUR PICTURE WITH TYRONE POWER AND IF IT'S EVERYTHING YOU HOPE IT TO BE THEY WILL NEVER EVEN REMEMBER OUR PICTURE. . . . ANN JOINS ME IN SENDING OUR LOVE TO YOU AND VIRGINIA. IN CLOSING, PLEASE DON'T TAKE OUR AIR PICTURE AND WHATEVER IT MAY BE AND YOUR IMPORTANT AIR STORY TOO SERIOUSLY. YOUR FRIEND. JACK.

JL TO FOY—READ WIRE I SENT TODAY TO ZANUCK IN ANSWER TO ONE I RECEIVED FROM HIM. DISREGARD IT BUT CARRY ON AND MAKE AS GREAT A PICTURE AS YOU CAN AT THE RIGHT BUDGET.

Both pictures were produced. Zanuck's film was a big success. International Squadron *scraped by as a not very good B picture.*

TO: Hal Wallis
FROM: Kurt [Curtis] Bernhardt
    [director]

DATE: May 9, 1941
SUBJECT: "The Man Who Came
    to Dinner"

Dear Hal:

You will notice in the tests of John Barrymore [for the role of Sheridan Whiteside], which you are going to see, that in one scene—the scene with the family and the doctor—he is mugging and hamming a lot, while in the other scene he is much better.

I think that, on the average, he can be gotten to be as good as in the second scene.

The reason for his not being so good in the first scene may be due to the fact that I only found out after working with him how to handle his business of placing blackboards [around the set with his dialogue on them] and of playing a scene in bits, rather than in one round, which, for him, is physically impossible.

Kurt Bernhardt

Monty Woolley, who played the role on the stage, was cast in the film.

From DAVID O. SELZNICK PRODUCTIONS, INC.,
Culver City, California*

TO: Mr. [David] Selznick
FROM: Mr. [Ray] Klune
    [Selznick's studio manager]

DATE: May 19, 1941
SUBJECT: Warner Brothers' Music

I have discussed the subject of music in Warner Brothers' pictures with a number of people. Most of the sound departments and a lot of theatre patrons think that the main thing that distinguishes Warner Brothers' music from that of all other companies is the volume of it.

There is nothing new or substantially different in their method of recording from that which is being used by most other companies. . . .

If you have seen one of their pictures in Warners' Hollywood or Downtown Theatre you will have found that everything sounds better, music and dialogue. This is because they are employing in these two houses a variation of the control track system about which I wrote to you some time ago. This, as you will recall, places the sound on the screen at the point from which such sound is visually coming. . . .

I see a good many pictures and I can't help feeling that the thing which distinguishes Warner Brothers' music more than anything else is

*This memo is from the David O. Selznick files, now at the University of Texas, in Austin.

that you hear more of it than you hear in most other pictures, and this by virtue of the volume at which they dub it. They represent the extreme school of thought on this method of handling music. Metro represents the other extreme where the music is just an incident of the picture and is handled as such and as a result the audience is not conscious of the music as such. I believe that, when it comes to comparing music departments, Metro's ranks very favorably with Warner Brothers' in all respects and I further have the feeling that audiences prefer the Metro policy on music.

TO: Warner, Wallis   DATE: May 22, 1941
FROM: Obringer   SUBJECT: Bette Davis "The Little Foxes"

This morning I talked to Dudley Furse, Bette Davis' attorney, and I am arranging to have Reeves Espy [Samuel Goldwyn executive] come over this afternoon, at which time I will get the Goldwyn side of the story.

 Furse advises me that while he is not familiar with what actually did take place, as far as he can find out there have not been many scenes photographed which can be used.* It appears there were many tests made as to make-up and wardrobe, and when they would see the tests, Wyler would say they were good or lousy and someone else would say the reverse—all of which upset Davis. Later on they photographed a dinner scene, and . . . Wyler criticized the scene and, according to Furse, stated it was the lousiest dinner scene he had ever witnessed and possibly they had better get Tallulah Bankhead [who originated the role on the stage in New York].

 It appears that Davis . . . made up her mind that she had better get off the lot. However, this situation was quieted down and Goldwyn stated he would not need her from May 12th up until last Wednesday, the 21st. . . .

 Furse talked to Goldwyn's insurance carriers insuring his picture, and the insurance carriers had their own doctors examine Davis and agreed that she should rest until June 5. That is the way the matter now stands, and Davis is at Huntington Beach. Furse states, however, that Davis, since having a week's rest, has taken a different slant on the picture and is showing more enthusiasm about going back and finishing it. At first she wanted simply to leave the lot and let Wyler and Goldwyn get whoever they wanted, but now she realizes that she could not deliberately walk out of the picture, and Furse believes that she will undoubtedly get back into the picture by June 5. He also stated that Goldwyn and Wyler had

*Davis had been loaned to Samuel Goldwyn for his production of The Little Foxes.

talked to Davis on the phone and more or less assured her that she would receive different treatment when she returned to finish the picture. . . .

R. J. Obringer

Davis returned and completed The Little Foxes.

TO: Elliott Nugent [free-lance DATE: September 16, 1941
   director]   SUBJECT: "The Male Animal"
FROM: Mr. Wallis

Dear Elliott:
   . . . I would, of course, like to have you here for the first preview, but I don't think it will be possible for us to have a sneak within a week after we finish shooting.
   We will, I am sure, be able to see the picture assembled within a few days of the date you finish shooting, but we do not dub or score our pictures as we go along as they do at some studios. Our procedure is to cut the picture as close as possible to what it will be for final release and then to score it and dub it and this takes anywhere from three to six weeks after a picture is completed.
   It will be okay for you to run the stuff with [film editor] Tommy Richards and to tell him how you see it.

Hal Wallis

TO: [Perc] Westmore   DATE: February 11, 1942
FROM: Wallis   SUBJECT: Bette Davis "In This
                                Our Life"

Last night we previewed *In This Our Life*. There were a number of cards turned in—far too many—commenting on Bette Davis' makeup and in most uncomplimentary terms. They . . . didn't like the hairdress nor the new style of cupid's bow lips on her.
   It is quite unusual for an audience at a preview to make comments of this kind about a star in a picture and I wanted you to know about it.
   In the future, before you change anyone's makeup as radically as you did Davis' in this picture, I would like to be informed of the fact so that we can discuss it carefully, make exhaustive tests, and then determine just how far we want to go.
   What we must keep in mind is that the characterizing of stars shall not reach the degree where it becomes objectionable or offensive to audiences.

Hal Wallis

TO: Mr. Warner   DATE: March 2, 1942
FROM: [Paul] Nathan   SUBJECT: Clifford Odets
     [secretary to Hal Wallis]

The writers are complaining about Odets. They say his phonograph is going all day with Gershwin records, and it becomes very difficult to try to concentrate.

    Should we move Odets and his phonograph into the bungalow (near the shine stand), or should we have him take his phonograph home and play Gershwin at night?

Paul Nathan

Odets was hired to work on the screenplay of Rhapsody in Blue, *the film biography of George Gershwin.*

TO: Col. J. L. Warner*   DATE: September 29, 1942
FROM: Mr. Obringer   SUBJECT: Hal B. Wallis Contract

The [new] contract provides that Wallis is to [personally] produce 4 Class A motion pictures each year of his contract, and the contract is for a period of 4 years commencing Feb. 2, 1942. The first year of the contract, however, was modified so that Wallis would do 6 pictures, i.e., *Now, Voyager, Desperate Journey, Casablanca, Air Force, Princess O'Rourke,* and *Watch on the Rhine.* . . .

    Wallis has first call and right to use the services of any director, actor or actress, writer, unit manager, cameraman and administrative assistants who are under contract with the company who are not otherwise actually engaged in other productions at the time Wallis may need them. . . .

    Wallis has the first right to the selection of stories owned or purchased by company. He has 14 days to accept or reject any stories purchased by us, and he is entitled to select up to 6 stories and have them in work at all times. If, within 10 weeks after he makes a selection of a story, the screenplay is not being developed to his satisfaction, he can release this story and select another. . . .

Hal Wallis in his 1980 autobiography said that "the job of supervising this vast and growing organization was becoming more and more exhausting. I had no rest, no home life. . . . My [new] deal with Jack Warner was that I would make no more than four pictures a year. The studio would provide the financing, and I would have a drawing account."

---

*In April of 1942, Jack Warner was appointed a Lieutenant Colonel in the Army Air Corps and was assigned as public relations officer in Los Angeles while continuing to function at the studio.

NOW, VOYAGER

TO: Hal Wallis   DATE: October 16, 1941
FROM: Jacob Wilk [story editor,
      New York]

Am enclosing a memorandum from Olive Higgins Prouty to [literary agent] Harold Ober, giving Mrs. Prouty's ideas of a screen treatment of her story, *Now, Voyager*.

FROM: Olive Higgins Prouty   [Undated]

You have asked me to write a brief outline of my idea for this picture version of *Now, Voyager*. I have in mind something I have never seen on the screen in any *sustained* action, that is a *combination* of a talking and silent picture in one production.

This combination, if adapted to the nature and subject-matter of the story portrayed, would offer, I think, a very unusual, if not unique performance. To a rather jaded moving picture audience I think it would be of much interest.

In my novel I tell my story by the method of frequent flashbacks—a not uncommon device to maintain interest and to increase suspense, used by writers of fiction, but difficult to adapt to a play, in which the chronological sequence of events is usually followed.

It has occurred to me, however, that by employing the silent picture for the flashbacks, in combination with the talking picture, similar results can be accomplished, and with much interest to an audience because of the novelty of the technique.

Charlotte's story is that of an escape from domestic tyranny, and tells of her amazing metamorphosis, and her moving love-story. In my novel, when Charlotte first appears, it is after her physical transformation has taken place. She is attractive in appearance, but her shy, unselfconfident manner offers a provocative paradox. This is explained by a "flashback" during her first meeting with "J. D." ["Jerry Durrance"] when she recalls her past.

In the picture version I propose that the flashbacks appear as a *silent* picture interlude with captions, accompanied by music, *or by a man's voice describing the scene as was done in Our Town*. The action of the talking picture would pause, the scene would fade, and Charlotte's memory would be portrayed by a silent picture scene. The audience would see on the screen what Charlotte was seeing in her mind's eye, and the man's voice, (or captions) would explain it. Low music would accompany the silent scenes.

This method suggests that used by the revolving stage in Gertrude

Lawrence's play, *Lady in the Dark* [1941], which showed the heroine's early life through her dreams. In my story there is no dream device used. The silent picture would depict simply a *memory* of Charlotte's—a common experience to every person in the audience.

I am one of those who believe the silent picture had artistic potentialities which the talking picture lacks. The acting, facial expressions, every move and gesture is more significant, and far more closely observed by an audience waiting for the explanatory caption or voice. The accompaniment of appropriate music to the silent picture is still another factor that plays on the emotions of an audience.

Of course the silent picture has "gone out" now, but I believe it has a place, for depicting what goes on in the *mind* of a character. In my story, Charlotte's memories of events in her early life play as large a part as her acts, therefore I think the combination would be an interesting and successful experiment in the case of *Now, Voyager*. The story opens, as I have stated, after Charlotte's physical metamorphosis has been accomplished. The first flashbacks will explain that metamorphosis. It will show her as she was before her illness—stoop-shouldered, big, shapeless, spectacled, submissive, the victim of the family's jibes, etc. Also the contrast between the bright, brilliant, blinding Italian sunshine of the opening scene, and the dour, dreary atmosphere of the heavily draped living-room on Marlboro [Marlborough] Street, which Charlotte recalls, will be very effective and affecting. Such sudden contrasts will occur frequently throughout the production.

As the story proceeds the method I suggest, in order to carry on the memory flashback device, is that of cutting short a scene at a certain dramatic juncture and leaping ahead to another scene, telling what happened in the previous one by a flashback.

For instance I suggest that what happened in Ravello between Charlotte and her lover, should not be disclosed to the curious audience until *after* Charlotte is at home again, and recalls (in a flashback) the idyllic Ravello setting, perhaps the bedroom, all of which could be done with far more artistic effect through the silent picture medium, as a memory, to the accompaniment of music, than as an actual event through the talking picture medium. . . .

Technicolor would be the most ideal, of course, the flashbacks being shown in subdued colors as if seen through a veil.

This is a very uncoordinated description of my idea, but I believe, in the hands of the right producer, it would be unusual and a great box office success.

Sincerely,
Olive Higgins Prouty

The suggestions were not used. Olive Higgins Prouty was also the author of the exceptionally popular novel Stella Dallas *(1923).*

TO: Mr. [Steve] Trilling [casting   DATE: December 24, 1941
   director]   SUBJECT: "Now, Voyager"
FROM: Hal Wallis

Two or three weeks ago I gave copies of the book *Now, Voyager* to [agent Charles K.] Feldman and requested that he submit them to Irene Dunne and to Norma Shearer. So far I have heard nothing from Feldman, and I wish you would get after him and ask for a decision. If the people are definitely not interested, we will forget them—but I think we should have an answer when we submit important properties.

In the meantime, will you send a copy of the book to [agent] Leland Hayward for Ginger Rogers—or, even better, to Ginger Rogers direct. Send it to her house and see if you can get an answer on this for me.

Hal Wallis

Irene Dunne, Norma Shearer, and Ginger Rogers were all free-lance stars at the time.

TO: Hal Wallis   DATE: February 2, 1942
FROM: Mr. Trilling   SUBJECT: "Now, Voyager"

Have been unable to get anything concrete out of the Feldman office regarding Irene Dunne, as they claim to be awaiting word from you regarding the Norma Shearer matter which they took up prior to your going to New York. I believe there was some "feeling" that they were in an embarrassing position because Shearer liked the story and if Irene Dunne did the part she would claim her agent—Feldman—was playing one against the other. I, therefore, thought it best to let it ride until you returned.

Ginger Rogers had almost completed the book and according to Hayward was crazy about it so far, and promised to let them know her complete reaction from her Oregon ranch, where she is now resting . . .

Steve Trilling

FROM OLIVE HIGGINS PROUTY

Warner Brothers Studio
Burbank, California

January 9, 1942

Gentlemen:

    This is about the title for the screen version of *Now, Voyager*. I understand . . . that the title is likely to be changed. If so, before you make a selection, perhaps you would like to have a list of the titles we considered before selecting *Now, Voyager*. Our object was, like yours, to get as arresting a title as possible, something brief, striking and appealing. The final choice was made after the book was finished and all ready to go to print. I planted the references to "voyaging," to "sailing forth to seek and find" *after* the title was chosen. Likewise I inserted Walt Whitman's lines* at the same time, to fit a title unanimously acclaimed by the salesmen handling the book as "packed full of human appeal". . . . This eleventh hour choice of *Now, Voyager* was made after at least four other titles (which I had considered excellent) had been discarded. . . .

I had my doubts about the title myself, at first. As I analyze it however I think it is because the very word "Voyage" has a peculiar lure for most people. The word "Voyager" brings in the human element, and "*Now*, Voyager!" suggests immediate action. . . .

Please let me know what titles are being considered. I realize the decision rests entirely with you. Do you wish to know any of the titles we *didn't* use?

Sincerely,
Olive Higgins Prouty

The studio already had decided to retain Now, Voyager *as the title.*

TO: Hal Wallis   DATE: April 6, 1942
FROM: Mr. J. L. Warner

Dear Hal:

I saw the Paul Henreid and Bette Davis test.

I am much afraid of Davis' hat, where you will have to guess what she is thinking about. A large hat may be all right and again it may not, but we must see the people's eyes when they are acting.

Jack

FROM GEOFFREY M. SHURLOCK [Production Code Administration]

Mr. J. L. Warner
Burbank, California

April 14, 1942

Dear Mr. Warner:

. . . As discussed with Mr. Wallis, it will be absolutely essential

---

*"Now, voyager, sail thou forth, to seek and find." From Whitman's poem "The Untold Want," in *Leaves of Grass*.

that in the finished picture, [*Now, Voyager*] it be quite clear that there has been *no* adulterous relationship between Charlotte [Bette Davis] and Jerry [Paul Henreid, borrowed from RKO]. Mr. Wallis was in thorough agreement with this, and stated that such was his intention. . . .

Cordially yours,
Geoffrey M. Shurlock

TO: Hal Wallis
FROM: Casey Robinson
[screenwriter]

DATE: May 5, 1942
SUBJECT: "Now, Voyager"

Dear Hal:

This morning I ran all available cut stuff on *Now, Voyager* [which Robinson adapted for the screen] as you suggested. I am convinced that we are on our way to a very, very good picture and the following comments are meant to be helpful rather than carping.

Boston Home: The mother [Gladys Cooper] played a little too hard, rather than aristocratic. Lisa [Ilka Chase] not gay enough. (Don't suppose anything can be done about this now.) One point bothered me considerably. In the scene with Mrs. Vale, Lisa, Dr. Jaquith [Claude Rains] and Charlotte, just after the latter's entrance, the point has been missed that Mrs. Vale deliberately reveals Dr. Jaquith's identity. I carefully wrote this as a motivation for Charlotte to break down and tell Dr. Jaquith her story later up in her room. But as it is played, there is not even any sharp reaction, either from Charlotte or from Lisa when Mrs. Vale spills the beans. I am afraid some unfortunate juggling of dialog was done here. I don't know if this can be corrected in the cutting, but if not, I feel strongly we need a couple of closeups to clarify. . . .

Charlotte's Cabin Before Cocktails: I think we badly need a closeup of Charlotte as she first enters the room. She should hesitate at the door and for a moment look at the bottle of perfume Jerry has given her. There should be a little breathlessness in her look, a little trembling, and a great deal of hesitation. Then she should make up her mind, walk into the room and start getting dressed. As the film is now, it appears that Charlotte rushes in, hardly able to wait till she gets to cocktails. This is the wrong impression. Charlotte was afraid to have cocktails with a man. It was the perfume that got her dressed, and it was the cablegram from Dr. Jaquith which gave her the final courage to meet Jerry again. Without these moments of hesitation clearly marked, Charlotte's later behavior at cocktails is inexplicable. . . .

Deck Scene and Rail Scene Coming Into Rio: I agree thoroughly that both of these scenes have to be re-shot. They are terrible. All of the heart and all the meaning of these scenes are lost and we have left just some damn dull exposition.

Possibly I'd better explain in some detail the way I see the scene played—and especially Charlotte's attitude throughout the scene. We must remember that she is hearing for the first time the truth about Jerry [that he is unhappily married]. It is true that Charlotte is not one to enjoy gossip about other people, therefore she should try to stop Deb [Lee Patrick] from telling her, but Deb persists. So Charlotte learns for the first time that Jerry, too, has had a rough and rocky time. Her sympathy for him wells up, and this attitude must be very clear to the audience. (I suggest the removal of the dark glasses so we can see her eyes.) But Charlotte would not reveal her feelings to Deb, hence her noncommittal lines which are a cover-up for her true feelings. But though Charlotte would not reveal her feelings to Deb, she would to Jerry, that is, her sympathy for him. He has helped her and she would try to help him. Hence it is very important that at the rail she tells him that Deb has told her about his home life, and when she sees the shadow of pain cross his face, she must place her hand on his, as he once placed his on hers, in a gesture of returning his gift of friendship. I am sure that this will never be misinterpreted as Charlotte's leading Jerry on if it is done with sincere feelings.

Now, the next point is most important, too. The contact of Jerry's hand this time affects Charlotte strongly, and in a way which, to her, is strange. A woman wise in the ways of the world would know that she is falling in love with Jerry and, in fact, might even be thinking, "Here's a man with whom I will have an affair, and no matter what we do, nothing will stop it." But not Charlotte. She only feels the strange stirrings of the first real love she has known, and these stirrings make her afraid and only unconsciously glad, too. She retreats. She deliberately talks about scenery, turning the subject, making him look away from her to Sugarloaf, etc. In this way we will re-capture the spirit of romance between these two— which is very important as a prelude to the night on the mountain which follows so closely in the film. . . .

After all of the above, I had better repeat that the general effect of the picture is very, very good, and [director Irving] Rapper and all the others are doing an excellent job.

Casey

Most of Robinson's suggestions were followed. Now, Voyager was Irving Rapper's fourth film as a director at the studio. He had been a dialogue director there since 1936.

TO: J. L. Warner · DATE: August 3, 1942
FROM: Harry M. Warner

Last night I saw the picture *Now, Voyager,* which is certainly a very fine picture. It has about as good a story and is as beautifully done as any picture could be. What I am going to tell you is not from the point of view of finding fault, but I think it would be much better if shortened about 20 minutes and if you took out nearly the entire scene of Bette Davis and the little girl going for the trip. This scene is silly and just spoils a good picture. If you use that scene you should not use over ten feet. There are a few other spots where this picture could be cut.

I am sending a copy of this note to Hal [Wallis]. In fact, I am going to talk to him personally about it. I hope you have Paul Henreid signed up. Also, there are several other people in this picture who are very good.

HM

The sequence remained. There may have been other cuts. With rare exception, correspondence from and to President Harry Warner does not appear in any of the studio files until 1942, at which time telegraph messages from and to the Warner Bros. Corporate Headquarters in New York began to be saved. Harry Warner spent more and more time on the West Coast during World War II, eventually moving there.

Warner Americana (1941)

THEY DIED WITH THEIR BOOTS ON

FROM JACK L. WARNER

Mr. Sam Goldwyn
7210 Santa Monica Blvd.
Hollywood, California

February 4, 1941

Dear Sam:

In answer to your letter of January 30, 1941, just received, I must definitely disagree with you regarding our phone conversation. At no time did I ever state that our proposed picture [*They Died with Their Boots On*] and any tradepaper or other publicity about it was merely a publicity stunt. It seems, Sam, that while you have innumerable excellent habits, you also have one bad habit, that is, you appear to hear over the phone only the things you want to hear.

You know that I definitely told you on two or three occasions that we were writing a story with a Custer background and that the title of it was *They Died with Their Boots On* and that we did not contemplate the production of this story in the near future. We have spent a considerable amount of money in developing our screenplay, and naturally, Sam, we do not want, nor do we propose, to be denied the right to produce this picture simply because you likewise have a story with a Custer background. . . .

As I have already told you, all the producing companies in the industry cannot sit back and be stopped from making a picture about the Royal Air Force just because one studio proposes to do so. Anything in the public domain belongs to everyone, and I know you realize this. However, I cannot permit you to put words in my mouth that I never said, as you are apparently trying to do and as indicated in your letter. Everybody loves you, Sam. You are a fine fellow, but you will have to realize that other companies are producing pictures besides yourself. . . .

Best wishes.

Goldwyn's Seventh Cavalry project was not produced.

FROM JACK L. WARNER

MARCH 7, 1941

TO WALLIS:

. . . REFERENCE "CONSTANT NYMPH" NEXT FLYNN PICTURE. MAKE FOLLOWING "DIED WITH BOOTS ON," AS FLYNN IN MODERN CLOTHES JUST DOESN'T SEEM TO GO OVER. "FOOTSTEPS [*in the Dark*," starring Flynn] DOING PRETTY GOOD, BUT NOT IMPORTANT. EVERYWHERE IT HAS OPENED IT IS UNDER "NO TIME FOR COMEDY" 20 TO 25 PERCENT. BELIEVE "NYMPH" WOULD BE ALL RIGHT FOR HIM, THEN AGAIN AM BIT FRIGHTENED AS SEEMS THEY ONLY WANT FLYNN IN OUTDOOR PRODUCTIONS WE HAVE BEEN HAVING HIM IN. THINK IT OVER. IF WE COULD GET "BOOTS ON" READY AS FLYNN'S NEXT, OR HAVE YOU ANY SUGGESTIONS OF DOING . . . [*Captain Horatio*] HORNBLOWER . . . ETCETERA, INSTEAD OF USING HIM IN MODERN CLOTHES. THIS VERY SERIOUS, THEREFORE GIVE ME YOUR REACTION . . .

Charles Boyer was cast in The Constant Nymph *(1943); Flynn did* They Died with Their Boots On; Captain Horatio Hornblower *was postponed for many years.*

TO: Mr. Wallis
FROM: Mr. Trilling

DATE: June 9, 1941
SUBJECT: Joan Fontaine

Inasmuch as Joan Fontaine had expressed herself as not liking the part [of Custer's wife] in *They Died with Their Boots On*, after reading the script, Dan O'Shea (David O. Selznick office) felt they did not want to make an issue of it with her. If it was an exceptionally dramatic part like *Constant Nymph*, they would try to sell her or compel her to do the part, but they felt this was merely a straight lead any one of a number of girls could do and they did not want to create a situation and try to force her to do it. We, therefore, will have to forget about her for *They Died with Their Boots On*.

Steve Trilling

Oliva de Havilland, Joan Fontaine's sister, played the role of Custer's wife. It was her eighth and final appearance with Errol Flynn. Joan Fontaine, borrowed from Selznick, played opposite Boyer in The Constant Nymph.

FROM LEE RYAN [captain, Security Department; apparently a history buff and friend of Robert Fellows, associate producer]

Undated

Bob:

Here's my reaction to the *Boots On* script, for what it's worth. Although you told me last evening that it is a "fairy tale," with no attempt at adherence to historical fact, I nevertheless feel that not enough stress is being placed on that part of the story (and the only part incidentally) with which the general public is familiar, i.e., the "massacre," which was not a "massacre" at all but a very fair fight in which the army was outmaneuvered and outgeneraled. . . .

I don't agree at all that you need a "young Indian" as your principal Indian character. That, as I see it, is an affront to the Red Men because their chiefs, their sages and their medicine men were not youngsters but mature men of wisdom for whom the tribe had great reverence and respect. The name of Crazy Horse means nothing to the average American, who is not a student of Indian history, but the name of Sitting Bull (truly a tremendous character) is known to everyone. For that reason I can't see how you can kiss him off with a mere mention of his name.

It's a bit gushy, I think, to have Custer as the last survivor and is not borne out by my conversations with Sioux braves who participated in the fight. I believe it is a fact that Custer was not scalped and it is also a fact that he did not wear his hair long in that particular scrap. But that's of minor importance. . . .

Sincerely,
Lee Ryan

FROM LENORE COFFEE [screenwriter]

July 4, 1941

Dear Mr. Wallis:

I started in this morning to read Mrs. Custer's book about her life with General Custer in Dakota and verified, at the same time, in the

Encyclopaedia Britannica, all the facts that seemed to bear upon the script and found a number of really shocking inaccuracies. Were they only technical matters, they could perhaps be dismissed, particularly as the picture is already in production, but these are distortions of truth which may lay us open to a libel suit on behalf of the descendants of General Custer and a reprimand from the Government for having impugned the honor of such a celebrated regiment as the 7th Cavalry. They are as follows—

1. The sequence in which Custer is promoted from a Second Lieutenant to a Brigadier-General as an error seems to have no foundation in fact. . . .

2. All the episodes to do with his drinking will lay us open to a libel suit, as, according to Mrs. Custer's own book: "The General never tasted liquor and we were both so well always we did not even keep it for use in case of sickness."

3. The episodes which show Custer out of the army at the end of the Civil War as unhappy and resorting to drink through the boredom of civilian life are entirely erroneous. Custer was *never* out of the army from the time he graduated from West Point until his death.

4. And this is important. Custer was in command of the famous 7th Cavalry for seven years before he went to Dakota with it. . . .

In the script, General Custer is taken from civilian life and sent out to Dakota where he finds the 7th Cavalry already in charge of a fort. . . .

Of course, these sections of the script *can* be rewritten and the faults corrected although with the picture in production, the pressure of time makes this a little difficult, but not impossible. . . .

Contract screenwriter Lenore Coffee was assigned by Hal Wallis to strengthen the scenes between Custer (Errol Flynn) and his romantic interest and, later, wife (Olivia de Havilland), in addition to other scenes involving Mrs. Custer. Coffee had written numerous screenplays since the early 1920s. Aeneas MacKenzie and Wally Kline wrote the original drafts of the script.

TO: Lenore Coffee   DATE: July 16, 1941
FROM: Bob Fellows [associate   SUBJECT: "They Died with
    producer]   Their Boots On"

Dear Lenore:

In the two books I am sending you there are references to Custer's drinking. Even though they were brief, I think there is justification enough for us to use them at the start of the second half of our picture, in underlining the unrest and dissatisfaction of a man of action, who is hedged in on all sides by his inactivity.

I know you are worried by his drinking, but if he did drink at any time, it doesn't make any difference if he drank in 1864 or 1868.

I am only bringing this point up in the event you feel we need any strong justification for Libby [Mrs. Custer] to go to [General Phil] Sheridan—that is, that her husband is degenerating because of his inactivity, and momentarily turns to drink.

Bob

TO: [Raoul] Walsh   DATE: July 10, 1940
FROM: Mr. Wallis   SUBJECT: "They Died with
         Their Boots On"

Dear Raoul:

Supplementing our talk on the phone last night, I do want you to watch this picture very closely and see that every scene is done with the utmost care and attention to detail and performance.

As I told you yesterday, the photography on the exterior was not good. . . . Also, the West Point Cadets seemed very sloppy, both in their dress and in their marching, etc. . . .

Also, the scenes so far have seemed a little choppy—broken up into short cuts—and you should watch this closely and get tieup shots and long shots wherever necessary.

This picture lacks the bawdy dialogue and humor of the modern type of story you have been doing, and being a period picture of a very well-known historical character, it must have a feeling of authenticity and it must be very well done.

I know you are working hard at it, but don't let your anxiety to hurry be the cause of unfinished or "sloppy" scenes. . . .

Hal Wallis

TO: Mr. Wallis   DATE: September 9, 1941
FROM: T. C. Wright   SUBJECT: #372—"They Died with
         Their Boots On"

Dear Hal:

Bob Fellows is going to present you with a list this morning of the shots that Walsh, [second unit director B. Reeves] Eason, and himself have made out, to be shot by Eason [for the climactic sequence depicting the Little Bighorn attack]. . . . Would you kindly proof-read this list and send me your marked copy, and then I will give Eason a list of just the shots that you have O.K.'d, as I do not want him to go out and shoot everything and then possibly have Walsh duplicate, or shoot more than you think is necessary. I have spoken to Eason and he says it will take him around 6 days to shoot this material. . . .

T. C. Wright

The schedule was cut to four days. Earlier and later Walsh shot a good deal of this sequence. Eason had codirected the final "charge" in The Charge of the Light Brigade *with Michael Curtiz. He was an action specialist, particularly with scenes involving horses.*

FROM WALTER MacEWEN

September 17, 1941

Mr. Wallis:

Wally [Kline] talked to Lenore [Coffee], and frankly told her that he and MacKenzie would appreciate her not holding out for [screenplay] credit beause it meant so much to them. She agreed to think it over and a little later she called me, saying that under the circumstances she would gladly withdraw—and would have done so three weeks ago if the boys had called her as originally planned, and been frank with her.

Mac

Coffee contributed substantially to the final script that was shot.

YANKEE DOODLE DANDY

TO: Hal Wallis   DATE: May 5, 1941
FROM: William Cagney [associate   SUBJECT: George M. Cohan
        producer] and Robert
        Buckner [screenwriter]

Dear Hal:

We have just completed a series of very concentrated story conferences on the Cohan material, with certain clear results that we would like to establish with you at this early point of development.

We are submitting this report in carefully considered detail, to show you each step in the problems we have encountered. Since the original conception of a picture based on Cohan's life, this is the first fully analytical study of the material which anyone has made.

(1) The extensive research record which Buckner brought back from New York, both in written form and that which resulted from his several conferences with Cohan, provides us with full coverage of all the essential elements of Cohan's life. It is extremely doubtful if there is anything of

dramatic importance about him which we do not know. The material itself, then, is well in hand. In addition, we have familiarized ourselves with most of his plays and music.

(2) We have systematically arranged and examined the factual material, eliminating what we could not use and building up those incidents which gave us good scenes. Then, with a rough knowledge of our general timing and direction, we started to put the pieces together.

(3) Very quickly one great problem became definite and clear. We needed a romantic personal story, or at least an honest and important statement of what Cohan was working for. As you know, Cohan has made quite clear that he does not want his private domestic life as a major element of this picture. He stated that in no uncertain terms to Buckner, and this is his main reason for reserving the right of final approval of the screenplay. . . .

(4) So we approached the personal story from other angles. First, at Cohan's own suggestion, we tried the Four Cohans, a famous trouping family, believing that the tight-knit story of a mother, father, son and daughter would sustain the line of George M. Cohan's career. The result was a good first four reels, the colorful and crowded childhood, then the lusty young manhood of a dynamic character. But beyond that point the family relation of the Cohans could not be made a believable or dramatic basis for the remaining years, as they were not in fact. Before abandoning this angle we explored every conceivable way to retain it, but at the age of 20 George Cohan was definitely on his own as a fighter in the ring, and the family was the least of his problems. Apart from this, it would be hard to swallow Jimmy Cagney as a guy with a mother or father complex.*

(5) The middle section of this story is unmistakably the most important part for picture purposes. From 1902 until 1921 were the years when Cohan was setting Broadway on fire with one hit after another. During this time he had no serious reversals of luck, except the Actors Equity fight, which made him very disliked, and which Cohan prefers not to be recalled. It is also very dull. The main feature of these years is simply that Cohan coined a fortune. He wrote many plays and musicals; directed, staged, produced and played in most of them. Superficially, this sounds like great picture material. It has color, music and action. But, as you know, those things are good only when they are tied tightly to a good personal story. At least, that is how we feel.

Cohan's shows, as read or reproduced today, are old-fashioned almost to the point of burlesque. They were purely products of their periods

---

*Although he later played (and played well) just such a role in the extremely successful *White Heat* (1949).

and all followed the same simple story formula—"A young man gets rich between 8:30 and 11 P.M." This was particularly true of his musicals. You should read them. They had not even the advantage of being "spectacles," such as Ziegfeld's shows. And even if we took the liberty of making one or two of them into elaborate production numbers would that of itself counteract the absence of an interesting personal story? We don't think they would.

(6) Next we developed the patriotic theme. George M. Cohan as the symbol of a dynamic and sincere American, a boy imbued with the true spirit of his country, who carried the same fervent feeling into his plays. And we gave this angle a tremendous workout. But it spreads too thin. He waved the flag for good dramatic effect and he wrote a couple of popular flag-waving songs. It was good showmanship but it was not the main theme of his life. Cohan was a good citizen, yes. He loved his country. But the evidence is neither complete enough or dramatic enough to ask any intelligent person to accept as the key to his character. It was a vital part, but again, it is not an honest substitute for a personal story. It is also dangerous as a bore to a modern audience, for today Cohan's flashy type of patriotism sounds as cornily theatrical as it was in 1910. And accidentally or not, the fact still blares at you that he made several million dollars with this act—*during the War.*

(7) We attempted next to develop a fictitious romance, assuming the liberty and trusting that its light-hearted handling might prove acceptable to Cohan. We found a girl who was a definite character. But a romance without conflict is a very dull affair in a motion picture. . . . Finally we convinced ourselves after much discussion that a romantic angle strong enough to be the backbone of the picture would be too violently contrary to the facts of Cohan's life ever to gain his approval. Cohan's attitude on such a suggestion has been too clearly stated by him for us to waste time with a lengthy development. The same old wall stared us in the face. We were fighting a purely personal blockade which paralyzed every inventive attempt at a warm, human and entertaining story.

(8) To summarize our position to date, it is briefly this: We have a good beginning and a good ending for the story, but the all-important middle is, at this point, insoluble to us because of Cohan's restrictions in personal matters. Furthermore, it is our very carefully considered opinion that the basic factual material of Cohan's career, unlike Rockne's for example, is not, without great hunks of sheer hokum, a naturally progressive story-line for a motion picture. Individual scenes are excellent, but they have no continuity of purpose. And this missing factor is the heart and soul of the picture. Even if Cohan were finally persuaded to give us complete liberty with the romantic angle, that would be only a partial cure of our problems. For a love story, unless fantastically fictional,

could never explain the big question of his life—Why? His career was purely and absolutely of the theatre. He had no outside interests. His only objective was success, and he achieved it with monotonous annual regularity, unhindered and unobstructed.

The only alternative we foresee to such a straight-jacket situation is to duck any fully developed personal story, or any real romance, and just tell the rise to fame and riches of Cohan the showman. But when we try to break that down into a continuity of scenes it does not seem to justify the effort or expense of production. Montages, business talk, gags, bustles and obsolete theatrics—even with music—do not add up to the sort of picture we all would care to make.

It must be said, to Buckner's credit, that he foresaw this serious complication from the beginning, and repeatedly requested to be relieved of the assignment. But for reasons which are understood, he undertook the personal contact and preliminary spadework.

We have given this job our most intense and honest efforts, and would continue to do so but for the dead-end of difficulties described above, and to avoid the running up of studio expenses in the face of factors beyond our control.

It is possible, naturally, that there is a solution which we have not discovered; and this report is not meant as any Supreme Court verdict on the possibilities of George M. Cohan's life as a good motion picture. It has many elements for a great piece of entertainment, but we have been unable to assemble them to our satisfaction, and we have worked like hell.

William Cagney
Robert Buckner

William Cagney, James's brother, was the associate producer of Yankee Doodle Dandy *under Hal Wallis.*

FROM HAL B. WALLIS, WILLIAM CAGNEY, AND ROBERT BUCKNER

Personal.
Mr. George M. Cohan
New York

August 29, 1941

Dear Mr. Cohan:

We greatly appreciate your extensive personal efforts in preparing a script for our guidance. Your indications and suggestions of preferred ways to handle certain individual scenes in your life-story are very clarifying. . . .

Our meeting-point seems to be this: a compliance with and correction of your principal objections to Mr. Buckner's script, while at the same time retaining as much as possible of the latter's advantages to the studio, and to the final picture. This is the spirit of your script, and so we are sure that you will help us in examining objectively these points of compromise. They are submitted only after long and careful analysis of your desires and our sincere efforts in creating a picture to our mutual satisfaction.

In our script we gave you an opposition to overcome, a Broadway that resisted you at first. This gave a sympathy to the character. You hoped he would win through because you knew that it was a New Order versus the Old. But when you state, as on Page 35, that you feel the boy has had enough trouble, that now the family's success is set and that the young fellow needs no further obstacles in his path to future success—we feel this is a serious mistake in dramatic construction. The problems of the boy, Cohan, are not those of the man, and this is the first time we have seen the man. All that preceded this scene is really but a prologue of background. Now begins the real story of your fight.

Under your construction the remainder of the story is concerned largely with your chronology of productions, interspersed with personal scenes to link them by explaining the factors surrounding their staging or casting. These scenes are unquestionably accurate as biography and interesting as history, but for the time-tested purposes of motion pictures, they do not seem to us to hold or build the interest in a central theme. We believe that the deep-dyed Americanism of your life is a much greater theme than the success story.

In order to do this dramatically we took several liberties in our script because we thought that was our mutual understanding. All that we ask is this: except in instances where your close personal relations, as with your wife, are disturbing to you in their misrepresentation, would you try to appreciate our sincerity of purpose and plan in building an organic structure which is true and honest to the spirit of your life, if not the letter?

In the life of Knute Rockne, which we believe you admired, we could never have produced as fine and well-rounded a picture had not his family so graciously permitted us to have some freedom in arranging a few elements in Rockne's life story. Many scenes in that picture never actually occurred as we showed them, but they were all true to Rockne's spirit. When the picture was shown to his family and friends their pleasure and gratitude at the warmly humanized results overcame completely any microscopic objections to literal facts. We did the same with Zola and Pasteur. Ziegfeld's life was given the same freedom for an excellent picture [*The Great Ziegfeld*, 1936]. . . . It is the only way in which a biographical picture can be made interesting and worthy. . . .

If you can see your way clear to approve the story we are trying to tell, we are positive that we can do it in a manner that would fully satisfy you. The love story can be changed as you wish, to bring the girl in more casually and to delay the courtship and marriage very much as you have indicated. . . .

Will you then examine our script in view of these many changes, which we understand to be those most important to you, and tell us if the resulting story would be acceptable to you? . . .

> Sincerely,
> Hal B. Wallis
> William Cagney
> Robert Buckner

TO: Hal Wallis
FROM: Robert Buckner

DATE: September 27, 1941
SUBJECT: "Yankee Doodle Dandy"

Dear Hal:

I'm taking the Cohan job home to work on over the weekend and will do my best to have the finished script in your hands by Tuesday or Wednesday.

[William] Cagney and I feel that the new script is a 50% improvement over our first one, and a 250% improvement over Cohan's egotistical epic. I have combined a great deal of his stuff into our lineup, all the points he was most touchy about, and have made every possible concession to his wishes which would not louse-up the picture. I have written it a little long, but deliberately, to get his okay on certain sequences as he wanted them spun out. But these can be cut down before we start to shoot, retaining only what's needed. I am convinced that this is the quickest and smartest way to get this approval and still protect ourselves fully. If he objects to anything now, we still have enough footage to close up the gap without having to originate completely new scenes—mail them to him—and wait interminably while we kick them back and forth by correspondence.

If Cohan is honestly sincere about giving us the necessary little freedom to tell his story as we've got to tell it, then this is the showdown, Hal. We've given in to him all down the line, and I've broken my neck to play fair with him. And he knows it.

If you want to settle this thing now with Cohan—yes or no—I believe strongly that I should take this new script back to him and lay our cards on the table. If he wants minor changes I will make them right there, or even major changes if they can be done. Only by this way can we get his final approval, a face to face settlement of every point. He will do this with me. . . .

I'll either come back with Cohan's unqualified approval, or we will know definitely that he will never let us make a good picture. And from his wires I think he wants to be square. . . .

But also, between ourselves, I am so damned tired and nervously exhausted after six months of wrestling with Cohan and a solid year without a day's rest, that I've either got to have a brief break or go nuts. I've been taking adrenalin shots for months to keep going, and I think you can sympathize with my present state. It's been pretty tough on Mary too, and I'd like to take her to New York with me. I think I've earned a small humane favor from Warner. It would be a life-saver to both of us.

Sincerely,
Bob Buckner

TO: Hal Wallis   DATE: November 25, 1941
FROM: Robert Buckner   SUBJECT: "Yankee Doodle Dandy"

Dear Hal:

. . . The sequence beginning on page 23 [of a revised script by contract writers Julius J. and Philip G. Epstein], between George and Mary [contract player Joan Leslie], will be a great shock to him. I can assure you firmly. . . . I had a terrific time persuading Cohan to let me introduce Mary when I did. You may recall that in his own script Cohan held her back until almost the very end of the story. These reasons are peculiarly personal to him, and my compromise was a great concession, reached only after hours of argument and persuasion.

But even this fact is less vital, from Cohan's viewpoint, than the manner in which this scene is now played. Mary showing her legs to him, his long look at them, his pinching and stroking her cheek—all this is in very bad taste and is taking an extremely long chance with Mr. Cohan's known personal attitude on this relation. Believe me, Hal, I am not guessing what he will do when he sees it. This scene is a fresh kid on the make, and is less funny than vulgar. Apart from that great reason, can you assume in this scene that Joan Leslie and Jimmy Cagney are approximately the same age? That is the clear implication, as I read it. . . .

Bob Buckner

The above was modified. James Cagney had requested a revision of the original Buckner script by the Epstein twins, at the time very important writers at the studio. Another contributor was Edmund Joseph.

FROM JESSE L. LASKY [producer]

Major Albert Warner [treasurer, in charge of distribution; brother of
Harry and Jack L. Warner]
Warner Bros.
321 West 44th Street
New York, New York

December 4, 1941

Dear Abe:

I am in receipt of your letter of November 24th and I am indeed
sorry that while I was in New York you did not take advantage of my
presence there to discuss the subject matter of your letter. As it is, it
will take a somewhat lengthy letter to express my feelings about this
situation—so bear with me and read the following:

First, as an old friend, I do not hestitate to disclose my present
personal situation to you. You will remember that when I left
Paramount in 1932, I lost my entire personal fortune. As a matter of
fact, when I arrived in California my affairs were so involved that I
retained Lloyd Wright, who has been my attorney ever since, and by
the time we were through settling with all my creditors, I had not only
lost my fortune and my home but I had to borrow considerable sums
on my life insurance. Since that time I have cleared myself of all
indebtedness, but this effort has left me without any cash reserve
whatsoever.

About this time, I conceived the idea of acquiring the picture
rights to Sergeant York's life. This cost me six months of negotiation
and four trips to Tennessee, during which time I was not drawing
salary from any company—a considerable investment on my part, you
must admit. When I finally persuaded York to sell his life story, I had
to make the first payment. I did not hesitate to do this because I knew
that I was acquiring one of the most valuable properties available to the
picture industry.

When I contacted Harry Warner with the object of producing the
picture for your company, I did not attempt to make a profit on the
resale of the picture rights which I might justifiably have done. Instead
of that, having absolute faith in the timeliness and box-office appeal of
this subject, all of which Harry immediately sensed, and my ability to
successfully produce it, I determined to gamble, and so was willing to
make a deal so that I would not get any profit until after the picture
grossed $1,600,000.

Your contention that Jack Warner estimated the picture could be
made for approximately $1,000,000 is true. He should not be criticized
because of the fact that the picture went over this amount, as many

unforeseen elements caused this overage—for instance: we were delayed for several months in starting production waiting to secure the services of Gary Cooper. Let me say, even then it would have been impossible to secure his services if Jack had not very wisely offered Bette Davis [for Goldwyn's *The Little Foxes*, 1941] in trade for Cooper, which gesture on his part I deeply appreciated. Also, we were producing the picture during the rainy season and lost about three weeks due to extraordinary rainy weather when we had nothing left to shoot but exteriors—battle scenes, etc. Other unforeseen conditions arose which further increased the cost of the picture. However, this is not a new situation. We, who understand the exigencies of picture production, realize it is not unusual for occasional big pictures to exceed their budgets by a very large percentage.

During the years I served Paramount as its First Vice President in Charge of Production, we had many instances of pictures exceeding their budgets from $500,000. to as much as $1,000,000. These very pictures, however, proved in the end to be our greatest money-makers—and I was always able to face my Board of Directors courageously because the eventual profit on these pictures that exceeded their budgets justified their enormous additional expenditures.

It seems to me that is the situation that now confronts you. Instead of apologizing or explaining the fact that *Sergeant York* [1941] cost approximately $600,000 more than was estimated, you should ask for a vote of thanks and confidence for first, having had the foresight to make the deal with me, and, finally, for the amount of profit that it will bring to your company even in spite of the percentage that will accrue to me.

Some years ago I faced a similar situation with Cecil deMille. I negotiated a deal with deMille for *The Ten Commandmants* [1923 version] in which I had agreed to give him a percentage of the net profit. Messrs. [Adolph] Zukor and Sidney Kent [Paramount executives] telephoned me that deMille was taking advantage of our close friendship to put over an unfair deal and that if I would not mind they would send Sidney Kent to attempt to negotiate a better deal with deMille. Kent arrived, and when he was through with his negotiations, he had given deMille a percentage of the gross after a certain figure. Kent did not know what deMille knew—that this great subject, if successful, could pile up a record gross return. The final result brought *The Ten Commandments* in for a cost of over $2,000,000, but the gross reached about $5,000,000, so that deMille's share eventually turned out to be as large or even larger than Paramount's. I was later asked to discuss the deal with Cecil for a possible adjustment but he and his attorney, Neil McCarthy, refused to even consider the matter, and the part I tried to play in these negotiations proved very embarrassing, and they both censured me severely for making them such an unbusinesslike proposition from their point of view. When the result of *The Ten Commandments* was calculated, even though deMille received more as his share than Paramount, it worked out that Paramount's share of the profits were so satisfactory that he was given a new contract at a greater remuneration and was regarded as a hero, and not as a heavy, for many years thereafter.

Where it was hard for Cecil to forgive me for attempting to repudiate my company's contract I, who am made of a different clay, do not blame you for writing to me and requesting a similar adjustment.

If your company were having a very bad year and if I had any surplus cash with which to protect my family in the event of my death, I would just be generous enough to meet your request; however, as Warner Bros. are having one of the biggest years in their history and your Board of Directors must be jubilant over the shrewdness with which the company has been operated, I don't think that you are going to apologize to your Board for Harry and Jack Warner having made the *Sergeant York* deal,— and frankly, by the way, I consider much of the success of the company's operation is due to their mature judgment, showmanship and hard work.

How I would like to have a chance to face your Board and justify this deal. I would tell them that, in the first instance, they should have paid at least $150,000 for the *Sergeant York* picture rights alone, which would have reimbursed me for my six months of time and financial outlay in acquiring the story—but I didn't ask for this sum because I was willing to gamble for my profit on the outcome of the picture itself. But why go on—I know you follow my thoughts. . . .

I can't help but smile as I conclude this letter because I am thinking back to the many times I was compelled to do the very thing, under similar circumstances, that you are attempting to do in order to placate your Board of Directors and serve the best interests of your company.

Please have no regrets over having written me as you did—and please do not blame me for turning down your request that I give up $120,000 soon to accrue to me. I am very glad that this matter came up because I feel it will create a better understanding between us— and, anyway, it is well that matters of this kind are brought out in the open for frank and honest discussion.

> With kindest personal regards, I am
> Sincerely yours,
> Jesse L. Lasky

P.S. I would appreciate it enormously if you would pay me the compliment of reading this honest expression of my thoughts and experiences to your Board of Directors.

Isolationist factions in Washington were investigating Hollywood's so-called "war mongering."

September 25, 1941

Prepared Statement [edited] of Harry M. Warner, President of Warner Brothers Pictures, Incorporated.

. . . Reckless and unfounded charges have been made before your committee against Warner Brothers and myself. These charges are so vague that, frankly, I have great difficulty in answering them. However, they have been widely disseminated and may be believed by the uninformed. I have tried to summarize the charges. They seem to divide into four allegations, as follows:

1. That Warner Brothers is producing a type of picture relating to world affairs and national defense for the purpose allegedly of inciting our country to war.

This, we deny. Warner Brothers has been producing pictures on current affairs for over 20 years and our present policies are no different than before there was a Hitler menace. The pictures complained of were prepared under similar studio routine to all Warner Brothers productions.

2. That the Warner Brothers pictures concerning world affairs and national defense are inaccurate and are twisted for ulterior purpose.

This, we deny. The pictures complained of are accurate. They were all carefully researched. They show the world as it is.

3. That Warner Brothers is producing pictures that the public does not wish to see and will not patronize.

The proof of the pudding is in the eating. All of the productions complained of have been profitable. To the point is *Sergeant York*, which, I believe, will gross more money for our company than any other picture we have made in recent years.

4. That, in some mysterious way, the government orders us to make this or that type of picture.

This, we deny. We receive no orders, no suggestions—direct or indirect—from the Administration. It is true that Warner Brothers has tried to cooperate with the national defense program. It is true that Warner Brothers, over a period of eight years, has made feature pictures concerning our Army, Navy or Air Force. It is true that we have made a series of shorts portraying the lives of American heroes. To do this, we needed no urging from the government and we would be ashamed if the government would have to make such requests of us. We have produced these pictures voluntarily and proudly. . . .

Our company has pioneered what, for a better phrase, I will call "Action" pictures. By that I mean we have tried to portray on the screen current happenings of our times. We have tried to do this realistically and accurately, and over a long period we have discovered that the public is interested in and grateful for this type of picture. . . .

I have no desire to infringe unduly on the time of this very preliminary hearing. I should like to read to you the case history of *Confessions of a Nazi Spy* [1939]. I have prepared similar summaries on *Sergeant York, Underground* [1941], and *International Squadron* [1941]. I will not take the time to read these latter summaries, but I would like to present them for your record, at the conclusion of my statement on the history of *Confessions of a Nazi Spy*.

Confessions of a Nazi Spy was exhibited to the public beginning April, 1939, or six months before the outbreak of the Second World War. The plot was not the creation of a fiction writer. Nor did we sit down to devise a story to show the dangers of Nazi espionage. *Confessions of a Nazi Spy* correctly portrays the operation of a Nazi spy ring in this country, as this operation was disclosed at a Federal trial which convicted the conspirators.

In June, 1938, certain persons were indicted in a New York Federal Court, charged with being Nazi spies and with violation of U.S. espionage laws. The spy ring was revealed by the Federal Bureau of Investigation and the charges attracted great attention in newspapers throughout the country. Before the trial began, the *New York Post* announced that it would publish a series of daily articles on the spy ring, authored by Leon G. Turrou, a former F.B.I. agent, who was active in developing the case. . . .*

Mr. [Jacob] Wilk, our New York story editor, noted the announcement of the *New York Post* articles and relayed this information to Jack L. Warner, who is in charge of production. The idea received a friendly reception in our production department and Wilk was authorized to inspect Mr. Turrou's material, with a view to making a motion picture. Mr. Turrou's material was impressive and we purchased the motion picture rights.

The *New York Post* articles were postponed until after the trial, which began on October 14, 1938. The defendants were convicted in a New York District Court on November 29, 1938, and sentenced on December

---

*A character based to a degree on Turrou was portrayed in the film by Edward G. Robinson.

2. The Turrou articles were then printed by the *Post* and syndicated in many newspapers throughout the country.

As the Federal trial progressed, the testimony was used by our company as a practical basis for the picture. In addition, our script writers had the Turrou articles which described in detail the F.B.I investigation preceding the trial. For additional facts, our writers referred to a great many current books, magazines and newspaper articles, particularly an article in the *American* magazine, written by Joseph F. Dinneen and captioned "An American Fuehrer organizes an Army", and articles in the *Chicago Daily News* written by John C. Metcalfe. Mr. Metcalfe was not writing hear-say. As a reporter for the *Chicago Daily News*, Mr. Metcalfe joined the German-American Bund, in order that he might have first hand knowledge of the Bund's operation.

The final script was rechecked for accuracy and the resulting effort was a carefully prepared picture, portraying—on the basis of factual happenings—Nazi espionage within this country, the semi-military German-American Bund camps within the United States and the tie-in of these bunds with Nazi Germany. . . .

I can not conceive how any patriotic citizen could object to a picture accurately recording a danger already existing within our country. . . .

There has been a great deal of loose talk that we are producing pictures, such as *Confessions of a Nazi Spy*, that the public does not wish to see. Civic, patriotic and labor organizations endorsed this picture. Hundreds of thousands of movie patrons paid to see it. Contrary to rumors, the pictures made a sizable profit. . . .

Of course, *Confessions of a Nazi Spy* was criticized by pro-Nazi sympathizers. For example, in its May 18, 1939, issue the newspaper of the German-American Bund said:

> The producer of this nightmarish concoction has drawn for his material on the choicest collection of flubdub that a diseased mind could possibly pick out of the public ashcan.

But loyal Americans of German descent reacted favorably to the picture. . . .

I want to point out that although we have produced 140 feature pictures in the last 2-½ years, only seven have been alleged to be propaganda. . . .

If Warner Brothers had produced no pictures concerning the Nazi movement, our public would have had good reason to criticize. We would have been living in a dream-world. Today 70% of the non-fiction books published deal with the Nazi menace. Today 10% of the fiction novels are anti-Nazi in theme. Today 10% of all material submitted to us for consideration is anti-Nazi in character. Today the newspapers and radio devote a good portion of their facilities to describing Naziism. Today there is a war involving all hemispheres except our own and touching the lives of all of us. . . .

There is one last charge against the motion picture industry that I have not mentioned. In essence, it is that we support Britain and oppose Naziism because we have a financial stake in Britain.

Warner Brothers receives a net revenue of approximately $5,000,000 a year from Britain. If we were to stop receiving this revenue, we would continue to operate, just as we did in 1932 through 1934, when our gross revenue declined by $50,000,000. If we were able to adjust our affairs to offset this loss in revenue, then I certainly am not worried about a drop of $5,000,000. In truth, this charge challenges our business judgment and our patriotism.

No one with any business judgment could possibly have acted on the assumption that the policy of this country towards England would be influenced by the relatively small investment of our industries in England.

Warner Brothers has certainly not acted on the theory that our government would pull our chestnuts out of the fire.

When we saw Hitler emerge in Germany, we did not try nor did we ask our government to appease him. We voluntarily liquidated our business in Germany. Business is based on keeping contracts, and Hitler does not keep his contracts with men, or with nations. No one can do business with Hitler's Germany. If, God forbid, a similar situation should arise in Britain, we would follow the same course as we did in Germany. . . .

In conclusion, I tell this committee honestly, I care nothing for any temporary advantage or profit that may be offered to me or my company. I will not censor the dramatization of the works of reputable and well informed writers to conceal from the American people what is happening in the world. Freedom of speech, freedom of religion and freedom of enterprise cannot be bought at the price of other people's rights. I believe the American people have a right to know the truth. You may correctly charge me with being anti-Nazi. But no one can charge me with being anti-American.

Thank you, gentlemen, for your courtesy in listening to me. (Applause)

Other industry figures such as Darryl Zanuck testified. Shortly thereafter the hearings collapsed.

TO: Hal Wallis   DATE: December 26, 1941
FROM: Vincent Sherman   SUBJECT: "Forced Landing"
        [contract writer-director]

Dear Hal:

Read *Forced Landing* [*Desperate Journey*, 1942] yesterday and thought it was very well written, in so far as the actual writing goes. The overabundance of German dialogue could be cut down, but it seems to me good that it remain in German since this would give a certain authenticity to the piece. However, as you may remember from our discussion after I read the treatment, it was my feeling that, while this was an excellent framework for a story, its greatest weakness was that it didn't have a story. And—what was true of the treatment is true, also, of the screenplay.

But I think I can explain a little better now what I mean by its lacking a story. Once the men make their first escape you could very easily leave out every following sequence and simply go to the end without losing anything in so far as story is concerned. They make one hairbreadth escape after another and at the end of the piece are at the same point they were in the beginning without anything of consequence having developed in between. Comparing it with *All Through the Night* [1942], there were many things that developed and transpired from the beginning of the chase to the end. . . .

Since the set-up in *Forced Landing* is so good, I think the story should and could be licked. . . .

Sherman, formerly a stage actor and director, signed with Warner Bros. as a writer, director, and actor in 1937. In 1939, he began directing at the studio. Desperate Journey, for the most part, remained a series of chases and escapes without a strong story development.

TO: Hal Wallis   DATE: February 13, 1942
FROM: Raoul Walsh   SUBJECT: "Desperate Journey"

Dear Hal:

The Epstein Boys [Julius and Philip] have added a little zip to the script, why not let them continue with it, and keep a little ahead of me.

In going over the script last night, I think for the story and laughs, we should try to carry [Alan] Hale a little longer in the script, and I would like to give him a more physical death; such as, a scene where he uses his brute strength, chokes a guard or something, or holds a closed door, and lets the others escape, and he could be shot through the door.

As there is quite a lot of joking in the script now, and I like it, I think it might be a good twist to have a sort of a "Musketeers" feeling of great comrad[e]ship between our men. Frankly, they don't think they have a Chinaman's chance of ever escaping, so they are going to have a "Roman" holiday, and do all the damage they can, blow up all the military equipment they can lay their hands on—

Raoul

Walsh's suggestions were followed.

Casablanca
(1941–1943)

Immediately after Pearl Harbor, a Warner story analyst named Stephen Karnot in the normal course of his working routine synopsized an unproduced play submitted to the studio.

Stage Play   "Everybody Comes To Rick's"
Rec'd Ms from NY   Reader: [Stephen] Karnot
12/8/41   12/11/41

Everybody Comes To Rick's
by
Murray Burnett & Joan Alison

Rick Blaine, American owner of de luxe Rick's Cafe in Casablanca, French Morocco, is a taciturn man of mystery to his patrons—wealthy French expatriates; refugees; French, German and Italian officers. Cynically indifferent, Rick enforces an atmosphere of strict neutrality in his powderkeg of political tension. Only Rinaldo, French. Prefect of Police, Rick's professed friend, knows of his background as a famous criminal lawyer in Paris, his affair with a woman, his divorce from his wife and children in '39, his abandonment of career and flight into oblivion. But only Sam, Rick's devoted Negro entertainer, knows what's in Rick's embittered heart. Ugarte, peddler of stolen exit visas, asks Rick to hold a pair of priceless letters-of-transit signed by Weygand. He plans to sell them for a fabulous sum this evening, and quit Casablanca and the racket. Rinaldo enters with Strasser, Gestapo agent, seeking to prevent recently arrived Victor Laszlo—wealthy Czech patriot hunted by the Nazis for his fearless underground activity—from buying the letters from Ugarte. Rick plays dumb, but Ugarte is arrested. On their exit enters Laszlo, accompanied by beautiful Lois Meredith. Rick is almost visibly shaken by her presence—their casual greeting betrays their past connection. Strasser privately gives Laszlo an ultimatum. Unless he signs over his foreign-banked millions to Germany, he will never leave Casablanca. Laszlo calmly defies him. Later, after all have left, Sam begs Rick to avoid re-entanglement with Lois. But Rick cannot. She soon returns alone, and spends the night with him. In the morning, torn between unquenchable love and deep distrust, Rick challenges her motives. Frankly admitting admiration for valiant Laszlo, she insists she loves Rick, wants to stay with him. But she owes Laszlo a debt. Rick promises to help Laszlo. Rinaldo enters, and with one remark makes it clear to Rick that Lois is playing him for a sucker. Rick tersely, viciously, rejects her re-assertion of love. That evening, when Laszlo, followed by Lois, comes seeking Ugarte, Rick, now drinking heavily, insults them both. Rinaldo brings news of Ugarte's suicide—bluntly charges Rick with possession of the letters, but Rick outbluffs him. Rinaldo introduces Jan and Annina Viereck, young, bewildered, newly-wed Bulgarian refugees. When Annina confides to Rick she has agreed to yield to Rinaldo for the sake of an exit visa for Jan, Rick's cynicism is pierced; he begins to understand Lois. Rinaldo makes passes at Annina, Jan knocks him down. As he screams for his gendarmes, the lights go out. When they come on, the Vierecks have disappeared. After a vain search, Rinaldo summarily closes the cafe, promising Rick trouble. Later Rick brings the Vierecks from hiding, refuses to let them leave. In the morning, as Sam brings plane tickets for Lisbon, Rinaldo appears, warning Rick he is closed and will not leave town until the Vierecks are found. On his exit Lois appears; she is leaving Laszlo for Rick. Without explanation he demands her aid in helping the Vierecks. She agrees. He calls Rinaldo, offers to surrender the Vierecks. Rinaldo arrives to find Rick and Lois in rapturous embrace. Rick makes another offer; he will trap Laszlo for him, with one of the letters, if the Vierecks are allowed to leave with the other. Convinced by the lovemaking, Rinaldo agrees, calls off his police, and the Vierecks leave with the letter and plane tickets. Rick then calls Laszlo, who comes immediately for the letter. Rinaldo emerges to arrest him as he takes the letter, but Rick covers Rinaldo with a gun. Just realizing that Rick is practically committing suicide, Lois frantically tries to prevent him, but Rick insists that she accompany Laszlo. Despairing, she does. Rick, his self-respect redeemed, surrenders to Rinaldo and furious Strasser.

TO: [Irene] Lee [story editor]   DATE: December 22, 1941
FROM: Wallis' Office   SUBJECT: "Everybody Comes
                                                   To Rick's"

Dear Irene:

   Mr. Wallis would like you to please get him a price on the story
Everybody Comes To Rick's and to get reactions on it from three or four
people.

Olga

TO: Irene Lee   DATE: December 23, 1941
FROM: Jerry Wald [associate   SUBJECT: "Everybody Comes
       producer]*   To Rick's"

Dear Irene:

   This story should make a good vehicle for either Raft or Bogart. I
feel it can be easily tailored into a piece along the lines of *Algiers* [1938],
with plenty of excitement and suspense in it.

   What dialogue I read in the synopsis was very good, and I think we
should be able to get a good commercial picture out of it.

Jerry

TO: Irene Lee   DATE: December 23, 1941
FROM: [Robert] Lord   SUBJECT: "Everybody Comes
                                                   To Rick's"

Dear Irene:

   I suspect that with enough time and effort a picture could be got
from this very obvious imitation of *Grand Hotel*.

   Since it is written as a play, why not contribute a little money to its
production as a play in exchange for priority on the motion picture rights?
If it turns out to be a successful play, it would certainly be worth doing
as a picture.

Bob Lord

TO: All Departments   DATE: December 31, 1941
FROM: Hal Wallis   SUBJECT: Title Change

The story that we recently purchased entitled *Everybody Comes To Rick's*
will hereafter be known as *Casablanca*.

Hal Wallis

---

*Wald recently had been promoted from contract writer.

TO: Paul Nathan [secretary　　　　DATE: January 3, 1942
　　to Hal Wallis]　　　　　　　　SUBJECT: "Casablanca"
FROM: Aeneas MacKenzie
　　[screenwriter]

I think we can get a good picture out of this play. But it isn't a pushover; because certain characterizations—such as Rinaldo [later changed to Renault]—need very definite strengthening and certain basic situations present problems from the censorship angle. The pre-action relationship between Rick and Lois, for example, is one which does not seem permissible in a film.

These, however, can be overcome, I believe. Because behind the action and its background is the possibility of an excellent theme—the idea that when people lose faith in their ideals, they are beaten before they begin to fight. That was what happened to France and to Rick Blaine.

The chances for action are limited. But possibilities present themselves for several very emotional scenes. And the conviction of the play can be materially strengthened by having the dialogue of the characters reveal their varying national attitudes, despair, decadence and courage.

Aeneas MacKenzie

TO: Hal Wallis　　　　　　　　　　DATE: January 5, 1942
FROM: Wally Kline [screenwriter]　SUBJECT: "Everybody Comes
　　　　　　　　　　　　　　　　　　　　to Rick's"
　　　　　　　　　　　　　　　　　　　"Casablanca"

Dear Hal:
　　In taking this apart I find that when the highly censorable situations, relationships and implications are removed, we have left an American ex-lawyer in Casablanca who owns a cafe—the reasons for which are lacking. A mild plot about selling exit visas illegally. A millionaire Czech who must get to Lisbon for reasons not supplied and his very beautiful paramour who once had a lengthy affair with the American but who leaves for Lisbon with the Czech—if the original ending is to be preserved—and it should be as it is the only dramatic situation worthy of survival.

　　It will be a tough job to get a satisfactory picture out of this material, but I believe it can be done.

Wally Kline

TO: Paul Nathan　　　　　　　　　DATE: January 6, 1942
FROM: Aeneas MacKenzie　　　　　　SUBJECT: "Casablanca"

Yesterday I took *Casablanca* to pieces and made an analysis of its structure and movements. The result caused me to revise the more favorable impression left by my first reading of the play. It presents some very serious problems indeed, and has certain defects which are slurred over in its present form but which will become very apparent in a picture.

In my opinion this material will require some drastic revision, because the situation out of which the action arises is a highly censorable one. Even in the play it is merely suggested through dialogue and, in the main, left to the audience's imagination.

This is a tough job for anyone to whom it may be assigned. I do hope it gets into the hands of a producer who is strong on the literary side of a picture.

This for your information, to supplement my previous report of January 3rd.

TO: Hal Wallis   DATE: January 6, 1942
FROM: Robert Buckner   SUBJECT: "Everybody Comes
                                       To Rick's"

Dear Hal:

I do not like the play at all, Hal. I don't believe the story or the characters. Its main situations and the basic relations of the principals are completely censorable and messy, its big-moment is sheer hokum melodrama of the E. Phillips Oppenheim variety,* and this guy Rick is two-parts Hemingway, one-part Scott Fitzgerald, and a dash of cafe Christ.

Reading this back, I sound free enough, don't I.

Bob

TO: Messrs. Kline & MacKenzie   DATE: January 9, 1942
FROM: [Paul] Nathan   SUBJECT: "Casablanca"

Gentlemen:

You are definitely assigned to *Casablanca*, and Mr. Wallis would like you to start working on it immediately.

Paul Nathan

cc: Mr. Warner

TO: Warner   DATE: February 4, 1942
FROM: Nathan   SUBJECT: "Casablanca" (Epsteins)

Mr. Wallis had discussed *Casablanca* with the Epsteins before they left here, and also while they were in New York. They are anxious to do this script, and he is anxious for them on it. . . .

Paul Nathan

---

*Oppenheim was a prolific British writer of early-twentieth-century mystery novels about secret international documents, shifty diplomats, and seductive adventuresses.

After MacKenzie and Kline finished their adaptation, Julius J. and Philip G. Epstein were assigned to write the script.

TO: [Steve] Trilling [casting director]
FROM: Hal Wallis

DATE: February 5, 1942
SUBJECT: "Casablanca"

In one of our proposed pictures, *Casablanca*, there is a part now written for a colored man who plays the piano in the night club. I am thinking of making this a colored girl, and when I was in New York I saw Hazel Scott at the Uptown Cafe Society. She would be marvelous for the part. I understand that there is a colored girl out here now appearing in a Felix Young night club and I wish you would see her and tell me what you think. The one out here is Elena [Lena] Horn[e].

Hal Wallis

Wallis stayed with the male piano player.

FROM NORMAN KRASNA [screenwriter]

Sun Valley, Idaho

Circa February 13, 1942

Dear Hal:
   Zanuck leaves here tonight and Wyler probably will be forced to read *Casablanca*. They both play gin-rummy until 2:30 a.m., which, you can see, leaves little time for anything else. He hasn't read Goldwyn's story either so you can't feel slighted.
   I read *Casablanca* and think it will make a hair-raising, wonderful picture. . . .

Norman Krasna

TO: Trilling
FROM: Hal Wallis

DATE: February 14, 1942
SUBJECT: "Casablanca"

   Will you please figure on Humphrey Bogart and Ann Sheridan for *Casablanca*, which is scheduled to start the latter part of April.

TO: Trilling
FROM: Hal Wallis

DATE: February 23, 1942
SUBJECT: Hedy Lamarr re "Casablanca"

   I spoke to [MGM executive] Ben Thau—he intends to call you anyway, but he is positive he will be unable to make any arrangements on Hedy Lamarr for *Casablanca* as L. B. Mayer is opposed to loaning her out to anybody.

Steve Trilling

FROM JACK L. WARNER

Mr. Roy Obringer [general counsel]

February 24, 1942

Dear Roy:

I understand the Epsteins are leaving tomorrow, Wednesday, and that they are to be taken off salary with the understanding that if we accept the script of *Casablanca*, which they are working on while they are away, we will give them a certain sum. . . .

J. L. Warner

The Epsteins went to Washington with Frank Capra to do some preliminary work on what was to become the Why We Fight *series.*

MARCH 12, 1942
JULIUS EPSTEIN TO WALLIS—HOPE TO BE BACK MONDAY BUT MAY BE DELAYED DAY OR SO. WORK ON "CASABLANCA" PROGRESSING. RE-GARDS.

TO: Mike Curtiz [director]   DATE: April 1, 1942
FROM: Hal Wallis   SUBJECT: "Casablanca"

Dear Mike:

We will go ahead with the test of Michele Morgan [for the leading female role].

Trilling is arranging for the Epsteins to tell the story to [Dan] O'Shea at Selznick and, if they like it, they will have Miss [Ingrid] Bergman come back from New York to go into the matter further.

Hal Wallis

"They" liked it, and Miss Bergman came back from New York to go into the matter further.

TO: Hal Wallis   DATE: April 2, 1942
FROM: Jack L. Warner

What do you think of using Raft in *Casablanca?*

He knows we are going to make this and is starting a campaign for it.

Jack

TO: Jack Warner   DATE: April 13, 1942
FROM: Hal Wallis   SUBJECT: "Casablanca"

Dear Jack:

I have thought over very carefully the matter of George Raft in *Casablanca*, and I have discussed this with Mike, and we both feel that he should not be in the picture. Bogart is ideal for it, and it is being written for him, and I think we should forget Raft for this property.

Incidentally, he hasn't done a picture here since I was a little boy, and I don't think he should be able to put his fingers on just what he wants to do when he wants to do it.

Hal Wallis

TO: Hal Wallis   DATE: April 14, 1942
FROM: Steve Trilling   SUBJECT: Ingrid Bergman
                         "Casablanca"

6:30 P.M.

Dan O'Shea called after just speaking to David O. [Selznick] in Pittsburgh—and the only deal they can effect on Ingrid Bergman is an even swap for Olivia de Havilland.

He refused to give us Bergman for two pictures but promised an "understanding" that should they make any outside deal—except for *For Whom the Bell Tolls*, which has been pending for some time—Warner Bros. would be given first consideration (which really means nothing but a courtesy).

They will give us 8 weeks time on Bergman and we in turn are to give them 8 weeks on de Havilland on a 30 days advance notice—services to be completed within the year commencing May 15, 1942. I promised to advise tomorrow around noon, so will you kindly give me your reaction.

Steve Trilling

Bergman was signed for Casablanca *on April 24, and she also made* Saratoga Trunk *(1945) for Warners. Instead of using Olivia de Havilland for a film, Selznick loaned her to RKO for* Government Girl *(1943).*

TO: Hal Wallis   DATE: April 14, 1942
FROM: Steve Trilling   SUBJECT: Part of "Capt. Heinrich
                         Strasser" in "Casablanca"

Have made an appointment for [producer-director-actor] Otto Preminger for 11:30 a.m., Wednesday (April 15th)—we had him in mind for "Capt. Heinrich Strasser" in *Casablanca*.

Steve Trilling

TO: Mike Curtiz   DATE: April 22, 1942
FROM: Hal Wallis   SUBJECT: "Casablanca"

Dear Mike:

I have been going over with Trilling the possibilities for the part of "Laszlo" and, aside from Philip Dorn, whom we cannot get, and Paul Henreid who I am sure will not play the part when he reads it, there is no one else that I can think of. I think you should satisfy yourself on this point; that is, that there is no one available, and then begin to adjust yourself to the thought that we might have to use someone of the type of Dean Jagger, Ian Hunter or Herbert Marshall, or someone of this type without an accent.

I am as anxious as you are to have a type like Philip Dorn in the part, but if there is no one available there is just nothing that we can do about it.

Hal Wallis

TO: Mike Curtiz   DATE: April 22, 1942
FROM: Hal Wallis   SUBJECT: "Casablanca"

Dear Mike:

The test of Dooley Wilson [for the role of "Sam"] is pretty good. He isn't ideal for the part but if we get stuck and can't do any better I suppose he could play it.

I didn't particularly like the way the scene was played however, and I think we should have a talk about this so that we are in agreement in the manner of characterization. I didn't like the flip, bouncy manner of the man and it was always my impression that he would be really worried about 'Rick' and that when he said: "Come on, boss. Let's go fishing. Let's get out of here—we'll go for a long drive," etc., etc., that he was pleading with the man, knowing what the results would be if he left him there for "Lois" [changed to "Ilsa"].

What happened to the test we were going to make of Clarence Muse? . . .

Hal Wallis

TO: Steve Trilling   DATE: April 23, 1942
FROM: Hal Wallis   SUBJECT: "Casablanca"

. . . I was going to talk to you about Joseph Cotten [for the role of "Laszlo"], after seeing him in *Lydia* [1941], and Mike told me this morning he had already discussed him with you. I think Cotten could do it, so let me know when you get your dope.

Hal Wallis

TO: Hal Wallis   DATE: May 1, 1942
FROM: Steve Trilling   SUBJECT: Clarence Muse "Casablanca"

We have a hold on Clarence Muse for the part of "Sam The Rabbit," in *Casablanca*, but Metro are now interested in testing him also for *White Cargo*, which starts around May 11, and will run around four weeks. The agent has asked we give him an answer by Monday as he does not want to lose out on both jobs. . . .

Steve Trilling

TO: Steve Trilling   DATE: May 1, 1942
FROM: Hal Wallis   SUBJECT: "Casablanca"

Clarence Muse is okay with me, and in view of the interest elsewhere, I think we should sign him.

Check with Mike, and if it is all right with him, go ahead and make the deal.

Hal Wallis

For reasons unknown the deal was not made.

TO: Hal Wallis   DATE: May 1, 1942
FROM: Steve Trilling

Re Paul Henreid for *Casablanca*:

Discussed making a separate picture deal with his agent first before talking to Henreid. As you know, we have been trying to work out a deal to take over his RKO contract—and one of the deterrents was Henreid's reluctance to assign himself here exclusively—and then possibly be relegated to small parts. In this respect, you are aware by this time, he is a bit of a ham—and until the negotiations for the RKO deal are behind us—which should be in the next few days—I think we should let this separate picture deal ride. . . .

An obstacle we encountered in consummating the original deal was the billing situation—and after great persuasion, we got him to accept a special billing clause for the first two pictures—thereafter, he was to be starred or co-starred and I think if he gets assurance of co-star billing with Bogart and Bergman, it would clinch the matter. This might not be such a bad idea if we really are attempting to build him.

Steve Trilling

TO: Steve Trilling   DATE: May 1, 1942
FROM: Hal Wallis   SUBJECT: "Casablanca"

If we can get Henreid for *Casablanca*, we will give him co-star billing with Bogart and Bergman.

Hal Wallis

TO: C. H. Wilder [comptroller]   DATE: May 3, 1942
FROM: R. J. Obringer   SUBJECT: "Casablanca"

We are borrowing the services of Dooley Wilson from Paramount Pictures, Inc. for our photoplay now entitled *Casablanca* commencing on or before June 1, 1942, for a guaranteed period of 7 weeks at $500.00 per week, and an 8th week free if necessary, and pro rata at $500 per week beyond 6 weeks.

R. J. Obringer

TO: Mike Curtiz   DATE: May 6, 1942
FROM: Hal Wallis   SUBJECT: "Casablanca"

Dear Mike:

The Epsteins are sending in the balance of the script covering the second act, and there will be a copy in your office tomorrow morning at 10:00 o'clock. I will also have a copy and will read it immediately and we will have a conference with the Epsteins at 11:00, as they feel that they cannot proceed with the last act without first having a conference. . . .

I should judge that the balance will take them another week or ten days.

Hal Wallis

TO: Mike Curtiz   DATE: May 8, 1942
FROM: Hal Wallis   SUBJECT: "Casablanca"

Dear Mike:

I wish you would immediately get together with [art director] Carl Weyl, make up a list of our sets in the picture, see what you can find standing [in stock] that will fit your action, and then I will go around with you so that we may definitely arrive at a decision on what sets you are going to use, and Weyl can then do whatever revamping is necessary.

Let's do this in the next two or three days.

Hal Wallis

TO: [Howard] Koch [screenwriter]   DATE: May 11, 1942
FROM: Hal Wallis   SUBJECT: "Casablanca"

Dear Howard:

I will appreciate anything you can do to speed up the balance of the script. We are starting production next Monday, and I am very anxious to get as much script out as possible.

I think this next batch of the Epsteins' stuff is for the most part good. There are one or two things that I did not like, and I understand from Mike that you too were opposed to them. These are the bus scenes around the Black Market and the hotel scene—the gargling, etc., which I am of course opposed to—but aside from this, I think almost everything of the Epsteins is useable.

Will you please step on it as much as possible and get this next batch through to me within the next two or three days if you can.

Hal Wallis

Koch was put on the script while the Epsteins continued to write their version.

TO: Hal Wallis   DATE: May 11, 1942
FROM: Howard Koch   SUBJECT: "Casablanca"

Dear Hal:

Although the Epstein script follows in a general way, the new story line, I feel it is written in a radically different vein from the work I've just finished on the first half of the picture. They apparently see the situations more in terms of their comic possibilities, while my effort has been to legitimize the characters and develop a serious melodrama of present-day significance, using humor merely as a relief from dramatic tension. I am not presuming to decide which is the better way to attack the picture, but certainly they are different from the ground up.

From my talk this morning with Mike, I was left with the impression that you and he both wanted me to continue with the more serious treatment, using whatever parts of the Epstein script coincided with this intention. I was proceeding to plan out the scenes in this next part along those lines, when I received your letter, which puts an entirely different complexion on the assignment.

If you are in favor of the approach taken by the Epsteins, it would seem to me best that they do the patching on the few places you don't like. Frankly, to a large extent, I've been writing, and would continue to write, a new screenplay, gladly availing myself of what material I feel I could use from their script and from the original play. With the best of intentions, I would be lost trying to do anything less.

As for speeding up the script, ever since I was called on the assignment I've been working as hard as I can—first on the construction of the story, then on the first half of the screenplay. I would continue to work hard, but I can't turn out a third of the screenplay in three days—not the kind of screenplay I thought you and Mike wanted.

Howard Koch

Wallis had asked contract writer Casey Robinson to read over the composite script of Casablanca *and offer suggestions. Robinson, years later, claimed that he had read the play while traveling East with Wallis, urged him to buy it, and was disappointed when he was not assigned the screenplay.*

TO: Hal Wallis DATE: May 20, 1942
FROM: Casey Robinson SUBJECT: "Casablanca"

NOTES ON SCREENPLAY "CASABLANCA"

Again, as before, my impression about *Casablanca* is that the melodrama is well done, the humor excellent, but the love story deficient. Therefore, my comments are almost all concerned with the latter. . . .

The first meeting between Rick and Ilsa must occur late that night in the cafe when she comes back to talk to him, much along the lines of the scene I wrote for the test. That is, it is Rick's bitterness, his brutality (which spring from his wounded pride) which stop Ilsa from telling him and make her angry enough and disillusioned enough to go home. In other words, her disillusionment in him and what he has become instead of the old Ricky she remembers, is for the moment enough to turn her away from him and send her home. . . .

The next scene between them should occur in Rick's apartment above the cafe that afternoon. Ilsa does come. She comes, as she tells Rick, because she was angry last night and even this morning, but she has been thinking it over and she can easily see why he thinks of her as he does. She wants to clear that up, because she loves Rick, because the days they had together in Paris were the most beautiful in her life. She does clear it up. She tells him Laszlo is her husband. She tells him all the background of their marriage, and tells him the real reason she didn't come to the train in Paris. She tells him she loves her husband and explains the quality of that love—her admiration, respect, even veneration. To her [Laszlo] is the personification of the best ideals of her nature, of honor, of sacrifice for a great cause. Rick understands, softens, is ashamed of himself. . . .

Right on top of this business comes the scene between Laszlo and

Rick. It should go as follows: After Ilsa has seen Rick this afternoon, she has gone home to Laszlo and told him that she thinks perhaps they have a friend, someone who may be able to help them. I don't think this scene need be shown. Laszlo tells it to Rick. To Rick it means one thing, that Ilsa, this afternoon when she has come and been nice and told him she loved him, was softening him up for this touch. He doesn't know this for a certainty, perhaps, but he suspects it. He suspects he has been played for a sucker, and if there is anything Rick doesn't like to be, it's a sucker. So he tells 'no' to Laszlo and when Laszlo wants to know why, he says, "Ask your wife". Now this speech has much more significance. . . .

I would play the beginning of the next scene between Rick and Ilsa pretty much as it is, but greatly alter the finish. Ilsa comes for the visas. She tries to be hard-boiled. She can't be. She breaks down completely. But completely. She tells Rick that she loves him and will do anything he wants. She will go anywhere, stay here, anything. She is absolutely helpless in the great passionate love she has for him. She will leave Victor. Rick can get him out of Casablanca. She knows that she's doing wrong, she even says so. She knows that in a way it is a violation of all the high idealism and honor of her nature. She knows she is being wicked but she can't help herself. This is a great scene for a woman to play.

At the end of the scene, she says that she will go home to her husband and tell him. With an enigmatic look on his face, Rick tells her not to do it. Better that she come with her husband to his place for the letters without telling her husband first, for otherwise he might not come. Better, anyway, that they tell him together.

Now you're really set up for a swell twist when Rick sends her away on the plane with Victor. For now, in doing so, he is not just solving a love triangle. He is forcing the girl to live up to the idealism of her nature, forcing her to carry on with the work that in these days is far more important than the love of two little people. It is something they will both be glad for when the pain is over. . . .

FROM JOSEPH I. BREEN,
[director of the Production Code Administration]

Mr. J. L. Warner
Burbank, California

May 21, 1942

Dear Mr. Warner:
. . . The present material contains certain elements which seem to be unacceptable from the standpoint of the Production Code. Specifically, we cannot approve the present suggestion that Capt. Renault makes a practice of seducing the women to whom he grants

visas. Any such inference of illicit sex could not be approved in the finished picture.

Going through this new material, we call your attention to the following: . . .

Page 86: The suggestion that Ilsa was married all the time she was having her love affair with Rick in Paris seems unacceptable, and could not be approved in the finished picture. Hence, we request the deletion of Ilsa's line "Even when I knew you in Paris".

We will be happy to read the balance of the script, and to report further, whenever you have it ready.

Cordially yours,
Joseph I. Breen

FROM JACK L. WARNER

May 23, 1942

Dear Mike:

These are turbulent days and I know you will finish *Casablanca* in top seven weeks.

I am depending on you to be the old Curtiz I know you to be, and I am positive you are going to make one great picture.

The budget was not exceptionally high for its time, nor would it be regarded as a cheap picture. A film that cost $1,000,000 and up was considered a big-budget picture then. For example, some comparison costs of Warner Bros. pictures produced about the same time: The Maltese Falcon—$375,000; They Died with Their Boots On—$1,357,000; The Sea Wolf—$1,013,217; Knute Rockne—$645,618; Kings Row—$1,081,698; The Great Lie—$689,253. Casablanca's *final cost was approximately $950,000.*

TO: [Arthur] Edeson [director of photography]
FROM: Hal Wallis

DATE: May 26, 1942
SUBJECT: "Casablanca"

I don't want to enter a complaint of your first day's efforts, because I know that you are trying very hard and because I know that you want to give me a top job.

However, I understand that the setup took an extraordinary length of time yesterday and that the little Montmarte Cafe scene which Mike lined up yesterday afternoon, but did not shoot, took about an hour and a half to light. This was a very small set involving only two people and, if it is true that it took an hour and a half to get the lighting set, I must say that it is unreasonable.

I, too, want a beautiful photographic job on this picture, which offers a great deal of background and color for a cameraman, but you were present at all the meetings we had about all the war emergencies and the necessity of conserving money and material, and I must ask you to sacrifice a little on quality, if necessary, in order not to take these long periods of time for setups. If we continue to move as slowly as we did yesterday, we will run way over on our time and money on the picture, and this we cannot have happen.

I appreciate your cooperation.

Hal Wallis

June 2, 1942

	BUDGET #410 CASABLANCA			
1.	*Story Cost*			20,000
1a.	*Continuity & Treatment*			
	W. Klein [Kline]	1,983		
	A. MacKenzie	2,150		
	J. Epstein	15,208		
	P. Epstein	15,208		
	H. Koch	4,200		
	L. [Lenore] Coffee	750		
	Secretaries	1,432		
	Script Changes	6,350		
				47,281
2.	*Director*			
	Michael Curtiz			73,400
2a.	*Producer*			
	Hal Wallis			52,000
3.	*Assistant Directors*			9,837
4.	*Cameramen & Assistants*			10,873
5a.	*Cast Salaries*			
5b.	*Contract Talent*			
	Rick-Humphrey Bogart	36,667		
	Martinez-Sydney Greenstreet*	7,500		
	Laszlo-Paul Henreid	25,000		
	Yvonne-Madeleine LeBeau 3½ @			
	100 dbl	700		
			69,867	

5c.	Outside Talent			
	Ilsa-Ingrid Bergman	25,000		
	Renault-Claude Rains 5½ @4000	22,000		
	Annina-Joy Page 2 @100	200		
	Strasser-Conrad Veidt	25,000		
	Carl-part 6½ @400	2,600		
	Sam-Dooley Wilson	3,500		
	Sascha-part 5⅔ @400	2,267		
	Ugarte-Peter Lorre 1⅓ @1750	2,333		
	Abdul-Dan Seymour 4 @250	1,000		
	Heinze-part 4 @400	1,600		
	Berger-part 1 @400	400		
	Farrari-part 4 @ 100	400		
	Tonelli-part 4 @75	300		
	Pickpocket-Curt Bois 1 @1000	1,000		
	Jan-H. Dantine 2 @400	800		
	Andreya-Corinna Mura 4 @500	2,000		
	Croupier-Marcel Dalio 1⅓ @500	667		
	Headwaiter-part 2 @150	300		
	Waiter-part 2⅓ @150	350		
			91,717	
				161,584
6.	Talent [extras, bits, etc.]			56,019
7.	Musicians [arrangers, etc.]			28,000
8.	Property Labor			10,150
9.	Construction of Sets			18,000
10.	Stand by Labor			15,350
11.	Electricians			20,755
12.	Striking			7,000
12a.	Make Up [Hairdressers, etc.]			9,100
13.	Art Department Salaries			8,846
14.	Cutters' Salaries			4,630
15.	Property Rental & Expense			6,300
16.	Electrical Rental & Expense			750
17.	Location Expense			1,252
18.	Trick, Miniature etc.			7,475

19.	Wardrobe Expense		22,320
20.	Negative Film		8,000
22.	Developing & Printing		10,500
25.	Camera Rental & Expense		400
26.	Meals		1,200
27.	Auto Rental Expense & Travel		5,000
28.	Insurance		2,800
29.	Miscellaneous Expense		3,350
30.	Sound Expense		2,200
31.	Trailer**		2,000
32.	Sound Operating Salaries		8,000
34.	Stills		850
34a.	Publicity Total Direct Cost		3,000 $638,222
35.	General Studio Overhead @ 35%		223,822
40.	Depreciation @ 2½% Grand Total Cost		15,956 $878,000

*"Martinez" was changed to "Farrari."
**A short publicity film made for theatres, which was usually preceded by the title, "Previews of Coming Attractions."

TO: [S. Charles] Einfeld [director   DATE: June 3, 1942
of publicity and advertising,   SUBJECT: "Casablanca"
New York]
FROM: R. J. Obringer

We have borrowed the services of Conrad Veidt from Loew's Incorporated [parent company of MGM] for our photoplay now entitled Casablanca, and have agreed that Mr. Veidt's name will be featured on the main title of all positive prints of said photoplay. . . .

R. J. Obringer

TO: Mike Curtiz　　　　　　DATE: June 3, 1942
FROM: Hal Wallis　　　　　　SUBJECT: "Casablanca"

Dear Mike:

There are a couple of new costume changes for Ingrid Bergman, evening outfits, and I wish you would look at them and then talk to me.

The outfits, in my opinion, are okay. I prefer the Number 11 with just a clip instead of all the necklaces. But my point in writing you is that we should think seriously about whether this girl should ever appear in an evening outfit. After all, these two people are trying to escape from the country. The Gestapo is after them; they are refugees, making their way from country to country, and they are not going to Rick's Cafe for social purposes. It seems a little incongruous to me for her to dress up in evening clothes as though she carried a wardrobe with her. I think it would be better for Henreid to wear a plain sport outfit, or a palm beach suit, and if she wore just a plain little street suit. Somehow or other these evening costumes seem to rub me the wrong way. . . .

Hal Wallis

FROM JOSEPH I. BREEN

Mr. J. L. Warner
Burbank, California

June 5, 1942

Dear Mr. Warner:

This is sent to you as a confirmation of the understanding reached yesterday with Mr. Hal Wallis with regard to the incomplete script for your production titled *Casablanca*. . . .

With a view to removing the now offensive characterization of Renault as an immoral man who engages himself in seducing women to whom he grants visas, it has been agreed with Mr. Wallis that the several references to this particular phase of the gentleman's character will be materially toned down, to-wit:

Page 5: The line in scene 15 "The girl will be released in the morning" will be changed to the expression "Will be released later." . . .

Page 75: . . . the word "joy" in Renault's line is to be changed to the word "like". "You like war. I like women".

Page 76: Renault's line "At least your work keeps you outdoors" is to be changed to "Gets you plenty of fresh air." . . .

Cordially yours,
Joseph I. Breen

TO: [John] Kotanan [accounting
    department]
FROM: R. J. Obringer

DATE: June 18, 1942
SUBJECT: Casey Robinson

Casey Robinson has, at the request of Mr. Wallis, interrupted work on the script presently assigned to him, to do some polishing work on our script *Casablanca*, and for his services on *Casablanca*, we have agreed to pay him 2 weeks' salary at $3000 per week. This compensation is, of course, outside of and in addition to his regular contract compensation. . . .

R. J. Obringer

Robinson worked on the script for three and a half weeks and contributed considerably to the romantic scenes (see "Notes" of May 20, 1942).

TO: Mike Curtiz
FROM: Hal Wallis

DATE: July 6, 1942
SUBJECT: "Casablanca"

Dear Mike:

I see that tomorrow you are shooting in the Cafe with Laszlo and Ilsa arriving and with Renault putting Laszlo under arrest. All of this in the new rewrite on which we are working with Koch is the same as in your present Revised Final Script. . . .

I think we have successfully licked the big scene between Ilsa and Rick at the airport by bringing Laszlo in at the finish of it.

It was practically impossible to write a convincing scene between the two people in which Rick could sell Ilsa on the idea of leaving without him. No arguments that Rick could put up would be sufficient to sway her from her decision to remain, and that, I think, is why we always had so much trouble in trying to write such a scene between the two people.

However, by bringing Laszlo in for the additional few lines, it makes it impossible for Ilsa to protest further and in this way the scene can be finished convincingly. . . .

Hal Wallis

TO: Leo Forbstein [music director]
FROM: Wallis' Office

DATE: July 11, 1942

Mr. Wallis would appreciate your sending him answers on the following about which he has previously written:

Can Mr. Wallis figure on [staff composer-conductor Max] Steiner doing *Casablanca*?

Mr. Wallis would like to know if you have set a double to do Dooley Wilson's songs for *Casablanca*. This sequence, and Wilson, are all finished, and Mr. Wallis would like to get this done and get the track made so he can see how it works cut.

Olga

In the final version, Dooley Wilson's singing was used. Max Steiner was assigned the score.

TO: T. C. Wright [studio   DATE: July 18, 1942
    production manager]   SUBJECT: "Casablanca"—Curtiz
FROM: Al Alleborn [unit manager]

Report for FRIDAY, 7-17-42. 45th shooting day.

Company had a 9:00 o'clock call on Stage 1 to shoot the EXT. AIRPORT. First shot at 9:50 AM and the last one at 6:14 PM. . . .

Cast worked: BOGART, BERGMAN, RAINS, HENREID. . . .

During the day the company had several delays caused by arguments with Curtiz the director, and Bogart the actor. I had to go out and get Wallis and bring him over to the set to straighten out the situation. At one time they sat around for a long time and argued, finally deciding on how to do the scene.

There were also numerous delays due to the cast not knowing the dialogue, which was a rewritten scene that came out the night before. . . .

Al Alleborn

TO: Hal Wallis   DATE: July 20, 1942
FROM: Al Alleborn   SUBJECT: "Casablanca"

I talked to Steve Trilling who was very much upset over the Sydney Greenstreet situation. This note will explain the reasons Greenstreet will go over his guarantee of two weeks at $3750 a week. . . .

We have not been concentrating on Greenstreet, because we have been attempting to finish Claude Rains at $4000 a week, Conrad Veidt at approximately the same figure, both of which finish in the Airport Sequence which we are shooting now. By the company remaining on Stage 8, shooting the Interior Rick's Cafe, we were working with most of our cast and finished a set that had costly rentals and was needed by another company.

We have been trying to save money on this company by taking advantage of the street on the back lot. It was built for *Desert Song*, and the idea was that the Curtiz Company would take it as it was after *The*

Desert Song Company finished it. At the present time, the [director Robert] Florey Company is shooting this exterior, and the set has not been available to the Curtiz Company. . . .

There is very little expense involved with the exception of talent for the balance of the picture, so I am sure this picture will come in well under the budget.

Al Alleborn

TO: Colonel Warner   DATE: July 23, 1942
FROM: Hal Wallis   SUBJECT: "Casablanca"

Dear Jack:

. . . The Epsteins have been asking payment of . . . money, and you will have to make the decision as to whether or not they are going to be paid.

You will recall that they went to Washington for [producer-director Frank] Capra, and that they were to work on the [*Casablanca*] script while they were away. It is true that they did bring back some script with them, but this was practically all rewritten and their three weeks' absence put us into the hole which necessitated bringing in the other writers, etc., etc.

TO: Mike Curtiz   DATE: August 3, 1942
FROM: Hal Wallis   SUBJECT: "Casablanca"

Confidentially, Ingrid Bergman is getting the part of "Maria" in *For Whom the Bell Tolls*. They wanted to send her on location to Sonora tonight, but I prevailed upon them to wait until Wednesday night, in case we had any retakes. Therefore, we will run the picture tomorrow night, or possibly tomorrow afternoon, at which time we will determine whether or not there will be any retakes with Bergman on Wednesday.

Hal Wallis

TO: Owen Marks [film editor]   DATE: August 7, 1942
FROM: Hal Wallis   SUBJECT: "Casablanca"

Attached is copy of the new narration for the opening of the picture.

There are also to be two wild lines made by Bogart. Mike is trying to get Bogart today, but if he does not succeed, will you get Bogart in within the next couple of days.

The two lines to be shot with Bogart, in the event that Mike does not get them, are:

RICK:
Louis, I might have known you'd mix your patriotism with a little larceny.

(alternate line)

RICK:

Louis, I think this is the beginning of a beautiful friendship. . . .

Hal Wallis

TO: Mike Curtiz   DATE: August 21, 1942
FROM: Hal Wallis   SUBJECT: "Casablanca"

The new line to be spoken by Bogart when we get him is as follows:

RICK:

OUR expenses—(pause)—Louis, I think this is the beginning of a beautiful friendship.

Hal Wallis

FROM HAL B. WALLIS

CUTTING NOTES
REEL #2
CASABLANCA

September 2, 1942

. . . Start the piano as Ilsa and Laszlo come in the door. You can stop the piano playing at the table with Ilsa when Renault brings Strasser over to the table. Then don't start the music again until Sam introduces the guitar player. When Ilsa calls Sam over to play, let that go on just as it is until the scene is interrupted by Renault coming back, saying: "Oh, you have already met Rick". Now, at that point, when Rick and Ilsa exchange glances, on the first of their close-ups, start an orchestration using "As Time Goes By". And *score* the scene. Let Steiner do this. And carry this until right through the Exterior until the lights go out.

Hal Wallis

FROM HAL B. WALLIS

MUSIC NOTES
CASABLANCA

September 2, 1942

. . . On the *Marseillaise*, when it is played in the cafe, don't do it as though it was played by this small orchestra. Do it with a full scoring orchestra and get some body to it. You should score the piece where the Gendarmes break the door in and carry that right through to the dissolve to the Police Station.

In the last reel, the last time that Bogart looks off and we cut to the plane I would like to see a dramatic pause in the music, just before the cut to the plane. Then as we cut to the plane, emphasize the motor noises and then, when you cut back to the scene, resume the music.

Hal Wallis

NOVEMBER 10, 1942

WARNER TO . . . [NEW YORK EXECUTIVES]—HAVE JUST RUN "CASA-BLANCA" AND IT'S IMPOSSIBLE TO CHANGE THIS PICTURE AND MAKE SENSE WITH STORY WE TOLD ORIGINALLY. STORY WE WANT TO TELL OF [allies] LANDING AND EVERYTHING WOULD HAVE TO BE A COMPLETE NEW PICTURE AND WOULD NOT FIT IN THE PRESENT FILM. IT'S SUCH A GREAT PICTURE AS IT IS, WOULD BE A MISREPRESENTATION IF WE WERE TO COME IN NOW WITH A SMALL TAG SCENE ABOUT AMERICAN TROOPS LANDING ETCETERA, WHICH AS I HAVE ALREADY SAID IS A COMPLETE NEW STORY IN ITSELF. . . . ENTIRE INDUSTRY ENVIES US WITH PICTURE HAVING TITLE "CASABLANCA" READY TO RELEASE, AND FEEL WE SHOULD TAKE ADVANTAGE OF THIS GREAT SCOOP. NATURALLY THE LONGER WE WAIT TO RELEASE IT THE LESS IMPORTANT TITLE WILL BE, WHILE "YANKEE DOODLE DANDY" WILL NOT DETERIORATE.

Allied forces had landed in Axis-occupied Casablanca just a few days earlier. New York executives were inquiring whether the completed film could be modified in any way to take advantage of the timely event.

TO: [Tenny] Wright   DATE: November 11, 1942
FROM: Hal Wallis   SUBJECT: "Casablanca"

There will be a retake on *Casablanca* involving Claude Rains and Humphrey Bogart, and about 50 or 60 extras. Free French uniforms will be required for all of these.

We will need the deck of the freighter on Stage 7. The scene is to be a night sequence with fog.

We will also require the Interior of the Radio Room of this same ship.

Rains is in Pennsylvania, and I am asking [his agent, Mike] Levee to get him out here as quickly as possible as I want to make these scenes this week if possible.

Curtiz will shoot and we will shoot nights until the work is completed. . . .

Hal Wallis

It was decided not to do the additional scene, erroneously referred to above as a "retake."

TO: Harold McCord [editorial   DATE: November 11, 1942
supervisor]   SUBJECT: "Casablanca"
FROM: Steve Trilling

Left word through Dan O'Shea, of the David O. Selznick office, that we will have a print of *Casablanca* back in the studio by this coming Friday, the 13th, and we would run it here at the studio only for David O., his wife and Dan O'Shea—but only for these limited few. . . .

Steve Trilling

NOVEMBER 12, 1942

DAVID O. SELZNICK TO HAL WALLIS—DEAR HAL: SAW "CASABLANCA" LAST NIGHT. THINK IT IS A SWELL MOVIE AND AN ALL-AROUND FINE JOB OF PICTURE MAKING. TOLD JACK AS FORCIBLY AS I COULD THAT I THOUGHT IT WOULD BE A TERRIBLE MISTAKE TO CHANGE THE ENDING, AND ALSO THAT I THOUGHT THE PICTURE OUGHT TO BE RUSHED OUT.

KNOWING WHAT THEY STARTED WITH, I THINK THE FIRM OF EPSTEIN, EPSTEIN AND KOCH DID AN EXPERT PIECE OF WRITING. EVEN THOUGH RICK'S PHILOSOPHY IS IN AT LEAST ONE INSTANCE WORD FOR WORD THAT OF RHETT BUTLER.

I HAVE A FEW MINOR SUGGESTIONS TO MAKE, AND IF BY ANY CHANCE YOU WOULD CARE TO HAVE THEM I WILL BE GLAD TO PASS THEM ALONG, ALTHOUGH I AM SURE THAT YOU WILL FIND OUT THESE THINGS FOR YOURSELF AT PREVIEW.

MIKE CURTIZ'S DIRECTION WAS, AS ALWAYS, SPLENDID. HE IS CLEARLY ONE OF THE MOST COMPETENT MEN IN THE BUSINESS. I AM MOST GRATEFUL TO YOU AND TO MIKE CURTIZ FOR THE SUPERB HANDLING OF INGRID. THANKS TO YOU TWO, AND OF COURSE TO INGRID, THE PART SEEMS MUCH BETTER THAN IT ACTUALLY IS; AND I THINK IT WILL BE OF BENEFIT TO HER, AND THEREFORE OF COURSE TO ME.

AFTER "FOR WHOM THE BELL TOLLS" INGRID IS OBVIOUSLY GOING TO BE WHAT I HAVE FOR SO LONG PREDICTED. ONE OF THE GREAT STARS OF THE WORLD.

CORDIALLY AND SINCERELY YOURS

JL TO [New York executives]— . . . "CASABLANCA:" WILL DEFINITELY NOT TOUCH PICTURE. PREVIEWED IT AGAIN LAST NIGHT AND AUDIENCE REACTION BEYOND BELIEF. FROM MAIN TITLE TO THE END THERE WAS APPLAUSE AND ANXIETY. HUNDREDS SAID DO NOT TOUCH PICTURE. MY PERSONAL OPINION IS IF PICTURE IS TOUCHED NOW IT WILL BECOME A PATCHED JOB. THEREFORE . . . SHIP YOUR NEGATIVES AND POSITIVES TO ALL FOREIGN COUNTRIES. . . .

Casablanca *opened with no further changes.*

FROM FREDERICK FAUST (MAX BRAND) [Contract Writer]
Wednesday [circa spring, 1943]
Dear Mr. Wallis,
Here are some brief comments on [writer Frederick] Stephani's
suggestions for a continuation of *Casablanca*. His sketch seems to me
to be about twenty per cent possible and eighty per cent overboard. I
haven't attempted to re-plot the story but merely to suggest a general
line which is closer at least to the *emotion* of *Casablanca*.
The first chunk of the rough draft of *The Conspirators* [1944] is
being typed to-day. . . .

Frederick Faust

*"Max Brand" was Faust's pen name. He wrote many successful
Western novels* [Destry Rides Again, *etc.*] *as well as books and* MGM *films
about Dr. Kildare.*

Report on Suggested Sequel to *Casablanca*

The Stephani story has elements of action that might be used but
the characters and the emotion seem wrong.
In the original, Rick is an outcast, a sort of outlaw-gambler, very
much of the type of the Bret Harte figures: a tough fellow with a heart
which nevertheless can be touched, a man with a secret sorrow in his
past and all that sort of thing. The toughness of Bogart made the sentiment
credible.
The moment Rick becomes, as in Stephani, an agent of the secret
police, the interest in his position and character largely evaporates.
Almost in the very opening, he is given an almost unassailable place.
The Frenchman in authority turns out to be Free French, and the flag
waves violently as the American troops land, to the great chagrin of our
German villains. In other words, the hand of Rick is filled with cards,
whereas in *Casablanca* he was walking a tightwire nearly all the way. The
shift in locale to Algiers seems of no very great importance, either. As a
matter of fact, the action could be pursued in Algiers, Tunis, or Lisbon
just as well. But why not keep it in Casablanca itself—a background
which we already know interests the picture audience.
There is no necessity, of course, to repeat the action of *Casablanca*,
but the emotional drive, which succeeded before, could be repeated or
increased in the new picture. The main point is that Rick made the first
picture. I would stick to the original lines of his character and keep him
the same man.

Here is our country at war, and in a far-off corner of the world there is a hard-boiled American with such a past that he can't return to his country. He can't put on an American uniform by enlisting, either. Criminals aren't allowed to serve.

Now that his place of business has been closed, he's an independent gambler, which always has been his main hold. He's a tough hombre who knows how to make the cards fall in the right way for him; and what chiefly distinguishes him from other people of his profession is that he has been capable of a great romance which remains in him an invisible wound. In Casablanca he is a sort of sub-rosa friend of Renault [Rains], and Renault is under fire from Vichy with his job at stake. The Germans are still the controlling factor in Casablanca and now they are more aggressively active than ever before, because they know that large preparations are going forward in America and England to strike a blow which, perhaps, will be aimed at Africa.

That's the background situation against which the story could open. Good sequels almost always try to repeat the chief characters *and* the setting.

Instead of putting the arrival of the Anglo-American armada at the beginning of the picture, where it overbalances all the rest of the action, should it not be placed at the very end?

One could run the line somewhat as follows, tentatively:

In spite of some friendship from Renault, the position of Rick in Casablanca is so uncertain and dangerous that he is ready to pull out with whatever he can salvage from the wreck of his business. He is detained because he gains some hint that very large events may be just over the horizon. Their exact nature is unknown to him, but the presence of new German agents and their extreme activity and personal importance intrigue him. Through Maria, the Fräulein Doktor of the piece, he comes to a still closer and more exact knowledge of what is going forward.

We don't make Rick a figure so important that the failure or success of the invasion depends upon him, of course, but he manages to drop a monkey wrench in the German espionage machine. He should not do this with the assistance of Renault, but working through Maria.

Stephani's idea of the two women might be worked out with some variation. To have the pair of them, in the end, fighting for Rick, saving his life, etc. seems very overboard; but it well may be that after the arrival of Ilsa (Madame Laszlo), following the death of her husband, Rick has to continue his affair with Maria, however it wounds him to keep away from Ilsa. What he has in sight is too important for him to consider his personal affairs. Besides, he's a gambler, and the cards he's playing now fascinate him.

He succeeds in being of service. But he probably should find that the arrival of the Americans make him once more, with greater emphasis, a man without a country. I can't imagine the heart of Maria being seriously fractured. At least, it's not too important to the story. As for Rick, he has to move on, and fast. If a happy ending is wanted, he is able to take Ilsa with him.

Based on the evidence in the studio files, the proposed sequel never was developed further.

7

Conflicts
and Changes
(1942–1946)

SEPTEMBER 3, 1942

EDMUND GOULDING [director] TO COL. J. L. WARNER—INSTINCTIVELY SENSING TROUBLE AHEAD. AM ON TRAIN TO TALK TO YOU ABOUT "OLD ACQUAINTANCE" SETUP. I WAS DISTURBED BY LETTER FROM BLANKE ON CAMERAMAN SITUATION. THIS IS NO TEMPERAMENTAL OR CHILDISH WHIM BUT VERY SOLID AND BUSINESS LIKE CONVICTION THAT I AM EITHER WORKING FOR WARNER BROS. OR MISS DAVIS, AND THERE IS A DIFFERENCE. STOP. URGE YOU NOT TO COMMIT YOURSELF TO ANY PROMISE UNTIL AFTER TALK WITH ME. THIS WOULD PUT ME IN POSITION OF DAVIS, [MIRIAM] HOPKINS, MOODS, FADS AND NON-SENSE. STOP. A SOLID SCRIPT, GOOD DISCIPLINE AND GENERAL UNDER-STANDING BY ALL OF LIMITATIONS, ETC. IS ONLY FORMULA NOW. I KNOW YOU KNOW WHAT I MEAN. STOP. IF DAVIS IS TOO GOOD FOR THE SET UP WE CAN STILL MAKE IT WITH ANOTHER GOOD ACTRESS. REGARDS-

EDDIE

Goulding wanted Cameraman Tony Gaudio and Bette Davis demanded Sol Polito. Goulding had a heart attack before filming began and Vincent Sherman was assigned to direct. Polito was the cameraman.

TO: Col J. L. Warner   DATE: December 19, 1942
FROM: Steve Trilling   SUBJECT: "Old Acquaintance"
[now Jack Warner's
executive assistant]

. . . Bette Davis was out today [from *Old Acquaintance*] partially illness
and in my estimation partially a little temperament. The old Hopkins-
Davis feud has flared up again but was very quickly stamped out by our
immediately calling the turn on both of them. With Blanke and Sherman
I had a good long talk with Davis last night from 6 PM to 8 PM and this
morning with Hopkins from 9 AM to 10:30. There were a lot of tears
and a lot of denials of any differences but there has been constant tension
on the set and all the old tricks of *The Old Maid* [1939] episode renewed.
I told Hopkins that any continuance of tactics would result in my turning
the entire matter over to the [Screen Actors] Guild and she would just be
banned from pictures; Davis is no white lily either, and I warned her and
she agreed to lean over a little backwards and cooperate to get this picture
over with and get performances exactly as directed with no nonsense—
and less takes. It all ended amicably with both parties vowing there would
be no re-occurrence. Davis' voice, however, was completely gone and as
we had nothing else to go to we were forced to close down for the day. . . .

As ever,

FROM JACK L. WARNER

April 16, 1943

Dear Leo [Forbstein, music director]:

Before the next picture is scored by any of your men I want to
have a good talk with you, as I definitely want to use a theme song for
our love motif between a man and woman, or husband and wife. For
example, in *Old Acquaintance* had we used the beautiful song from
[*Thank Your*] *Lucky Stars*, [1943] entitled "How Sweet You Are", for
Davis and [John] Loder, I am sure we would have had a good chance
to repeat the success we have had with "As Time Goes By."

Whenever Steiner, [Franz] Waxman, or any of your other men,
try to write an original love theme it just doesn't come off and is only a
series of music well played and well conducted. However, if you have a
song like "How Sweet You Are," "Jealousy," or a good Cole Porter
tune, similar to any one of hundreds of songs our music companies
own, for our love theme, no matter how old it may be, we should be
able to do the same thing that we did in *Casablanca*. People remember
the words and music of these old songs, and you can't expect Steiner,
Waxman, or any one else to compete with "As Time Goes By", etc.,
and still write a complete score for a 12,000 foot picture. . . .

J. L. Warner

TO: Colonel Warner
FROM: Steve Trilling

DATE: February 11, 1943
SUBJECT: Notes for Tonight
[meeting with staff
producers and directors]

. . . Writers not to work at home anymore, no matter what the reason! For the few good rarities to get anything accomplished, it does not compensate the failures that occur with this method. . . .

Cannot re-write scripts on set! Of course understand a line must be changed because it does not play right or does not work out due to physical action, but we cannot and will not permit complete re-writes of paragraphs and pages while the script is in production, except for extraordinary reasons. We formerly would get completed scripts and the film would be identical with the pages. Now, there are constant consultations with Producers and Writers (and Directors sometimes) during the shooting of the picture—both on the sets and in the Producer's office. This causes writers to be on picture preparation and then they are not much use on anything else while the picture is in the 7 or 8 weeks of production. Everyone of the Producers are guilty, so the blame cannot be put on individuals. . . .

Directors:

Number of takes—After all the warnings and promises, everybody is taking unnecessary takes again—8, 9, 10, as high as 12, and they must understand that it is not only a question of cost but there is a war going on and a conservation of film. Each studio is allotted only so much film and when we exhaust that, we cannot get any more—therefore, they are putting themselves and the rest of the employees out of jobs.

Number of days shoot picture—Everybody is going over schedule now; taking it as a joke. Schedules are laid out giving longer time—7 or 8 weeks—and they are going over as much as 20 and 30 days, even longer—for which there is no excuse. (Elaborate on this).

All pictures are running over budgets and we must try to keep within bounds or we will not know what the devil we are doing. Although we deserve a lot of praise and credit and are making money, we have to keep some semblance of sanity and not run hog-wild. . . .

Steve Trilling

FEBRUARY 22, 1943

WARNER TO [New York executives]— . . . AGAIN WANT TO REITERATE HOW TOUGH IT IS TO GET PICTURES STARTED. THERE'S NOTHING SHOOTING AT STUDIO NOW. THIS FIRST TIME IN 15 YEARS THAT STUDIO IS DARK. NEXT WEEK WE START TWO PICTURES, ONE STARTING DOUBTFUL. JUST CANNOT GET PEOPLE TO WORK [on] ACCOUNT [of government] SALARY CEILING HYSTERIA IN EVERYONE'S MIND [on] ACCOUNT [of]

WORLD CONDITIONS, ETCETERA. THAT'S WHY AS GOOD AS WE ARE
DOING WE MUST EVEN DO MORE TO PROLONGATE THE RUNS [at theatres]
OF EVERY PICTURE WE RELEASE. PROFITS FOR WHOLE YEAR IS WHAT
COUNTS, NOT JUST ANY ONE WEEK OR DAY. . . .

*This was a temporary condition based on the immediate reaction to
the government-imposed salary ceiling brought on by America's partici-
pation in World War II.*

SARATOGA TRUNK

TO: T. C. Wright   DATE: March 13, 1943
FROM: Eric Stacey [unit manager]   SUBJECT: "Saratoga Trunk"

Report for [director Sam] Wood, SARATOGA TRUNK, for FRIDAY—
16th shooting day. . . .

    As you know. . . . we got only two long shots by lunch time and
we did not finish on the stage until approximately 4:00 o'clock. We then
moved out to the Street and lined up, the sunlight being off most of the
buildings. When we got to the Street MR. WOOD informed me that he
had forgotten to make two shots in the CATHEDRAL and when the light
on the Street wasn't good suggested going back to the CATHEDRAL,
which we did, to make an additional long shot, which he had forgotten. . . . This bears out what I told you at the beginning of the picture—
how much he misses someone like BILL MENZIES to make up his mind
and tell him things. . . .

Eric Stacey

    *Production designer–art director William Cameron Menzies had worked
with free-lance director Wood on* Gone With the Wind, Our Town, Kings
Row, For Whom the Bell Tolls, *and* The Devil and Miss Jones.

TO: T. C. Wright   DATE: April 1, 1943
FROM: Eric Stacey   SUBJECT: "Saratoga Trunk"

Report for WOOD, SARATOGA TRUNK, for WEDNESDAY—32nd
shooting day.

    Company finished the RESTAURANT at approximately 2:40 PM
and moved to Stage 3 where they spent the balance of the day rewriting
and rehearsing for the scene involving COOPER and BERGMAN (Scene
111).

    This scene was changed around and MISS BERGMAN, as is her
practice most all the time, has injected certain dialogue from the book

into this scene. I advised MR. WALLIS' office that this was going on and he sent CASEY ROBINSON down to get in on it. They wound up by rewriting the scene, a copy of which has been sent to MR. WALLIS and he is informed as to the fact that the company did not shoot anything yesterday afternoon. . . .

Eric Stacey

TO: T. C. Wright　　　　　　DATE: April 9, 1943
FROM: Eric Stacey　　　　　　SUBJECT: "Saratoga Trunk"

Report for WOOD, SARATOGA TRUNK, for THURSDAY—39th shooting day.

　　Company called to continue the RAILROAD STATION on Stage 6, which was finished. . . .

　　We had thought that we would finish this set before lunch, but in the morning MR. WOOD started to re-stage a scene that he had shot the day previous, which was the reason for spending the balance of the day on this set. As I have told you, on many occasions he is very vague about how he is going to stage scenes, and after he has done a scene, goes home and sleeps on it, gets another idea and does it again the next day. . . .

Eric Stacey

TO: T. C. Wright　　　　　　DATE: April 30, 1943
FROM: Eric Stacey　　　　　　SUBJECT: "Saratoga Trunk"

Report for WOOD, SARATOGA TRUNK, for THURSDAY—57th shooting day. . . .

　　The company is shooting today, FRIDAY, on Stage 4 the HOTEL SUITE. . . . As I have told you many times before, it is practically impossible to get MR. WOOD to select people for this picture and when they are selected and have been in the picture for several days he decides he doesn't like them and wants to get them out—even talking about trying to replace FLORA ROBSON after 9-1/2 weeks of shooting. . . .

　　MR. WALLIS is considering another director to take over the sequences involving GARY COOPER and the train wreck. . . .

　　They are putting into the script the part of "MISS FOROSINI", who was formerly taken out, and we are having a lot of trouble getting an actress for the part; MR. WALLIS wants [contract player] FAYE EMERSON—MR. WOOD does not like FAYE EMERSON and wants MAUREEN O'HARA!!! This scene, as far as I know, when it is written will consist of about four lines for this character.

　　Picture 20 days behind schedule.

Eric Stacey

Maureen O'Hara at the time was a star under contract to both Twentieth Century-Fox and RKO Radio Pictures. Jacqueline De Wit was cast in the role.

TO: T. C. Wright DATE: May 6, 1943
FROM: Eric Stacey SUBJECT: "Saratoga Trunk"

Report for WOOD, SARATOGA TRUNK, for WEDNESDAY—62nd shooting day. . . .

The company is shooting today, THURSDAY, the EXT. of the first RAILROAD STATION on Stage 6.

I am trying to get a clear picture from MR. WALLIS as to how much of the picture he will permit [contract second unit and montage director] DON SIEGEL to shoot. My understanding at the moment is that SIEGEL shall make the actual FIGHT SEQUENCE after the two trains collide and any other close montage style shots that may be required in the sequence. . . . We will only have WOOD shoot parts of these scenes where it is necessary to keep the company shooting while BERGMAN is ill—and we expect her to return to work on SATURDAY. Will report to you later in the day on this situation.

Picture 23 days behind schedule.

Eric Stacey

TO: T. C. Wright DATE: June 19, 1943
FROM: Eric Stacey SUBJECT: "Saratoga Trunk"

Report for WOOD, SARATOGA TRUNK, for FRIDAY—96th shooting day. . . .

SIEGEL UNIT:

The SIEGEL UNIT continued on Stage 6. . . . I had a talk with DON SIEGEL yesterday and he tells me that he is making far more scenes than he normally would if he didn't have *two bosses.* WALLIS wants him to make scenes one way; WOOD wants him to make them another. . . .

Picture 40 days behind schedule.

Eric Stacey

TO: T. C. Wright DATE: June 21, 1943
FROM: Eric Stacey SUBJECT: "Saratoga Trunk"

Report for WOOD, SARATOGA TRUNK, for SATURDAY—97th shooting day

Company called to continue the EXT. & INT. of CLIO'S [Bergman] HOME on Stage 3. . . . The reason they are taking so long is because

WOOD visualizes the sequence on the principals' backs and WALLIS wants their faces, so consequently we are shooting this entire sequence in the LOWER FLOOR two ways—one from their backs, one from their faces. . . .

Picture 40 days behind schedule.

Eric Stacey

TO: T. C. Wright DATE: June 22, 1943
FROM: Eric Stacey SUBJECT: "Saratoga Trunk"

Report for WOOD, SARATOGA TRUNK, for MONDAY—98th shooting day. . . .

SIEGEL UNIT:

. . . For your information, this unit has shot for 19 days and has covered 3 pages of script and no allowance was made in the budget for such an operation; in the figures that you can see on the Cost Report where we have gone over on extras, this is entirely due to insufficient allowance being put in for a unit of this kind. You remember, we only budgeted 1 day with 100 people for this entire FIGHT SCENE.

Picture 41 days behind schedule.

Eric Stacey

Saratoga Trunk *was not released until March 1946. Several nontopical films made during this World War II period were held up for release by the studio in favor of more timely material. Also, Warners was accumulating a large backlog of finished films because of longer runs in theatres.*

Warner Bros. records indicate that the following conversation between Humphrey Bogart and Jack L. Warner took place on May 6, 1943, between 4 and 4:30 p.m.

B. Hello, Steve.
W. This is not Trilling, Humphrey. This is Jack Warner. How do you feel?
B. I feel dandy, thanks. I just want to tell you I don't want to get into any personal fight with you.
W. This is nothing personal. I'm running a big business and try to call the shots for the good of all concerned, as it is a herculean task to get everyone paid each Wednesday.
B. This is personal between you and me, Jack. I am more serious than I have ever been in my life and I just do not want to do this picture [*Conflict*]. If you want to get tough with me you

can, and I know how tough you can get, but if you do get tough and do the things you say you will, I will feel that I have lost a friend. I ask you as a favor to me to take me out of this picture, for I feel very strongly about it. I am very sorry I ever gave my word to you that I would do it, for if I had stopped and thought for a minute I would never have agreed to do this picture.

W.   Well, we have everything all set, people engaged to work in the picture, so come on and come to work tomorrow.

B.   I'm sorry, Jack; I just can't do it. My stomach will not let me. I am an honest man and I have to be honest with myself in this matter.

W.   You came through on a picture called *The Big Shot* [1942] and I am positive that you can more than come through on this. If it's Bill Jacobs, the producer, you are worried about, everybody produces the pictures here and I watch what everyone does, and not one person is responsible. Just because Jacobs happens to have this story should not worry you a bit. Vincent Lawrence, who is a pretty good writer, thinks the story is great.

B.   Nothing you can say will convince me it is a good picture, or is in good shape, or for me. I consider you a personal friend of mine and do not think you will do all the things you say you will.

W.   All I know is, if you are the artist you think you are, and I know you are, you should do this picture.

B.   But, Jack, it is not any good. It is not constructed for me and no thought has been put into it. I was surprised when you sent it to me in Brawley, and just can't do it no matter what you do to me; I just can't do it.

W.   When we bought *The Pentacle* [retitled *Conflict*], I pictured you in it. At that time Blanke was originally assigned to it, but he had so many other stories I gave it to Jacobs in an effort to give him some good stories. But believe me, Humphrey, I bought it for you exclusively.

B.   Then allow me the same privilege, Jack, for I know something about this business and do not think it is good. This thing has upset me more than anything else in this town. I think Warner Bros. is the best studio in the business, and always want to work at Warners. You are a good salesman and can get people to do things that may not be good for them, but that is your job. I also have my career at stake.

W.   Well, I cannot let everybody do what they want and I have to go by the contract. You were successful by doing things that Muni and Raft refused to do, and I think this story is good for you.

B. I will ride along any other time, but I am tired and all in and just can't do this picture.

W. You must remember, Humphrey, it is not Jack Warner that is asking you to do this picture. You are doing this for the company, and the same thing would happen in the steel business.

B. It isn't the same as the steel business; you are selling people with feelings, and I tell you sincerely I can't do it. You can do all kinds of things to me, but I just can't do this picture.

W. I think somebody is advising you about capital gains, and all that sort of business, and I say you are making a serious error in not making this picture. Besides, once in a while you must give and take, and so far you haven't done this. I think you are just stubborn.

B. I am no more stubborn than you are.

W. Well, you start this picture next Monday and you won't regret it.

B. Both Wallis and Curtiz told me I should not do this picture before the next one [*Passage to Marseille*].

W. Did Wallis and Curtiz tell you not to do this?

B. Wallis and Mike never said a word to me [not to do *Conflict*].

W. Well some of the greatest things in life have happened to people when they did not realize it.

B. You know the way the business is run better than I do, Jack.

W. In this business you can't always take the apples off the tree; you have to take some of them that are on the ground.

B. Then you admit that this is a rotten apple.

W. No, I don't admit any such thing. You may think it is not good for you, but I think it will be great, and want you to rely on my judgment.

B. I know you can't always have good apples all of the time, and am perfectly willing to take some that are rotten, but not this time.

W. In my opinion, from a professional standpoint, this picture now called *Conflict* will be one of the important pictures, because it is so different from anything that you or we have done, and I am willing to wager a big sum of money that it will be an important picture. I have been in this job longer than you have, and you must believe me. I have heard the same talk from twenty people who talk just like you are doing, and I know one of them is now trying to get a job as just an extra. You must ride along with us and do what we think best.

B.   But why do I have to do this picture? You wrote me a letter
that this was a democratic world, so why force me to do this?
You take a gamble in this business—many of them. Allow
me the privilege of making a decision. I work for Warner Bros.
and am willing to die for Warner Bros. When you asked me
to appear at the [Hollywood] Bowl on Easter Sunday at 4 a.m.,
and dance in a musical comedy, I did so. I will do anything,
but I cannot do this picture. I realize what you are doing by
telling me this, and I appreciate it, but I just can't do the
picture.

W.   Don't make the mistake that some people have made.

B.   What are you doing? Threatening me?

W.   No, I am not threatening you, but if you don't want to play
ball I will have to think along certain terms contractualwise.
We will have to suspend you and we will not put you in *Passage
to Marseille*.

B.   I know what you can do to me, and am thoroughly aware of
this.

W.   Please understand that I am not threatening you. I don't threaten
anyone.

B.   I am glad that you are not making this a personal thing, for I
would be very sorry, but you are saying that you as a representative of a company must protect it. You would never have
offered this script to Flynn, Bette Davis, or anyone else, but
you think I am a sucker, and because I signed that contract
you are forcing me to do this.

W.   Not only did I buy this story, I have faith in it, and thought
only of you when we bought it. You should not sacrifice
everything you have accomplished, and all I can say is if you
don't want to live up to your contract we will have to take
steps that are provided in our agreement.

B.   All I am doing is talking to you as a man. What the lawyers
do I cannot help. You are telling me what happens if I don't
do the picture. You have suspended other people on the lot;
why be so tough with me?

W.   I am trying to convince you to do something that is good for
you, and that I feel in my heart is swell. I told your agent I
do not want to hurt you, but I also told him we are not going
to keep this other picture and are going to hold *Conflict* until
you come back and work on it.

B.   Well, let me come back and work on it. Did you ever read a
book called *Hangover Square*? That is what this picture should
be.

W.   All I can say is Vincent Lawrence read the script and pronounced it perfect. We engaged him for four weeks to work on it, and he could not find any more than three weeks' work to do even though we are paying him for four.

B.   I don't want to get into a fight with you, Jack. I like you even though I do not ever work for you again [sic].

W.   I am going to New York tomorrow and wanted to get this behind me, for the good of everyone. Please believe me you are making a very serious error if you do not do this picture.

B.   But, Jack, your business is to get people to do things.

W.   Well, come on then and get down from that stepladder. Start the picture Monday. We have to pay you for six more years win, lose or draw, so there is no reason why you should not do it.

B.   Jack, I like the way the studio is run, and I have always liked it, but I do not think I am the right guy to play it.

W.   I am positive you can do it. When I read the script I thought you were the only man in town who could play it, and we will just have to hold it until you come back and make it. Naturally, when these things happen I lose a little of the faith in human nature, particularly after the agreement we made.

B.   I thought it was a gentleman's agreement and I was to be taken care of. Why don't you give it to [John] Garfield? I know what I can do. I don't think Trilling or anyone knows what the hell they are talking about. I know I can direct or produce a picture better than most of the people you have on the Lot.

W.   I am not detracting from your ability; all I ask you to do is to come in Monday, and five or six weeks will go by, then you can go back on your boat.

B.   I am sorry, Jack. I just can't do it. I can only say what I have said.

W.   Well, you are your own keeper.

B.   Turn your dogs on me; get [general counsel Roy] Obringer to send over the letter.

W.   This is a potent business, that is why people respect the motion picture industry, and I know you are making an awful error.

B.   What are you doing, frightening me? You have suspended other people; why don't you suspend me, for I do not think the picture is carefully prepared.

W.   Well, that's where you are wrong and I can only say you are making an error. You call a doctor to give you a treatment because he knows his business, and that is why you should take my word and do the picture.

B. Yes, but you are working for Warner Bros.

W. Certainly I am working for Warner Bros. the same as everyone else connected with this company is working for Warner Bros. I am working the way I am because I have faith in the company. . . .

B. Why don't you burn this script up and forget about it?

W. I have burned up hundreds of scripts of stories that we have never done, but I know you can do a great job in this picture.

B. Well, I am sorry, Jack, but I can't do it.

W. Well, I have said everything I can. Goodbye and good luck.

B. Goodbye, Jack.

Bogart did Conflict. *It is not generally recognized as one of his better films.*

NOVEMBER 28, 1943

WARNER TO WALLIS— . . .PER L.A. "DAILY NEWS" ARTICLE 23RD, I RESENT AND WON'T STAND FOR YOUR CONTINUING TO TAKE ALL CREDIT FOR "WATCH ON RHINE", "THIS IS THE ARMY," "GOD IS MY COPILOT," "PRINCESS O'ROURKE" AND MANY OTHER STORIES. I HAPPENED TO BE ONE WHO SAW THESE STORIES, READ PLAYS, BOUGHT AND TURNED THEM OVER TO YOU. YOU COULD HAVE AT LEAST SAID SO, AND I WANT TO BE ACCREDITED ACCORDINGLY. YOU CERTAINLY HAVE CHANGED AND UNNECESSARILY SO.

NOVEMBER 30, 1943

WARNER TO [Charles] EINFELD—WIRED WALLIS RE DAILY NEWS STORY. HE ANSWERED AS FOLLOWS: "STORY IN NEWS WAS LOCAL PUBLICITY TO TIE IN WITH 'O'ROURKE'. LACK MENTION OF YOU WAS NOT DUE ANY OMISSION MY PART. I GAVE YOU ALL DUE CREDIT. HAVE SEEN MANY INTERVIEWS WITH [producers Jesse L.] LASKY, [Jerry] WALD, OTHERS IN NEW YORK TIMES, OTHER PUBLICATIONS, ALL SIMILAR TO MINE WHERE I'M SURE THEY TOO MENTIONED YOU AS I DID, BUT ARTICLES APPEARED WITHOUT YOUR PROPER CREDIT DUE UNFORTUNATELY TO OMISSION BY INTERVIEWERS. SORRY YOU FEEL I HAVE CHANGED. I HAVE NOT CHANGED AND DON'T WANT TO IN MY REGARD FOR YOU, HAL." MEAN WHAT I SAID [in] MY WIRE AND WILL DEFINITELY TAKE LEGAL ACTION IF THIS ISN'T STOPPED. WANT YOU INFORM ALL PRODUCERS DIPLOMATICALLY IN GIVING STORIES OR INTERVIEWS THAT I SHALL BE DEFINITELY ACCREDITED AS EXECUTIVE PRODUCER OR IN CHARGE PRODUCTION. SICK, TIRED EVERYONE TAKING ALL CREDIT AND I BECOME SMALL BOY AND DOING MOST OF WORK. . . .

NOVEMBER 30, 1943

WARNER TO WALLIS—STOP GIVING ME DOUBLE TALK ON YOUR PUB-LICITY. THIS WIRE WILL SERVE NOTICE ON YOU THAT I WILL TAKE LEGAL ACTION IF MY NAME HAS BEEN ELIMINATED FROM ANY ARTICLE OR STORY IN ANY FORM, SHAPE OR MANNER AS BEING IN CHARGE PRODUCTION WHILE YOU WERE EXECUTIVE PRODUCER AND IN CHARGE PRODUCTION SINCE YOUR NEW CONTRACT COMMENCED. SO THERE WILL BE NO MISUNDERSTANDING IT WILL BE UP TO YOU TO PROVE AND SEE THAT MY NAME IS PROPERLY ACCREDITED IN ANY PUB-LICITY.

FROM JACK L. WARNER

Undated, circa August 12, 1943

OLIVIA de HAVILLAND CASE

Want to sue Miss de Havilland for non-performance of services in the 26 weeks that she refused to work. . . .

Miss de Havilland's claim that she did not want to do the pictures because they were not up to her standards is ridiculous. She made no complaint about the pictures she did make, and which were successful, so we certainly knew what we were doing equally as much in the pictures we wanted her to do that she would not appear in. If Miss de Havilland wants to compare all pictures with *Gone With the Wind* I will get David Selznick . . . and every other top producer to testify that such a comparison would be absurd.

We brought her from obscurity to prominence and can show that we made a profit on every picture she has ever been in and made it possible for her to get $125,000 for each picture which she is now getting. If she is worth that now she certainly was worth that much during the last year of her contract with us. In fact we turned down offers to rent her for this sum, therefore, she was worth that much to us for each picture. . . .

Selznick is also going to sue Joan Fontaine when her contract expires for non-performance of services along same lines.

At the end of Olivia de Havilland's seven-year contract in May of 1943, she had accumulated and begun serving six months of suspension extension time by going to RKO (via Selznick) on a loan-out. Jack Warner then loaned her to Columbia for a film, according to de Havilland, "that had twenty pages of script and a starting date the following Monday. I took another suspension—on extension time. Shortly thereafter . . . [attorney] Martin Gang told me that there was a California law which forbade an employer from enforcing a contract against an employee for more than

*seven years. The issue was whether or not seven years meant calendar years
or years of work. It seemed to mean calendar years." Just as Jack Warner
was about to sue de Havilland for "non-performance of services" (see above),
she and Martin Gang petitioned the court for an interpretation of the law
as it applied to an actor's contract. Finally, eighteen months later in
February, 1945, the Supreme Court of California ruled that there was no
reason to review the case as she had won in two lower courts. The seven-
year law was called the Anti-Peonage law and the calendar year ruling is
referred to as "the de Havilland decision" in the law books.*

JUNE 7, 1944

HM [Warner] TO JL [Warner]—AFTER THINKING IT OVER, BELIEVE YOU
WILL HAVE TO FIND SOME WAY OF DISCONTINUING SUSPENDING PEO-
PLE. IF THEY DON'T WANT [to] WORK IN ONE PICTURE, MAKE SOME
OTHER PICTURE WITH THEM, BUT FOR GOODNESS SAKE MAKE A PIC-
TURE. YOU DON'T GAIN ANYTHING BY SUSPENDING, AND YOU JUST
LOSE A PICTURE WITH A BIG DRAWING STAR. YOU MUST BEAR IN MIND
THAT EVERYONE IS PREACHING LIBERTY AND FREEDOM AND THE AC-
TORS ARE GETTING TO BELIEVE IT, AND THEREFORE WANT TO PLAY
ONLY THE PARTS THEY WANT TO PLAY. WHEN THE WAR IS OVER AND
ALL THE ACTORS AND HELP HAVE COME BACK, YOU CAN AT THAT TIME
SUSPEND ANYONE YOU WANT—INCLUDING ME, BUT RIGHT NOW DON'T
CUT YOUR NOSE TO SPITE YOUR FACE. IF IT WERE ME AND THEY
WOULDN'T PLAY IN ONE PICTURE THEN I WOULD HAVE THEM PLAY IN
ANOTHER.

JUNE 7, 1944

JACK WARNER TO HM [Warner]—AGREE WITH YOU WHOLEHEARTEDLY
ABOUT NOT SUSPENDING ANYONE, BUT ALL YOU HAVE TO DO IS LET
ACTORS PLAY PARTS THEY WANT TO AND YOU WON'T BE IN BUSINESS
VERY LONG. YOU MUST ALSO REMEMBER IT ISN'T ALWAYS THEY DON'T
WANT TO PLAY PARTS, BUT MAJORITY TIMES HAVE FOUND THEY USE
THIS AS ALIBI TO GET MORE MONEY OR REWRITE CONTRACT. THAT'S
MY OPINION, HOWEVER WILL TRY YOUR METHOD AS MAYBE I AM ALL
WET. ALSO, EVERYBODY ISN'T SUSPENDED EVERY TIME BECAUSE THEY
DON'T PLAY IN PICTURE. IF THEY WERE, WE WOULDN'T BE MAKING
PICTURES AT ALL. WE PLAY BALL WITH THEM BUT WHEN PEOPLE
BECOME ORNERY LIKE BOGART, DE HAVILLAND, THIS TYPE, YOU HAV-
EN'T ANY ALTERNATIVE.

TO HAVE AND HAVE NOT

TO: Colonel Warner   DATE: December 9, 1943
FROM: Steve Trilling   SUBJECT: "To Have and Have Not"

Dear Colonel:
   . . . Spoke at great length to [producer-director] Howard Hawks re
your letter and notes on *To Have and Have Not*. . . .
   Naturally, it ran long as he wanted to retain some of the Hemingway
flavor and dialogue, and as soon as he is through with [writer Jules]
Furthman—which he thinks will be within a week or ten days—wanted
to hop a plane and take the complete script with him to Cuba, meet
Hemingway (who has promised he would write on it for nothing) and
have everything cleared there.
   Hawks, too, was concerned about the possible ramifications of the
Cuban situation and had contacted the local Consul. . . . Hemingway
has already talked to the State Department in Cuba and sent Hawks a
long letter covering it. Hawks felt he could get this all clarified when he
arrived there with these top men, with whom Hemingway is very friendly,
probably [dictator Juan] Batista himself. . . .
   Re the two girls, Sylvia and Corinne—He is going over the tests of
our various young people and [I] will try, as much as possible to talk him
out of Betty Bacall—the girl he has under personal contract and was
willing to share with us if she played the part. No decisions will be made
without your knowledge, and before he leaves he plans to make some
tests of our own people. . . .

My best,
Steve Trilling

   *The Office of the Coordinator of Inter-American Affairs objected to
Warners' plan to make a film that could place a strain on Cuban-American
relations. The locale of the novel was changed from Cuba to Martinique
in the summer of 1940, shortly after the fall of France. Hemingway did
not work on the script. The two names "Sylvia" and "Corinne" were
changed to "Marie" and "Helene."*

TO: J. L. Warner   DATE: January 17, 1944
FROM: Mr. Obringer   SUBJECT: Howard Hawks

. . . With respect to *To Have and Have Not* . . . we agreed that no producer credit would be given on the screen or advertising to any person
other than Hawks, except that we can give you credit as executive producer
of the picture. Also, we have to display "A Howard Hawks Production"
in 60% of the title [size]. . . .
   Therefore, while you could appoint a producer . . . your problem

would arise in not being able to give the producer credit as you are the only one that this credit can be given to in addition to Hawks. . . .

R. J. Obringer

TO: Colonel Warner   DATE: February 7, 1944
FROM: Steve Trilling

Dear Colonel:

. . . Hawks had an hour's conference with [producer] Mark Hellinger this morning, and then talked to me later.

It does not seem to be a question of who is going to produce . . . but a question as to whether he [Hawks] will have to work under a Producer if he continues working at Warner Bros.

Hawks feels it has taken him all these years to reach the position where he can work on his own pictures without such Producer's supervision—said he always does most of the work himself anyway, and when there is a difference of opinion as to how the script should be developed or scenes played, it creates friction and makes for "bad pictures"—from Hawks's viewpoint. . . .

Steve Trilling

TO: Roy Obringer   DATE: February 11, 1944
FROM: Steve Trilling

Dear Roy:

. . . Hawks does not want Jack to be surprised if he signs somewhere else. He started out without a producer on *Air Force* [1943], then life was made hell for him [when Wallis was assigned]—he doesn't function as well with a producer and if he hasn't proven by this time that he can work without a producer, he doesn't want to continue—he'll get a job somewhere else to show he can do it as a lone producer. . . .

Steve Trilling

Hawks received producer and director credit on To Have and Have Not.

FROM HAL B. WALLIS

EDWIN SCHALLERT [critic and movie editor]
LOS ANGELES TIMES
202 W FIRST STREET
LOS ANGELES CALIF

MARCH 4 1944

I HAVE BEEN WITH WARNER BROS FOR TWENTY YEARS AND DURING THIS TIME IT HAS BEEN CUSTOMARY HERE AS ELSEWHERE FOR THE

STUDIO HEAD TO ACCEPT THE ACADEMY AWARD FOR THE BEST PRO-
DUCTION. NATURALLY I WAS GLAD TO SEE JACK WARNER ACCEPT THE
AWARD THIS YEAR FOR "CASABLANCA," AS HE DID FOR "THE LIFE OF
EMILE ZOLA" [in 1939]. I AM HAPPY ALSO TO HAVE CONTRIBUTED MY
BIT TOWARD THE MAKING OF THAT PICTURE. YOUR COMMENT IN YOUR
COLUMN THIS MORNING ON RIVALRY AT WARNER BROS. IS TOTALLY
UNJUSTIFIED. I WOULD BE GRATEFUL IF YOU WOULD CORRECT THE
MISLEADING IMPRESSION CREATED BY IT. . . .

HAL B. WALLIS

*Wallis's version of the rift with Jack Warner and the circumstances
behind the Academy Awards imbroglio are taken from his 1980 autobiography,* Starmaker:

Jack did not live up to the terms of our contract [see page 165].
He often acquired material I never saw and never had an opportunity
to consider for my own productions. This was totally unacceptable
to me. Then Jack began to inject himself into my company's decision
making, attempting quite arbitrarily to overrule me in some cases. . . .

Matters came to a head that Oscar night. After it was announced that *Casablanca* had won the Academy Award for Best
Picture of the Year, I stood up to accept when Jack ran to the stage
ahead of me and took the award with a broad, flashing smile and a
look of great self-satisfaction. I couldn't believe this was happening.
Casablanca had been my creation; Jack had absolutely nothing to
do with it. . . .

I was miserable . . . and felt I could no longer work under the
conditions imposed upon me by Jack Warner. I broke clean, left for
New York without any plans, and holed up at the Waldorf Towers
for eight weeks. . . .

*After leaving Warner Bros. Wallis set up his own independent unit
at Paramount, and for many years that studio released his films.*

HM [Warner] TO JL [Warner] . . .

APRIL 18, 1944
MY ADVICE TO YOU IS NOT TO MENTION THAT PARTY'S NAME [Hal
Wallis] EVEN IN FORM OF KIDDING. ATTEND TO YOUR OWN BUSINESS.
I ASSURE YOU HE WILL DO VERY WELL. IT COMES ACROSS THE WIRE,
MANY PEOPLE SEE IT AND THEY THINK YOU ARE JEALOUS. YOU ARE
SUPPOSED TO BE A BIG MAN. . . .

The Cagney clan at the Warner Hollywood Theatre World Premiere of *Yankee Doodle Dandy* (May 29, 1942). Left to right: Mrs. William Cagney (the former Boots Mallory), Producer William Cagney, Jeanne Cagney, Mrs. James Cagney, and James Cagney. (USC Archives of Performing Arts)

Producer Hal B. Wallis, screenwriter Casey Robinson, and Bette Davis discuss a scene for *Now, Voyager* (1942) on the set. (Warner Bros. Archives)

Producer Mark Hellinger (left), Ida Lupino, and Jack Carson at the time of *The Hard Way* (1942). (Warner Bros. Archives)

Bogart and Paul Henreid play chess between scenes on the set of *Casablanca* (1943) while Claude Rains (left) observes with a characteristic expression. (IMP/GEH Still Collection)

Director Raoul Walsh (right) makes a point to Errol Flynn during the filming of *Desperate Journey* (1942). (Warner Bros. Archives)

Non-Warner stars Ingrid Bergman and Gary Cooper are directed by non-Warner director Sam Wood (center) in *Saratoga Trunk* (1945). Cinematographer Ernest Haller on the right. (Warner Bros. Archives)

An oddity: Ann Sheridan, who may have made an unbilled, unrecognizable appearance in *The Treasure of the Sierra Madre* (1948). Seen here with Bogart and Director John Huston after her scene was photographed on the set (see page 287).

Joan Crawford, as was her custom, knits on the set of *Mildred Pierce* (1945) while talking with Director Michael Curtiz.

Bogart, John Huston, and Lauren Bacall (Mrs. Bogart) on a studio set for *Key Largo* (1948). (Warner Bros. Archives)

Writer (and later Director) Richard Brooks (left) and Bogart confer with Producer Jerry Wald during the making of *Key Largo* (1948). (Warner Bros. Archives)

Free-lance star Vivien Leigh, Playwright Tennessee Williams, and free-lance Director Elia Kazan evidently amused while rehearsing A *Streetcar Named Desire* (1951). (The Museum of Modern Art/Film Stills Archive)

Agent-producer Charles K. Feldman (*The Glass Menagerie, A Streetcar Named Desire*) talking with Jane Wyman at a party in 1950.
USC Archives of Performing Arts

Left to right: Walter MacEwen, Story Editor and later Executive Assistant to Hal Wallis. Roy Obringer, General Counsel at Warners' Burbank Studios. (James Silke/"MUKY," Warner Bros.) Producer-writer Robert Lord. (James Silke)

Joseph I. Breen, Director of the Production Code Administration (1934 photo). (USC Archives of Performing Arts)

Steve Trilling, Casting Director and later Executive Assistant to Jack Warner. (USC Archives of Performing Arts)

Right: Screenwriters Seton I. Miller and Norman Reilly Raine discussing research for *The Adventures of Robin Hood* with Associate Producer Henry Blanke (1937).

Contract writer Lenore Coffee (*The Great Lie, Old Acquaintance, Beyond the Forest*, etc.). (USC Archives of Performing Arts)

Contract writer John Monk Saunders (*The Dawn Patrol, The Last Flight, The Finger Points*, etc.). (USC Archives of Performing Arts)

Contract writers Philip and Julius Epstein (*The Strawberry Blonde, Yankee Doodle Dandy, Casablanca*, etc.). (Culver Pictures)

Contract writer and later producer Robert Buckner (right (*Dodge City, Yankee Doodle Dandy, Life with Father* etc.). Harry Warner, left. (Warner Bros. Archives)

Contract writer Catherine Turney (*My Reputation, The Man I Love, A Stolen Life*, etc.). (USC Archives of Performing Arts)

Contract writer Howard Koch (*The Sea Hawk, The Letter, Casablanca*, etc.).

Contract writer Ranald MacDouga (*Objective, Burma!, Mildred Pierce The Breaking Point*, etc.). (Floy McCarthy, Warner Bros.)

MR. SKEFFINGTON

FROM BETTE DAVIS

December 5, 1940

Dear Jack:

. . . I have also heard rumors that [Mr.] *Skeffington* with Mr. [Edmund] Goulding [directing] was my next. This, I would be forced, for my own future career, to refuse. It is *physically* impossible for me to play this woman of fifty—I am not old enough in face or figure, and I have worked too hard to do something that I know I would never be convincing in. *The Old Maid* and Elizabeth [in *The Private Lives Of Elizabeth and Essex*] were different. They were very eccentric characters and wore costumes which always helps age. This is a chic modern woman.

If your action in these matters is suspension, or if you decide to give me my three months vacation for next year in January, February and March, I would appreciate knowing as soon as possible so I can open my house in New Hampshire.

Sincerely,
Bette Davis

Bette Davis was 32 at the time of this letter. Mr. Skeffington was not produced with Davis until 1943, at which time the thoroughly revised script (by a different writer) represented an entirely new approach to the material. However, the character of Fanny Skeffington still aged during the course of the film.

FROM THE OFFICE OF WAR INFORMATION

MR. SKEFFINGTON (Warner Bros.)
Revised Temporary Script (pp. 178)
9/26/42

February 16, 1943

This story presents problems from the standpoint of the war information program.

(1) *The reactions shown by other Americans toward a minority group are undemocratic.*

Mr. Skeffington [Claude Rains] is intelligent, generous, devoted to his wife and family. Yet he is never accepted by the majority of characters in the story. . . . Fanny [Bette Davis] seizes upon the first pretext to divorce him; her suitors partake of his hospitality but ignore him personally.

Why? It is implied throughout the story that the reason for this is that he is a Jew (pp. 10-30-31-57-60-66-116). Regardless of how sympathetically Mr. Skeffington is characterized, this portrayal on the screen of prejudice against the representative of an American minority group is extremely ill-advised as it adds nothing to our understanding of a minority question, but only focuses attention on this social problem without examining or interpreting it. The screen today has been entrusted with the tremendous responsibility of clarifying the issues of the war. Does this presentation help Americans to a better understanding of one of the four freedoms—freedom of worship—for which Americans today are fighting and dying all over the world?

(2) *The characterization of Skeffington unwittingly confirms the Nazi Propaganda line.*

The Nazi propaganda contention that the Jews control the money interest in all countries would seem to be confirmed in this story by the portrayal of Skeffington as the richest and most powerful man on Wall Street. This is given added emphasis by the fact that Skeffington is the only representative of Wall Street with whom we have any major contact. Any characterization which substantiates the Nazi propaganda line is a disservice to the country.

(3) *The practices of American financiers are characterized as "shady."*

Wall Street appears as a minor villain in the story. According to Mr. Skeffington, the richest man on the Street—"the line between stealing and a smart deal is almost non-existent." He further states that "a man who has stolen only twenty-four thousand dollars has no future in Wall Street. If it had been one hundred and fifty thousand, several firms would make him offers."

This is a period when national unity is vital. This characterization of our financial leaders *as a group* is a disservice to that unity. . . .

The script reinforces the Nazi propaganda line in another respect. Nazi world propaganda states that although we condemn the Fascists for discrimination against races and creeds, we practice it ourselves. . . .

Fanny's suitors react much the same way to her marriage. Thatcher [Bill Kennedy] says with some satisfaction (p. 57) that Fanny will find out that as Mrs. Skeffington there will be one or two hotels she won't be able to get into. Later, they continue to court Fanny, completely ignoring the fact that she has a husband, because according to Skeffington (p. 66) they feel they have to "rescue" her. . . .

This is just the kind of picture of America which the Fascists would like to see. They have deluged the world with propaganda about the money-mad Americans, and today are using this line to create a breach between us and our allies. Is this the picture we want to give other peoples as representative of America and the American way? . . .

For the most part, the "problems" discussed above were only slightly muted in the released film.

JL [Warner] TO TRILLING

MAY 26, 1944

SAT THROUGH "SKEFFINGTON" LAST NIGHT WITH PACKED HOUSE. AUDIENCE REALLY ENJOYED IT. . . . EXPLAIN TO EPSTEINS, SHERMAN AND EVERY DIRECTOR, WRITER, PRODUCER OUR STUDIO THAT THEY MUST STOP TRYING PUT SO MUCH IN EVERY SCRIPT AND PICTURE . . . AS THAT IS WHAT IS WRONG WITH "SKEFFINGTON." IT ISN'T FEW FEET YOU CAN CLIP HERE AND THERE, IT'S COMPLETE SCENES THAT ARE SO ROUNDED AND TAKE SO LONG TO TELL IN SO MANY SEQUENCES. WHILE SEEING PICTURE LAST NIGHT, WANTED TAKE OUT THREE OR FOUR SEQUENCES BUT COULDN'T AS THEY WERE PLANTS FOR NEXT SEQUENCE, WHICH AGAIN MEANS BUT ONE THING: EVERYBODY TRYING WRITE TOO MUCH SCRIPT. THEREFORE, OUR PICTURES ARE SO LONG. . . . OUR PICTURES HAVE BEEN IMPORTANT FOR THEIR RAPIDITY AND AVOIDING STALLING IN TELLING STORY. "SKEFFINGTON" COULD HAVE BEEN TWO TO THREE THOUSAND FEET LESS IN PHOTOGRAPHING ALONE. . . . DON'T LET ANYONE TELL YOU IT'S BECAUSE WE DIDN'T CUT PICTURE, THAT ISN'T IT. IT'S BECAUSE OF COMPLETE TEMPO OF PICTURE AND METHOD IN WHICH IT WAS WRITTEN AND DIRECTED. SHOULD BE VERY BITTER LESSON TO ALL, AND SEE WE GET TEMPO IN ALL OUR PICTURES WHICH I AGAIN WANT REITERATE IS WHAT WE HAVE BEEN FAMOUS FOR. . . .

NEW YORK NY

JUNE 1, 1944

HM [Warner] TO JL [Warner]—HAVE GIVEN CONSIDERABLE THOUGHT TO REMAKING OF "PETRIFIED FOREST" [1936]. I CANNOT FOR THE LIFE OF ME UNDERSTAND HOW YOU CAN MAKE A WORTHWHILE PICTURE OUT OF THAT STORY. AM ALSO OF THE OPINION THAT YOU SHOULD NOT MAKE ANY REMAKES AT ALL AT PRESENT TIME. THERE ARE PLENTY OF ORIGINAL STORIES YOU COULD MAKE. WOULD ADVISE YOU TO STOP "PETRIFIED FOREST." THE MINUTE YOU ANNOUNCE A REMAKE THE EXHIBITORS GET WISE TO IT AND IT JUST MAKES IT HARDER TO SELL. BELIEVE YOU CAN DO BETTER BY REISSUING PICTURES THAN BY REMAKING THEM. WISH YOU WOULD THINK THIS OVER. "BETWEEN TWO WORLDS" [1944] SHOULD BE A LESSON TO YOU BECAUSE ANYONE WHO REMADE "OUTWARD BOUND" [1930] DON'T KNOW WHAT IT'S ALL ABOUT, AS THIS WAS A FAILURE IN THE FIRST PLACE AND YOU TOOK ONE FAILURE AND MADE ANOTHER FAILURE OUT OF IT. THIS HAS NOTHING TO DO WITH THE QUALITY OF THE PICTURE. IT IS JUST THAT THE

SUBJECT MATTER ISN'T WHAT PEOPLE WANT. "PETRIFIED FOREST" IS OF THE SAME TYPE SUBJECT MATTER. THIS WAS A FAILURE ONCE AND WILL BE A FAILURE AGAIN. DON'T CARE HOW MUCH YOU INTEND CHANGING STORY. IN ONE BREATH YOU SAY YOU HAVE BUILT UP AN ORGANIZATION TO PRODUCE GREAT PICTURES AND IN SECOND BREATH YOU WANT TO DO THINGS TO MAKE IT HARDER FOR YOURSELF SELLING ORGANIZATION AND EVERYONE ELSE BY MAKING PICTURES OF RE-MAKES. YOU CAN'T DO THIS AND SUCCEED . . . THAT IS ALL RIGHT WHEN YOU ARE MAKING FIFTY OR SIXTY PICTURES AND SHOOTING THEM OUT LIKE CHEESE, BUT WHEN YOU HAVE BUILT UP A REPUTATION SUCH AS YOU HAVE YOU CANNOT CONTINUE IT IF YOU KEEP ON MAKING REMAKES. . . .

Despite the above, The Petrified Forest *became the basis of a remake,* Escape in the Desert *(1945); One More Tomorrow (1946) was based on* The Animal Kingdom *(1932); A Stolen Life (1946) derived from the 1939 British film of the same name;* Of Human Bondage *(1946) originally was made in 1934;* The Unfaithful *(1947) was based partially on* The Letter *(1940);* Escape Me Never *(1947) stemmed from a 1935 British film with the same title;* One Sunday Afternoon *(1948) was a musical version of* The Strawberry Blonde *(1941), which in turn had been based on* One Sunday Afternoon *(1933);* My Dream Is Yours *(1949) was adapted from* Twenty Million Sweethearts *(1934); and* Colorado Territory *(1949) was a remake of* High Sierra *(1941), etc. Some did well at the box office; more did not.*

Warners also reissued a great number of past successes to theatres from 1943 to 1953. Most did exceptional business; the melodramas and action-spectacles being the most popular. Often double bills were released with potent title combinations such as Crime School *and* Girls on Probation, The Sea Hawk *and* The Sea Wolf, Alcatraz Island *and* San Quentin, Dodge City *and* Virginia City, Little Caesar *and* The Public Enemy, *etc.* The Adventures of Robin Hood *was reissued in Technicolor and on a single bill; the other films which were originally made and released in Technicolor were reissued in black and white. The running time of some of the pictures was trimmed—sometimes considerably—for reissue.*

HM [Warner] TO JL [Warner] AND [Charles] EINFELD
NEW YORK, NY

SEPTEMBER 20, 1944

IF BETTE DAVIS OR ANYONE ELSE WANTS TO APPEAR AT ANY RALLY, WHETHER REPUBLICAN OR DEMOCRATIC, THAT IS THEIR BUSINESS. PEOPLE ARE NOT GOING INTO THEATRES BECAUSE DAVIS IS REPUBLICAN OR DEMOCRATIC, BECAUSE IF THAT WERE THE CASE NO ONE WOULD

GO SEE PICTURES AS ANY PERFORMER IS ONE OR THE OTHER. I ADMIRE
PERFORMERS OR ANYONE ELSE WHO FIGHT FOR WHAT THEY THINK IS
RIGHT. ARE WE THE SAME PEOPLE WHO MADE "CONFESSIONS OF A
NAZI SPY," "MISSION TO MOSCOW" AND MANY OTHER PICTURES WHICH
EVERYONE CONDEMNED US FOR MAKING? WE THOUGHT IT WAS RIGHT
TO MAKE THESE PICTURES, SO WE MADE THEM IN SPITE OF WHAT
EVERYONE ELSE THOUGHT. HEREAFTER WHEN IT COMES TO MATTERS
OF THIS KIND PLEASE DO NOT MAKE ANY DECISIONS UNLESS YOU HAVE
FIRST DISCUSSED THE MATTERS WITH ME. I CAN'T RUN THIS COMPANY
PROPERLY WITH EVERYONE TRYING TO DECIDE THINGS I SHOULD DE-
CIDE. THIS IS A VERY SERIOUS THING AND IF IT IS AT ALL POSSIBLE
FOR ME TO ARRANGE FOR DAVIS TO APPEAR TOMORROW NIGHT SHE
IS GOING TO BE THERE IF SHE WANTS TO. IT IS NONE OF OUR BUSINESS
AT WHICH RALLIES THEY APPEAR.

*Davis did appear and speak at a meeting to reelect President Franklin
D. Roosevelt in Madison Square Garden, sponsored by the Independent
Voters Committee of the Arts and Sciences.*

FROM PRESS RELEASE December 11, 1944

NEW YORK NY
RELEASING TUESDAY [to] TRADES AND NEWSPAPERS:
HARRY M. WARNER BEFORE RETURNING TO COAST OVER WEEKEND,
DISCLOSED THAT IN A SURVEY OF POST-WAR PLANS OF FORMER EM-
PLOYEES NOW IN ARMED FORCES IT WAS FOUND THAT 67% PLAN TO
RETURN TO COMPANY, 9% WILL COME BACK IF OFFERED A BETTER
POSITION, 13% ARE UNDECIDED AT PRESENT, WHILE 11% DO NOT IN-
TEND TO RETURN.

THIS BELIEVED TO BE FIRST SURVEY, IN FILM INDUSTRY AT LEAST,
TO ASCERTAIN PLANS, SENTIMENTS AND PROBLEMS OF SERVICE MEN
AND WOMEN WITH REGARD TO FUTURE.

MR. WARNER STATED QUOTE FOR A LONG TIME I HAVE BEEN
INTERESTED IN PROBLEMS OF RETURNING SERVICE MAN. LONG BEFORE
IT WAS REQUIRED BY LAW, OUR COMPANY PROMISED THAT ANY BONA
FIDE WARNER EMPLOYEE RETURNING FROM ARMED FORCES COULD
HAVE HIS (OR HER) JOB BACK IF HE WANTED IT. WE ARE STICKING BY
THAT PROMISE, BUT WE WANT TO DO MORE THAN JUST GIVE A VETERAN
HIS JOB BACK.

I HAVE ALWAYS FELT THAT PROPER READJUSTMENT OF VETERANS
TO CIVILIAN LIFE IS RESPONSIBILITY OF EVERY CIVILIAN, AND THIS
SURVEY IS ONE STEP WHICH OUR COMPANY HAS TAKEN TO MEET THE
RESPONSIBILITY. WE CIVILIANS ARE ONES WHO MUST GO MORE THAN

HALF WAY TO MAKE WHATEVER ADJUSTMENT MAY BE NECESSARY. WE OWE THAT MUCH TO OUR SERVICE MEN AND WOMEN. AFTER ALL, THEY ARE THE ONES WHO HAVE BEEN DOING THE JOB THAT MAKES IT POSSIBLE FOR US AT HOME TO LIVE IN PEACE. IT IS THEIR COURAGE AND THEIR SACRIFICE THAT MAKES IT POSSIBLE FOR US TO HAVE A FREE WORLD FOR OUR CHILDREN TO GROW UP IN UNQUOTE. . . .

QUESTIONNAIRE SENT TO APPROXIMATELY 3,600 FORMER EMPLOYEES, WITH OVER 1,100 REPLIES RECEIVED UP TO DECEMBER 6. . . .

THE BIG SLEEP

TO: T. C. Wright
FROM: Eric Stacey [unit manager]   DATE: November 20, 1944

Report for [Howard] Hawks, *The Big Sleep*, for Saturday—33rd shooting day.

Company called to shoot the INT. of MARLOWE'S [Humphrey Bogart] OFFICE on Stage 8. First shot at 4:30 PM; finished at 6:00 PM. . . .

You will observe that this company did not make a scene until 4:30 in the afternoon. Mr. Hawks rewrote the entire scene and they are continuing with this scene today, Monday.

Picture 15 days behind schedule.

Eric Stacey

TO: T. C. Wright   DATE: December 26, 1944
FROM: Eric Stacey   SUBJECT: "The Big Sleep"
                                    (Humphrey Bogart)

The Hawks Co., while waiting for Mr. Bogart this morning about 9:15 (the assistant director had called the Beverly Wilshire Hotel where he had been staying and was told he had left), received a phone call for Mr. Hawks from Mrs. Bogart [Mayo Methot] saying that Bogart had shown up at the house at 8:30 this morning very drunk.

I went out to the house with [assistant director] Bob Vreeland, talked to Mrs. Bogart relative the situation, having previously contacted Sam Jaffe (Mr. Bogart's agent), asking him to please come along. According to Mrs. Bogart, Bogie was in a very bad condition and sleeping by the time we arrived—approximately 10:00 o'clock. . . .

Mr. Bogart himself appeared and the atmosphere became extremely strained and I felt that my presence there would serve no useful purpose since Bogart himself kept asking, "Are we holding a wake?" . . .

I really do not feel that Bogart's condition can be straightened out over night since he has been drinking for approximately three weeks and it is not only the liquor, but also the mental turmoil regarding his domestic life that is entering into this situation. . . .

Eric Stacey

TO: Obringer   DATE: December 26, 1944
FROM: T. C. Wright   SUBJECT: "The Big Sleep"—Pro-
                                                        duction delays due
                                                        to Humphrey Bogart

. . . Dec. 20th—EXT. of HIDEOUT (Stage 19)—Thirty minute delay, from 1:20 to 1:50 P.M.—conference. It was necessary for Mr. Hawks to speak with Mr. Bogart for a half hour and straighten him out relative the "Bacall" situation, which is affecting their performances in the picture. . . .

In checking this situation with [assistant director] Bob Vreeland, who has been on the picture since it started (I have only been connected with it for the last few weeks), was informed that outside of four or five cases Bogart has always shown up on time and has not had a day off during the entire picture, but I understand there have been several instances when Hawks has had to take him to one side and talk with him at great length because he was dissatisfied with his performance, which was no doubt caused by his domestic troubles—and, naturally, these delays cannot be itemized.

T. C. Wright

Bogart and Lauren Bacall had fallen in love during the filming of To Have and Have Not. *They were costarred again in* The Big Sleep. *Bogart was still married to Mayo Methot, but at this point was living away from home (most of the time) and trying to work out a divorce agreement.*

TO: T. C. Wright   DATE: December 29, 1944
FROM: Eric Stacey   SUBJECT: "The Big Sleep" (Hawks)

Report for Hawks, *The Big Sleep*, for Thursday—64th shooting day.

Company called to resume production, shooting the EXT. of the HIDEOUT on Stage 19, which was finished. . . .

As already reported to you, during the day that this company did not work due to Mr. Bogart's absence Mr. Hawks had time to sit down with his writers and completely rewrite the end of the story.

Also, this rewrite means that the company will never return to the STERNWOOD HOME on Stage 12, nor will they use the INT. of the GENERAL'S BEDROOM, which was especially built at Mr. Hawks's request; however, the rewrite has eliminated approximately four or five days of shooting, which in itself is a great saving.

Mr. Bogart returned to work—apparently in good shape. . . .

Picture 30 days behind schedule.

Eric Stacey

With the exception of the above instances on this picture, Bogart was usually on time and ready to work through the years.

TO: T. C. Wright   DATE: January 6, 1945
FROM: Eric Stacey   SUBJECT: "The Big Sleep" (Hawks)

Report for Hawks, *The Big Sleep,* for Friday—70th shooting day.

Company called to continue the INT.-EXT. of GEIGER's HOME on Stage 7. . . . As Hawks is rewriting this entire ending, and nobody has a copy of the script except the actors, it is very difficult to estimate how long it will take. . . .

Eric Stacey

TO: T. C. Wright   DATE: January 13, 1945
FROM: Eric Stacey   SUBJECT: "The Big Sleep" (Hawks)

Report for Hawks, *The Big Sleep,* for Friday—76th shooting day.

Company called to continue the PROCESS [rear projection] of MARLOWE'S CAR on Stage 5, which was finished, and also a retake of the opening sequence in VIVIAN'S [Lauren Bacall] SITTING ROOM on Stage 12, which was finished. Incidentally, this sequence has already been retaken completely and this will be the second retake of this episode. . . .

This finishes the picture in 76 days—34 days behind its 42-day schedule.

It is interesting to observe that in spite of the fact that this show has run over 34 days, the last Daily Cost Report shows the picture only $15,000 over the budget, so it is reasonable to expect that, with $35,000 budgeted for music, which has yet to be spent, and the normal post-production charges, this show might not go over the budget much more than $50,000.

Eric Stacey

The Big Sleep *went considerably over budget as a result of additional retakes, as explained in the following pages.*

FROM ROY OBRINGER

Ralph Lewis, Esq.
Freston & Files [attorneys]
1010 Bank of America Bldg.
Los Angeles 14, California

April 30, 1945

Dear Ralph:

Last Wednesday I had an interview with . . . the Salary
Stabilization Unit with respect to a new contract for Betty Bacall.

As you know, we are the assignees of a contract dated May 3,
1945 between Howard Hawks and Betty Bacall. . . .

The consideration for Howard Hawks assigning the contract to
Warner Bros. was our agreement, which was effected by way of a
lending agreement with Hawks, to cast Miss Bacall opposite Humphrey
Bogart in the picture *To Have and Have Not*. This was the first picture
in which Miss Bacall appeared. After the assignment of the contract,
we again co-starred Miss Bacall with Humphrey Bogart in the picture
directed by Howard Hawks entitled *The Big Sleep*, which picture has
not as yet been released.

Recently we made application to the SSU [Salary Stabilization
Unit] and received approval to pay Miss Bacall a $5000 bonus for her
outstanding performance in the picture *To Have and Have Not*. . . .

In my discussion, I pointed out that while Miss Bacall did not
have a lengthy picture background, having only appeared in two
pictures, nevertheless she has developed into star material overnight, so
to speak.

This is a situation which . . . happens once in a lifetime, where
you have a personality develop overnight and become a terrific box
office value. Obviously, it became very impracticable to have Miss
Bacall co-star with top-notch male stars in the business at $350 a week,
and particularly when her value is appraised as equal to that of Ingrid
Bergman. . . .

We desire to make a contract with Miss Bacall as follows: 52
weeks straight, no layoff, at $1000; with yearly options at $1250,
$1500, $2000, $2500, $3000 and $3500 [per week]. . . .

Will you please prepare the necessary application.

Very truly yours,
R. J. Obringer

*The government Salary Stabilization Unit (set up during World War
II) approved the new contract as outlined above.*

FROM JACK L. WARNER
TO [Ben] KALMENSON [general sales manager, New York].

AUGUST 23, 1945

INSTEAD OF "THE BIG SLEEP," DEFINITELY WANT RELEASE "CONFIDENTIAL AGENT." LATTER IS TOPICAL PICTURE THAT HAS SOMETHING TO DO WITH SITUATION IN SPAIN. . . . FURTHERMORE, BACALL ABOUT HUNDRED TIMES BETTER IN "CONFIDENTIAL" THAN SHE IS IN "BIG SLEEP," AND WE WANT TO KEEP THIS WOMAN ON TOP. ALSO, INSTEAD OF "NOBODY LIVES FOREVER," WHICH WILL NEVER GET OLD, WE MUST PUT IN "JANIE GETS MARRIED" ON MAY 25TH AS THIS PICTURE IS TOPICAL TOO. CONTAINS NOTHING ABOUT WAR, HOWEVER IT'S ABOUT MEN WHO COME BACK FROM WAR AND TEN OTHER PICTURES BEING MADE AT STUDIOS NOW WITH SOLDIER RETURNING HOME THEME. BELIEVE THIS IS GOOD SPACING AND GOOD BUSINESS.

FROM CHARLES K. FELDMAN [agent and packager]

Mr. Jack L. Warner
Warner Bros.
400 West Olive
Burbank, California

November 16, 1945

Dear Jack:

You will recall that during the filming of *The Big Sleep* I came to your house and urged you to make retakes with Bacall. You allowed Howard [Hawks] to make three or four days additional scenes with some retakes. After viewing the picture in its entirety I asked you again to re-do the scene where Bacall wears a veil but in the last analysis you allowed the scene to stay in.

Before the retakes were made I suggested to Howard, and in two or three instances he followed my suggestions, that he give to Bacall certain scenes that were previously shot with the butler and made other substitutions of a similar nature. All of the foregoing I did because I felt that Bacall only had a "bit" in the picture.

After reading the write-ups in the New York papers, Jack, and the general comments regarding the girl with which you are probably familiar by now,* I urge you (and that is the reason for this letter) to view the film again with the following in mind:

1. Make whatever photographic retakes are necessary and by all means re-do the veil scene.

2. Give the girl at least three or four additional scenes with Bogart of the insolent and provocative nature that she had in *To Have and*

*Regarding *Confidential Agent*, made after *The Big Sleep* but released before it.

Have Not. You see, Jack, in *To Have and Have Not* Bacall was more insolent than Bogart and this very insolence endeared her in both the public's and the critics' mind when the picture appeared. It was something startling and new. If this could be recaptured through these additional scenes with Bacall and Bogart, which frankly I think is a very easy task, I feel that the girl will come through for you magnificently.

Bear in mind, Jack, that if the girl receives the same type of general reviews and criticisms on *The Big Sleep* [as the poor ones on *Confidential Agent*] which she definitely will receive unless changes are made, you might lose one of your most important assets. Though the additional scenes will only cost in the neighborhood of probably $25,000 or $50,000, in my opinion this should be done even if the cost should run to $250,000. I am writing this note to you as a friend and trust that you will not think that I presume to tell you how to run your business.

Rushing to see a show so had dictated this letter without rereading same.

Best,
Charles K. Feldman

FROM JACK L. WARNER

NOVEMBER 20, 1945

TO [Samuel] SCHNEIDER [vice president, New York]: HOW MANY PRINTS HAVE YOU MADE UP ON "BIG SLEEP?" IF YOU HAVEN'T MADE ANY, DON'T. IF YOU HAVE, ADVISE FOREIGN DEPT NOT TO MAKE UP ANY PRINTS UNTIL WE SEND THEM REPLACEMENTS. . . . AS HAVE ALWAYS FELT WE SHOULD TAKE OVER SEVERAL SEQUENCES WITH THIS GIRL. KEEP THIS CONFIDENTIAL. . . .

FROM JACK L. WARNER

NOVEMBER 21, 1945

RELAY TO CHARLES FELDMAN, SHERRY NETHERLAND: DEAR CHARLIE: . . . THANKS YOUR LETTER 16TH RE "BIG SLEEP" RETAKES. YOU MUST BEEN READING MY MAIL AS WAS THINKING ABOUT THIS AT VERY TIME WAS OPENING YOUR LETTER. AM DEFINITELY ARRANGING TO SO DO. . . .

FROM JACK L. WARNER

JANUARY 3, 1946

TO [Samuel] SCHNEIDER: RAN "THE BIG SLEEP" AGAIN LAST NIGHT. WE ARE TAKING OUT A THOUSAND FEET TO IMPROVE THE TEMPO AND

ADDING TWO NEW SULTRY SEQUENCES WITH BOGART AND BACALL. IN
MY OPINION, PICTURE WILL BE IMPROVED FIFTY PERCENT AS WELL AS
PROTECT LAUREN BACALL. . . . SEE THAT ALL FOREIGN NEGATIVES
AND PRINTS ARE RETURNED TO STUDIO . . .

FEBRUARY 9, 1946
FROM JACK WARNER TO [New York executives] . . . HAD FINAL SNEAK
PREVIEW "BIG SLEEP" LAST NIGHT. THIS NEW VERSION WHICH HAS
NEW SCENES PROTECTING BACALL COMES OFF GREAT, AND IN MY
OPINION WE HAVE ONE HUNDRED PERCENT BETTER PICTURE . . .

SEPTEMBER 6, 1945
FROM JACK L. WARNER TO [Samuel] SCHNEIDER: . . . "RHAPSODY [in]
BLUE" . . . ABOUT LENGTH OF PICTURE: THIS BUGABOO AND MEANS
NOTHING BECAUSE "ANCHORS AWEIGH" [MGM] HAS BEEN RUNNING
SEVEN STRAIGHT WEEKS HERE IN THREE THEATRES AND TRY TO GET
IN! IT RUNS TWO HOURS FIFTY MINUTES AND SEEMS LIKE IT WILL
NEVER STOP. LIKEWISE, SEEMS LIKE AUDIENCE WILL NEVER STOP
GOING TO THEATRES, SO THAT OLD ADAGE OF PICTURES BEING TOO
LONG DOESN'T HOLD WATER. SO WAS "GONE WITH WIND" LONG, ETC.
TRUE, SHORTER PICTURES MEANS FASTER TURNOVER BUT IT ISN'T ANY
MEASURING STICK. . . .

SEPTEMBER 7, 1945
FROM JACK L. WARNER TO [Mort] BLUMENSTOCK [head of publicity and
advertising, New York] . . . CONFIDENTIALLY, IMPOSSIBLE SIGN UP [John]
GARFIELD AFTER HE MAKES ONE MORE PICTURE FOR US. HE HAS
FORGOTTEN DAYS WHEN I PICKED HIM UP WHEN MAKING SIX BITS
WEEKLY. NEVERTHELESS, WE WILL GET ALONG WITHOUT HIM AND
DON'T WANT SLOWDOWN ON HIS PUBLICITY BECAUSE NATURALLY WE
HAVE HIM IN "NOBODY LIVES FOREVER" [1946], WHICH IS IN VAULTS,
PLUS ONE MORE TO MAKE [Humoresque, 1947] AND DON'T WANT TROUBLE
WITH HIM WHEN WE MAKING LAST ONE, AS HE NO PUSHOVER. . . .

FROM WILLIAM FAULKNER, Oxford, Mississippi

To Col. J. L. Warner

15 October, 1945

Dear Colonel Warner:
     . . . I still feel that I should not . . . commit myself further to
studio work, and that if possible I should sever all my existing studio
commitments. . . .
     I feel that I have made a bust at moving picture writing and

therefore have mis-spent and will continue to mis-spend time which at my age I cannot afford. During my three years (including leave-suspensions) at Warner's, I did the best work I knew how on 5 or 6 scripts. Only two were made and I feel that I received credit on these not on the value of the work I did but partly through the friendship of Director Howard Hawks. So I have spent three years doing work (trying to do it) which was not my forte and which I was not equipped to do, and therefore I have mis-spent time which as a 47 year old novelist I could not afford to spend. And I don't dare mis-spend any more of it.

For that reason, I am unhappy in studio work. Not at Warner's studio; my connection with the studio and all the people I worked with could not have been pleasanter. But with the type of work. So I repeat my request that the studio release me from my contract. . . .

Waiting to hear from you, I am
Yours sincerely,
William Faulkner

One week later, the request was denied via Warners' legal department. Altogether, Faulkner worked on seventeen Warner Bros. projects since signing a contract in 1942, but received screen credit on only two, To Have and Have Not *(1945) and* The Big Sleep *(1946). The future Nobel prize-winning novelist also worked on* Air Force *(1943),* Background to Danger *(1943),* Northern Pursuit *(1943),* Mildred Pierce *(1945),* Stallion Road *(1947),* Deep Valley *(1947), and* Adventures of Don Juan *(1949), in addition to some projects that were not realized.*

The Rise of Jerry Wald (1944–1947)

TO: Jerry Wald   DATE: December 9, 1944
FROM: Alvah Bessie [screenwriter]   SUBJECT: "Objective, Burma!"

Dear Jerry:

I'd like to put on the record what we were discussing yesterday on the phone. Namely—the scene in *Objective,Burma!* in which the newspaper correspondent says the Japanese should be "wiped off the face of the earth."

I've discussed this with [screenwriter] Lester Cole, and he feels precisely the way I do about it—that the statement, as used, can be a very dangerous one and, in a film that so sedulously avoids political statement of any kind, this one highly political statement sticks out like a sore thumb.

It seems to me that if you are going to dramatize Japanese atrocities— and I think they *should* be dramatized—then you owe it to yourself to make it plain that such atrocities are not the private property of one nation or one race of people.

You will recall that in the story I wrote for you the atrocities were dramatized, and a character did state that "these are not men—they are beasts." And that Nelson [Errol Flynn] correctly answered: "There's nothing especially *Japanese* about this. . . . You'll find it wherever you find fascists. There are even people who call themselves Americans who'd do it, too."

I am not asking for a complete explanation of these things. But I assure you that if you do not answer the racist statement: "They ought to be wiped off the face of the earth," you are falling into the enemy's trap. Wiping people off the face of the earth is the private idea—and policy— of fascists. The Italians tried it in Ethiopia. Franco is doing it in Spain; the Germans have tried it with the Jews, the Poles, the Russians. And even the Russians, who have suffered more from fascist bestiality than any other people, are not talking about wiping the Germans off the face of the earth.

I quote you Roosevelt's recent statement on this: "In all people, without exception, there lives some instinct for truth, some attraction toward justice, and some passion for peace—buried as they may be in the German case under a brutal regime. . . . We bring no charge against the German race, as such, for we cannot believe that God has eternally condemned any race of humanity."

You handled this idea very well indeed in *Destination Tokyo* [1943] when Cary Grant made it plain that people can be trained from childhood to be brutes—or they can be trained to be decent human beings.

Of course, you might argue that the correspondent's statement refers only to the Japanese Army. But it seems quite likely to me that even if this *is* the intention, the phrase is quite ambiguous, and could be interpreted to mean the Japanese people. And since this is obviously not the policy of our government or any of the other Allied governments, a very bad impression indeed could be created.

I would strenuously urge that if it is technically impossible for Nelson to answer the correspondent's [Henry Hull] remarks, then the correspondent's speech should be cut. The scene carries enough impact as it is, without Henry Hull's hysterical commentary.

P.S. I'm taking the liberty of sending copies of this memo to Mr. Warner and Steve Trilling, as I believe I owe it to them to let them know what I feel. Also, I am sure neither Warner nor Trilling would want our film to be misinterpreted, or to apparently carry the tone of a typical Hearst editorial.

The line of dialogue remained in the film. Alvah Bessie wrote the original story and Lester Cole shared screenplay credit with Ranald MacDougall.

MILDRED PIERCE

TO: T. C. Wright   DATE: November 6, 1944
FROM: Jerry Wald   SUBJECT: "Mildred Pierce"

Dear Tenny:

The closer we come to production on *Mildred Pierce* the more worried Curtiz and I are becoming about the cameraman.

First let me point out to you that the following men have made tests of Miss [Joan] Crawford with not very satisfactory results:

1—Ernie Haller
2—Bert Glennon
3—Sol Polito
4—Carl Guthrie

On Tuesday we are making additional tests with Pev Marley.

This note is not written to you in criticism but rather to ask your advice. We do know that somewhere along the line these cameramen are missing. Both Curtiz and I looked at the film she made at Metro and there is no doubt that men like Bob Planck and Ray June managed to capture on the screen what we are trying to get for Miss Crawford. What is worrying me at the present time is what happens if Pev Marley doesn't work out? As you know, both Curtiz and I feel that Jimmie Howe would be the logical man for this picture but from my past conversation with you regarding his availability, you hold very little hope that we'll have him in time for our picture. What suggestions have you in mind after Marley?

As I told you, Miss Crawford is most anxious to make tests with any and every cameraman you can suggest because she is just as anxious as we are to look right on the screen and she certainly has no objection to using one of our own cameramen, if they do right by her, so in fairness to everybody concerned, would you let me know what you think we can do?

Jerry Wald

Ernest Haller photographed Mildred Pierce. *Joan Crawford had been under contract to MGM for eighteen years before going to Warner Bros. in 1943. Mildred Pierce (1945) was her first picture at Warners (other than an appearance in the all-star Hollywood Canteen, 1944).*

*The following study was made as a result of another legal compli-
cation, which finally was determined to have no basis.*

TO: Roy Obringer   DATE: March 4, 1949
FROM: Tom Chapman [assistant   SUBJECT: "Mildred Pierce"
    story editor]

THE GENESIS AND DEVELOPMENT OF MILDRED PIERCE
   . . . From the first, *Mildred Pierce* presented a difficult problem in
adaptation. As [James M.] Cain originally wrote the novel all the characters
in it, including Mildred, were unpleasant. It is well known that in a
successful motion picture the audience must be able to identify itself with
the interests of certain good characters as against certain bad ones. At the
same time the immoral activities of Mildred actually were unscreenable
because of the Production Code. Since it was clear that Mildred must be
the heroine of this story it was necessary to clean up her character. For
this reason she was made a member of the upper middle class instead of
the lower middle class; vulgarisms were dropped from her speech; she was
made more the victim of circumstances than a sinner. At the same time
her affair with Wally [contract star Jack Carson] was dropped and her
relationship with her husband [contract player Bruce Bennett] made deeper
and more honest so that the audience could feel, when the end of the
film was shown, that there was a real basis for Mildred and her husband
Bert to find happiness together.
    Mildred's antagonists in this story were [her daughter] Veda [Ann
Blyth, borrowed from Universal] and Monty [contract star Zachary Scott].
For purposes of heightening this dramatic conflict they were both made
a little more villainous than they are in the novel. Mr. Cain's book gave
Veda the saving graces of a passionate devotion to music and a genius for
singing. We did not wish Veda to have these saving graces and so eliminated this from the picture. In order to emphasize her villainy further,
and for other reasons which are outlined below, we made her the murderer
of Monty. In order that Monty should be shown up as little better than
a gigolo, and to justify this murder, we introduced a scene in which
Mildred Pierce openly buys him as a husband, and further made him
responsible for Mildred's losing her business.
    It is clear, we think, that these changes were dictated by the logical
dramatic necessity of establishing a group of characters fighting for the
good as against a group representing evil. Mr. Wald informs us that he
had such changes in mind from the first. . . .

TO: Roy Obringer
FROM: Tom Chapman

DATE: November 8, 1949
SUBJECT: Genesis and Development of "Mildred Pierce"

WALD'S METHOD OF WORK

Mr. Wald does not develop a story from script to script in chronological fashion. He employs the services of a number of writers, many of them working without previous acquaintance with the work of others on the same script, in order that a full scale original contribution may be made by each writer. Mr. Wald organizes the story in his own mind on the basis of his selection and synthesizing of the work of the different writers. He must, therefore, be considered the originator and organizer of the story, regardless of a chronological line of development.

THE PURCHASE OF "MILDRED PIERCE"

. . . Ever since the publicaton of *Mildred Pierce* in 1941, Mr. Wald had been interested in this novel as a story property. He keeps a file of over 2000 such stories, all of which have aroused his interest and all of which present problems in adaptation which are difficult to solve. From time to time, Mr. Wald informed us, he tried to persuade the front office to purchase this story. They were not unwilling to purchase it, but pointed out that Wald would have to find a way of organizing it dramatically and getting it by the Breen office before serious purchase consideration was justified. In the summer of 1943, several months before our purchase of the novel, Mr. Wald conceived the idea of creating suspense in the story by telling it in flashback and providing the missing dramatic climax through a murder. Wald discussed this matter with James Cain himself, and suggested that Cain prepare a treatment of the story, starting it with a murder and telling it in flashback. On September 22nd, 1943, Mr. Cain wrote Mr. Wald a letter in which he said he had struggled with this problem and had not solved it to his own satisfaction. The letter credits Wald with the idea of starting the story with a murder and doing the main part by means of flashback. . . .

Following Cain's inability to solve the problems mentioned, Mr. Warner wrote Mr. Wald a memo in which he suggested that the project should be dropped. . . . However, Mr. Wald's belief in the story was so great that he did not give up. He tells us that he discussed the matter with James Geller, then our Story Editor, who is also a personal friend of Cain's, and that Geller suggested that Thames Williamson, a well known writer who was then on our staff as a screen story analyst, might have some ideas for treatment. . . .

Williamson's treatment . . . employs the flashback technique which was in Wald's mind from the first and it has a murder in it—Mildred murders Veda after discovering her in a compromising position with

Monty . . . and that as a result of this murder certain police characters would have to be introduced. These ideas did not come to him from Wald, to whom they had already occurred, because Wald does not work that way. Any writer he assigns to a script develops it independently, in order that Wald may have the benefit of the original thinking of a number of people. . . .

THE BREEN OFFICE GETS THE WILLIAMSON TREATMENT

Mr. Warner transmitted the material to Mr. Breen, requesting his opinion. Mr. Breen's opinion, expressed in a letter to Mr. Warner dated February 2nd, 1944, was that you dismiss this story from any further consideration.

Accordingly, Mr. Trilling, Mr. Warner's assistant, advised Mr. Wald to forget the project. . . .

On February 7th Williamson sent Wald another memo in which he said that the novel, *Mildred Pierce*, was so rich, strong and dramatic that it could be played from start to finish on a higher level, and that this approach could solve the Breen office objections. . . . The Breen office accepted this line of approach, while at the same time pointing out that there would be a number of problems later on, no doubt, in handling subsequent scenes and sequences. . . . On February 25th, 1944, Mr. Warner authorized the purchase of the novel. . . .

THE CATHERINE TURNEY SCRIPTS

Williamson was not given the job of doing the screenplay because Wald felt he was not the person for the assignment. *Mildred Pierce* was designed as a "woman's picture" and Wald wished to assign it to [contract writer] Catherine Turney who, at the time, was one of our best developers of this type of material. . . .

Miss Turney worked from the Cain novel. She also saw Thames Williamson's treatment and [contract writer] Albert Maltz's [62 pages of] notes, though she did not base her work on these. . . .

It was with great reluctance that Miss Turney acceded to Mr. Wald's insistence upon dropping Veda's interest in classical music; she felt that this was an integral part of Mr. Cain's story. Mr. Wald felt, however, that audience sympathy might be lost for Mildred if Veda had this much talent and ability, and he therefore insisted that she go into a low dive and become a night club singer. Under protest Miss Turney made these changes. Then Mr. Wald broached to Miss Turney the idea of telling the story in flashback, beginning with a police situation. Miss Turney thought that he had gotten this idea from seeing the motion picture, *Double Indemnity* [Paramount, 1944] (made from the James Cain novel of the same name). . . . Miss Turney refused to tell *Mildred Pierce* in flashback, because she felt that this was not fair to the Cain book, and so there is no flashback in her version, and she subsequently went off the script. . . .

THE MARGARET GRUEN SCRIPT

It became necessary for Mr. Wald to find another writer. . . . He approached James Cain to do the job. Cain refused, and suggested Margaret Gruen. . . . Mrs. Gruen's script also follows the novel very closely, except for some changes which were never used. . . .

By this time, it had become obvious to Mr. Wald that for reasons of dramatic structure it was necessary to include the elements Mrs. Gruen omitted from her version and her version was therefore dropped. . . .

After seeing the picture Mrs. Gruen discussed it with James Cain, who, she asserts, told her at the time he considered the picture a splendid version of his novel. . . .

RANALD MACDOUGALL AND THE PREPARATION OF THE FINAL SCRIPT

. . . Mr. Wald asked Ranald MacDougall to develop a script. According to Mr. MacDougall, he independently arrived at the idea of telling the story in flashback, etc. (Mr. Wald hopes writers will arrive at such ideas independently, for they turn out better scripts. Sometimes, however, he must help them do so in conference, through carefully led discussion.) From the evidence we have been able to analyze, it appears that the police and other elements in the story, which came into it as soon as the flashback and murder were employed, are his creation. . . .

MacDougall's approach to the script includes all the basic changes from the novel which appear in the completed film. . . .

OTHER WRITERS ON THE SCRIPT

From time to time other writers were employed on the script, for purposes of polishing and sharpening rather than affecting the basic line, which had now been shaped. These writers were Margaret Buell Wilder, Louise Randall Pierson and William Faulkner. So far as we can make out, they all had access to each other's work, and while everybody was revising everybody else's work Wald was synthesizing everything. . . .

Mrs. Wilder was not available to answer . . . questions, since she is in New York. . . .

Mrs. Pierson worked under the supervision of Jerry Wald and Mike Curtiz. She explained that Curtiz had some ideas which he wished incorporated in the picture and she was supposed to do this. Wald, who differed with Curtiz on some of these points, had Ranald MacDougall trying to get Wald's ideas in the script. Mrs. Pierson said that Wald won out. . . .

Mrs. Pierson worked from the Cain novel, the Catherine Turney script, and the Ranald MacDougall script. She explained that she was revising MacDougall's copy at the same time Faulkner was revising MacDougall's copy, and that she also preceded MacDougall on some scenes of connective copy. At the same time MacDougall and Faulkner were revising each other's and her copy. . . .

Mr. Faulkner is not on good terms with the studio. He has not been contacted. . . . We did not feel that he would be of much assistance. . . . He is living at home in Oxford, Miss. . . .

JERRY WALD

In discussing the opening of *Mildred Pierce*, in which Mildred has an impulse to suicide, Mr. Wald said that Miss Turney had thought this suicide impulse a logical extension of Mildred's feelings when she discovered Monty with Veda. Opening the picture with this impulse had been suggested, Wald thought, by Mr. Curtiz, and in adopting the suggestion Wald was influenced by the success of this particular opening in a previous film of his [Wald's], *The Hard Way* [1943]. . . .

He [Wald] said that he had discussed the picture with James Cain and that Cain was delighted with it. He believes that Cain wrote Joan Crawford, who starred in the film, a letter to this effect. His purpose throughout, he asserted, was to bring the Cain novel to the screen in suitable dramatic form, and the novel was his only original source material. . . .

MICHAEL CURTIZ

[Curtiz] worked from the Turney and MacDougall scripts and also consulted with several of the writers who were polishing. It was he who suggested the beach house sequence. He was living at [director] Anatole Litvak's house at the time,* and thought it would be colorful to show on the screen. Our art director, he said, went down to the Litvak house so that he could virtually duplicate some of it for our screenplay. He also claims that it was his idea that Mildred should operate a drive-in instead of a restaurant. . . .

He [Curtiz] telephoned James Cain himself and told him the story as our final script presented it. . . . Mr. Curtiz asserts that Mr. Cain was most enthusiastic about this line of treatment, and said that in his opinion our final screenplay constituted an improvement over the book, because it was better dramatically and brought out the book's values. . . .

*Litvak was in the Army.

TO: Obringer   DATE: February 12, 1950
FROM: Chapman

Dear Roy:

. . . It is commonplace in this business that authors who sell us stories often feel that their material has been destroyed by the vultures of Hollywood; this thesis, as you know, has been the subject of a good many novels and plays. Authors tend to place an equal value on every aspect of their stories, with the result that so much as changing an adjective will lead the author to conclude that his story as a whole has been changed unrecognizably. In writing *Mildred Pierce* James Cain presumably believed that he had written a serious genre study of the middle class. The introduction of the murder, the police element, flashback form, might well have convinced him that we had changed his "serious study" into a murder mystery. When the story is examined in its structural aspects and in its characterization it is clear that all of these are substantially as they were in the Cain novel. What has been altered here is the *method*, the screenplay technique of telling the yarn.

A slight written substantiation of my above theory—and it is only a theory as I have seen no word from Cain that this was his feeling—may be found in an article he wrote in *Modern Screen* for August 1946, entitled, "Why Did Mildred Pierce Do It?" (page 33). In this article, Cain mentions a visit of his to Joan Crawford and says in part, "By the time we had crossed the hall we were friends, which wasn't surprising, as we had a profound bond, which was *Mildred Pierce*, which I wrote and she played. . . ." Later, referring to the novel *Mildred Pierce*, and quoting Joan Crawford, Cain states, " 'I had read it when it was first published, and I went through it again. They did several scripts, each one a little better than the last, and at last there was one that seemed right.' "

" 'Nice, except for the murder.' " (This is Cain quoting Cain.)

" 'You want to know about that? All I can say is, they tried it without the murder, and the thing seemed flat. The murder pulled it together somehow.' " (This last was Crawford's statement.)

As you will see from the answers to some of the questions below, there is ample reason to believe Cain was quite pleased with the film at the time it was in work and released, regardless of what he says now. . . .

It is certain that Wald did *not* get the idea of a flashback treatment of *Mildred Pierce* from seeing the picture, *Double Indemnity*, as *Double Indemnity* was released by Paramount on April 24, 1944. We know from Cain's letter to Wald, dated September 22, 1943, that the flashback idea was in Wald's mind at that time.* It is, however, possible that the success

---

*It is possible, of course, that Wald was aware of the structure of *Double Indemnity* from a reading of the script, discussions with people involved in the project, an advance screening of parts or all of the film, or word via the industry grapevine.

of the motion picture, *Double Indemnity*, helped to confirm Wald's conclusion that this was the correct line of approach to *Mildred Pierce*. Cain's novel *Double Indemnity*, is not told in flashback but straight line. The flashback treatment was a necessary screenplay device to help build up suspense in the case of the Paramount release, as well as in the case of *Mildred Pierce*. . . .

Curtiz telephoned Cain [and] he arranged to meet him at the Brown Derby in Beverly Hills for dinner. Wald also went along (Wald had forgotten this but recalled it when it was brought to his attention). Curtiz says this dinner took place between three and six weeks prior to the start of shooting (shooting began December 7, 1944). . . . Curtiz says he and Wald told Cain the story line as it would appear in the final script. . . . Curtiz says Cain was delighted and said "I couldn't write it better. You have improved it. Excellent. . . ."

For Cain's side of the story, see Roy Hoopes' biography Cain *(1982), which goes into considerable detail based on Cain's correspondence.*

FROM JACK L. WARNER

January 1945

NOTES FOR MEETING WITH CAMERAMEN AND ART DIRECTORS

Must preface remarks by pointing out that we are not finding fault in any manner but must be realistic. Although times are good and quoted box office figures are high, we must not believe all the publicity we read. We must remember that pictures, even though they too are made with all the technical perfection—excellent sets and photography, etc.—can sustain losses, such as *Action in the North Atlantic* [1943]—*Passage to Marseille* [1944]—*Mission to Moscow* [1943]—*[The Adventures of]* Mark Twain [1944] and others.

Also, technical perfection does not necessarily mean the success of a picture. Some of the best commercial successes and pictures that have received high critical acclaim do not necessarily reflect the greatest technical perfection, such as *Going My Way* [1944], which was not outstanding photography, nor highly important sets, nor new or tricky devices from a technical standpoint. It missed a lot of those things our perfectionists insist on in pictures. . . .

With rising costs, must use your ingenuity and devise new means of cutting corners without losing any of the quality. By this we do not mean we have to "cheat" but we all have to use our imagination wherever possible. . . .

. . . On construction of sets we possibly go into too much detail. Half of the time it is in the background and unnoticed. On the sets we try to show adjoining rooms which entails construction, lighting, etc., when shooting—whereas we can confine our action in the single room.

When plans are being sketched and models made, if the Art Director can visualize action being played in slightly different manner that might save constructing a set or telescoping three sets into two, he should speak up and tell the head of the department, or [Tenny] Wright, so the idea can be thoroughly explored.

We try more and more for the low camera angles and ceiling shots, which take time to light and slow us up.

Once a master shot is okayed by the director, the cameraman should not call for another take because the cameraman noticed a slight technical fault. It isn't just taking another shot but you find that in redoing it there is "talent breakdown" and other mechanical faults, so instead of one shot it goes into 4 or 5 additional takes. Most of the time these master shots are only used for a flash, as we break it up into the closer shots—and if there is a little mechanical fault it is covered anyway. Let the Director call the turn and if it is necessary to go back and reshoot it later on we will do it—but only if necessary.

Have heard comments from cameramen that because of the ceilings it is more difficult to light sets. Is there any remedy arrived at by the Art Directors after this was brought to their attention? . . .

NEW YORK NY

JULY 24, 1945

JL [Warner] TO TRILLING—INFORM JERRY [Wald] I DEFINITELY DO NOT WANT ANY MORE MEMOS SENT YOU, MYSELF OR ANYONE WHERE HE BEGINS BY STATING QUOTE NO ONE ON THE LOT HAS A PROPER CONCEPTION OF THE MAGNITUDE OF OUR PROJECTED FILM UNQUOTE. TELL JERRY EMPHATICALLY THIS TYPE OF LANGUAGE UNCALLED FOR AND I DO NOT WANT ANY MORE. INSOFAR AS YOU AND I CONCERNED, WE HAVE A CONCEPTION OF EVERYTHING THAT'S BEING DONE INCLUDING [Wald's production of] "TASK FORCE" [1949]. HE SHOULDN'T PUT THESE THINGS IN WRITING OR IN HIS MIND. . . .

FROM ROBERT LORD

Mr. J. L. Warner
Warner Bros. Studio
Burbank, California

August 29, 1945

Dear Jack:

I have just got the first definite information about the possibility of my release from the Army. This is not official yet but it could be classed as "probable."

It seems likely that I will be released sometime in October. After almost four years of getting beat over the head, I feel wonderful—was never healthier. But I do have about four weeks of concentrated dentistry to suffer through. . . .

I could go back to work around the first of December. I prefer not to start back to work until the first of next year but we won't argue about that. You tell me which date you prefer.

Now, a few words as to my relationship with Warner Brothers: In the time that I have been gone, the company has made more money, and I believe, more pictures than ever before in its existence. Never before has the company been more solid, prosperous, strong, etc. If I never went back, it would not make the slightest difference to Warner Brothers. Not only am I not the "indispensable man"; I am not even slightly important to the studio. I realize this clearly and am suffering from no illusions of grandeur.

Furthermore, I realize that I have a perfectly legal and valid contract with Warner Brothers. If you order me to come back and complete that contract, I have no reason to refuse and, of course, I will comply with the terms of the contract.

If you wish to release me from that contract, I can make a very fine deal for myself in practically any one of the major studios. I am sure you know this to be true and that I am not bluffing. If you want me to sign a new contract and continue with Warner Brothers in the future, here is what I propose:

I think that I could function as Executive Producer of your studio, build a great deal of good will amongst your employees and amongst the other studios in this community. I think that I can be instrumental in helping to produce some pictures of high quality and strong box-office appeal. I think I can administer the studio quietly, politely, efficiently and without attempts to become a God, as several of your previous Executive Producers have attempted. For this job, my salary would be $250,000 per year; a straight five year contract with no options. You can fire me at any time on 60-day notice. I can quit any time on 60-day notice.

If you are not interested in the Executive Producer idea, I will function as a Producer for $3,500 per week and two percent of the gross receipts (world distribution) of the pictures I produce. A straight five year contact, no options. But you can fire me and I can quit any time on 60-day notice. In case I get fired or quit, it goes without saying that I get my percentage of the gross on pictures I have completed.

If we make a new deal, I have the right to have my attorney inspect the contract before I sign it. If we do not make a new deal, that has nothing to do with our friendship or mutual esteem. I have the warmest feelings toward H. M. [Warner] and toward yourself. The Warner organization is a magnificent one and I will not work anywhere else if Warners will give me, even remotely, as good a break as I can get at other studios. My terms to you are rather steep, I know. But we both know that I can do as well and even better at other studios.

Naturally, I expect to hear from you after you have had a chance to digest this letter and discuss it with all the people concerned. In the meantime, you know that I wish you all the luck and happiness in the world, and that I am grateful for everything you have done for me in the past.

> Cordially and sincerely,
> Robert Lord
> Lt. Colonel, Signal Corps

FROM JACK L. WARNER

Lt. Col. Robt. Lord
157 N. Las Palmas
Hollywood Calif.

August 31, 1945

Dear Bob:

First, in behalf of all those who helped make the great pictures and the important progress of our Company possible since you went into the Army, I want to thank you for your good wishes. Second, your statement about having a valid and legal contract with our Company is, of course, perfectly true. However, the balance of your letter is completely opposite to the last talk we had in the private dining room, and the monies you asked for plus a percentage with a sixty-day notice of cancellation by either party, etc., are terms in which we would definitely not be interested.

Therefore, since you have asked for your release from your existing contract, I have no objection to granting your request, and I am attaching three release forms, two of which you can execute and return to us in order that proper company records can be had of our mutual agreement in this respect.

I wish you every success in the world wherever you may become associated, and want you to know my brother and I have the very warmest feelings towards you and always will have. I also want to thank you for all the splendid work you did for our Company prior to your entrance into the service.

> Kindest regards.
> Sincerely,

Robert Lord had been with Warner Bros. since 1927. He went to
MGM and then teamed with Humphrey Bogart to form Santana Productions in 1948.

HUMORESQUE

TO: Steve Trilling   DATE: March 12, 1945
FROM: Jerry Wald   SUBJECT: "Humoresque"

Dear Steve:

I spoke to [writer] Barney Glazer and he will have the treatment
finished on Friday of this week. I hope you realize that the screenplay
will go much faster, inasmuch as we are using tremendous hunks out of
the "Humoresque" story [by Fannie Hurst] and the original Odets script
on *Rhapsody in Blue* [1945].

I am enclosing a note from Barney, which he wrote to me when he
originally started working on this treatment, which explains the whole
Jewish problem. The fact that you want to make the family Jewish is okay
with me. We will leave the rest of the treatment in the Italian atmosphere
but in the screenplay we will go back to a nondescript foreign family, just
as was done in *Rhapsody in Blue*.

                                   Jerry Wald

In 1942 playwright Clifford Odets was hired by Warner to write a
script loosely based on the life of George Gershwin (Rhapsody in Blue,
1945). Since very little of Odets's script was used in the final version of
that film, Wald took a large portion of the script, changed the names of
the characters, and retitled it Humoresque.

TO: Jerry Wald   Undated, circa early 1945
FROM: Barney Glazer [screenwriter]

Dear Jerry:

You have asked me to put down a story line which shall include:

(a) The fruit of our several conferences.
(b) What can be salvaged from the Odets script of *Rhapsody in Blue*.
(c) What can be retained of the story and [the 1920 silent] picture *Humoresque*.
(d) Ideas of my own to supplement the rest.

I remind you that what has not yet been decided is the important
question of the hero's racial origins. I want to keep him a Jew, as Ferber

[sic; Fannie Hurst] and Odets did. You are not sure that is wise. I say we are too sensitive about putting the real Jew on the screen the way they put the Irish Catholic on the screen in *Going My Way* [1944]; that stories like *Abie's Irish Rose* and *Children of the Ghetto* were so enormously successful because they pulled no Jewish punches; that even "Humoresque" owed its popularity largly to the Yiddisha Momma who dominated its story. You answer that we are doing a study of young genius; that for the greater part of it our hero must be portrayed as an out-and-out little sonofabitch; that the same color and sympathy can be had from say an Italian-American family portrait. It is an open question. It ought to be decided before we go much further. Perhaps you may want to consult the opinions of Jack Warner, Charley Einfeld and Steve Trilling. After all it is a matter of policy too.

In this outline I am going Italian, but do not blame me too much if the Jewish creeps in. It is more than a choice between serving spaghetti or gefeulte fish; the ingredients I have to cook with *are* Jewish as Ferber [*sic*; Hurst] and Odets contrived them. And musically, Jerry, it could well be a choice between Paganini's "Perpetual Motion" or the "Hebrew Melody" of Achron, as Heifitz plays it, or the Kaddish Death Song.

Faithfully,
Barney

In the final version of the screenplay, the character portrayed by John Garfield came from an Italian family.

TO: Jerry Wald
FROM: Mary Lou Mitchell
[secretary to Roy Obringer]

DATE: June 27, 1945
SUBJECT: "Humoresque"

. . . Insofar as Odets is concerned, we took all right, title and interest in and to his screenplay and can do with it whatever we like. However, the script was based on the life of George Gershwin and under our contract with the Gershwin estate, we have the right to make only one picture; therefore, in using the Odets script, you cannot use any material which pertains to the life of Gershwin. In other words, the only material which you can use is that which is fictional and this should be thoroughly checked so that absolutely none of the Gershwin material appears in the *Humoresque* script.

Mary Lou Mitchell

Only Odets's fictional material was used.

TO: Steve Trilling DATE: December 1, 1945
FROM: Jerry Wald SUBJECT: "Humoresque"

Dear Steve:

If you wish to start *Humoresque* a week from Monday, I think you are making a mistake that is going to cost this company eventually an extra $100,000 on the picture. Let's face the facts for a moment:

MUSIC: John Garfield arrived in the studio Tuesday. You expect him to know how to play the violin in two weeks—or even give the impression that he is able to play this instrument. For your information, nobody in the history of the music world or the picture business has been able to accomplish this feat, unless he has had some previous knowledge of the instrument. The studio is certainly placing a handicap on Mr. Garfield's performance when they ask him to fake violin-playing in a picture which concerns itself primarily about a violinist, without giving him a reasonable amount of time to get up on it.

After Mr. Garfield learns how to handle the bow and the violin, he must next learn how to get the proper fingering for each number he is supposed to be doing in the picture.

Robert Alda, in order to play the piano in *Rhapsody in Blue*, studied four hours a day, seven days a week for one month. Cornel Wilde studied for six weeks, four hours a day, seven days a week to play the piano in the Chopin picture [*A Song to Remember*, 1944]. As you well know, learning to fake playing the violin is a much more difficult job than the piano, because with a piano you can fake so much with the keyboard.

Although we have been desperately trying to get set on who is to play the violin, we have not decided on anybody as yet, due to our anxiety to get a violinist whose tone has the quality that [Jose] Iturbi's piano-playing had in the Chopin picture. By Monday night, we will have test recordings from New York which we ordered last week.

[Music Director Leo] Forbstein and [staff composer and conductor Franz] Waxman are desperately trying to get music clearances. A lot of the numbers are in public domain, but we must be sure they are cleared in Europe for us. Forbstein and Waxman are pushing ahead on this as fast as they can.

Once the violinist and the music are set, the numbers must be rehearsed and pre-recorded so we don't have to wait around on the set wondering what number we have to shoot.

Oscar Levant arrives here Tuesday. A lot of the numbers will have to be worked out with him. None of this can be done until we know what our music is going to be.

MAKEUP: We have to make comparative makeup tests of [Joan] Crawford and Garfield together. Hair-tests of Crawford have to be done. . . .

WARDROBE: . . . All Crawford's wardrobe must be tested before we start the picture.

To my way of thinking, I would recommend that this picture start on December 17. This week's delay will not only save us time in shooting but it will rid everybody of a tremendous amount of confusion and pressure that is being exerted to put this picture into production before it is completely ready. . . .

Jerry Wald

Humoresque *was rescheduled to commence shooting on Friday December 14.*

TO: Bernie Newman [wardrobe   DATE: December 22, 1945
      department]   SUBJECT: "Humoresque"
FROM: Jerry Wald

Dear Bernie:

We ran the first four clothes test changes on Crawford. In general they are excellent, except that the shoulders are still too broad. . . .

The dress that was designed for Helen's [Crawford's] party, with the puffed sleeves, is much too exaggerated in the shoulders and the skirt is too full. . . . To us, it looks too much like the Joan Crawford who was left behind at Metro.

We have in our hands a woman who is being recognized for her acting ability, and nothing should be done to distract from that. We know she is a good actress and we shouldn't make the fatal mistake that Metro did by trying to over-dress her. . . .

Jerry Wald

Gilbert Adrian designed Crawford's wardrobe for Humoresque.

TO: Steve Trilling   DATE: December 28, 1945
FROM: Jerry Wald   SUBJECT: "Humoresque"

Dear Steve:

Today we photographed Isaac Stern playing the eight numbers that are to be done in the picture. We would like to have these reduced to 16 mm so that Garfield can run them at his house at night on his own machine. By running these at night, he can practice his violin at home and imitate Stern's fingering and bowing. This will save us a tremendous amount of time and energy on the set.

Jerry Wald

LIFE WITH FATHER

FROM MICHAEL CURTIZ

MRS. WILLIAM GRANT SHERRY [Bette Davis]
PLAZA HOTEL
LAREDO TEXAS

DECEMBER 14, 1945

DEAR BETTE: JUST RETURNED FROM NEW YORK AFTER PROJECTING YOUR TEST [for the role of Mrs. Day] TO THE GROUP THAT OPERATES "LIFE WITH FATHER." BETTE, IT WAS WORSE THAN THE POTSDAM CONFERENCE. I WAS NOT BORN TO BE A DIPLOMAT, SO PROBABLY HURT A FEW PEOPLE'S FEELINGS. I WAS AND STILL AM HONESTLY CONVINCED THAT YOU ARE THE WOMAN TO PLAY THE PART BUT I COULD NOT OVERCOME OBJECTIONS OF THESE CRITICS USING ALL THE TECHNICAL TERMS OF THE THEATRE, SUCH AS THE CHARACTERIZATION IS TOO POWERFUL, TOO DOMINATING, TOO SUPERIOR AND WITHOUT ANY NAIVETE, ETC., ETC. I EXPLAINED THE CIRCUMSTANCES UNDER WHICH WE MADE THE TEST WITHOUT MUCH PREPARATION. TRIED TO CONVINCE THEM THAT BEING THE GREAT ARTIST YOU ARE YOU COULD OVERCOME ALL OBJECTIONS AND YOU COULD EASILY CHARACTERIZE THE PART AS IT SHOULD BE PLAYED BUT I WAS NOT VERY SUCCESSFUL; WAS OVERRULED, AND I AM AFRAID BETTE, WE WILL HAVE TO JUST CONSIDER IT FOR THE TIME BEING FORGOTTEN, UNLESS I CAN CHANGE THEIR MINDS WHEN THEY COME OUT TO THE COAST AND INSIST UPON OTHER TESTS. ALL I CAN TELL YOU IS THAT I AM HEART-BROKEN AS I HAD LOOKED FORWARD TO WORKING WITH YOU AND I HOPE SOME DAY WE CAN START ON A MOVING PICTURE WHICH WILL NOT HAVE TO BE APPROVED BY SUPERIOR PREJUDICED CRITICS OF THE THEATRE. MUCH LOVE AND HAPPINESS TO YOU AND YOUR HUSBAND—MICHAEL CURTIZ

Robert Buckner produced Life with Father *for Warners.*

TO: Obringer   DATE: April 1, 1946
FROM: Mr. Trilling   SUBJECT: "Life with Father"

Dear Roy:

We have arranged to borrow William Powell from MGM to portray the part of Father in *Life with Father*, with a starting date of April 8th, and are to compensate MGM in the amount of $200,000 for the engagement. Powell is to be co-starred with [free-lance star] Irene Dunne. We are to endeavor to crisscross the names of Powell and Dunne on all main titles and publicity, but if in our sole judgment this method of billing is unsatisfactory, then we are to endeavor to persuade Miss Dunne to permit alternate first billing on all main titles and lithograph, i.e., 50% with Powell's name first, 50% with Dunne's name first. Failing which we can resort to Powell being co-starred in second position.

In consideration of the above, we have agreed to loan MGM the services of Errol Flynn for a picture to be made within two years [*That Forsyte Woman*, 1949] at the salary we are then paying Flynn, which I estimated to Ben Thau to be $150,000. We would permit them the same number of weeks, without overage pro rata, as we were required to use William Powell. . . .

Steve Trilling

The alternate first billing on main titles, publicity, advertising, and theatre displays was used (at least during the film's initial release).

TO: [Irving] Kumin [assistant   DATE: May 29, 1946
    to Tenny Wright]   SUBJECT: Elizabeth Taylor—
FROM: [Phil] Friedman [casting   "Life with Father"
    director]

Dear Irving:

Billy Grady [MGM casting director] tells me that Elizabeth Taylor [borrowed from MGM and cast as one of the children in *Life with Father*] is a nervous, highstrung youngster whose condition has caused her to absent herself fairly frequently from the pictures which she worked in for them. This has been aggravated somewhat recently by a natural condition in girls of her age.

Phil Friedman

Elizabeth Taylor at the time was fourteen. She did play the role.

TO: Steve Trilling   DATE: February 20, 1946
FROM: Leo F. Forbstein [music   SUBJECT: Max Steiner—
    director]   Contract Renewal

Dear Steve:

Thought I would send you this note to remind you about [staff composer and conductor] Max Steiner. . . .

I think we should start a new contract with him for five years beginning March 1st. . . . As you know we have been receiving as high as $3500.00 a week for his services on loanout and I am getting many calls every day for his services at other studios with price no object and I assure you that with the Warner spirit, if he lives for ten years, it will be a miracle. . . .

I assure you that I will always try to sneak in an extra picture or two for Steiner to do during each year which would compensate not having to bring in someone else to do them. He also has been here for the past eight years with us and in those eight years he has scored over eighty pictures which is a pretty good record for any man to do. . . .

Many thanks.

Sincerely,

Steiner signed a new contract and remained at Warners until 1954. He then continued to do scores for the studio on a nonexclusive basis until 1965.

JL TO TRILLING—NEW YORK NY—DECEMBER 11 1946
DEFINITELY MUST MAKE ACTION SWASHBUCKLING FILMS WITH [Errol] FLYNN HEREON. ["Never] SAY GOODBYE" [1946] BAD BUSINESS [in] THEATRES. . . . "DON JUAN" SHOULD BE NEXT . . . PICTURE AT MINIMUM COST. . . . PREPARE "DON JUAN" NOT WITH CURTIZ BUT WALSH. . . .

JOHNNY BELINDA

TO: Steve Trilling DATE: June 15, 1946
FROM: Jerry Wald SUBJECT: "Johnny Belinda"

Dear Steve:

Despite the fact that [theatrical producer] Elmer Harris is asking fifty thousand dollars for [the play] *Johnny Belinda*, I feel that we should make him a counter offer and try to secure an option on the material so that I can work out a treatment for you.

I can't stress to you enough the great box-office picture there is in this material. The other night, as I told you, I saw *To Each His Own* [Paramount, 1946] which, as you know, is cleaning up at the box-office, because it is an out-and-out woman's story. The basic story of *Johnny Belinda* is a thousand times more commercial than *To Each His Own*. The emotional values of *Belinda* are vastly superior to *His Own*. Why nobody has purchased this property before this is somewhat beyond my powers of comprehension. In a very slick fashion, you are dealing with the most primitive emotional subject in the world—an unwed mother who is having her child taken away. The mother, in order to defend her child, kills the man who is attempting to do this.

In contrast to the *Belinda* story, here, in a few words, is the story of *To Each His Own*: Olivia de Havilland during World War I, meets a young flier and falls in love with him. The flier goes off to war and, after he has gone, Miss de Havilland without benefit of clergy, finds herself with child. Now get this great twist—the pilot is killed before they have a chance to get married. Where have you seen that before?

The story from there goes on to show Miss de Havilland allowing the baby to be adopted so it will not have a bad name. One guess as to who adopts the baby. No one else but her very good friend. This is deliberately made convenient, of course, so that Miss de Havilland can go over to her friend's house on Thursdays and Sundays, when the nurse is off, to take care of the baby. Of course, the parents don't know that this is Miss de Havilland's child, and the boy grows up not knowing that his real mother is the nice lady who takes him for a walk every Sunday.

For eighteen years, this situation goes on, and, finally, in the last five feet of the film, the boy recognizes her and calls her "Mother." And, believe it or not, the fade-out of the picture is mother and son dancing gaily while the son is saying, "Mom, Mom."

The little epic quoted on the preceding page is one of the biggest grossers that Paramount has. It is corn on the cob without any attempt to convert it into succotash. Contrast *Johnny Belinda*, which has the same basic story ingredients, except that it has in addition the value of a killing and the sensational characterization of a deaf and dumb girl. . . .

Don't you think it's high time that you guys acknowledged that I do have a good mind for stories?

There is no need to worry about the censorable angles of this picture. You have only to look at *To Each His Own* to see how the same situation was handled and was given an okay by the [Eric] Johnston Office [formerly the Hays Office].

Consistently, Steve, I've had to sell you and Warner on properties. . . .

You know, frankly, what I should do is take the notes I wrote you on *Mildred Pierce* and just substitute *Johnny Belinda*, because they all run down the same road, primitive stories told in a slick, new fashion. When are you going to get wise to the fact that you can tell a corny story, with basic human values, in a very slick, dressed-up fashion? When you tell a corny story in a corny fashion, you end up with junk. Certainly there is no cornier story than *Humoresque*. Let's face it. But it is so slickly mounted that you forget this is the tired, old mother-love story and find, as a substitute, a triangle story with a mother, son and married woman.

Okay, Doctor—I'll go quietly.

Jerry Wald

TO: T. C. Wright

FROM: Jerry Wald

DATE: August 25, 1947

SUBJECT: "Johnny Belinda"

Dear Tenny:

We would like to make additional wardrobe and makeup tests for [contract star] Jane Wyman in *Johnny Belinda*. The second batch of tests we made with Miss Wyman, I feel, are heading in the wrong direction. Her hair was curled and she looked like something that stepped out of Perc Westmore's Beauty Salon. Somewhere between our first tests and these second ones, the right wardrobe and makeup is to be found. Certainly what we have seen on the screen in the second makeup tests in no way resembles the type of people who live in Newfoundland. In fact, any resemblance is purely coincidental.

Surely the character Belinda does not use lipstick and does not curl the ends of her hair as seen in our present test. If this film is to have any honesty at all, Belinda and her family should look like farmers and not like fugitives from Hollywood.

I'm genuinely distressed by the new tests because Wyman has lost a quality of warmth that was present in the first one. . . .

Tenny, if you remember, when we were doing *The Hard Way* [1943] years ago with Ida Lupino, there was a good deal of yelling around at the studio about Miss Lupino doing her role without any makeup for the first part of the picture. After a great deal of argument with Wallis, we finally sold him on the idea of having Lupino do the picture realistically. The result was that Lupino and the picture won all sorts of critical awards, and these notices gave the picture additional box-office impetus.

Anything you can do to help me capture this quality will be greatly appreciated.

Jerry Wald

Jane Wyman had been under contract to Warners since 1936, but began playing important starring roles in the mid-1940s.

FROM JACK L. WARNER

undated, circa June 1947

Notes for talk with [MCA agent Lew] Wasserman
regarding Errol Flynn

. . . So there will be no further misunderstanding, our company is reserving the right to keep track of the things that transpire during each day the picture [*Silver River*] is in production.

If Flynn is late, if liquor is being used so that from the middle of the afternoon on it is impossible for the director to make any more scenes with Flynn, if liquor is brought on the set or into the Studio—

we must hold Flynn legally and financially responsible for any delay in the making of this picture.

We may go so far as to abrogate the entire contract and sue him for damages. . . .

We will never again make pictures where Flynn or any other artist becomes incoherent due to liquor or whatever it may be. When a director informs Production that it is impossible to shoot further because the actor or actress cannot properly handle their assignment we may as well quit. This has happened repeatedly during the last pictures we have made in which Flynn has appeared and we cannot permit it any longer.

Apparently, from all evidence, the practice continued—or at any rate resumed a short while later.

TO: T. C. Wright   DATE: July 5, 1947
FROM: Eric Stacey [unit manager]   SUBJECT: "Romance in High C"
     [released as *Romance on the High Seas*]

Report for Thursday, July 3rd, 27th shooting day. . . .

Mike's [Curtiz] progress on this show is phenomenal, due to great measure to the wonderful cameraman he has, [staff director of photography] Woody Bredell, who takes very little longer in Technicolor than most people do in Black and White. Which proves the point I have so long been telling you, that the Black and White and Technicolor cameramen routine we have been stuck with around here so long is a lot of nonsense; it makes everything take twice as long. . . .

Of course, Mike himself plans his work so well and knows exactly what he is going to do several days head of time, which most directors on this lot do not do. . . .

Picture 3 days ahead of schedule.

Eric Stacey

In the 1930s and early 1940s, per agreement with the Technicolor Corporation, a cameraman employed by Technicolor was either the director of photography on a film using the Technicolor process, or he worked with the studio's director of photography assigned to the film. In the mid-1940s, more and more studio cameraman began working without Technicolor cameramen.

NOVEMBER 8, 1947
FROM JACK L. WARNER TO [New York executives] . . . CONFIDENTIAL:

LAST WEEK CUT PAYROLL [at Burbank studios] EIGHTY EIGHT THOUSAND
NOT INCLUDING OVERHEAD. . . . AIMING TO SAVE HUNDRED THOU-
SAND OR MORE INCLUDING OVERHEAD. . . . SORRY HEAR BILLINGS
DOWN, BUT UNDERSTAND NOT ONLY PICTURES NOT CLICKING BUT
CONDITIONS GENERALLY BAD, AS YOU EXPLAINED TO HM [Warner] ON
PHONE. . . .

*Attendance at movie theatres dropped dramatically in 1947 following
the boom war years.*

The Return
of John Huston
(1946–1948)

THE TREASURE OF THE SIERRA MADRE

TO: Mr. Wallis
FROM: Mr. Obringer

DATE: November 14, 1941
SUBJECT: "The Treasure of the
Sierra Madre"

As you know, purchasing the story *The Treasure of the Sierra Madre* by B. Traven is developing into a complicated proposition. In the first place, the deal is with some sort of a spook in Mexico, as Traven apparently will not sign any documents but wants it all done through a Power of Attorney. Secondly, the copyright status on this work with a half dozen different people copyrighting translations of it, etc., will have to be thoroughly examined.

However, I know you want to get this property. . . .

R. J. Obringer

Henry Blanke and John Huston persuaded Jack Warner to buy the novel for Huston to direct earlier in 1941.

FROM ROY OBRINGER

Mr. Morris Ebenstein [Legal Department, New York]
Warner Bros. Pictures, Inc.
321 West 44th St.
New York City, N.Y.

January 15, 1942

Re: *The Treasure of the Sierra Madre*
Dear Morris:

I am still struggling with [agent Paul] Kohner and the phantom spook, Traven, his being a citizen of the U.S., his contractual arrangements with the various publishers and translators of this story. I presume I need not tell you that I am having little or no success. I am enclosing epistle #17 from Traven which is at least amusing to read and is rather conclusive that Traven cannot or will not provide the necessary information and contracts. . . .

I recently discussed with Messrs. J. L. Warner and Wallis the risks involved of producing a motion picture based on this property and particularly in view of the questionable title we would be getting from Traven, and even as to Traven there is a question as to his identity and citizenship. . . .

When we get the Swedish publisher out of the way then it will be definitely up to Mr. Warner to decide as to the risk involved with respect to the other foreign publications.

I should like very much to hear from you on this.

Sincerely,
R. J. Obringer

FROM MORRIS EBENSTEIN

Mr. Roy J. Obringer
Warner Bros. Pictures, Inc.
Burbank, California

January 29, 1942

Re: *The Treasure of the Sierra Madre*
Dear Roy:

. . . Traven's letter, of which you enclosed a copy, convinces me more than ever that in this case a great big Senegabian [sic] is hibernating in the lumber.

First of all, it is almost impossible for me to believe that the author of that letter is, as he claims, a native born American. He may be one but he certainly does not write like one. Certain terms and phrases betray a Germanic rather than any other origin. . . .

Unless I know more about Traven, who he is, the terms of his contract with his translator and the various publishers, I would not touch this deal with a ten foot pole. It is like buying a piece of real estate from an anonymous person and then putting a million dollar building on it. No title company in the country would give you five cents worth of insurance under such circumstances.

My point is, Traven may be exactly what he represents himself to be, a native born American citizen who really owns all the rights in his book as he claims, but in the circumstances here given, it reduces itself to a matter not merely of taking his word for it, but rather of taking the word of a letter. . . .

Of course, I realize that in the long run the question is one of taking a business risk and that is essentially a question to be determined by our executives. Viewed from the legal point of view, my personal opinion is that there are too many unknown factors in this situation.

> Sincerely yours,
> Morris Ebenstein

FROM ROY OBRINGER

Mr. Morris Ebenstein
c/o Warner Bros. Pictures, Inc.
321 W. 44th St.
New York, N.Y.

> June 30, 1942

Re: *The Treasure of the Sierra Madre*
Dear Morris:

From all indications, Colonel J. L. Warner is determined to produce a motion picture based upon the above story property by B. Traven. I believe we both appreciate the rather muddled status of this property, and which I have on numerable occasions explained to Col. Warner. He feels, however, that if we can secure a copyright assignment from the Swedish publishers and a disclaimer letter from the translator, plus the assignment of the copyright of Traven, he will take a chance with respect to the various other translations. . . .

I should appreciate hearing from you on this.

> Yours very truly,
> R. J. Obringer

TO: [Jim] Geller [story editor]   DATE: July 14, 1942
FROM: Mr. Blanke   SUBJECT: Edward G. Robinson
　　　　　　　　　　　　　　　and "Treasure of the
　　　　　　　　　　　　　　　Sierra Madre"

Dear Geller:

Your note of July 10th states that you have to submit by August 29th three stories to Edward G. Robinson. I know that he likes the book of *The Treasure of the Sierra Madre* very much and in case you cannot run up three scripts for his consideration, I advise that you make *The Treasure of the Sierra Madre* one of them with the notification to him that in case he should like the property it cannot be made until the rights are cleared.

Blanke

Warners acquired the motion picture rights, but by now John Huston was in the Army.

TO: Robert Rossen, [screenwriter]   DATE: December 28, 1942
FROM: Mr. H. Blanke   SUBJECT: "Treasure of the Sierra Madre"

Dear Robert:

I am sorry I got sore on the telephone, but my temperament got away with me.

I see from the record that you have been on this story for six weeks. So far I have not seen a single line written by you. I have had some very successful pictures but, as I can prove to you by the record, none of them has taken that long a time. I am saying here and now that I cannot afford any longer to have scripts take six months or more to be finished. Life is too short for that, and if you cannot promise me better time for this script, I really think it would be best that I try to find another man to do the job.

Kindly advise me what you think will be the overall time you need to complete this screenplay, and if whatever time you give me will be satisfactory to Mr. Warner, it will be okay with me. But I don't think it is fair, nor worth it, that I take it on the chin just to cover up other people.

Henry Blanke

Treasure eventually was postponed until John Huston returned from active duty at the end of World War II.

FROM B. TRAVEN, Mexico

John Huston, Esq. [now out of the Army]
Hollywood
California

September 2, 1946

Dear Mr. Huston:

. . . Before anything else I want to tell you that I am delighted over your script. It goes as close alongside the book as a picture ever will allow. And that's something. In most cases you don't recognize your own novel when you see the picture on the screen. There are two items which I particularly well like about the script. One is, that you didn't sugar-coat it and that you saw no reason doing so. The other item is, that you didn't bring in a skirt, just a photograph which will do just as well. This photograph and Pat's [Barton MacLane] dame will furnish the missing link and that's just as it ought to be. It reminds me that when I offered the MS of the book it came back with an editor's remark, saying that because it had no woman's interest they could not accept it in spite that the novel was very good. When, years later, the book had sold by another publisher more than 100,000 copies a check-up was made and it was found that more women had read the book and liked it than men. . . .

Your script is so good, almost too good, that it could remain as it is without any change at all.

However, a few changes will, and of this I am positive, make the picture better still. And what I have to say in this respect is by no means a sort of criticism. Far from it. These are merely suggestions which you may accept or forget about. But if I were to direct the picture I would follow my suggestions.

Here it goes.

If I were to direct the picture I would give no date but make it timeless instead.

You start with springing the date August 5, 1920 at the audience. In 1920 you could not find one white man without a very well paid job, not in Tampico. That time I made as much as thirty dollars a day, of course working like hell, sixteen, eighteen hours, no Sunday, every day was weekday and a hard day it was every day. You went to Tampico only to blow your money, and once it was gone you had another well paid job next day if not the same day. The slowing down started by 1923/24, and began to be felt by 1925. So if you must give a date, put it 1924. But I think it would be better not to state any date.

John, now look here, you've never been on the bum. Right? I have, back home in the States, and over here also. And [sic] Englishman from Manchester or a British subject from South-Africa perhaps might approach another white man, a gentleman, as does Dobbs. But from my own experience I know that no American unless he is very bashful will use this phrase "Will you lend a helping hand to a fellow. . . ." Why? No busy gentleman, and they are all busy, in Tampico in particular, will stop long to listen to that sermon of a bum. It's too long. Before Dobbs is through saying it, the gentleman will be a half block away. Of course, John, in a picture you can hold him long enough, in real life you can not.

In real life it goes this way: "Brother, can't you spare a dime?" or "Buddy, h'about a cup of javy, 'wfully down o'my luck." If you don't

get your dime at this moment or at least you see the gentleman
fumbling in his pocket, brother, you never make it. . . .

Know what I'd do if I were directing? I would have Dobbs only
mumble a few words with the audience not understanding one single
word, but fully understand what Dobbs really wants from the
gentleman. At the first time the audience, at least part of it, will
wonder what Dobbs may have said, but after this, everyone in the
audience will know, more or less exactly, what Dobbs says, because
what he says is international language. . . .

Page 26. Here you let the partners fire their revolvers. Try it in
Mexico as an American and board a train with guns sticking out at
your hip and see what happens to you.

If you want to have them fire at the bandits, make them pick up
revolvers which Mexican wounded or killed dropped and can no longer
use.

It's little details like that which Hollywood mostly overlooks and
which makes many otherwise good picture look so very ridiculous in
Latin American countries. If the partners want to travel with their shot
guns and revolvers, they have to be packed inside their baggage. In
times of political unrest every baggage even in your own car is searched
by soldiers for arms and ammunition. . . .

It was a very good idea to let the natives now and then speak
Spanish and the way you did it makes it possible for anybody who does
not understand Spanish to grasp the meaning. More isn't necessary.
But suppose there were a few cases where Spanish is spoken to some
extent you could overprint the scene with a caption in English as it is
done here in Mexico with English or French talkies.

It also was a grand idea of yours to bring in, or better still, invent
that scene where Curtin saves Dobbs' life after the cave-in of the
tunnel. Very good. . . .

I don't think it is to be recommended that Dobbs is attacked by
three of the train robbers among whom is the man with the gilded hat.
In my opinion whoever was connected with that train assault will for a
long time stay away from cities where they easily might be recognized
by people who were passengers on that train. But of course they might
take such a chance.

It would perhaps be more effective that these three thieves who
murdered Dobbs were the lowest, lowest footpads one can imagine.
They should be the filthiest and lousiest scum as if of the outskirts of a
very large city in China. Unwashed, unkempt, their hair pitch black
and wild around their heads, their eyes only ugly slits, a constant
sneering grin or snarl on their lips, faces such that you shudder,
barfooted [sic], only ragged pants and a ragged shirt all covered with

dried mud. They should be between sixteen and nineteen, not older. The bandits would most likely recognize that the sand in the bags is pay-dirt or at least they would guess that, whereas these youngsters never think that the sand might be of some value other than giving more weight to the pelts, an idea which only this kind of hoodlums would come upon. At certain sections of Mexico City and if you look for you'll find the type I have in mind for that scene. But if you prefer to have three of the bandits already known by the audience, no objections.

It would perhaps heighten the effect of this scene by adding, just before, a certain suspense to build up a contrast which will make some in the audience jump from their seats. It's this.

A minute or so before Dobbs spots that huge shade spending tree and when he is physically at his lowest, his mouth full of dust, his eyes red-rimmed, his dirty, dust covered face ridiculously smeared because of sweat wiped off in every direction, his tongue practically hanging out of his mouth, he is just about to drop onto his knees and give up, when his eyes catch the gilded cupolas and towers of the churches of the city of Durango. Seeing that he is so close he gains some new energy. He has a vision Out of Scene. He has arrived at a fonda, an inn, at one of those sections of the city where travelers with animals will find lodgings. With the help of stable boy he has unloaded his burros, he sits down at a table and is served a meal and a huge glass of beer is set before him with a earthen vessel beside filled with chunks of ice of which he picks up one and drops it into his beer and then with both his hands he grabs the beer and by one swallow he drains the glass, sighing with a satisfaction as that of an animal. Hardly has he put down the empty glass when scene flashes back to where we left Dobbs on the dusty road under a blistering sun and we see him wiping his mouth with the back of his hand just to wipe off an unrush of dust blown into his face by a wave of furnace hot air. It is at this moment that he spots the tree and comes to life again as if actually strengthened by the vision he had. If you decline that, okay by me; it is not essential.

Perhaps you had a reason why you changed Lacaud's name to Cody. I think we could leave the name Lacaud intact.

The way you wind up the whole thing is very, very good if you consider that it is to be a picture. The reader of a novel has lots of time to ponder about what idea is behind. In the book I left both survivors a little bit of money as you know. You cut even that little bit and leave them not one single ounce. By so doing you drive the message clear cut home. You see, no matter how hard you work, no matter how ferociously you fight, no matter how intensively you struggle for your existence you can never be sure of your gains or your property unless you have consumed it. Only what is in your tummy and what is in your brain is really yours.

I would also suggest that after you have run the credit title you offer the audience the same introduction the book has, that is:

> The real and genuine treasure you are hunting and also the ideal happiness are always and forever on the other side of the mountain—

but if you prefer, offer it in the same wording as you find in the book, only I think for a regular movie audience it is too long and too difficult to grasp in so short a time as that title will run.

And, John Huston, I must say that pp. 48 to 58 is just super excellent writing and letting the whole script flash through my mind for a few seconds I simply feel obliged to say that I don't know anybody or can imagine anybody who could have written a script better liked by me than the one you wrote. John, what next?

B.T.
[B. Traven]

FROM JOHN HUSTON

December 30, 1946

Dear Mr. Traven,

. . . First, let me bring you up to date as to plans and expectations re *Treasure in [sic] the Sierra Madre.* So far the cast includes my father [free-lance actor Walter Huston] in the role of the old man and Humphrey Bogart as Dobbs. These two are set. Ronald Reagan for Curtin and Zachary Scott for Lacaud (or Cody) are very strong likelihoods. Production is to begin on March 15. I am flying down to Mexico on the tenth or eleventh of January to look for possible locations, and I'll be two or three weeks in Mexico. I think it would be very good for the picture if we could get together. I certainly feel a need for your wise counsel. . . .

As to your criticisms and suggestions, I'll take them up in the same order that you wrote them down. The first has to do with the date I used, August 5, 1920. Of course it would be much better if no date is given at all and that's how it will be in the final script unless the Mexican government should insist upon a date thereby placing the period when bandits were knocking over trains and such like as definitely past. If this should be the case I shall certainly use the date of your choosing—1924.*

---

*The date established in the film is 1925.

Your point about the approach of a fellow on the bum to an American gentleman is very well taken. I was only on the bum once in my life and that was in England where one is graded for politeness rather than for brevity. Your notion of having the audience not hear Dobbs's actual words but fully understand what he wants is excellent— and that's the way it shall be.*

I will do as you say about having the partners pick up revolvers dropped by wounded or killed Mexicans to fire at the bandits attacking the train.**

Now as to the three who attack Dobbs being the train bandits, let me tell you my reasons for doing this. For one thing, it was my hope that this also would serve to bring out the fate that pursued Dobbs. It's a rather precious point to be sure, but back toward the beginning of the story had the train not lurched at the wrong instant and spoiled Dobbs's aim Gold Hat would have been a dead bandit. From that moment on their destinies are paired in some mysterious way. But all that is not even a secondary reason for employing the bandits as I have. The primary purpose was to give the moving picture a certain dramatic unity which novels don't necessarily require to be great novels. Pictures and plays, however, seem to fall apart when new characters and incidents are introduced in final scenes. I know very well what you meant the three thieves to be like, lower than the low, and I like the idea of Dobbs falling by the hand of such. Can't we make the bandits every bit as unwashed and filthy—not the leatherclad spurred desperadoes that audiences are familiar with.

As for our flashing back during Dobbs's time of thirst . . . such devices are apt to be awkward and even a little on the old-fashioned side. Not that I would ever discard an idea purely for the latter reason. We might shoot it and see, but I am inclined to think it would be discarded in the cutting.

I changed Lacaud's name to Cody only for the reason that Lacaud is unfamiliar and that American audiences might think that they had not heard correctly. This likelihood is all the greater because of the scene in which the story is laid—a foreign country.

I like very much the introduction you have written, i.e., the real and genuine treasure, et cetera, et cetera, and it shall certainly be used.***

Let me now mention my chief criticism of the script I have written. It seems to me it's on the black and white side. Dobbs is a pretty thorough rotter and Curtin pretty goddam virtuous. In the novel

*In the film Dobbs mumbles, "Hey, mister, could you stake a fellow American to a meal?"
**In the film, the guns are taken out of their luggage.
***Not used.

the difference between them is not nearly so marked. I would like, if it
were possible, to have at least one dramatic scene in which Curtin is
on the verge of yielding to temptation and then doesn't. It strikes me
that not only would this add another dimension to Curtin's character
but would further dramatize the message of your book that all men are
subject to certain pulls and temptations and that one man is better than
another only in so far as he has the strength to resist. I have pored over
the script, juggled existing scenes and searched for places where such a
new scene might be introduced but without very much success I am
afraid. Maybe I'll have a last minute inspiration but it's ten to one
I won't. On the other hand it's ten to one you will. I hope you'll give
it to me in person as I am greatly looking forward to a meeting with
you.

Yours,

FROM B. TRAVEN, Mexico

John Huston, Esq.
Tarzana
California

January 4, 1947

Dear Mr. Huston:

Thanks for your extensive letter.

Bogart will be great as Dobbs. Besides that he will draw the
public as no one else would do better. Ronald Reagan and Zachary
Scott I do not know sufficiently to judge them but as they have your
approval, so it seems, they will be good. As to Walter Huston, I
haven't seen him for a long time—fact is I do see pictures only
rarely—but I think he is too robust, too healthy and looks too young
for the part. My idea would have been somebody like Lewis Stone,
really old, stocky, looking sickly somehow, more short than tall,
inclined to stoop, making the impression that he might drop down any
minute, unable to get up on his feet again without outside help. The
contrast between Walter and Bogart is too narrow, they may be well
apart in years but not much in real toughness. The surprise should be
that an old man like, let's say again, Lewis Stone, when it is a matter
of resistance beats any of those who brag about their being the tough
guys. Of course I know, Stone is with MGM and therefore cannot be
had so I believe. But now, Walter is one of my preferred stars, always
was. . . . So if you can make him look over seventy and make him act
as if he were to give up his ghost any minute and all unexpected snap
out of it when he is needed in full to show the four-flushers how weak
and useless they in fact are, this part will add tremendously to his fame
and get him in the fore again. You know as well as I do that Howard

["the old man"] not Dobbs, is the heart and soul of the picture, the only one who is to get all the sympathy and the love of the audience.

Of course I noted the difference in character you mention. . . . The change appears to me easier than you think. . . .

I got two places where we can work it out.

One is the scene when Dobbs is buried inside the caved-in mine. Curtin sees what has happened. Howard is not around and knows nothing. Curtin looks at the broken-down gallery, horrified, jumps toward it to help Dobbs out of which inside a few minutes might well be his grave. But halfway to the mine, he abruptly stops to hesitate. Closeup of his face which expresses what is going on in his mind. To make it surer still for the less imaginative audience, he turns half-way round toward where he knows Dobbs had hidden his little fortune. He scratches his chin, grins rather diabolically, nods to himself, pats his pants-pockets where he soon will have this extra money, whistles nonchalantly a tune and tries to sneak away as if he had not been near when it happened should Howard come upon the scene. But to the good fortune of Dobbs, Howard comes up to the camp. . . . They rush to the mine and get busy like hell.

The second chance we have.

This occurs when Dobbs suggests to Curtin, when they are without Howard now, on their way to Durango and sit by the fire at night, that it would be a great idea to take Howard's earnings and make their getaway, disappearing so that Howard will have no chance ever finding them. Curtin listens to the proposition, thinks it over, and says to Dobbs that this is a great idea, the more so as Howard is old and won't live long, he doesn't need all that money, while they, young and enterprising can really enjoy the old man's money and build up a great business. It seems that is settled for good. But sometime later, or the following day, Curtin tells Dobbs that he thinks it unfair to rob the old man, perhaps he has some people depending on him who he can make happy. And so Curtin winds up, saying that Dobbs should count him out. . . .

Now of course, we need only one of these two episodes, because if we brought both it would seem too obvious even to a yokel what we have in mind to drive home. . . .

I do hope that you agree with the suggestions made in this letter.

B.T.

[B. Traven]

Bogart and Walter Huston were cast, but free-lance actor Tim Holt played "Curtin" and contract player Bruce Bennett was "Cody." In the film, there is a hesitation (in closeup) on Curtin's part when he learns that

Dobbs is buried inside a caved-in mine. He starts to walk away, changes his mind and rescues Dobbs before Howard, "the old man," comes back on the scene. None of the other suggested indications of Curtin's "yielding to temptation" was used.

TO: Roy Obringer   DATE: March 20, 1947
FROM: Don Page [assistant director]   SUBJECT: "Treasure of the Sierra
                                                Madre"

There is a silent bit in this picture that works one day, Page 6, Sc. 7. Ann Sheridan has agreed to do this for Huston as a good-luck gesture.

This bit works tomorrow, Friday. I believe they have contacted Miss Sheridan and she has agreed to come in and do this. Is there anything in her contract whereby we would become involved by using her?

Will you please advise me on this as soon as possible.

Thank you.

Ann Sheridan did the "silent bit." After Dobbs (Bogart) leaves the barbershop in Tampico, he notices a passing prostitute who returns his look. In studying the scene carefully, it is difficult to believe that the woman in the foreground walk-by is Ann Sheridan. After the actress exits the foreground frame, the camera lingers on Bogart, and then as Bogart starts toward her she is again picked up in the frame—but in the distance— going into a rooming house. It is possible that the switch was made to Sheridan at that point, or an alternate take without Sheridan may have been used.

FROM JACK L. WARNER

MR. BENJAMIN KALMENSON [General Sales Manager, New York]
WALDORF ASTORIA HOTEL
NEW YORK CITY

AUGUST 1, 1947

DEAR BENNY: THIS IS THE FIRST TIME I HAVE EVER DONE THIS BUT LAST NIGHT I RAN, IN 12,500 FEET, THE TREASURE OF THE SIERRA MADRE. I WANT YOU AND THOSE ASSEMBLED TO KNOW THIS IS DEFINITELY THE GREATEST MOTION PICTURE WE HAVE EVER MADE. IT IS REALLY ONE THAT WE HAVE ALWAYS WISHED FOR. . . . A FEW YEARS BACK THIS ONE PICTURE WOULD VIRTUALLY PUT OVER A WHOLE SEASON'S PRODUCT, THAT'S THE SIZE OF IT. HOPE EVERYTHING GOING GREAT AT THE CONVENTION. MY BEST TO ALL.

JACK

FROM JACK L. WARNER, edited statement and edited testimony

October 20, 1947

HEARINGS (REGARDING THE COMMUNIST INFILTRATION
OF THE MOTION PICTURE INDUSTRY) BEFORE THE
COMMITTEE ON UN-AMERICAN ACTIVITIES, HOUSE OF
REPRESENTATIVES.

Los Angeles, California

It is a privilege to appear again before this committee to help as much
as I can in facilitating its work*. . . .

I believe that I, as an individual, and our company as an organization
of American citizens, must watch always for threats to the American way
of life. History teaches the lesson that liberties are won bitterly and may
be lost unwittingly. . . .

Ideological termites have burrowed into many American industries,
organizations, and societies. Wherever they may be, I say let us dig them
out and get rid of them. My brothers and I will be happy to subscribe
generously to a pest-removal fund. We are willing to establish such a fund
to ship to Russia the people who don't like our American system of
government and prefer the communistic system to ours.

That's how strongly we feel about the subversives who want to over-
throw our free American system.

If there are Communists in our industry, or any other industry,
organization, or society who seek to undermine our free institutions,
let's find out about it and know who they are. Let the record be spread
clear, for all to read and judge. The public is entitled to know the facts.
And the motion-picture industry is entitled to have the public know the
facts. . . .

Many charges, including the fantasy of "White House pressure,"
have been leveled at our wartime production *Mission to Moscow* [1943].
In my previous appearance before members of this committee, I explained
the origin and purposes of *Mission to Moscow*.

That picture was made when our country was fighting for its existence, with Russia as one of our allies. It was made to fulfill the same
wartime purpose for which we made such other pictures as *Air Force,
This Is the Army, Objective, Burma!, Destination Tokyo, Action in the
North Atlantic*, and a great many more.

If making *Mission to Moscow* in 1942 was subversive activity, then
the American Liberty ships which carried food and guns to Russian allies
and the American naval vessels which convoyed them were likewise en-

*Warner had secretly testified before the Committee in May 1947.

gaged in subversive activities. This picture was made only to help a desperate war effort and not for posterity. . . .

Mr. [Robert] Stripling [chief investigator for the House Committee on Un-American Activities]. Shall we proceed with your testimony on *Mission to Moscow?*

Mr. Warner. Very well. . . .

Mr. Stripling. Now, when the picture *Mission to Moscow* was made, were you aware that there were certain historical events which were erroneously portrayed in the picture? . . .

Mr. Warner. I told you, I don't know if it was all correct or not. . . .

Mr. Stripling. The point is this, Mr. Warner, that here was a picture which was produced and shown to the American people, and it was shown in other countries, I presume, was it not?

Mr. Warner. I think it was shown in England and several other countries.

Mr. Stripling. It was also shown in Moscow, to Mr. Stalin?

Mr. Warner. In Moscow and to Stalin; yes.

Mr. Stripling. Here is a picture, however, which portrayed Russia and the Government of Russia in an entirely different light from what it actually was?

Mr. Warner. I don't know if you can prove it, or that I can prove that it was . . .

Mr. Stripling. Well, is it your opinion now, Mr. Warner, that *Mission to Moscow* was a factually correct picture, and you made it as such?

Mr. Warner. I can't remember.

Mr. Stripling. Would you consider it a propaganda picture?

Mr. Warner. A propaganda picture—

Mr. Stripling. Yes.

Mr. Warner. In what sense?

Mr. Stripling. In the sense that it portrayed Russia and communism in an entirely different light from what it actually was?

Mr. Warner. I am on record about 40 times or more that I have never been in Russia. I don't know what Russia was like in 1937 or 1944 or 1947, so how can I tell you if it was right or wrong?

Mr. Stripling. Don't you think you were on dangerous ground to produce as a factually correct picture one which portrayed Russia—

Mr. Warner. No; we were not on dangerous ground in 1942, when we produced it. There was a war on. The world was at stake. . . .

Mr. Stripling.	Well, do you suppose that your picture influenced the people who saw it in this country, the millions of people who saw it in this country?
Mr. Warner.	In my opinion, I can't see how it would influence anyone. We were in war and when you are in a fight you don't ask who the fellow is who is helping you.
Mr. Stripling.	Well, due to the present conditions in the international situation, don't you think it was rather dangerous to write about such a disillusionment as was sought in that picture?
Mr. Warner.	I can't understand why you ask me that question, as to the present conditions. How did I, you, or anyone else know in 1942 what the conditions were going to be in 1947. I stated in my testimony our reason for making the picture, which was to aid the war effort—anticipating what would happen.
Mr. Stripling.	I don't see that that is aiding the war effort, Mr. Warner—with the cooperation of Mr. [Joseph E.] Davies [former ambassador to Russia and author of the book *Mission to Moscow*] or with the approval of the Government—to make a picture which is a fraud in fact.
Mr. Warner.	I want to correct you, very vehemently. There was no cooperation of the Government.
Mr. Stripling.	You stated there was.
Mr. Warner.	I never stated the Government cooperated in the making of it. If I did, I stand corrected. And I know I didn't. . . . Certainly there are inaccuracies in everything. I have seen a million books—using a big term—and there have been inaccuracies in the text. There can be inaccuracies in anything, especially in a creative art . . .

Jack Warner was one of many representing the film industry to testify before the Committee. By 1947 the Cold War had begun; President Truman had pledged American aid to governments in Europe resisting Communist aggression.

Some HUAC sympathizers ascribed Communist beliefs to Franklin Roosevelt and the New Deal. Mission to Moscow was criticized by several sectors because it glorified Stalin, rewrote history by justifying acts of aggression, and whitewashed and distorted the purge trials of the late 1930s.

In his 1964 autobiography, Jack Warner revealed that it indeed was Roosevelt who requested that Warner make the film as propaganda to generate support for Stalin from the American people. Warner recalled the President saying to him, "We simply can't lose Russia at this stage."

FROM JACK L. WARNER

DECEMBER 15, 1947

TO [Samuel] SCHNEIDER [New York] STRICTLY CONFIDENTIAL:
FROM PRESENT INDICATIONS APPEARS TO ME WE GOING HAVE LOT TROUBLE WITH JOAN CRAWFORD, TEMPERAMENT AND SUCH THINGS. . . . MAY HAVE SUSPEND HER THIS WEEK. SECONDLY, WHAT DO YOU THINK OF DROPPING HER ENTIRELY. WE HAD SEMI FAILURE IN "HUMORESQUE" [1947] AND EXCEPTIONAL FAILURE IN "POSSESSED" [1947]. INSTEAD WORRYING ABOUT HER COULD BE DEVOTING MY TIME TO WORTHWIIILE PRODUCTIONS AND NEW PERSONALITIES. . . . HOW-EVER, THIS ONLY WAY I FEEL TODAY. IF SHE STRAIGHTENS OUT BY END WEEK MAY NOT FEEL THIS WAY BUT FACTS MUST BE FACED AS THESE THINGS TAKE ALL YOUR TIME. . . .

Joan Crawford's next film was the successful Flamingo Road *(1949). According to trade paper and magazine reports,* Humoresque *and* Possessed *did well commercially.*

NEW YORK NY DEC 26 1947
JL TO TRILLING—STEVE, I CAN'T IMPRESS ON YOU EMPHATICALLY ENOUGH THE IMPORTANCE OF CUTTING THE BUDGETS. JUST IMPOS-SIBLE TO GROSS THE MONIES WE ARE EVEN SPENDING "[One] SUNDAY AFTERNOON," "DON JUAN," AND EVERYTHING MUST COME DOWN, AND ANYONE WHO DOESN'T WANT TO COOPERATE WILL JUST HAVE TO. THIS IS A MUST. THERE CAN BE NO PRESTIGE AND ALL THAT STUFF THAT GOES WITH IT. WE ARE FIGHTING HELLUVA BATTLE AND YOU MUST TELL EVERY DIRECTOR AND WRITER IN NO UNCERTAIN TERMS.

Attendance at movie theatres continued to drop dramatically.

KEY LARGO

FROM STEPHEN S. JACKSON [Production Code Administration]

Mr. J. L. Warner
Warner Bros. Pictures
Burbank, California

November 28, 1947

Dear Mr. Warner:
We have read . . . your proposed production *Key Largo*, and hasten to advise that the objections expressed in our brief letter of Nov.

13, 1947, still seem to hold. It is our considered judgment that this material is still very much objectionable under the provisions of the Production Code.

Much of the objection, of course, stems from the fact that the Murillo character is definitely a gangster surrounded by his henchmen and his kept woman.

As you must well be aware, the public reaction to gangster stories, particularly where the gangster can be identified as some past or present gangster, is extremely violent and vociferous. We feel that this story might very well call forth such a public reaction.

Hence, we urge upon you the advisability of serious reconsideration of the story line of this script as well as the characterizations of the various people before proceeding any further. Otherwise, the story could not be approved under the provisions of the Production Code. . . .

> Sincerely,
> PRODUCTION CODE ADMINISTRATION
> By: Stephen S. Jackson

TO: Steve Trilling   DATE: November 29, 1947
FROM: Jerry Wald   SUBJECT: "Key Largo"

Dear Steve:

The attached [Jackson's letter] is serious enough for us to get together immediately with the Breen office and discuss it at greater length.

They mention in this note that Murillo's character is definitely "a gangster surrounded by his henchmen and his kept woman." Apparently the Breen office has not seen *Brute Force, Kiss of Death, Desert Fury, The Strange Love of Martha Ivers, The Gangster, Ride a Pink Horse*, etc. [all current films].

They go on to say in their note that the public reaction to gangster stories, particularly where the gangster can be identified, is extremely violent and vociferous. Again, I call your attention to such productions as *The Killers* [1946], and a picture of that type.

To my way of thinking, the Breen office is narrowing our range of properties down to where we can either make a musical or a comedy. It is becoming more and more apparent that each story we do faces the same problem—we might offend some vocal minority. As you know, the Breen office condemned *John Loves Mary* [1947] in toto. You have seen the play and you know there is nothing in it that is immoral. . . .

To me it becomes more and more distressing, as a producer, in an attempt to find material that will cash in at the box-office, to learn that you are limited in the type of material you can secure—material that will please the Breen office. Must we find *Going My Ways?* [1944].

The Breen office is good in many ways, but somewhere along the line we should get together and try to find out exactly what we can make and cannot make. The Breen office today goes by a production code that was written in 1930. Many important events have taken place since the code was written. Is it possible that the code is dated? Certainly a re-examination is due. The industry today is feeling the box-office slump with bowed heads and long faces, but yet I notice that *Body and Soul* [1947] and *Gentleman's Agreement* [1947] are both doing stand-out business. I understand that both these pictures had quite a job of getting past the Breen office. Certainly *Body and Soul* is cluttered with gangsters and henchmen and their kept women. It is also good box-office because it has guts and vitality. The story we are trying to tell in *Key Largo* is a moral one and certainly there is no better way to point a moral than to use a gangster as a symbol of everything that we are trying to avoid going back to.

Frankly, Steve, I am depressed and distressed at this note from the Breen office . . . How [writer Richard] Brooks and [writer-director John] Huston can be expected to follow the line of a play written by a very eminent playwright [Maxwell Anderson] and eliminate all that was in the play, is something beyond my powers of comprehension.

No wonder the industry is continually being ridiculed—no wonder it has to continually apologize for itself. . . .

This piling up of continuous censorship is what is making all our pictures empty, and running along with a competent mediocrity. We could never have made *Odd Man Out* [1947] in this country, or *Shoeshine* [1947], or *Open City* [1946], or many other outstanding films. Must we try to copy films like *Unconquered* [1947]?

You've got to help us. This is serious.

Jerry Wald

The following memo was instigated by another legal complication of the time.

TO: Obringer   DATE: July 29, 1948
FROM: McDermid [story editor]   SUBJECT: "Key Largo"

[Jerry Wald's] first memo to J. L. Warner, written at the time we purchased the play *Key Largo*, July 25, 1947, states that he sees the picture as a sort of combination of *Petrified Forest* and *To Have and Have Not*, both of them, of course, successful pictures in which Humphrey Bogart appeared. Examination of our picture discloses that there is a very definite thematic resemblance to *Petrified Forest* and that the ending is taken from the Ernest Hemingway book, *To Have and Have Not*. . . .

Wald *customarily* uses a process of *literary blending* in developing a screenplay . . .

[Richard] BROOKS' STATEMENT

On August 4, 1948, I was assigned to write the screenplay of *Key Largo*, the Maxwell Anderson play which Warner Bros. had recently purchased. The producer on the picture was Jerry Wald and I was informed that John Huston was to be the director and would work with me on the screenplay, which was to be a starring vehicle for Humphrey Bogart and Lauren Bacall. I have seen and read *Key Largo*. It is a play in blank verse about a man who had fought in the Spanish Civil War and returned to this country completely disillusioned. On one of the Florida keys he finds himself once more face to face with dictatorship—in the form of a gambler and his mob who have taken over a small hotel. The hero, largely influenced by the faith of a girl—the sister of a fellow soldier who had died in Spain, finally realizes that he must continue his fight against dictatorship even though he knows he will lose his life by doing so. The principal adaptation problems were these: Anderson's play was written in blank verse, which is a difficult medium for the screen; the Spanish background was dated; I believed the motion picture would require an authentic background.

I sent to our research department for guide books and other sources of information about Florida and consulted with John Huston and Jerry Wald. We decided to make the hero a returning veteran from World War II. We also thought that, since the analogy existed in the Maxwell Anderson play between a foreign dictator and the local gambler, we substitute a big shot gangster. (During the war a great many analogies had been drawn between Hitlerism and gangsterism.) In discussing gangsters, Huston and I recalled the then recent story about Lucky Luciano, who had been seen in Cuba. We speculated as to whether he was trying to return to this country. I sent to Research Department for the *Time* Magazine account of Luciano's visit to Cuba, together with other magazine articles written at the time of Luciano's trial and deportation. From the "Luciano conception," Huston and I developed the character, Rocco [Edward G. Robinson], as a substitute for the gambler character [Murillo] in Anderson's play.

Likewise as a substitute for the two molls in the play we developed a single character, Gaye [Claire Trevor]. Huston and I discussed at some length a number of women who had been mistresses of ganglords and notorious public figures. We agreed that, in most cases, time and fashion had passed these women by. Most of them, unable to maintain an aura of glamor and success, had taken to whiskey or drugs as a substitution for former beauty and talent. Rocco's mistress was supposed to represent happier days of long ago—now faded. She also was to be a foil for Rocco's sadism. Gaye Dawn (in film) was a natural consequence based on real life and from out of our combined personal experience.

There was in the play no spectacular weather phenomenon, but in the guide books there were repeated references to hurricanes and particularly to the disastrous hurricane of 1935 which struck Key Largo. Just as in making a screenplay of *The Petrified Forest*—a play very similar in theme to *Key Largo*—the screenwriters had inserted a sandstorm, we decided to use a hurricane as a display of violence on the part of nature as opposed to man-made force.

We had written two thirds of a screenplay and an outline to the end by October 14 and then went to Key Largo for checking of background material. The second draft of the screenplay was written in Key Largo. We saw the plaque describing the 1935 hurricane and were still in Florida when a hurricane struck. We also ascertained that stock film of a hurricane was available to use from another unreleased Warner picture *Night Unto Night* [1949].

For the ending of our screenplay, Huston and I decided upon the ending of the book *To Have and Have Not*. This ending had *not* been utilized in the Warner picture of the same name. In it the protagonist agreed to take to Cuba in his boat a gang of criminals, escaping after a Florida bank robbery, even though he realized they planned to kill him as soon as the boat was within sight of Cuba. The robbers do not realize that the protagonist had a gun; he manages to kill them all but is himself mortally wounded and dies after the Coast Guard picks up the boat. We followed the same pattern, but later decided to let our lead stay alive— bowing to the motion picture penchant for happy endings.

Various other modifications in the script were made at the behest of the Breen Office. Some of these, such as the deletion of references to dope and vice made our character Rocco less like Luciano but left him a composite of Luciano and Capone . . .

HUSTON'S STATEMENT

I completed work on the picture *Treasure of the Sierra Madre* on July 22, 1947, and a few days later was assigned to direct and collaborate in the writing of *Key Largo*, a play by Maxwell Anderson. I had never particularly cared for this play and its post-Spanish war setting was dated, but the theme appealed to me. I feel that it is no less important now than it was ten years ago that we continue to fight against dictatorship or gangsterism—as Anderson points out in his play.

I have read the statement by Richard Brooks and herewith endorse it. I might add two comments: The action ending in the boat was something which would not only appeal to the star, Humphrey Bogart, who is a boat owner and had made one of his big successes in *To Have and Have Not*, but it would also show him in the kind of action which his fans expect of him.

In the discussion about gangsters' mistresses mentioned by Brooks, I recall, among others, mentioning Luciano's mistress Gay Orlova, an American showgirl I met in London in the early 1930's. She was with a troupe known as the Dorchester girls. From time to time, thereafter, I saw her name in the newspapers—when she made the statement she would follow Luciano out of the country if he were deported, the occasional alcoholic difficulties she encountered, etc. The last item I recall was that she had been sentenced to be executed by a German or French firing squad. . . .

Hard Times and Farewells (1948–1950)

10

TO: Col. J. L. Warner
FROM: Jerry Wald

DATE: January 8, 1948
SUBJECT: "Look for the Silver Lining"

Dear Jack:

It is incredible to me that you want to take [*Look for*] *The Silver Lining* project away from me, after bringing this idea to you, and putting in many extra hours to help get the songs cleared. I don't understand this decision.

While it's true I'm doing more pictures than any of your other producers, this is no way to repay my loyalty to you. The dirty work has been done on *The Silver Lining*. The job of physically putting the film into production is an easy one. What has been done up to date was the tough work.

If this was the first time that a project thought up by me was taken away from me, I wouldn't be so angry, but the story is a familiar one. On *Air Force* [1943] Charlie Einfeld called me in to say I should let Wallis do it because it was for the good of the company. On *Rhapsody in Blue*, Jesse Lasky didn't have too much work to do. *Shine on Harvest Moon* [1944]—Bill Jacobs needed a couple of pictures. On *Casablanca* Wallis thought it best that he do it. The same goes for *Desperate Journey*, and a few other projects which I can't think of at the moment.

If you plan to take the *Silver Lining* project away from me, I promise you that it will be the last idea you'll ever get from me. Just because I happen to be more efficient than some of the other boys working around here is no reason why you should fatten them up with easy assignments. . . .

I'm not anxious to be the busiest man in the cemetery, but I am very desirous of holding onto the few script ideas I get.

Jerry Wald

Look for the Silver Lining *(1949)* was produced by Warner staff producer William Jacobs in order to spread assignments more evenly. Wald was very prolific in initiating potential films.

ADVENTURES OF DON JUAN

FROM ERROL FLYNN

March 26, 1945

Dear Jerry [Wald],

Although at this date the studio hasn't given me any starting date for [*Adventures of*] Don Juan to go before the cameras I am worried about the script. We agreed, if you recall, several months ago, that the script lacked certain vital qualities which you thought at the time could be remedied. So far out of our discussions has come thirty four pages we decided could be improved—as clearly outlined in our conference of the 23rd. March, with [director Raoul] Walsh.

I am now getting concerned about the rest of the script—not even having seen a revision of the first thirty four pages so far. I feel your true interest in this story; I feel our joint concern about making it good; I feel your enthusiasm. But where, quite apart from conferences, discussions, etc., is the script—in writing? We still have some weeks it appears, but are we going to start shooting this kind of difficult movie without a good and solid full treatment? I don't have to tell you that this is one movie we cannot possibly start making just as soon as Mr. [Tenny] Wright has a faint clue as to where to begin having somebody else build a set. That might be alright for some pictures, but not this one. I personally feel helpless without more than thirty four pages of an opening that already needs revision.

The best—sincerely
Errol

Adventures of Don Juan *was postponed for various reasons, including a lengthy industry strike.*

TO: Colonel J. L. Warner   DATE: April 9, 1947
FROM: Jerry Wald   SUBJECT: "Adventures of Don Juan"

Dear Jack:

[Director] Jean Negulesco came up with an excellent suggestion yesterday to have Viveca Lindfors play the Queen in *Don Juan*.

As you know, the part of the Queen has been tailored into the major love story of the piece, and I concur with Jean that she would be excellent. . . .

Jerry Wald

Viveca Lindfors, imported from Sweden by Warner during the heyday of Ingrid Bergman, did play the Queen.

TO: Jerry Wald   DATE: May 6, 1947
FROM: Jean Negulesco   SUBJECT: "Don Juan"

Dear Jerry:

Following our conversation yesterday regarding the story outline of *Don Juan*, I believe you understand how important it is for us to realize that there come moments in the show business when the tide of public taste has changed its direction. As much as you are talking about things which you should give to the public, or should give as an Errol Flynn starring vehicle, and about trying to run away from formulas which have been proven flops, I believe maybe we should look at what makes box-office today with the public. For that reason we should approach maybe in a little more unusual manner our story, I am giving you a few little general ideas about our story.

I am against Don Juan being called home because he has been an ambassador of bad will. That brings up the point I worried about in the first script—Don Juan (and Errol Flynn, our star) appears then in the light of an unnecessarily quarrelsome fellow, which I think is just as bad as having him a deliberate seducer of women and breaker of homes. It would seem to me advisable that he appears not so much as a chippy chaser as a chivalrous fellow who cannot refuse when a pretty woman or an ugly one or a good old:man like Don Polan or a dwarf asks him for help. What gets him involved in love affairs and duels is his physical attraction, his legend, which knocks the pretty girls for a loop, even when he is not trying to court them. As I said yesterday, he is like a fellow walking past a pack of dogs with a big piece of roast beef under his arm and being puzzled why all the dogs are running along and jumping at him. He is not doing anything, or he thinks he isn't, to attract all the attention he gets. Of course, once Don Juan has started to help out some pretty woman who is not being treated right by her rascally lover or husband and he ends up in a clinch with her, he is much too courteous a fellow, and he is ardent too, to go away without a kiss or two. But that is unfortunately where he always gets into a conflict with some other man who can be expected to see that Don Juan has gotten into the boudoir in chivalrous answer to the woman's call, and that the romance is really the woman's fault rather than that of good old, kind hearted and terribly magnetic Don Juan. It is not that he takes the women away from other guys. It is rather that the women leave the other guys.

As to the queen. A good characteristic of her will be for her to be a philosopher queen. She sees from the reports she is getting from all over Europe and particularly from her own Spain that the legend of the wandering lover threatens the institution of the family upon which society and her government rest. So, when Don Juan returns home and is given the reception of a hero by the whole of Spain, she holds a great court, and in reproving him, she addresses a corrective message to all her subjects. . . . As the story goes along, and when the queen falls for him, he argues with her in the end that this must not be, because her early philosophy is obviously right, and if she should desert her kingdom and king for love, her example will ruin all Spain.

If you have seen *Monsieur Beaucaire* [1946] or *The Bandit of Sherwood Forest* [1946], you will realize how a very simple, melodramatic story could make a picture ordinary and unimportant. I cannot tell you how much in the beaten path our melodrama is. Or, at least if we use a simple straight line, we should have it presented so that it feels different, it reads different. . . .

Again I want to repeat to you one thing, that I try to force myself to get excited about any of the characters of our script, and I do not succeed. The plot idea of a man in search of love, and when he meets it, it is unobtainable, is still the right line of our story. Do not dismiss lightly, dear Jerry, the short, clever scene of Don Juan making love in different countries with women answering him in their native language and Don Juan talking the language of love. . . .

Sincerely,
Jean Negulesco

The last idea was not used.

TO: Steve Trilling	DATE: July 2, 1947
FROM: Jean Negulesco	SUBJECT: "Johnny Belinda"

Dear Steve:

Jerry Wald gave me a copy of *Johnny Belinda* to read this morning. I read it very carefully and I must say it's one of the most exciting, human and colorful scripts I have read in a long time. I am terribly enthusiastic about the possibility of doing it, because I know I could make a good job of it. . . .

Of course, I was sorry to have lost the *Don Juan* assignment after having put a good deal of work on it; but if Mr. Flynn feels I am not suited for the job, I would prefer getting off now to going through the mental torture of doing a picture with a man who didn't want me.

You know, from my past pictures around here, that I'm a hard worker, that I'm willing to be economical and at the same time, by the proper use of the camera, get unusual production values on the screen.

I certainly demonstrated to Jerry Wald and Tenny Wright that there were ways of cheating *Don Juan*. I put a lot of work into this project, and all I can do is hope that the studio will make a great picture out of it. In fact it can't miss being a tremendous box-office film; that's why I regret not being connected with it.

However, I feel that *Johnny Belinda* offers the same possibilities, and that's why I would like to be assigned to it.

> Warmest personal regards—
> *Jean Negulesco*

At Errol Flynn's request Vincent Sherman was assigned to direct Adventures of Don Juan.

TO: Steve Trilling   DATE: August 20, 1947
FROM: Vincent Sherman

Dear Steve:

The lack of enthusiasm I displayed yesterday in your office, which fortunately was amusing, arises out of the fact that I still am dubious about spending from two and a half to three million dollars on *Don Juan*.

It is true that [writer Harry] Kurnitz has suggested many improvements, and while I have great faith in his ability, at the moment I feel that our story is still rambling and weak in suspense and conflict. Many of my fears may be dispelled as Harry is writing, but on this 20th day of August in the year 5000 of our Lord, I am a worried Jewish boy.

You asked me the other day why I accepted the story in the first place. Let me reply bluntly that I accepted it, not because I was enthusiastic about the script, but because I was ashamed to keep on turning down stuff. I had read *Rebel Without a Cause*, *Young Man with a Horn*, the first script of *Flamingo Road*, and *The Last Fling*, and being a very conscientious guy, I said to myself, "I should try to do this one." You may also recall Mr. Warner's words to me, and I quote: "For Christ sake, will you please try to like this because Jerry Wald says you run down all of his scripts."

There it is, Steve, the simple truth. I am deeply worried and depressed, but I assure you that I have hope that one of us will get a brain inspiration and find some simple and effective line for the story. There is one last point I wish to make: Harry Kurnitz has a very good reputation and, therefore, I am counting heavily on his rescuing us, but we are planning to shoot on unwritten scenes at the moment.

Sincerely,
Vincent

P.S. I would appreciate your keeping this letter to yourself since I don't want to do anything to discourage Harry or Jerry and I am doing everything I can to bolster my own courage.

TO: Mr. Wald DATE: November 8, 1947
FROM: Mr. Trilling SUBJECT: "Adventures of Don Juan"

Dear Jerry:

I am amazed at your persistence, as you and Vince are over-evaluating the amount of work and importance of Don Rodrigo. This character is a glorified bit—appears in five scenes throughout the picture for a total of 11 lines of dialogue, one line each scene except one in which he speaks 7 lines. . . . after which he is run through by Don Juan and dies. . . .

You fellows evidently still do not understand what we meant in these talks about economy. If we use a free-lance actor, and I question whether you are going to do any better in type or quality, it will cost $500 to $750 or more weekly with a 6 or 7-week carry. If [contract player Douglas] Kennedy can't do this, essentially a silent bit with a few scattered lines, then we should have our heads examined for carrying people like him under contract.

In our original discussions when Claude Rains was planned for de Lorca, we did say we would try to get an expert swordsman and a big physical heavy for Rodrigo's part and make it more important, as he would have to be the menace and carry all the dueling, but now that Robert Douglas is set for de Lorca, you must revise your views when you realize how little Rodrigo actually has to do and how easy it is to make Kennedy look physically correct.

Please don't make it so tough for yourself and all concerned.

Kennedy played "Rodrigo"—essentially "a glorified bit."

TO: T. C. Wright
FROM: Frank Mattison [unit manager]

DATE: March 27, 1948
SUBJECT: "Don Juan"—Sherman

Report for Friday, March 26th, 93rd shooting day . . .

We are to proceed this morning, Saturday, and complete the close-ups necessary for the duel on Stage 21. When I went to the set at 5:15 P.M. yesterday Flynn called me to his dressing room and told me he was "pooped" and that the only way we could get the closeups was to do them today, Saturday. Also that I would have to get someone to fence for him with [actor] David Bruce in addition to the double.

I got [fencing master and duel choreographer] Fred Cavens and we are fitting him up to step in this morning to get the sequence finished. Flynn said he was unable to cope with either the double or Bruce. I told Errol that no matter what he threw at Cavens with his sword that Cavens would take it and that it would make Errol look good. This is the only way we are going to get this sequence finished. . . .

Frank Mattison

TO: T. C. Wright
FROM: Frank Mattison

DATE: April 10, 1948
SUBJECT: "Don Juan"—Sherman

Report for Friday, April 9th, 105th shooting day. . . .

Shooting the INT GRAND STAIRCASE on Stage 7.

The reason for getting so few shots yesterday was due to the fact that we were using Robert Douglas duel with Errol Flynn. As you know, Douglas . . . could not rehearse but a very little part of the shooting of the scene, with the result we have had Cavens doubling him in every possible foot of the picture where we did not actually come to a head closeup. Douglas has a very bad leg due to the war and is not as agile as he should be for this picture. However, I am sure it will turn out all right.

This picture is now 33 days behind schedule. And will run an additional 8 or 9 days before we finish. . . .

Frank Mattison

NEW YORK NY APRIL 30, 1948
H. WARNER TO JL—HAPPY ABOUT "DON JUAN" [finally finished shooting] BUT WITH PICTURES AT A COST OF "DON JUAN" AND [Flynn's] "SILVER RIVER" [1948] IT IS IMPOSSIBLE TO GET YOUR MONEY BACK. SEE YOU WEDNESDAY . . .

NEW YORK NY JANUARY 7, 1949
[Mort] BLUMENSTOCK [publicity and advertising director, New York] TO JL— WE ISSUING SUPPLEMENTARY [advertising] PAMPHLET ["Adventures of] DON

JUAN" TO AVOID PREVALENT CONFUSION AS WHETHER THIS IS OLD OR NEW PICTURE. SO MANY REISSUES ON MARKET, CONFUSION WIDESPREAD.

NEW YORK NY JANUARY 24, 1949
[Mort] BLUMENSTOCK TO JL—YOU EVIDENTLY DID NOT SEE NEW SUP-PLEMENTARY AD SECTION WHICH LAST WEEK WENT TO ALL BRANCH MANAGERS, DISTRICT MANAGERS AND EARLY DATES IN WHICH WE HEADLINED NEW SET OF ROMANTIC TYPE ADS WITH LINES LIKE "HE MADE HISTORY WHEN HE MADE LOVE," "BIG AND BOLD AND BREATH-LESSLY TOLD; THE STORY OF HISTORY'S GREATEST LOVER," "THE BIG LOVE THRILL OF 1949 IS HERE." IN EVERY ONE OF THESE, ROMANTIC ANGLE COMPLETELY DOMINATES AND WORD "NEW" IS PLAYED UP BIG AND IN SOME CASES USED TWICE IN BODY COPY. IN ADDITION, OVER TWO WEEKS AGO WE MAILED ADAPTATION OF TITLE WITH WORD "NEW" ENORMOUSLY ENLARGED AND SET UP IN SUCH WAY IT WOULD FIT EVERY MAT [ad] IN PRESSBOOK. ALSO ON THIS SHEET WE FURNISHED NEW HEADLINES WITH WORDS "BRAND NEW" WHICH COULD BE DROPPED INTO EVERY AD. . . . DESPITE ALL THIS, IN BROOKLYN WHERE WE USED ADS WITH WORD "NEW" POPPING NEARLY TITLE SIZE AND IN BODY COPY AND FRONT OF THEATRE AND LOBBY, PEOPLE STILL CAME OUT OF THE-ATRE SAYING THEY HAD SEEN THIS PICTURE SOMEWHERE BEFORE.

The Sea Hawk (1940) *had been an extraordinarily successful reissue in 1947,* The Adventures of Robin Hood (1938) *did exceptionally well as a 1948 reissue, and innumerable other swashbucklers (old and new) had recently glutted the market. Also,* Don Juan *with John Barrymore had been produced by Warner Bros. in 1926 as a milestone silent film with a synchronized sound-on-disk score, and Alexander Korda made* The Private Life of Don Juan *in 1934. To compound the situation, for the new Ad-*ventures of Don Juan, *a few stock shots from Warners'* Robin Hood *were used, and an entire sequence was liberally embellished with scenes from* The Private Lives of Elizabeth and Essex (1939).

FROM RALPH E. LEWIS [attorney]

CONFIDENTIAL
Mr. R. W. Perkins
Legal Department
Warner Bros. Pictures, Inc.
321 West 44th Street
New York 18, New York

April 19, 1948

Dear Mr. Perkins:
I am writing to you direct on the specific instructions of Mr. J. L. Warner. He has become very much disturbed over the situation now

existing with Michael Curtiz Productions, Inc. He does not want any of the studio staff other than Mr. Obringer to have knowledge of the situation.

Curtiz, under the contract of October 7, 1946, has made two pictures and is now making a third. Mike Curtiz himself has no administrative talent whatsoever, and . . . the corporation seems to be falling further behind financially all the time. It owes Warners approximately $1,500,000 in advances, in addition to the Warner charge of 35% for overhead and other miscellaneous items. I am enclosing a tentative balance sheet as of April 3 which will show you the picture.

As you know, Warners own 49% of the stock and Curtiz owns the balance. Apparently the only purpose in initiating the deal in 1946 was to protect Mike Curtiz in the future and allow him to accumulate a nest egg on a capital gains basis. Mr. Curtiz had his own legal advisors and tax men at the time. It is now obvious that the nest egg will not develop and Mike is apparently sacrificing his directorial abilities to his worry about the financial and administrative problems.

J. L. wants to give Mike some kind of a nest egg with a capital gains factor. He wants to deal individually with Mike and purchase Mike's 51% of the stock for a total price of $500,000, payable in installments of $100,000 per year. He then wants Mike to cancel his existing director's contract with Curtiz Productions and enter into a direct employment agreement with Warners on the basis of, say, $3,500 per week plus 10% of the gross. The only motivation that I can see is the desire to keep Mike on the job as a director without other duties, and at the same time give him half a million dollars spread out over five years on which he would not be heavily taxed. . . .

Warner's proposal, or a variation of it, was worked out with Curtiz.

FROM BARBARA STANWYCK

JACK WARNER
WARNER BROTHERS STUDIO

JUNE 21, 1948

DEAR JACK: A COUPLE OF YEARS HAVE GONE BY SINCE I MADE A FILM FOR YOU AND SINCE THEN I AM SURE YOU WILL AGREE THAT THE SCRIPTS SUBMITTED TO ME HAVE NOT COMPARED WITH "THE FOUNTAINHEAD." I READ IN THE MORNING PAPERS TODAY YOUR OFFICIAL ANNOUNCEMENT THAT MISS PATRICIA NEAL IS GOING TO PLAY THE ROLE OF "DOMINIQUE" IN "THE FOUNTAINHEAD." AFTER ALL, JACK, IT SEEMS ODD AFTER I FOUND THE PROPERTY, BROUGHT IT TO THE ATTENTION OF THE STUDIO, HAD THE STUDIO PURCHASE THE PROP-

ERTY, AND DURING THE PREPARATION OF THE SCREENPLAY EVERYONE ASSUMED THAT I WOULD BE IN THE PICTURE, AND NOW I FIND SOME-ONE ELSE IS DEFINITELY PLAYING THE ROLE. NATURALLY, JACK, I AM BITTERLY DISAPPOINTED. HOWEVER, I CAN REALISTICALLY SEE YOUR PROBLEMS, AND CERTAINLY BASED ON ALL OF THESE CIRCUMSTANCES, IT WOULD APPEAR TO BE TO OUR MUTUAL ADVANTAGE TO TERMINATE OUR PRESENT CONTRACTUAL RELATIONSHIP. I WOULD APPRECIATE HEARING FROM YOU. KINDEST PERSONAL REGARDS.

BARBARA STANWYCK

FROM JACK L. WARNER

Miss Barbara Stanwyck
807 North Rodeo Drive
Beverly Hills, Calif.

June 22, 1948

Dear Barbara:

I have your telegram of the twenty-second and, while I know you brought *The Fountainhead* to Mr. [Henry] Blanke's attention, I want to make it very clear to you that we have a huge Story Department here in the Studio as well as in New York that covers every book, periodical, etc.

The Fountainhead was called to the attention of our studio through the regular channels. I personally knew about it long before you suggested it to Mr. Blanke, and we were considering it for purchase and subsequently closed for it.

Naturally your interest in this property is well understood, but our studio does not confine its operations to cases where people bring in books or other stories and we buy them solely on their suggestion. It operates through regular channels, and did in this case as in most cases.

However, since our actions have offended you and you desire to terminate your contract with us, it may be that under the circumstances this would be the best thing to do.

It is with regret that I accede to your request and, if you will have your agent or attorney get in touch with our Legal Department here at the studio, the formalities of terminating your contract can be arranged.

Kindest personal regards,
Sincerely,
Jack

The contract was terminated. Since returning to Warner Bros. with a nonexclusive contract, Stanwyck had starred in The Gay Sisters *(1942),* Christmas In Connecticut *(1945),* My Reputation *(1946),* The Two Mrs. Carrolls *(1947), and* Cry Wolf *(1947). However, the studio was committed to the building of Patricia Neal, who had recently signed a contract.*

TO: Mr. Trilling—Wald   DATE: June 30, 1948
FROM: Sylvia Fine [writer of special   SUBJECT: "Happy Times"
   musical material and wife   [*The Inspector General*]
   of Danny Kaye]

In thinking of various conversations I have had with you both recently, I find that there are several things I would like to reiterate. While there are many things in the production of the picture in which I have bowed and will continue to bow to your years of experience—i.e., choice of locations, sets, etc.—there is one phase in which I think it would be foolish not to profit by my previous experience—and that is Danny's numbers, in relation to when they should be shot, how they should be shot, and the musical and choreographic planning involved.

As far as special effects are concerned (specifically the triple mirror number), I found in working on [Goldwyn's] *Wonder Man* [1945] that the most efficient way to get the most original and satisfactory result is to go to the special effects department with the number planned in detail, and then throw in their lap the problem of how to do it. If you ask them first what can be done, you immediately put limitations on the imagination of the choreographer, Danny and myself, because they will naturally tell you in advance that only things they have done before are possible. This obviously is not true, or new things would never be done.

Since the mirror number will be one of the last things shot in the picture, since it involves nobody but Danny, and therefore will be much less expensive to shoot when you are carrying nobody else on the picture, we certainly have plenty of time for me to first work with the choreographer and then go to the special effects department.

As far as music is concerned, you will find it far less expensive to have one man in complete charge, because Danny's numbers will not be recorded in any routine fashion. They will be half pre-recorded, half done standard and scored later. I think I need not point out that unless this procedure is carefully pre-planned, it can easily run into duplication of time and effort on the part of both the music and sound departments, plus considerable confusion in rehearsal and shooting, all of which runs into a great deal of M-O-N-E-Y. Nobody, unless they have lived through the planning, shooting and recording of Danny's numbers, can understand how very much different the procedure is from that used in other musicals.

In view of all of this, I don't think it a very wise plan to use both Johnny [Green] and Ray Heindorf on the picture unless you have them working jointly—in which case, I don't see what saving is effected.

Sylvia Kaye

Green was assigned as musical director.

NEW YORK NY OCTOBER 1, 1948
[Robert W.] PERKINS [Legal Department] TO HM . . . JL—GOVERNMENT IS SERVING TODAY PAPERS. . . . NOT YET RECEIVED BUT WE UNDERSTAND THEY CONTAIN FOLLOWING: FIRST, DEMAND COMPLETE DIVORCE [of] PRODUCTION AND DISTRIBUTION FROM EXHIBITION, AND IN ADDITION DIVESTITURE BY THEATRE SUBSIDIARIES OF SUBSTANTIAL NUMBER OF THEATRES. SECOND, COMPANIES TO HAVE ONE YEAR TO FORMULATE PLANS FOR DIVORCE AND DIVESTITURE AND FIVE YEARS TO CARRY OUT PLAN. THIRD, ALL JOINT AND PARTNERSHIP INTERESTS TO BE DISPOSED OF IMMEDIATELY. FOURTH, BEGINNING IMMEDIATELY IN 250 TOWNS WHERE GOVERNMENT CLAIMS MONOPOLY EXISTS, NO AFFILIATED COMPANY SHALL LICENSE MORE THAN HALF OF ITS PICTURES TO ANY OTHER AFFILIATED COMPANY. FIFTH, IMMEDIATE INJUNCTION AGAINST ANY THEATRE ACQUISITIONS. WE WILL KNOW MORE WHEN WE SEE ACTUAL COURT PAPERS. YOU PROBABLY WILL BE ABLE TO READ ABOVE IN THIS AFTERNOON'S PAPERS. . . .

By the mid-1950s the major motion picture companies completed their divorcement of production and distribution from exhibition as a result of the government antitrust decree. This marked the beginning of the end for the studio system of the time. It was no longer necessary for the movie companies to mass-produce films in order to supply their theatres with constant product.

TO: Vincent Sherman [in London   DATE: November 19, 1948
      directing *The Hasty Heart*]
FROM: Steve Trilling

. . . You probably will read soon about our "slow down" at the studio here. We definitely are not going to shut down but we want to carefully analyse and estimate the values of our future properties before going into production, so that we are able to meet present world picture conditions, and as they will be in the future. We will not start a picture until the script, cast, and *price* are right. If we feel a picture will cost too much or present difficulties, we will fold it rather than hazard any extreme gamble. In short, we will be much more selective and choosie, much the way we find the public is now in their picture buying. We cannot take any more chance now making a picture just for the mere sake of making a picture—without having some definite conclusion as to the end result and *cost*. Further, we don't want to just keep jamming pictures through and find ourselves overloaded with an inventory of expensive pictures which, when released, might prove to be on the moldy, untimely side. You and I have discussed this innumerable times, and I know you will heartily concur in this concept. . . .

Attendance at movie theatres continued to drop as a result of modifications in post-World War II America's recreational needs—including the beginning of TV.

TO: Steve Trilling
FROM: Harry Kurnitz [screenwriter]

DATE: December 7, 1948
SUBJECT: "Little Sister" by
Raymond Chandler

Dear Steve:

[Story editor] Bud Kay asked me to give you my reaction directly on this property.

It is of course impossible to analyze the plot, which is not typical of Chandler's work but in proper hands that is not necessarily a drawback.

I think it is important to remember about these stories that the plot or story line has *absolutely nothing* to do with their success or failures, as pictures. The best story Chandler ever wrote, *The High Window*, made the worst picture [retitled *The Brasher Doubloon*, 1947] because of the way it was cast and directed. Both *Murder My Sweet* [1944] [from Chandler's novel, *Farewell, My Lovely*] and *The Big Sleep* [1946] equally bizarre and confusing, were so treated in the writing, playing and direction that the story-line became incidental to the individual scenes. It is generally true of these stories that if the individual scenes pack a wallop and present intriguing characters, the sum total of plot is incidental. . . .

Harry Kurnitz

FROM STEVE TRILLING

Mr. Vincent Sherman
Warner Bros. Pictures, Ltd.
Warner House
Wardour Street
London, W.I.

February 5, 1949

. . . The Studio still remains inactive—no picture shooting. We hope to start March 1st a picture with Jane Wyman and Dennis

Morgan, a Harry Kurnitz opus called *The Octopus and Miss Smith*
[*The Lady Takes a Sailor,* 1949] with Mike Curtiz directing—then slip
into a Bette Davis vehicle, *Beyond the Forest* [1949] with King Vidor
doing the chores. Thereafter it will be a gradual return to more
production . . .

We are paring down our contract list—more streamlining—a few
of the lesser lights are departing. Bette Davis has signed a new type of
deal—one picture a year if and when we can catch her or want her.
Errol Flynn is also on a one picture a year deal from now on similar to
Bogart's.

We made a bargain package loan-out deal with David O.
Selznick and during the next year will have Gregory Peck, Jennifer
Jones, Joe Cotten, Shirley Temple, Louis Jourdan, Valli, and a few
other lesser lights for a picture. . . .

As ever,

[Mort] BLUMENSTOCK TO JL

APRIL 21, 1949

"INTERIORS," ARCHITECT'S MAGAZINE, BELTS WHISKERS OFF SETS IN
"FOUNTAINHEAD" [1949]. FROM NUMBER OF SCREENINGS WE HAVE HAD
ON THIS PICTURE SO FAR WE CAN TELL THAT MIDDLEBROW AND LOW-
BROW AUDIENCE LIKE IT. HIGHBROWS DO NOT. SINCE MIDDLEBROW
AND LOWBROWS OUTNUMBER HIGHBROWS THOUSAND TO ONE THIS
WOULD NOT SEEM LIKE GREAT COMMERCIAL RISK. JUST TO BE PRE-
PARED FOR WHAT I THINK IS COMING UP WOULD YOU HAVE ALEX
[Evelove] TELL ME IF WE EVER CONTACTED [architect Frank] LLOYD WRIGHT
AS CONSULTANT ARCHITECT ON THIS PICTURE OR IF HE EVER INDI-
CATED THAT HE WANTED TO WORK ON STORY. AM INFORMED THAT
WRIGHT GOES AROUND TELLING EVERYBODY THAT PICTURE IS BASED
ON HIS LIFE, WHICH ISN'T BAD, AS WRIGHT DID THINGS IN HIS LIFE
THAT WOULD FRIGHTEN EVEN ROARK [the principal character in *The Foun-
tainhead*]. . . .

FROM JACK L. WARNER

JULY 13, 1949

TO BLUMENSTOCK: THE CAMPAIGN ON "FLAMINGO ROAD" [1949] WITH
THAT HOT PHOTO OF CRAWFORD WITH CIGARETTE IN MOUTH, GAMS
SHOWING, ETC HAD MUCH TO DO WITH PUBLIC GOING FOR THIS PIC-
TURE. TRY USE THIS TYPE PHOTO ON ANY PICTURE YOU CAN IN FU-
TURE. . . .

FROM JACK L. WARNER

Mr. Roy Obringer
Studio

May 3, 1949

Dear Roy:

This morning I told Lew Wasserman [Bette Davis's agent] over the telephone that Bette Davis said she would not do the picture, *Rose Moline* [*Beyond The Forest*], with [Joseph] Cotten, to [director] King Vidor, Henry Blanke and Trilling.

In view of this situation I told Wasserman to let me know the maximum settlement she would make on the contract, which she could pay us over two years, otherwise we may have to go to court as everyone was suing us so we were going to try it once.

J. L. Warner

FROM BETTE DAVIS

WARNER BROS PICTURES, INC.
ATTN: JACK L WARNER

MAY 3, 1949

I HAVE BEEN ADVISED BY MY AGENT TO THE EFFECT THAT YOU ARE CONSTRUING MY STATEMENTS AND ATTITUDE IN THE MEETING YESTERDAY, REQUESTED BY ME AND ATTENDED BY TRILLING, BLANKE, VIDOR AND MYSELF AS A RESULT OF AND IN CONNECTION WITH YOUR HAVING NOTIFIED ME TO APPEAR IN THE PICTURE "ROSE MOLINE" [*Beyond the Forest*] STARTING MAY SECOND, AS A REFUSAL TO COMPLY THEREWITH. IT IS TRUE THAT I EXPRESSED MYSELF [to] THE EFFECT THAT THE CAST, SCRIPT, AND CERTAIN OTHER MATTERS PERTAINING TO THE PICTURE WERE LIKELY TO CAUSE DIFFICULTIES AND UNDESIRABLE RESULTS, WHICH OPINION I UNDERSTAND IS LIKEWISE SHARED BY OTHERS AND DID NOT COME AS ANY SURPRISE TO YOU, BUT I APPRECIATE THAT THE FINAL DECISION IS WITHIN YOUR PROVINCE, AND MY POSITION WAS PROMPTED, AS IN THE PAST, BY A SINCERE DESIRE TO ASSIST AND PROMOTE OUR MUTUAL INTERESTS BY A FRANK DISCUSSION TO THE END THAT UNHAPPY SITUATIONS, DIFFICULTIES AND DISAPPOINTMENT MIGHT BE AVOIDED, AND IN ORDER THAT THERE BE NO MISUNDERSTANDING YOU ARE HEREBY ADVISED THAT I DID NOT EXPRESSLY NOR DID I INTEND BY INFERENCE TO IMPLY SUCH A REFUSAL.

BETTE DAVIS

Davis asked for and received a release from her Warner Bros. contract in July—just prior to the completion of Beyond the Forest. *The picture was released in October to generally poor reviews and business.*

THE BREAKING POINT

FROM JOHN GARFIELD

Mr. Michael Curtiz
Warner Bros. Studios
Burbank
California

January 16, 1950

Dear Mike:

I am most happy to have heard from you. The only reason I didn't answer sooner was because I wanted to re-read the Hemingway book [*To Have and Have Not**], which I did.

I quite agree with you about doing it very realistically without the phony glamor, so that there is a real quality of honesty and truthfulness which, by the way, I feel [screenwriter] Randy MacDougall captured from the book [in his screenplay].

He has followed the book quite honestly, I think, and some of the questions I would like to kind of throw out for consideration or discussion are:

The deepening of the relationship with the wife [Phyllis Thaxter], so that you get a sense of a man who although he is married for many years has a real kind of yen for her, which is usually very rarely shown in films. As Randy indicates, very warm love scenes are played with the man and the wife. I feel, however, that these scenes can be still deeper without making it too slick.

The other girl [Patricia Neal], I feel has to be carefully gone over in the sense that Harry [Garfield] should be tempted, as most men are, and almost goes through with it, but in the end kind of gets cold feet. I feel this relationship can be a little clearer.

Since Eddie [Juano Hernandez] is to be a Negro, I am of the opinion that the relationship between Eddie and Harry can also be gone into in a little more detail to show that Eddie has similar problems to Harry's, which Randy also indicated in the script, but not with enough detail. Their regard for each other, without being too sentimental, can be kicked up a bit more.

*Upon which *The Breaking Point* was based. The 1945 Bogart-Bacall version of *To Have and Have Not* deviated considerably from the novel.

One of the interesting features of the book is that Harry loses his
arm. That might be a little too morbid, but it has a wonderful quality,
particularly later on in the book where he makes love to his wife. This
kind of a relationship, if you want to include the loss of the arm, has
never been shown. It might seem a little grotesque talking about it, but
I certainly think it's worth considering, as it will kick up the whole
latter part of the script, purely from a characterization point of view. Of
course, Mr. Warner might think it's a little too morbid. However, I
feel as long as Randy has stuck so close to the original story in many
respects, there is no reason why this couldn't be included. . . .

The main theme which seems to me quite simple and direct is:
the struggle of a man who tries to make a living for his family and to
discharge his responsibilities and finds it tough. . . .

I, too, am anxiously looking forward to working with you again
and I think with Randy and Jerry [Wald] we might come up with
something which will be a little off the beaten path, but also excellent
entertainment and a real joy to do.

With much love and regards,
Johnny G.

*Garfield's suggestions were reflected to a degree in later drafts of the
script. Near the end of the film the character is so seriously wounded that
his life can be saved only through amputation of his arm. It is on this note
that the picture ends.*

TO: Ranald MacDougall DATE: April 19, 1950
FROM: Jerry Wald SUBJECT: "The Breaking Point"

Dear Randy:
On P. 63, Sc. 87, I wish you'd explore this scene again. I think we
could make it emotionally much stronger at the end of the scene where
Harry, irritated, is talking about enjoying killing a man and not being
able to sleep nights. . . .

The other day I was having lunch with Audie Murphy,* and he
brought up the same point, that during the war killing became a matter
of something that was run of the mill. After the war was over, he found
himself gradually losing his desire to kill, and became irritated when he
was aroused by reading a headline or talking about somebody having been
killed in civilian life. He told me that the reason he goes hunting so much
is because he gets an emotional outlet for any desire he might have for
killing. . . .

Jerry Wald

*World War II's most decorated GI, who began a film-acting career in the late 1940s.

From *Los Angeles Mirror*

January 6, 1950

STAR TO PICK FUTURE FILMS
by Bob Thomas
Associated Press Correspondent

Seldom do film stars have an opportunity to stand off and take a long gaze at their careers. Ronald Reagan is the exception.

The chance befell Reagan last year when he and [actor] George Tobias engaged in a bit of horseplay during a charity baseball game. Tobias bumped Reagan at first base and the crowd roared with laughter—until it was discovered that Reagan had busted his leg.

"After spending most of last year in bed," he declared, "I'm going to concentrate on my career in 1950. And there'll be some changes made."

Reagan, now working on his first post-accident picture, *Storm Center*,* is lining up a select schedule.

"I'm going to pick my own pictures. I have come to the conclusion that I could do as good a job of picking as the studio has done. At least I could do no worse," he said.

"With the parts I've had, I could telephone my lines in and it wouldn't make any difference."

After reflecting on his statements, Reagan shrugged:

"Well, I can always go back to being a sports announcer."

TO: Mr. Warner   DATE: February 17, 1950
FROM: Obringer   SUBJECT: Ronald Reagan

I talked with Ronald Reagan today in his dressing room at Universal relative to his interview with Bob Thomas of the Associated Press which appeared in the L.A. *Mirror* on January 6, 1950.

Reagan, while not unfriendly, stated that he felt he was the one who had the beef about his treatment at the studio, about his playing second lead to [Richard] Todd in *The Hasty Heart* [1949], that he was more or less blamed for the poor showing of *That Hagen Girl* [1947], and that he did not want to do it but gave his promise to do it with the assurance that he would not be criticized if it did not come off as we admitted it was not the best script, and about his wanting to do a Western and our promise to put him in one if he would bring in a good Western story and which he did—*Ghost Mountain* [and retitled *Rocky Mountain*, 1950 starring Errol Flynn]—but it was never given to him, etc. etc.

After he got the steam off I told him that the implications from the

*Released as *Storm Warning* (1950).

interview were very damaging to his pictures, practically all of which were produced here, that it undoubtedly reflected his attitude with respect to future pictures and that, while you considered him a very good personal friend, you felt from a business standpoint that if he were going to be unhappy and not have his heart in his work and was not going to accept our judgment of story selection, it would be best if the present 2-picture agreement could be amicably called off.

Reagan went into some more alleged abuses and particularly the fact that he lay in the hospital for 6 weeks with a broken leg without anybody from his studio contacting him or ascertaining his condition except at the last moment when *The Girl from Jones Beach* [1949] was released.

Reagan stated, however, that he would think the matter over and discuss it with [agent] Lew Wasserman and we would undoubtedly get his decision in a few days from Wasserman.

R. J. Obringer

Shortly afterwards Reagan left Warner Bros., where he had been under contract since 1937.

TO: Vincent Sherman   DATE: November 11, 1950
FROM: Jack Warner

Dear Vince:

After talking to you on the telephone last night, Friday, I am depending on you to finish the picture [*Goodbye, My Fancy*, 1951] by next Saturday, November 18th. . . .

As I told you, other companies are making the same type of picture in 21-28-36 days with important casts. As you know, Metro made *Father's Little Dividend* [1951] with Spencer Tracy, Elizabeth Taylor and Joan Bennett in 21 days and I am sure the Director had the same problems you have had. . . .

You will just have to do this. Otherwise, we cannot stand off this type of cost and delay in making a picture. Those days are gone and no one is going to stay on the team unless they can carry the ball. Get in there and finish the picture by next Saturday or before and stop trying for perfection. No one is interested but yourself and I am sure you are not going to pay to see the picture. . . .

If you would only realize the seriousness of our position.

Director Vincent Sherman left Warners in 1951.

FROM RAYMOND CHANDLER

6005 Camino de la Costa
La Jolla, California

November 2, 1950

Dear Mr. [Finlay] McDermid:

I am a cad not sooner to have made acknowledgment of your two letters dated July 7 and August 22. I remember very well the time when you (at the ungodly hour of 9:30 in the morning) conducted me to a projection room where I sat alone and watched *The Big Sleep* [based on Chandler's novel]. I was trying to do a script on [Chandler's novel] *The Lady in the Lake* [1946] for M.G.M. then, and we were very anxious to be sure that we did not imitate any effect which Warners had got in the Howard Hawks picture.

As to the week for which I did not receive payment working on *Strangers on a Train* [1951], was I a damn fool about that! I had had a touch of food poisoning, incurred in the course of duty at a lunch with Hitchcock; and for three days I just sat around and gloomed, although I did work the rest of the week including Saturday and Sunday. In fact I worked Saturdays and Sundays all the time I was on this assignment. What strange delicacy of conscience induced me to give any weight to this, I wonder. It must have been that I thought I was dealing with people as precise as myself in these matters. . . .

Are you aware that this screenplay was written without one single consultation with Mr. Hitchcock after the writing of the screenplay began? Not even a telephone call. Not one word of criticism or appreciation. Silence. Blank silence then and since. You are much too clever a man to believe that any writer will do his best in conditions like this. There are always things that need to be discussed. There are always places where a writer goes wrong, not being himself a master of the camera. There are always difficult little points which require the meeting of minds, the accommodation of points of view. I had none of this. I find it rather strange. I find it rather ruthless. I find it almost incomparably rude. And I think in your heart of hearts you would be very apt to agree with me.

Yours very sincerely,
Raymond Chandler

Chandler's screenplay was rewritten by Czenzi Ormonde.

11

Two by Tennessee (1949–1951)

THE GLASS MENAGERIE

FROM TENNESSEE WILLIAMS

Mr. Jerry Wald
Producer Warner Bros.

Mr. Charles Feldman
Charles K. Feldman Group Productions

May 31, 1949

Dear Mr. Wald and Mr. Feldman:

I am writing you jointly because I understand that you are jointly concerned as producers in the filming of my play, *The Glass Menagerie*, and my topic is the present condition of the film script which I have recently had the chance to read again.

I first saw an earlier version of the script in the summer of 1947, in Hollywood, and at that time I expressed to Mr. Feldman an agreeable surprise at the extent to which the material of the play had been kept in the film version. I understood that this was an early, preliminary draft of the screen-play and that it was still in a fluid state. My second reading of the play, quite recently, was a good deal less agreeable, for this is much closer to the date of actual filming, and I find that certain grave and important faults are still in the script, and I think it is a matter of great concern to all of us that these things should be rectified before you start shooting the picture, and that some rewriting will have to be done.

Let me say, before making specific allusion to these defects, that I am only as concerned as I am because of the conviction, which I have always held very strongly, that this "property" has every chance of becoming a really great picture, and one that would surpass its dimensions as a play on the stage. However, the *basic* qualities of the play *must* be kept if it is going to be transferred successfully to the screen. The qualities that made it successful, and widely appealing, as a play were, primarily, its true and fresh observation, its dignity, its poetry and pathos, for it had no great dramatic situations as a play nor has it any as a film-story, and the plot was slight and simple as it still is and must remain.

Now I feel that a great deal of the truth, dignity, poetry and pathos of this story has gone out of the window, and this loss occurs through the insertion of certain little sequences and devices which can easily and quickly be cut out and replaced by something in keeping with the tone and quality of the original. I think you all know that I have no reputation for being "arty" or highbrow, and that, on the contrary, I am known to be a believer in sound and popular theatre that gets across to a large public, and nothing that I object to or suggest is going to hazard the popular appeal of the screen-play, but is actually meant to preserve and increase it.

First of all, I specifically object to all the sequences involving "the other young man," the one who teaches art to children and who provides the so-called "happy ending." I object to him, first of all, because he is such a Sunday-school sissy of a character with no reality or interest, who brings into the story nothing but tedium and incredibility. He is a most palpable "device" and one that serves no constructive end from any point of view.

Now the whole play, in mood and quality and essential meaning, is keyed to the original kind of ending, and when something like this occurs, the poetry and the pathos which are so carefully built up in the preceding scenes are brought crashing to earth in splinters, and the final effect is one of bathos and sentimentality.

If the play had not been widely read and extensively toured through the country and presented by many little theatres, this distortion of its story and quality would not be so dangerous. But [it] is very well known as a play, and all who liked or admired it as such will deeply resent the loss of its basic dignity on the screen, and the reviewers will be likely to attack it.

The heartening message in the character of Laura is to those thousands of girls who do *not* find the dream-boy who sets everything magically right in the final sequence. This heartening message can be underscored and played up in the screen version without violating the essential meaning and truth of the play, and that is what I am appealing for in this letter. It is not a difficult (although very important) change to make, and although I am deep in other works and it is naturally hard for me to revert to something I worked on five years ago, I will be happy to undertake these revisions, either alone or in collaboration with another writer who shares my views, provided that I have the assurance from you, the producers, that it is equally your will to make this a really true and dignified picture. . . .

Cordially,
Tennessee Williams
American Express, Rome, Italy

The character of "the other young man" as described above was modified in the next revision of the script, on which Tennessee Williams collaborated.

FROM: Mr. Harry Mayer
     [Warner Bros., New York]
TO: Mr. S. B. Trilling

DATE: August 22, 1949

For Steve:

By the time this letter reaches the coast, you undoubtedly will have seen the [Tallulah] Bankhead–[Ralph] Meeker tests [for *The Glass Menagerie*]. She worked extremely well all day Thursday and Friday morning and the temperament was at a minimum. However, there was a big change at noon Friday when she was faced with finishing the last scene with Pamela Rivers, who played "Laura" and then going on to the Ralph Meeker scene. She claims she had insufficient time to prepare the material for the Meeker scene and pointblank refused to go any further. At this point we were all quite sure she had been drinking in her dressing room and became quite difficult. Through the intervention of her secretary, we were able to secure her promise to let Meeker do his scene while she remained out of camera view and fed him the lines. During the rehearsal of this scene having finished her own material, she drank quite a lot more and in her enthusiasm for Meeker and after reiteration that this boy was going to be a great star she constantly interfered with the direction and made it almost impossible to get the few rough feet of film that we were so anxious to secure. I think it is really lamentable after all the desire we have shown to get Meeker to test that the circumstances should have been so inauspicious. If anything good shows on this film, it will be quite miraculous. If interested then you might be able to get further film by flying him from San Francisco where he will be playing in *Streetcar* [*Named Desire*] commencing this coming weekend.

There is no chance at all of using Meeker with [Miriam] Hopkins on Wednesday because he has a matinee on that day and leaves that night. Anyway, it will take a complete day to shoot the Hopkins test. . . .

Sorry this whole thing turned out in the fashion it did but you have absolutely no idea of the disgraceful state Miss Bankhead was in late Friday afternoon. Incidentally, it was this that caused us to go into two full hours of overtime at the studio. [Director] Irving Rapper agrees that in his experience he has never seen a star behave in this fashion.

Regards,

Gertrude Lawrence, Arthur Kennedy, and Jane Wyman played the roles tested by Tallulah Bankhead, Ralph Meeker, and Pamela Rivers.

FROM TENNESSEE WILLIAMS

Messrs. Jack Warner,
Jerry Wald, and
Charles K. Feldman

May 6, 1950

Dear Sirs:

I have now seen the picture [*The Glass Menagerie*, 1950] three times, twice in a private screening room and finally with a regular audience in New Jersey and this letter is meant to convey as clearly as possible my own reaction to it, based on these three showings. I know and truly appreciate the tremendous enthusiasm that you have all felt and expressed for this picture, which you have made with great care. It was perhaps unfortunate that I had received nothing but highly laudatory comments on the film before I saw it, as I was not prepared to find any faults in it whatsoever. Consequently the first time I saw it, in the cold light of a private screening, my reactions were unavoidably more critical than those that you had expressed to me in your wires. . . .

Now I would not be willing to make any adverse comments at all if I didn't feel that certain things can still be done to protect and enhance the property as it now exists. . . .

The things that I object to most strenuously, and very strenuously indeed, are certain changes that were made in the script after I left Hollywood and which came to me as a complete and very distressing surprise when I first heard them from the screen. I understand why you decided to dramatize Amanda's [Gertrude Lawrence] recollection-scene, but it has the unfortunate effect of making her seem not just a romanticist, which she was to some degree, but an out-and-out liar. I am thinking particularly of her statement that she had "twenty-three proposals in a single evening." Of course the background for this fanciful reminiscence is much too elaborate and somehow it seems to lack any real nostalgia or poetry, it is more like a bit of an MGM musical suddenly thrown into the middle of the picture.* . . .

A really strong objection concerns an insertion that has been made after Tom's [Arthur Kennedy] final exit from the apartment. Laura [Jane Wyman] follows him out into the alley and calls him back for the exchange of some lines from the cornball department. It is the only scene in the entire picture where Miss Wyman's performance really weakens. Rapper has exact notes on this passage. The worst of these lines is "Send me your poems so I may travel with you." I would prefer the entire elimination of this little scene, which is anti-climactic and saccharine, but I particularly beseech you to eliminate the two or three utterances that Irving and I have noted upon the script.** . . .

About the "new" gentleman-caller. In my script he was never visible on the screen. At the most, he was the sound of approaching footsteps and perhaps a shadow stretching before him as he came up the alley. This gives him a quality of poetic mystery and beauty which the picture badly needs in its final moments. Now we not only see him very plainly, his whole figure, but he is also provided with a full name, Richard *Henderson*. This little touch is going to stand out like a sore thumb and will gravely affect your critical reception, particularly in all those cities where the *Menagerie* has been known as a play. The light in Laura's eyes, and in her mother's, their glad "hellos" from the fire-escape were absolutely all the up-beat that the traffic could bear. As I remarked when I left my script with you, any more upbeat at this point is the straw that breaks the camel's back. I urge you most seriously to consider eliminating the shot of the actual figure coming up the alley and to remove the last name, both totally unnecessary to giving the picture its final "upbeat" and both extremely dangerous to a respect for the film's integrity among that relatively small, but terribly important, segment of the film public to which such things make a

*This mateial remained.
**This scene was deleted.

difference. (I don't think we should dismiss from our minds the possibility of an Academy Award, for instance.)* . . .

The lines I think should be restored are the best, most lyric lines in the entire narration—"Then all at once my sister touches my shoulder. I turn around and look into her eyes . . . Oh, Laura, Laura! I tried to leave you behind me. But I am more faithful than I intended to be. . . ."**

[Director] Irving [Rapper] tells me that Breen made the disgustingly prurient charge that these lines (!!!!) contained a suggestion of *INCEST!* I cannot understand acquiescence to this sort of foul-minded and utterly stupid tyranny, especially in the case of a film as totally clean and pure, as remarkably devoid of anything sexual or even sensual, as the *Menagerie*, both as a play and a picture. The charge is insulting to me, to my family, and an effrontery to the entire motion-picture industry! And I think you owe it to motion-pictures to defend yourselves against such prurience and tyranny by fighting it out with them. If I ever work in pictures, in America, I must know that my work is not at the mercy of the capricious whims that seem to operate in this office.

Well, boys, I have had my say! I am sure that you wanted me to have it, and I deeply appreciate your wanting me to have it and giving me the chance to have it. You have what is *almost* a fine picture. Don't let it remain anything less than what you are still able to make it, with only the exercise of a little scissors and paste.

Cordially and gratefully,
Tennessee Williams

A STREETCAR NAMED DESIRE

MARCH 20, 1950

[Charles K.] FELDMAN TO J.L.: (PERSONAL) AM TRYING TO GET FINISHED VERSION OF "STREETCAR" FROM TENNESSEE BY APRIL 15 . . . CONTRACT WITH GADGE [director Elia Kazan] WILL PROVIDE IF WE DON'T SEE EYE TO EYE WHEN FINISHED SCRIPT COMES IN FROM TENNESSEE EITHER PARTY CAN CALL OFF DEAL. AS OF THE MOMENT, GADGE IS STILL HIGH ON DE HAVILLAND AND BRANDO BUT FRANKLY DON'T BELIEVE WE SHOULD MAKE ANY COMMITMENTS UNTIL AFTER APRIL 15 UNLESS YOU DECIDE TO CONTRARY. . . .

---

*Compromises were made in revising this scene.
**These lines were restored.

Kazan had directed the New York stage production. Vivien Leigh was eventually cast in the role of "Blanche." Feldman, an independent packager and agent, bought Streetcar *for filming and then made an arrangement with Warner Bros. for financing, coproduction, and distribution. A similar situation applied to* The Glass Menagerie.

FROM THE BREEN OFFICE

April 28, 1950

Memo to Warner Bros. Studio with reference to A *Streetcar Named Desire*
. . . Mr. Shurlock and Mr. Vizzard [of the Breen Office] set forth the following three points as representing the three principal problems posed by this material under the code.

Number 1: The script contains an inference of sex perversion. This principally has reference to the character of Blanche's young husband, Allan Grey [not seen in the play or film]. There seems little doubt that this young man was a homosexual.

Number 2: There seems to be an inference of a type of nymphomania with regards to the character of Blanche herself. Her peculiar and neurotic attitude toward sex and particularly to sex attraction for young boys has about it an erotic flavor that seems to verge on perversion of a sort.

Number 3: The third problem has reference to the rape which is both justified and unpunished.

With reference to the first point, the solution lies in affirmatively establishing some other reason for suicide which will get away entirely from sex perversion, which is absolutely forbidden by the code. It was felt that this could not be achieved simply by eliminating dialogue: that something else would have to be added which would effectively establish that this boy's problem was not one of homosexuality.

With reference to the second problem, it was felt from a standpoint of the code that Blanche's problem be more on an emotional basis and not from a standpoint of physical sex promiscuity. The suggestion was offered that, in her approaches to the various men referred to in the course of the story, she would be searching for romance and security, and not for gross sex. It would be indicated that this was the reason that she had been asked to leave the hotel, and this point would be further emphasized by the way her scenes were played with the young newspaper collector, and with Mitch [Karl Malden]. We felt that this could be achieved with a minimum of rewriting. In any scenes in which Blanche approaches men, she, at some time during the conversation, calls the man, Allan, the name of her first husband. This will carry the inference that Blanche is seeking for the husband she has lost in any man she approaches.

With regards the problem of the rape the following suggestion was made: the big scene of the assault on Blanche by Stanley [Marlon Brando] would be kept relatively intact as now written. In the sequences which follow in which we find Blanche now completely demented, we also find that she is hinting that Stanley actually raped her. On the other hand, Stanley, when this accusation comes to his attention, violently denies this and proves positively that he did not rape her. The device by which he proves himself is yet to be invented.

The point of this suggestion is that Blanche in her pitiable state is making one last effort to assault the security and well-being of her sister, Stella, of whom she is so envious; that even with her broken mind she is endeavoring to achieve her objective—which was her goal through the entire play—of wrecking her sister's home with a lie.

Mr. Shurlock and Mr. Vizzard said, that it seemed that this would very likely be a solution to the rape as now written. But, that this connotation would have to be brought to the attention of Mr. Breen and given further consideration before any final judgment is passed on such a device. An alternate suggestion was made, that it is clearly established to the audience during the course of the rape scene, that Blanche is, at this time, demented. She calls Stanley by the name, Allan; she imagines the rape; the rape does not actually take place, and this is known by the audience. Another suggestion was, that the scene could be told from Stanley's point of view, and that although he contemplates rape he does not go through with the act, and leaves the room when he realizes that Blanche is demented. It was agreed by Mr. Shurlock and Mr. Vizzard, that this would be far the most satisfactory solution to this difficult problem. . . .

FROM TENNESSEE WILLIAMS

[Undated, circa late August 1950]

Dear Mr. Breen:

. . . *Streetcar* is an extremely and peculiarly moral play, in the deepest and truest sense of the term . . . The rape of Blanche by Stanley is a pivotal, integral truth in the play, without which the play loses its meaning, which is the ravishment of the tender, the sensitive, the delicate, by the savage and brutal forces of modern society. It is a poetic plea for comprehension. . . .

Please remember, also, that we have already made great concessions which we felt were dangerous, to attitudes which we thought were narrow. In the middle of preparations for a new play, I came out to Hollywood to rewrite certain sequences to suit the demands of your office. No one involved in this screen production has failed to show you the cooperation, even the deference that has been called for.

But now we are fighting for what we think is the heart of the play, and when we have our backs against the wall—if we are forced into that position—none of us is going to throw in the towel! We will use every legitimate means that any of us has at his or her disposal to protect the things in this film which we think cannot be sacrificed, since we feel that it contains some very important truths about the world we live in. . . .

FROM ELIA KAZAN [director]

[Undated]

Dear Jack:

I've been meaning to write you for a week now and tell you how grateful I am for the generosity you have shown me. I know it would be a damned sight easier to plan this picture with me if I were living in California. . . .

[Vivien] Leigh lives in England and I am terribly worried about her costumes. I had thought for a while that we might be able to use the clothes she wore on the stage. I had seen a couple of pictures, but when I saw the complete set that she sent me, I pretty quickly changed my mind. To put it in one word: they were "English." I mean stuffy, dull, ultra-conservative and—"English." They have to be completely redesigned, in order to get the best out of Leigh. As you know I want Lucinda Ballard. All I can say about her is that she is the best. There are two things we could do, bring Leigh here early or ship Ballard over to England now. I'd like to give Leigh as much rest as possible—as you know she has been tubercular and generally not well. Nothing slows up a shooting schedule like an easily exhausted woman. And if we brought her here something like the end of July, or even the middle there would be a last minute rush.

I'd very much like to send Ballard to England right now. She could carefully work over the costumes with Leigh, so that when Leigh came to this country they would be all ready for a fitting. And Leigh would be happy with the clothes, instead of worrying about them all the time I was trying to get great scenes out of her. I know it is an added expense, but really a very small one compared with any delay or slow up in the shooting, even if it were only half a day. . . .

I'll test [contract star Ruth] Roman this week. I'll test anyone else whom you think a strong possibility [for the role of Stella, Blanche's sister]. I still think [Fox contract star Anne] Baxter is our best bet, but there's time yet on this. . . .

My very best to you.
Gadg [Kazan]

FROM ELIA KAZAN

[Undated]

Dear Jack:

You know I like old Charlie [Feldman] personally very much. . . . In fact I liked him so much that despite the fact that I disagree with every single thing he ever said about the picture, I never raised my voice to say a harsh word to him. . . . By the way, on the *Menagerie* he did do exactly what he's trying to do here: bring the thing down to the taste HE THINKS the audience has. (As if any but a small percentage of our movie going populace was made up of bobby soxers, autograph waterheads and preview minded water-brains!)

The last time I met this good old fashioned type of thinking was from old L. B. Mayer [head of production at MGM] who came to New Haven and tried to influence me in his best and most persuasive manner to have a happy ending tacked on to the play and make Blanche the heavy. He said it would never never go as is. (P.S. last week I got a substantial royalty check from the touring company of *Streetcar* which is playing some towns in the South that I never heard of. They seem to catch on to it there just as they did everywhere else. In fact they seem to like it.) . . .

What made it a Pulitzer Prize winner—the poetry—must be kept in, untouched so that it will appeal to those who don't want to admit that they are interested in the moist seat department. (Everybody, of course, is!)

Well Jack, one thing you got to say for me, I *give* a damn! The fact is that I've never been this way about a picture before. This is the only picture I ever made that I'm completely proud of.

I'll be talking to you Wednesday.

Gadg

Again Thanks. I mean for everything

TO: Jack L. Warner DATE: October 19, 1950
FROM: Elia Kazan SUBJECT: "Streetcar Named Desire"

Dear Jack:

. . . One thing about the picture itself. I just saw it again and I liked it. You will have your own impression, of course, but I thought it completely clean. Whatever there is of sex and violence is truthfully done, never exploited or sensationalized. And, I think it is full of the very Christian feeling of compassion and charity.

I don't know what Mr. Joseph Breen will say but may I, before we sit down with him, recall to you the conversation we all had in your trophy room, after lunch, several months ago. That was the occasion when Joe said that the "rape" could not be in the picture—and I withdrew from the project. If you remember, Charlie Feldman asked me directly, "You mean to say that if the 'rape' is not in, you will not do the picture?" Whereupon, I said he was absolutely right and to count me out. You were there and will remember this. You will also remember that later we got together on a basis that I suggested. And this, too, was very clearly put. It consisted of (1) The rape would be in, but done by suggestion and delicacy (2) Stanley would be "punished" and that the punishment would be in terms of his loss of his wife's love. In other words, that there would be a strong indication that she would leave him.

On this understanding, I embarked on the project. And on the basis of these points, I made the picture.

At several subsequent meetings, Joe [Breen] seemed to waver from this understanding, but since I had already come into the project, it was too late to bring up the *very basis* of our understanding. I never again discussed this with Joe. Charlie Feldman has known from weekly re-statement how I was proceeding. So has Finlay McDermid [story editor]. The picture you will see is in line with what we discussed that afternoon in your trophy room.

I do not really think we will have much trouble with Joe Breen; however, it seems to me that if he has objections that are basic, why this is an opportunity to put up a worthwhile fight. Everything is on our side. The picture is good! The stage property won every prize known in the World Theatre. We can have a perfectly clean conscience about the "sensationalism" in the picture—for absolutely none of it is for its own sake. And, I really think the picture's theme is deeply moral. . . .

Yours, with gratefulness,
Gadg

FROM STEVE TRILLING
RELAY TO ELIA KAZAN, 167 EAST 74TH STREET, NYC.

NOVEMBER 14, 1950

DEAR GADG: WE WANT TO GET MAIN TITLE AND BILLING UN-DERWAY ON "STREETCAR" SO WOULD APPRECIATE HEARING FROM YOU IF WE ARE TO REMOVE YOUR PRODUCTION CREDIT ["An Elia Kazan Production"] AND STICK TO THE DIRECTOR CREDIT. . . . WOULD AP-PRECIATE YOUR FOLLOWING THROUGH ON THIS. BEST WISHES. STEVE TRILLING.

FROM ELIA KAZAN COLLECT
STEVE TRILLING
WARNER BROS

NEW YORK NY NOVEMBER 17, 1950

ALL MY ADVISORS, LAWYERS, AGENTS, AND THOSE SUPERIOR INTEL-
LIGENCES WHO DETERMINE MY FATE ADVISE ME TO KEEP THE BILLING
AS IN THE CONTRACT. I ASK YOU, STEVE, WHAT CAN I DO AGAINST
SO MUCH SUPERIOR INTELLIGENCE, BUT KEEP THE BILLING IN THE
CONTRACT. GIVE MY VERY BEST TO JACK. YOURS.

GADG

FROM JACK L. WARNER

NOVEMBER 22, 1950

DEAR GADGE: TO MY RECOLLECTION CHARLEY FELDMAN BOUGHT THE
PROPERTY AT A TIME WHEN WILLIE WYLER AND OTHERS WANTED TO
PURCHASE IT. TO MY RECOLLECTION CHARLEY FELDMAN WENT TO
NEW YORK AND SPENT SEVERAL WEEKS WITH YOU IN ORDER TO PRO-
CURE YOU TO DIRECT THE FILM. FURTHERMORE IT IS MY UNDER-
STANDING THAT FELDMAN AT ALL TIMES WANTED VIVIEN LEIGH FOR
THE ROLE WHILE YOU WANTED OTHER STARS FOR THE ROLE. I ALSO
HAVE A COPY OF THE WIRE THAT TENNESSEE WILLIAMS SENT TO
CHARLEY WHEN CHARLEY ASKED HIM WHAT HIS REACTION TO VIVIEN
LEIGH WAS, AND THOUGH INITIALLY IT WAS IN THE NEGATIVE, SUB-
SEQUENTLY AND BEFORE CHARLEY'S SECOND TRIP TO NEW YORK WIL-
LIAMS AGREED WITH CHARLEY. THEN I UNDERSTAND THAT AT A MEETING
IN NEW YORK WITH BOTH YOU AND WILLIAMS YOU ALL AGREED TO
CHARLEY'S ORIGINAL SUGGESTION, NAMELY, VIVIEN LEIGH. I ALSO
UNDERSTAND THAT CHARLEY WENT TO KEY WEST TO SEE BOTH WIL-
LIAMS AND [writer] OSCAR SAUL IN CONNECTION WITH THE SCREENPLAY.
I KNOW THAT CHARLEY WENT TO GREAT LENGTH IN TRYING TO PRO-
CURE ANNE BAXTER FOR THE ROLE [of Stella] AS WELL AS OTHERS. ALSO
THAT HE SECURED BOTH THE ART DIRECTOR AND CAMERAMAN FROM
GOLDWYN AFTER HE FIRST TOLD YOU THAT HE DIDN'T WANT THE ART
DIRECTOR PROPOSED BY YOU. I ALSO UNDERSTAND THAT CHARLEY
TRIED TO MEET YOUR EVERY WISH IN PROCURING THE OTHER MEMBERS
OF THE CAST AND BELIEVE ME, HE WENT TO VERY GREAT LENGTHS
WITH THE STUDIO TO FULFILL YOUR EVERY REQUEST WHICH I AGREED
TO. THIS IS A FAITHFUL TRANSLATION OF THE PLAY. EVERYTHING YOU
WANTED WAS PROCURED FOR YOU BY CHARLEY, AND I KNOW IT TOOK
A GREAT DEAL OF TIME, EFFORT AND MONIES ON HIS PART AND HE
HAS CONSIDERABLE MONEY TIED UP IN THIS PRODUCTION. I DON'T
KNOW WHAT FUNCTION A PRODUCER IS SUPPOSED TO GIVE TO A PIC-
TURE BUT I DO KNOW IN THIS INSTANCE HE MET WITH YOU AT EVERY

TURN, MET WITH THE BREEN OFFICE MANY, MANY TIMES AND STAYED WITH THIS PRODUCTION FROM THE BEGINNING TO THE FINISH. . . . HE GAVE YOU A FREE HAND AND DID NOT BOTHER YOU WITH DETAILS. . . . IN ADDITION, HIS COMPANY IS THE PRODUCING COMPANY OF THE PICTURE. HE IS THE PRODUCER OF THE PICTURE AND HE OBVIOUSLY MUST REGULATE THE CREDITS. I THINK YOU HAVE DONE A FINE JOB, BUT IN TAKING DUE CREDIT WHICH YOU ARE ENTITLED TO I DON'T THINK YOU SHOULD MINIMIZE THE EFFORTS OF CHARLEY IN THIS RECARD AND THAT IS WHY I URGE YOU BECAUSE OF THE APPARENT CONFLICT THAT YOU TAKE THE MAXIMUM CREDIT THAT ANY IMPORTANT DIRECTOR IN THE INDUSTRY TAKES.

FROM ELIA KAZAN
J L WARNER
WARNER BROS STUDIOS

NEW YORK NY NOVEMBER 22, 1950
DEAR JACK: SINCE I RECEIVED YOUR WIRE I HAVE REVIEWED THE PROBLEM OF CREDITS AND DID IT THIS TIME WITHOUT BENEFIT OF ADVISORS. I TRIED TO THINK IN TERMS OF WHAT ACTUALLY WAS DONE ON THE PICTURE. IN OTHER WORDS, I THOUGHT NOT OF THE LETTER OF THE CONTRACT [which entitled Kazan to "production" credit] BUT OF WHAT FUNCTIONS I ACTUALLY FULFILLED. YOU WERE MOST GENEROUS AND COOPERATIVE WITH ME AND I HAVEN'T FORGOTTEN THIS IN THE LEAST AND I WON'T. BUT YOU WILL AGREE, I'M SURE, THAT WHAT I ASKED FOR AND THE THINGS YOU MADE IT POSSIBLE FOR ME TO HAVE WERE ALL RECKONED TO GIVE YOU AND YOUR COMPANY THE BEST POSSIBLE PICTURE AND NOTHING ELSE. THE RESULTS SPEAKS FOR ITSELF. IN REVIEWING THE ACTUAL JOB OF WORK, IT SEEMED TO ME THAT I CHOSE EACH ARTIST WORKING ON THE PICTURE AND GUIDED HIM OR HER TO DO HER BEST WORK. THIS COVERED EVERYONE FROM THE PEOPLE WHO PREPARED THE SCREENPLAY RIGHT DOWN TO THE CHOICE OF THE BITS [players] YOU SO WISELY ENABLED ME TO BRING FROM NEW YORK. IN OTHER WORDS, I FUNCTIONED AS THE PRODUCER ON THE PICTURE AND I THINK IT'S JUST THAT IT BE CALLED "AN ELIA KAZAN PRODUCTION" AND THAT I TAKE WHATEVER CREDIT OR BLAME THERE MIGHT BE AND FULL RESPONSIBILITY. I THOUGHT OVER THE MATTER OF BAD TASTE AND REMEMBERED THAT I DID HAVE THE SAME CREDIT ON STAGE REVISION AND ALSO ON "DEATH OF A SALESMAN" HERE, AND THESE CREDITS WERE NOT IN BAD TASTE BECAUSE THEY WERE ACCURATE. AGAIN I THANK YOU FOR EVERYTHING. . . .

BEST ALWAYS
GADG

FROM JACK L. WARNER

Mr. Charles K. Feldman
Famous Artists Corporation
9441 Wilshire Boulevard
Beverly Hills, California

December 4, 1950

Dear Charlie:
    . . . About the Elia Kazan credit on *Streetcar*. As you know,
Kazan's billing on the film and in advertising matter requires that he be
given "An Elia Kazan Production" credit in 40% of the size of the
title. Then we have "A CHAS. K. FELDMAN GROUP
PRODUCTION" credit at 35%, plus a Chas. K. Feldman Group
Production copyright notice and, in addition, your "Produced by Chas.
K. Feldman" credit.
    I would appreciate it if you would drop the "Chas. K. Feldman
Production" credit. The Chas. K. Feldman Production copyright notice
on the film definitely protects you as to copyright ownership of the
picture, subject only to our distribution agreement.
    Also, you will be receiving sole credit as the producer, i.e.,
"Produced by Chas. K. Feldman." I could have placed someone else as
co-producer with you,* but did not do so because I knew you could do
the job, so, if you get the important credit "Produced by," in my
opinion, it will do more good than one hundred Chas. K. Feldman
Group Production credits. Am sure you will agree with me. . . .
    We cannot have an Elia Kazan Production and a Chas. K.
Feldman Group Production. It will be a little ludicrous, I think, with
two production credits and will look as though we are making a series. . . .
    Best wishes.

Sincerely,

The final credits dropped "A Charles K. Feldman Group Production."

FROM JACK L. WARNER

Mr. Elia Kazan
167 East 74th Street
New York, New York

December 11, 1950

Dear Gadg:
    Thanks for your letter of the 7th reference the publicity treatment
on *Streetcar*. . . .

---

*As he did by teaming Feldman with Jerry Wald on *The Glass Menagerie*.

I am not taking away from Goldwyn but he could do nothing
with *Edge of Doom* [1950]. Seriously though, Gadg, if the picture is
everything we all believe it is, it will tell its own story. If the public
will not accept a picture, you can spend eight million dollars and they
still will not come to see it. If it is what they want (which again I feel
Streetcar is), we will be very discreet, and I assure you there won't be
any tearing of clothes, as in *Johnny Belinda*, which by the way, was a
tremendous success irrespective of what you and many others thought
was a bad campaign. The two [Fox] pictures *Pinky* [1949] and *No Way
Out* [1950] did not do business of any consequence despite the great art
work. So, again, this is the story of where beautiful art in the ads
was—beautiful art in the ads!

Every good wish.

Sincerely,

FROM ELIA KAZAN

July 27, 1951

Dear Steve [Trilling]:

I spoke to [agent] Abe Lastfogel yesterday about how disturbed I
was at what was going on in New York. I mean with the Legion* and
the picture. I am more disturbed than I can possibly tell you. Abe
thought that since I felt so upset and anxious I should communicate
this to you (and through a copy to J. L.) by mail. Put it all on record
as it were.

What disturbs me is the silence. The fact that SOMETHING is
being done to my picture—*I don't know what!* And, this above all, that
it is being done without consultation with me and without even in-
forming me. I do believe you when you say that you knew nothing
about Dave's [editor David Weisbart] mission to New York when I first
asked you about it last week. I only believe you however because I
know you and like you personally. If I didn't trust you as a person you
can see how difficult it would be to believe that the executive of a
studio, through whose office practically all company business passes,
should not know about something as pressing as this. However, as I
say, I do believe you.

At the same time on last Sunday I called Dave Weisbart in New
York, on my own, at the Sherry Netherland hotel. He told me then
that he was not in New York on *Streetcar* business, although it might
develop into that. He said nothing had happened so far, but something
might, etc., etc., in other words the conversation was full of innuendo,
and the clear implication that he had been instructed NOT TO TELL

*The Legion of Decency, established by Catholic Churchmen and lay members in 1934 in
order to impose standards of morality.

ME ANYTHING. I cannot believe that *he* did not know what the hell he was doing in New York or standing by for in New York, although clearly that is what he and his wife were telling me. Of course Warner Brothers Business is W.B. Business. But since I put everything I have into a picture, isn't it perfectly and completely inevitable that I should be terribly anxious when it reaches me by dribs and drabs, that some fenagling is going on? To say that I got burned up is an understatement.

I called Charlie Feldman too last week. He said he knew nothing about it; that Warners were not telling him either.

Then I spoke to you yesterday. You said that the Legion had seen it once and had asked for certain deletions. You were not sure what these were, but you felt they were minor, and to quote Charlie F[eldman], "nothing to worry about." You know very well, Steve, that as far as I am concerned they are plenty to worry about. I don't want any meddling by these people into the guts of my picture, or of YOUR picture either. If the deletions really are minor, they might be o.k. with me. And they might not. What might seem minor to you and Jack, may not seem minor to me. I'd like to know. I think I should have been told.

You also said yesterday that you thought the Legion had asked for another showing, and that "This was serious." How serious you weren't sure. You thought it might turn out, probably would, that their requests were minor, but their request for a second showing was always serious. And you stressed the thing Charlie always stresses—that I should shut up, or to put it more gently—keep a discreet and watchful silence.

This always means only one thing to me. That a *fait accompli* is being prepared, if you'll excuse the French. In other words, that the hope is that the cuts will be made in conformance with the Legion, that they will then give us a B rating* and I will be so informed after the fact. And that I'll then be a good guy and let that be that. Well I may feel that way, and I may not. I want to put myself on record with you and Jack that I may be sore as hell about what the hell is done to please the Legion and if I'm sore as hell nothing in this wide world will keep me silent. To quote an old Jewish proverb, if someone spits in my face, I will not say it's raining.

If you think I'm overboard, or if Jack does, I will listen and try to understand, because I like you all, but if I'm overboard you really have only your own silence to blame. The picture is very, very dear to me. I think it's the finest picture I've ever made, bar none. I put a hell of a lot into it, and I don't want it castrated.

---

*Rather than a C rating ("condemned").

Let me know.

You know, Steve, I was raised a Catholic. I went to Catechism school for two years. I think Jack Vizzard [from the Production Code Administration] is just the wrong person to have sent to New York. He was trained for the priesthood. The very fact that he was sent meant that you were all ready to do anything necessary to knuckle under to them. That they only had to name it. The Catholics are not as tough as they sound. Also to condemn *Forever Amber* [1947], a piece of out and out garbage, is one thing. But to condemn something that has received every prize worthy of the name, and a picture that every self-respecting, intelligent person in this land will want to see, is something else. The Catholics are like everyone else. They want to be respected and, like everyone else, they also despise no one as much as the person who licks their boots. . . .

Your friend,

Some modifications were made to satisfy the objections made by the Legion of Decency, and the picture was given a B rating ("objectionable in part for all").

Editor's Postscript

A Streetcar Named Desire *was a harbinger of things to come. Charles K. Feldman, an agent-producer-packager, purchased the property and brought it to Jack L. Warner. Elia Kazan was not a contract director and Tennessee Williams was not a house writer. Neither Vivien Leigh nor Brando—nor, indeed, any of the cast members—were Warner contract players (the only actor to sign a term contract was Karl Malden). The director of photography, art director, costume designer, and composer were brought in from the outside on a one-film basis.*

Here was a major modification of the studio system as practiced and presented in the preceding pages: a far cry from the presold three Cagney pictures, three Davis, three Bogarts per year, etc., designed and executed as vehicles for the star and designed and executed by full-time company employees. The traditional house style and assembly-line methods gave way to individually tailored films.

The old studio system, somewhat modified, survives only in TV film production, because of the heavy demands of product, frequency, and air dates. Talent and technicians are either under contract or employed regularly. The grind is continuous, and art is necessarily sacrificed for expediency.

Most of the stars, directors, and producers under contract to Warner

Bros. in the late 1930s and through the 1940s were gone by the early or mid-1950s—Davis, Bogart, Flynn, Cagney, Wyman, Reagan, Lupino, and others. John Huston had departed in 1948. Raoul Walsh left (except for an occasional picture) in 1951. Mike Curtiz, after being asked to take a salary cut, walked out in 1953. Jerry Wald was gone by 1950. Henry Blanke stayed until 1961.

As for Harry, Albert (Abe), and Jack—the Warner Brothers—Harry died in 1958, Albert in 1967, and Jack in 1978. Jack Warner had sold his interest in the studio in 1966, but continued to be a familiar figure in and around Hollywood and New York, occasionally becoming involved in a film or Broadway show.

Although the company has undergone continuous transitions through the past three and a half decades since A Streetcar Named Desire, Warner Bros. remains one of the most important of the major studios and still occupies the same lot in Burbank.

Appendixes

Appendix A

The following cablegrams to and from director Ernst Lubitsch, a 1930 deposition from writer John Monk Saunders, and two early memos dealing with the problems of foreign versions of American dialogue films shortly after the changeover from silent to sound films, while of great (but rather special) interest, seemed to me to interrupt the flow of the narrative when they were in chronological order near the beginning of the book. Therefore, rather than delete the material, I have opted to place it here in the relative calm of the Appendix.

TO HARRY M. WARNER [president of Warner Bros.],
    SAVOY HOTEL, LONDON
FROM JACK L. WARNER [vice president in charge of production],
    HOLLYWOOD

                              [Circa January 23, 1926]

[Producer-director Ernst] LUBITSCH* THREATENS SIGNING WITH [Mary] PICKFORD [to] PRODUCE SPECIAL [under] HER SUPERVISON [at] UNITED ARTISTS. LUBITSCH INCENSED, MADE VERY LITTLE MONEY THIS YEAR. STATES MUST MAKE BIG PICTURE AFTER NEXT. CLAIMS YOU STALLED HIM CONTINUOUSLY. LOW DOWN IS [Joseph M.] SCHENCK GIVING HIM

*Under contract to Warner Bros. since 1923.

BIG SUM AND PERCENTAGE, USING PICKFORD SUBTERFUGE. . . . LU-
BITSCH TRUTHFULLY STATES SHORT MONEY. . . . THIS SERIOUS. HIS
REASON [is that] SMALL DIRECTORS MAKING TWICE MONEY HE MAKING,
AND HE GREAT LUBITSCH. ADVISE IMMEDIATELY. IMPORTANT. . . .

TO JACK L. WARNER, HOLLYWOOD, CALIFORNIA
FROM HARRY M. WARNER, LONDON, ENGLAND

JANUARY 24, 1926

CABLED LUBITSCH FOLLOWING: "NOT INTERESTED SEPARATING UNTIL
EXPIRATION CONTRACT. DON'T ACT HASTY ABOUT THEREAFTER. WILL
DISCUSS SAME WHEN I RETURN. SHOW JACK [Warner] CABLES YOU SENT
AND MY REPLIES." DON'T DISCUSS PARTING WITH HIM; HE'S LOOKING
FOR OUT. ALSO TELL HIM NOT TO CABLE; WON'T ANSWER. DON'T START
BIG PICTURE WITH HIM UNTIL I RETURN. WILL THEN HANDLE HIM
PERSONALLY. . . .

FROM ERNST LUBITSCH
     HOLLYWOOD, CALIFORNIA
TO H M WARNER, SAVOY HOTEL, LONDON

JANUARY 27, 1926

JACK SHOWED ME YOUR CABLE CONCERNING MYSELF. AGREE WITH
YOU THAT EUROPEAN MARKET EXPECTS ONLY BIG PICTURES FROM ME.
IT IS VERY UNFORTUNATE FOR ME THAT FOR PAST THREE YEARS I HAD
NEITHER MEANS NOR CHANCE TO MAKE BIG PICTURES AND YOU HAVE
NO ONE BUT YOURSELF TO BLAME THAT MY TALENTS ARE WASTED
THUSLY. SITUATION HAS REACHED POINT WHERE BOTH OF US ARE
EQUALLY DISSATISFIED, AND I TAKE THIS OPPORTUNITY TO SUGGEST
THAT FOR OUR MUTUAL BENEFIT WE SEPARATE AFTER NEXT PICTURE.
EXPECT AND HOPE THIS PROPOSITION AGREEABLE TO YOU. PLEASE
CABLE ANSWER. REGARDS LUBITSCH

HOLLYWOOD, CALIF.
TO H M WARNER   SAVOY HOTEL, LONDON

JANUARY 29, 1926

YOU ARE MISTAKEN WHEN YOU THINK MY PROPOSAL CAUSED BY EX-
CITEMENT. IT WAS RESULT OF CAREFUL DELIBERATION. YOU HAVE
ALWAYS BEEN COMPLAINING OF BEING UNABLE TO MAKE MONEY WITH
MY PICTURES. AND MY OWN EARNINGS CERTAINLY FAR BELOW AMOUNT
I COULD GET EVERYWHERE ELSE. AM VERY SKEPTICAL REGARDING
YOUR PLANS OF BIGGER PICTURES BECAUSE THEY REQUIRE DIFFERENT
FACILITIES AND ACTING MATERIAL FROM WHAT YOU HAVE. FULLY
REALIZE WHAT WORLD EXPECT FROM ME AND THEREFORE REPEAT
PROPOSAL OF SEPARATING AFTER NEXT PICTURE. BEST REGARDS . . .

LUBITSCH

TO JACK L. WARNER, HOLLYWOOD
FROM HARRY M. WARNER, LONDON

JANUARY 25, 1926

. . . LUBITSCH MUST MAKE MORE THRILLING PICTURE AND NOT WORRY
SO MUCH ABOUT STORY. HIS PICTURES ARE OVER PEOPLES' HEADS
HERE. "KISS ME AGAIN" [1925] TAKEN OFF WHEREVER PLAYED AFTER
THREE DAYS. SHOW HIM THIS. . . . REPORTS SHOW SAME STORY WEAK-
NESS IN GERMANY AND CENTRAL EUROPE. . . . KEEP ME POSTED

HARRY

TO ERNST LUBITSCH, LOS ANGELES CALIFORNIA
FROM HARRY M. WARNER, LONDON

JANUARY 26, 1926

UNNECESSARY [for you to] GET EXCITED. . . . OUR SUCCESS IS ALSO
YOURS. YOU HAVE PICKED YOUR OWN STORIES AND MADE YOUR OWN
PICTURES WITHOUT INTERFERENCE BUT MADE THEM TOO SUBTLE. THE
WORLD WANTS THRILL AND EXCITEMENT. AS DISCUSSED WITH YOU,
WE WANT YOU TO MAKE STILL BIGGER PICTURES HEREAFTER BUT YOU
SHOULD LISTEN TO WHAT THE WORLD WANTS TO PROTECT YOUR OWN
REPUTATION. WE ARE THOROUGHLY SATISFIED WITH YOU AND PIC-
TURES, AND WHEN I RETURN WILL ENDEAVOR TO MAKE VERY LONG
TERM CONTRACT WITH YOU TO START AT EXPIRATION OF PRESENT
CONTRACT. LOVE TO FAMILY AND YOURSELF AND BEST TO ALL.

WARNER

FROM ERNST LUBITSCH
H M WARNER   HOTEL SAVOY, LONDON

FEBRUARY 23, 1926

WILLING TO PURCHASE CONTRACT MYSELF. WILL TRADE IN MY IN-
TEREST IN ALL MY WARNER PRODUCTIONS. WIRE YOUR TERMS. RE-
GARDS.

LUBITSCH

Lubitsch, who had been directing films since 1914, left Warners after So This Is Paris, *released in August 1926. He continued to make sophisticated and largely successful films for various studios—mostly Paramount.*

Appendix B

Howard Hughes, who recently had released his expensive World War I *aviation spectacle,* Hell's Angels, *was suing Warners. He claimed that certain story ideas and techniques in* The Dawn Patrol *(about to be released) were based on those in* Hell's Angels.

FROM JOHN MONK SAUNDERS [writer]

August 1930

Deposition

. . . At the conclusion of my training as a pursuit pilot I was sent to Bolling Field, Washington, D.C., where I served as an instructor until March 1919, when I resigned from the air service. In the fall of 1919 I was elected Rhodes scholar to Oxford University, England from the State of Washington. At Oxford I met flyers from the Canadian, British and French Air Corps and during my two years' residence at Oxford discussed with them frequently and in detail their own experiences and fears and hopes, adventures and activities while flying at the front during the war, and heard from them many recitals of the experiences and activities of other pilots. They told many instances of lone pilots being sent on missions of danger, ammunition dumps, food supply bases and railroad heads being blown up behind the German lines, the terrific responsibility resting upon the squadron commanders, the excessive drinking of intoxicating liquors indulged in by the pilots at the front by reason of the nervous tension under which they operated and so many other phases of flying activities at the front. . . .

Upon my return to this country I was for a time a resident at the American Flying Club in New York, where I daily heard recitals by former pilots of their experiences and adventures at the front, so that by the time I wrote my first war in the air story . . . I can truly state that I was saturated with first-hand, authentic information regarding activities of flyers at the front and the atmosphere and conditions in which they carried on.

Shortly before I went abroad in 1919 I attended a dinner at the apartment of the well-known author Irvin S. Cobb, at his apartment at No. 830 Park Avenue, New York City. Mr. Cobb had been a distinguished war correspondent at the front during the war. During the dinner Mr. Cobb was asked what impressed him as being the most tragic and terrible thing connected with the war. He replied that his most vivid recollection was a night spent in the company of young British pilots in a combat squadron in an airdrome at the front. He was impressed by the gallant manner in which each of these young, inexperienced and untrained pilots flew out in the morning to face almost certain death in aerial combat with veteran German air fighters. Between themselves and death these young British flyers hung up an alcoholic curtain of laughter, song and card playing. Mr. Cobb said that he would never forget the magnificent courage and spirit which those young Englishmen displayed. I was profoundly impressed by the statements made by Mr. Cobb and when I was at Oxford later I questioned the English pilots whom I met there, particularly as to the matters referred to and the conditions described by Mr. Cobb.

In the year 1923 I wrote a story of the war in the air which later took the title of *Wings* and was produced as a photoplay by Famous-Players-Lasky Corporation [Paramount] in 1927 in cooperation with the War Department of the United States Government. This was the first story involving the war in the air produced as a motion picture. This picture cost $2,100,000.00 to produce and required two full years to make. . . .

In July or August 1929, Howard Hawks . . . told me that he would like to obtain an air story with a war atmosphere as a starring vehicle for the well-known actor Ronald Colman. He stated that Samuel Goldwyn would buy such a story for the purpose of starring Mr. Colman and would employ Howard Hawks to direct it. At that time I knew that Howard Hawks had recently finished directing an air picture for the Fox Company called *The Air Circus* and was himself a pilot.* I then told Hawks the idea Mr. Cobb had given me at a dinner party at his apartment in New York and which I had further investigated at Oxford and during my travels in France and Germany. I told Mr. Hawks that I had in mind a story involving that tragic atmosphere of which Mr. Cobb had spoken, that to my knowledge the subject of a British airdrome at the front and the comradeship and attitude of mind of the British pilots had never been shown on the screen and that we had therefore a story which was in background and atmosphere altogether original. Mr. Hawks stated that he believed that the part would be suitable for Mr. Colman and that Mr. Colman's producer would be interested in the purchase of such a story. I then gave Mr. Hawks a synopsis of the story which I had in mind [*The Flight Commander*] and which was later produced on the screen under the title of *The Dawn Patrol* [1930]. . . .

Into the story outline as given by me to Howard Hawks and which has remained almost identical as it was first told and now so appears in the completed photoplay, were introduced minor suggestions, revisions and pieces of business which have not affected the theme, pattern or meaning of the story as a whole.

The treatment of the central theme of my story and the idea of sending a lone pilot on a dangerous mission to blow up an enemy munitions dump as a part of the development of that central idea were and are original with me, and nothing contained in my story, *The Dawn Patrol*, either as originally conceived or as it appears upon the screen, was copied or taken from *Hell's Angels* [1930], or from any part thereof. . . .

During the period of two or three months commencing about July

*During World War I Hawks was a member of the American Air Service and afterwards continued flying and spent considerable time with aviators who served in the American, British and French Air Forces during that war.

or August 1929, I told or read or submitted for reading my story *The Dawn Patrol* to various producers, directors and actors actively engaged in the motion picture industry in Los Angeles County, California, and among others to the following named persons: Howard Hawks, Sidney Howard, Arthur Hornblow, Samuel Goldwyn, Ronald Colman, John Gilbert, David Selznick (a producer at Paramount Studios), Louis Lighton, a writer for motion pictures and supervisor at Paramount Studios, Hector Turnbull, an associate producer at Paramount Studios, and Richard Barthelmess, a motion picture star. . . .

About the middle of October 1929, I offered to sell to Samuel Goldwyn . . . my story *The Dawn Patrol* as a starring vehicle for Ronald Colman, as had been suggested to me by Howard Hawks. At that time Sidney Howard, a well-known playwright and novelist was at Samuel Goldwyn's Studio preparing screen plays and writing dialogue for motion pictures for Mr. Goldwyn. I told Mr. Howard the story of *The Dawn Patrol* in detail and so far as the plot is concerned substantially as it now appears in the finished photoplay and discussed the story with him thoroughly and at length. Mr. Howard had been himself a flight commander in the American air service and was fully familiar with the theme and types of character which I was attempting to portray. In discussing the episode in my story in which a single aviator goes out to blow up a rail head at which munitions are concentrated, he told me that he had led just such an excursion himself at the front during the war; that he had been commanded to bomb a rail head inside the German lines in squadron formation; that he carried out his mission and was attacked by enemy planes and lost several members of his flight in the "dog fight" which ensued. In discussing this incident he pointed out that a single plane flying low to the ground would have a better chance than would a squadron of penetrating the German lines, of reaching its objective and returning to its airdrome. He pointed out also that for dramatic and pictorial purposes the explosion of an ammunition dump presents an exciting spectacle to the eye of an audience.

Shortly after my discussion with Mr. Howard I told the story of *The Dawn Patrol* to Samuel Goldwyn in the presence of Mr. Howard, Ronald Colman and Arthur Hornblow and at that time told them the incident of the single bombing plane going out to blow up a German munition dump, executing the mission and being shot down substantially as it now appears in the completed photoplay. . . .

John Monk Saunders

Hawks and Saunders took the property to First National (Warner Bros.) and it was decided to produce the film there as a Richard Barthelmess vehicle. Howard Hughes lost his suit. The Dawn Patrol *was remade in* 1938 *with Errol Flynn (see page 73).*

Appendix C

FROM H.A. BANDY [manager of foreign distribution, New York]

Mr. J. L. Warner
First National Productions Corp.,
Burbank, Calif.

November 18, 1930

Dear Mr. Warner,

   . . . 1. THE FOREIGN MARKET TODAY:
When "talkies" first came into being, the entire world was anxious to see and hear the new novelty. Our customer in Greece summed up the situation when he wrote: "My audiences naturally do not understand the English language—but they like to hear them talk anyway." However, the novelty has worn off and the non-English speaking countries now demand entertainment. Manifestly, a dialogue picture in a language which they do not understand possesses little or no entertainment value. . . .

   2. VERSIONS OF PICTURES IN NON-ENGLISH SPEAKING COUNTRIES:
Italy and France prohibit foreign dialogue but accept songs in any language. Other Central European countries have no laws on this subject but desire to eliminate a large part of the dialogue. Cuba, Mexico, Central and South America now prefer our present "X" versions,* with a sufficient number of titles added to clearly tell the story. Many of the Central European countries are ordering our rescored versions,** but substituting certain reels of the "X" version. . . .

   3. . . . Only a small part of each season's productions is successful abroad. The pictures which are appreciated do a phenomenal business. Those pictures which are unsuitable sometimes do not gross print cost. Therefore, we must use greater care than ever in selecting the pictures which we adapt in future. . . .

   6. SUMMARY FOR THE PRESENT SEASON:
Making foreign dialogue versions in America [usually with foreign cast members and director at the same time the American version is being

---

*The original American dialogue version.
**Nondialogue versions with synchronized music, sound effects, and dialogue titles.

shot or immediately following] is an experiment which we all hope will prove a financial success. However, none of us can tell at the present time what the results will be, as we have not as yet received the reaction to the pictures already finished and which are now being released in the foreign countries. We do know, however, approximately the revenue we can secure, providing the pictures satisfy, and even if all the pictures are successful, our margin of profit will be small. . . .

    7. DUBBING:

While [foreign language voice] dubbing is not considered as part of program for adapting our 1930–31 productions, I think we should nevertheless keep it in mind for perhaps the following season. . . .

Very truly yours,

H. A. Bandy

FROM HENRY BLANKE [Foreign Department, Burbank]

Mr. H. A. Bandy
First National Pictures, Inc.
321 West 44th Street

March 7, 1932

Dear Mr. Bandy:

    . . . It is very hard for me to decide or tell you whether [foreign language voice] dubbing should be done here or in Europe. . . . However, I must say that a studio like MGM, who first started dubbing, and has more experience in that line than any other studio in the world, continues working here in Hollywood—and, this year even on a larger scale than ever. Since the last five months, they have had Mr. Geo. Kann combing Europe for suitable actors, whose voices will match the voices of Garbo, Shearer, etc., for dubbing purposes, and so far he has sent over three French actors, and one French writer. . . .

    Besides importing all of these people from Europe, they have under contract most of the foreign colony in Hollywood.

    Germany is supposed to be very far advanced in dubbing, but, according to all the French newspapers and tradespapers, the Universal pictures, *Dracula*, etc., dubbed into the French language in Germany, were panned in comparing them technically to the MGM product dubbed in Hollywood. All the French tradespapers repeat and repeat—according to what I have read here, and have had shown me—that the MGM product, in regards to the technique of dubbing, is far superior to any other studio, and therefore, meets with success. . . .

    I firmly believe that dubbing is or will be, and very soon at that, the only salvation of the foreign market. With changing the cuts a little—for instance—by using cutouts—if [James] Cagney in *The*

Crowd Roars, in a big closeup is speaking to his brother Eric Linden for a length of time, one could easily play the bigger parts of Cagney's speech (the American version shows Cagney in closeup speaking) over Linden's closeup listening to the speech. In this way one could make darned good dubbed versions, and it would hardly be detectable—that the actor's lip movement is not actually the one whose language is dubbed in. . . .

Very truly yours,
H. Blanke

Eventually, foreign versions of American dialogue films consisted of dubbed voices for multi-language versions and/or, with certain films, superimposed titles.

Index

Note: Job descriptions of Warner executives and employees (excluding players) are included next to their names.